CAE

A SURVEY OF STANDARDS, TRENDS, AND TOOLS

Stephan A. Ohr

WILEY

John Wiley and Sons

New York • Chichester • Brisbane • Toronto • Singapore

This publication is designed to provide accurate and authoritative information in regard to the subject matter covered. It is sold with the understanding that the publisher is not engaged in rendering legal, accounting, or other professional service. If legal advice or other expert assistance is required, the services of a competent professional person should be sought. FROM A DECLARATION OF PRINCIPLES JOINTLY ADOPTED BY A COMMITTEE OF THE AMERICAN BAR ASSOCIATION AND A COMMITTEE OF PUBLISHERS.

Library of Congress Cataloging–in–Publication Data

Ohr, Stephan A.
    CAE: a survey of standards, trends, and tools/Stephan A. Ohr.
    p. cm.
    Bibliography: p.
    ISBN 0-471-63366-6
    1. Computer–aided engineering. I. Title
    TA 345.037 1990
    621.3'028'54—dc20

Printed in the United States of America
89 90 10 9 8 7 6 5 4 3 2 1

Preface

Computer Aided Engineering, or CAE, is revolutionizing the practice of electronics engineering at every level. Yet, up until now, there has been no centralized source for printed information on the myriad aspects of CAE, nor any guide to the perplexing pitfalls barring the way of a company wishing to implement CAE. This book, the author hopes, fills this void.

CAE: A Survey of Standards, Trends, and Tools offers a survey of all CAD/CAM tasks, focusing on ECAD tasks. Input from various highly visible companies in the field make this book particularly handy. CAE is rapidly becoming an essential tool in all phases of the engineering process—from design through development and testing. This sourcebook covers a broad spectrum of CAE technologies and applications in order for the reader to better understand the machinery and software that have become CAE standards.

The author acknowledges help from the following companies, who participated in the preparation of this book—CAECO, Digital Equipment Corporation, EDA Systems, Electronic Engineering Software, FutureNet, Hewlett–Packard, Integrated Measurement Systems, P–CAD, Racal–Redac, Test Systems Strategies, Valid Logic Systems, Viewlogic Systems.

Trademarks

The names of the products and company names listed below, to which reference is made in this work, may be protected by Federal, State, or Commonlaw trademark laws.

1104 terminal (Seiko)
1105 terminal (Seiko)

2900-processor family (AMD)

3090 mainframe computer (IBM)
32032 chip set (National Semiconductor)
3270 terminal (IBM)

4111 graphics terminal (Tektronix)
4125 graphics terminal (Tektronix)
4129 graphics workstation (Tektronix)

5080 terminal (IBM)

68000 microprocessor (Motorola)
68010 microprocessor (Motorola)
68020 microprocessor (Motorola)
68030 microprocessor (Motorola)
68881 floating–point processor (Motorola)

7400–series chips

80186 processor (Intel)
80286 microprocessor (Intel)
80386 microprocessor (Intel)
8080 processor (Intel)
8088 microporcessor (Intel)
88000 chip (Motorola)

9500–series VLSI testers (Tektronix)

ABEL universal compiler (Data I/O)
Adept algorithm (Silicon Design Labs)
A/D Lab circuit simulator (Daisy)
Aegis operating system
Allegro design system (Valid & Telesis)
AMAZE compiler (Signetics)
Analog Designer CAE package (Valid)

Analog Workbench (Analog Design Tools)
Analog Workbench Parametric Plotter module (ADT)
Analog Workbench Smoke Alarm module (ADT)
Analog Workbench Statistics module (ADT)
Andi circuit simulator (Silvar–Lisco)
APAR automated–layout system
ARPA/BSD networking service
ASPEC circuit simulator (Control Data)
ATG option (Genesil) ATG software
ATPG test–synthesis program (Aida)
AutoCAD software package (Autodesk)

Balance 21000 parallel processor (Sequent)
BILBO test–synthesis program (Virginia Polytechnic)
Blocks place–and–route program (Caeco)
Board Station PCB–design system
BORIS simulator (Siemens)
Bristle Blocks silicon compiler

CADAT simulator (HHB Systems)
CADDS 4X software (Computervision)
Cats hardware–modeling system (HHB Systems)
CDX–760 board (Cadnetix)
CDX–7900 hardware–modeling system (Cadnetix)
CGP 200X hardware (Computervision)
ChipMaster (Daisy)
CIF format (Calpoly)
Clipper chip set (Integraph)
CMOSY library (NEC)
Concorde silicon compiler
COS operating system
CoSim SDE (Aida)
Cray–1 computer
Cray–2 computer
CSMA/CD protocol
C–VAX computer (DEC)
Cyber computers (CDC)

Daisy Logic Simulator (DLS) (Daisy)
DataSource hardware–modeling system (Teradyne)
DECnet network architecture (DEC)
Design Kit (part of microCMOS)
DN3000 workstation (Apollo)
DN580 graphics accelerator (Apollo)
DNIX operating system (Daisy)
DO Loops math kernel (Lawrence Livermore)
Dragon experimental workstation

ÊCARDS PCB–design system (Scientific Calculation)
Eclipse computer (Data General)
EDS design system (HP)
EDS/3065 test–program generator (HP)
EE Designer 3 PCB–layout program (Visionics)
EGA graphics controller (IBM)
E–logic circuit simulator (Berkeley)
EMBOS operating system
Ethernet data–transfer method
Expanded Memory Specification Version 4.0 (Intel, Lotus, Microsoft)
Extended Memory Interface (Intel, Lotus, Microsoft)

FAST semiconductor–fabrication process (Fairchild)
FutureDesigner program (FutureNet)

GDS–11 computer–graphics system (Calma)
GDT compiler for compilers (Silicon Compiler Systems)

Hardware Modeling Library (Mentor)
Hardware Verification System (Mentor)
HDLC data–transfer protocol (IBM)
Helix simulator (Silvar–Lisco)
HiChip hardware–modeling system (GenRad)
HILO–3 simulator (GenRad)
HP–1000 minicomputer
HP–3000 mainframe computer
HP–3065 PCB testers
HP–9000 Model 840 computer
HP–930 computer
HP–950 computer
HP–UX operating system
HSPICE simulator (Meta–Software)

IC Design Tool Kit (Analog Design Tools)
Idea CAE turnkey system (Mentor)
IEEE 802.3 standard
IEEE 802.4 standard
IEEE 802.5 standard
Insight router (part of Allegro) (Valid)
Interpro 32C workstation (Integraph)
ISPICE simulator

Kermit file–transfer protocol

L language (Silicon Compiler Systems)
LASER–6 simulator (Teradyne)

Layout Synthesis program (Caeco)
LE 1032 logic evaluator (Zycad)
Linpack equations (Argonne)
LINT compiler (AT & T)
Logic Master ST prototype tester (IMS)
Logic Masters prototype testers (IMS)
LogicCompiler (part of Genesil) (Silicon Compiler Systems)
Logician 386 (Daisy)
Lsim simulator (Silicon Compiler Systems)
LSS logic–synthesis program (IBM–Watson)
LSSC self–test technique (IBM)
LVS

Mach 1000 SDE (Silicon Solutions)
Macintosh II (Apple)
Macintosh (Apple)
MacPitts silicon compiler
Macro Cell Library (part of microCMOS) (National Semiconductor)
MacroEdge standard–cell placement program
Master Designer 386 PCB–design system (PCAD)
MegaGatemaster accelerator (Daisy)
Megalogician hardware accelerator (Daisy)
Merlin S VR software
MicroCMOS (National Semiconductor)
MicroVax 2000 computer (DEC)
MicroVax II computer (DEC)
MicroVax III computer (DEC)
MP2D automated–layout system (RCA)
MPXL operating system (HP)
MSPICE+ simulator (Mentor)
MS–DOS operating system (Microsoft)
MS–DOS Release 2.1 (Microsoft)
MS–DOS Release 3.0 (Microsoft)
Multimax parallel processor (Encore)
MVS operating system (IBM)
NAS 9080 computer (National Advanced Systems)
NFS file–transfer protocol (Sun)

Omniroute II autorouting program (Omnicad)
OS/2 operating system (IBM & Microsoft)

Package Station design system (Mentor)
Pacsim simulator (Simucad)
PAL field–programmable array (Monolithic)
PALASM compiler (Monolithic)
Parts program (Microsim)
PCB Engineer PCB–design program (Integraph)

PC/AT computer (IBM)
PC/XT computer (IBM)
PC–CARDS Release 2.0 PCB–layout system (PCAD)
PC–DOS operating system
PerSim accelerator board (Aida)
Personal Logician 286 (Daisy)
PFG fault–simulation program (Caedent)
PLD Design System logic–synthesis program (HP)
PLD Master design system (Daisy)
PLDesigner logic–synthesis program (Minc)
Plogic simulator
PMX hardware–modeling system (Daisy)
Precise ADS analog simulator (EES)
Precision Architecture (HP)
Professional PCB Designer (Computervision)
PSPICE hybrid simulator (Microsim)
PS/2 Model 80 computer (IBM)

Quicksim simulator (Mentor)

R2065 chip set (Mips)
RealChip hardware–modeling system (Valid)
RealModel simulation subsystem (Valid)
Renaissance (HP–9000 Model 320SX) (HP)
RT–PC workstation (IBM)

Saber circuit simulator (Analogy)
SCALD schematic–entry program (Lawrence Livermore)
SCICARDS PCB–layout system (Scientific Calculation)
Sentry IC prototype tester (Schlumberger)
Sentry IC tester (Fairchild)
Simon circuit simulator (ECAD)
Slice circuit simulator (Harris Semiconductor)
SNA data–transfer protocol (IBM)
Socrates logic–transfer program (Calma)
SPARC chip set (Sun & Fujitsu)
SPICE simulator (Berkeley)
SPICE 2 simulator (Berkeley)
SPICE 3 simulator (Berkeley)
SPICE+ simulator (Analog Design Tools)
SRX 3–D workstation (HP)
Standard Cell Library (part of microCMOS) (National Semiconductor)
Star computer (Xerox)
STM4000 functional tester (Cadic)
Stream format (Calma)
Sun–3/160 computer
Sun–3/200 workstation

Sun–3/60 computer
Sun–4/200 computer
SYCOMORE silicon compiler
Symbad symbolic layout editor (ECAD)
SYSCAP circuit simulator
S–1 supercomputer (U.S. Navy)

TanTest test–synthesis program (Tangent)
TEGAS 5 simulator (Calma)
TEO/Electronics design system (Data General)
Thermo–STAT thermal–analysis program (Valid)
Titus test–synthesis program (AT & T)
Transcribe schematic–generation Tool (Valid)

UNICOS operating system
UNIX operating system (AT & T)
UNIX Relaease 4.2 BSD operating system (Berkeley)
UNIX System V operating system (AT & T)
UNIX System V.3 operating system (AT & T)

ValidPACKAGER (Valid)
Valid GED schematic editor (Valid)
ValidSIM logic simulator (Valid)
ValidTIME timing–analysis checker (Valid)
Vanguard Release 3.2 PCB–layout system (Case)
Vanguard Stellar CAE Design System (Case)
VAX 11/750 computer (DEC)
VAX 11/780 superminicomputer (DEC)
VAX 11/785 computer (DEC)
VAX 8200 computer (DEC)
VAX 8300 computer (DEC)
VAX 8800 computer (DEC)
VAXBI bus (DEC)
VAXstation 2000 computer (DEC)
VAXstation GPX workstation (DEC)
VAX–GPX computer (DEC)
Verilog–XL simulator (Gateway)
VGT100 library (VTI)
ViewSim hybrid simulator (Viewlogic)
Virtual Lab circuit simulator
VISULA PCB/CAD program (Racal–Redac)
VMS opreating system
VM/CMS operating system (IBM)
VT 100 remote terminal (DEC)
VT 200 remote terminal (DEC)
VT 300 remote terminal (DEC)
VTI workstation (VLSI Technologies)

VTIsim digital simulator (VLSI Technologie)

X.25 protocol
X/MP computer (Cray)
X–Window networking service (MIT)

Z80 processor (Zilog)
Zodiac cell family

Contents

CHAPTER 3:   SCHEMATIC ENTRY

CHAPTER 4:   ENGINEERING DATABASES AND NETLIST GENERATION

CHAPTER 5:   LOGIC SIMULATION

CHAPTER 6:   ANALOG–CIRCUIT SIMULATION

CHAPTER 9:   TESTABILITY ISSUES

CHAPTER 10: THE FUTURE OF COMPUTER–AIDED ENGINEERING

CHAPTER 1

ENGINEERS AND COMPUTERS

• **The World of Electrical Engineers** •

Several years ago, a trade magazine advertising campaign depicted an engineer—presumably in a fit of creative inspiration—ignoring his wife and other guests at a restaurant by drawing circuits on the back of a paper napkin. In another incarnation of the same ad campaign, the engineer was shown holding up a supermarket checkout line as he attempted to work out circuit ideas on the back of a paper shopping bag. I forget what product was being advertised, but I assume it was something to promote CAE—computer–aided engineering.

I have seen engineers draw circuit blocks on paper napkins in restaurants, but this was largely to illustrate points to their business companions—not to shut them out. Since paper napkins tear easily under the points of the fine-lined pencils engineers are fond of using, grid paper and notebooks are the preferred tools for sketching circuits. Advocates of CAE would replace the grid paper and notebooks with graphics tablets attached to personal computers (PCs) and graphics workstation screens. However, much more than graphics is required to automate the engineering process.

Outside the back rooms of corporations and defense plants, little is known about the world of electrical engineers. Author Tracy Kidder won a Pulitzer Prize for his earnest attempt to describe an engineering world in *Soul of a New Machine*. But his middle–distance perspective had a tendency to treat engineers as if they themselves were black boxes: The *input* was competitive market pressures on Data General Corporation to build a 32–bit computer; the *output* included a great deal of personal unhappiness. In the story told by Kidder, one young engineer abruptly abandoned the debugging process on the new machine to become a ski bum in Vermont. Not being close enough to the technology, Kidder could not possibly understand how someone could go crazy staring at a logic analyzer 18 hours a day.

Engineering circuits, many people assume, is a *creative* process—like painting a picture or writing a novel. This misconception persists even in the world's electrical–engineering capitals, like Massachusetts' Route 128 Circle and California's Silicon Valley. Consequently, there has been a proliferation of computerized equipment and software that are little more than mechanized paint brushes, designed to replace napkins and paper bags with $110,000 boxes. The partial success of CAE vendors is testimony to how well they understand the engineering process. It has little to do with creativity.

Typically, engineering is a matter of resolving conflicts or trade–offs between a product's performance and its manufacturability. Whatever is being designed should be high performance—it should run fast and should integrate many features and functions. But it also should be durable, easy to manufacture, and cheap. Engineering is less a matter of designing an original product and more a matter of juggling these trade–offs. It is cold, calculating work. Engineers may look like bohemians; they may forsake family and friends to go to the laboratory at 4 A.M. But the kind of creativity they exercise is roughly equivalent to that of an accountant wrestling with a knotty tax problem.

We mention this not to disparage engineers or engineering work, nor to devalue the amount of mental and emotional energy these people may invest in solving their problems, but rather to pull CAE away from the notion of creative or artistic design. Now that microprocessor chip technology has reduced a roomful of mainframe computer equipment to a small box that fits on top of a desk, and CRT (cathode–ray tube) technology has made it possible to create and view near–photographic images on a small screen, many people have assumed that engineers use this equipment the way artists and painters use an easel—as an electronic sketchpad. This assumption by CAE hardware and software vendors (and some corporate purchasers) has resulted in the proliferation of somewhat expensive computer–graphic equipment that has had little impact on the way engineering work is performed.

Frequently, for example, the rough design of an electronic product is formulated not by engineers, but by the marketing group within a company. Using inputs from the sales staff, the marketing department of an electronics company determines what a box, board, or semiconductor component should do; how fast it should work; what kind of package it should come in; and what kind of ASP (average selling price) it should have. Only then is the engineering department engaged.

To understand the product–development process, it is important to recognize that it is not just the interaction between black boxes labeled marketing, engineering, or manufacturing, but also an intensely human drama. Under most circumstances, engineers are reticent people who may resent the slick, smooth–talking marketing types (who may earn more money with less technical knowledge or training). This resentment may surface in a subconscious desire to sabotage a marketing plan, to prove that in the area of electronics expertise, the marketing people have a lot to learn. Frequently, design engineers will wage guerrilla warfare on the marketing departments: They will turn up again and again at milestone meetings with solid evidence that the electronic product that marketing executives envisioned cannot possibly run at 50 MHZ (megahertz), produce 100 MIPS (million instructions per second), sell for $10,000, and/or reach the market in a reasonable period of time.

The test and manufacturing engineers, similarly, tend to view design as a glamorous activity, one that garners much praise for designers who come up with hard–to–manufacture parts. Ironically, the test engineers frequently are recruited from the ranks of designers with substantial pay raises. Part of the reason to use a design engineer for test engineering is that the designer of a circuit typically knows best how to exercise it to prove its functionality. Unfortunately, the new test engineer often will need to learn the Pascal programming language in order to write the program for an automatic (read: computerized) manufacturing tester, and the finished part could be kept off the market for yet another year until the test program is completed.

Pressures in the Electronics Industry

Organizational conflicts that delay the introduction of a product can be extremely costly in this incredibly fast–paced industry. The pressures to get a sellable product idea into volume production before a competing company steals the market take an enormous psychological toll, forcing the most polished managers to cast their people–handling skills to the wind. Marketing, design engineering, manufacturing, and test frequently are pitted against each other like political interest groups. The management style within Silicon Valley's largest semiconductor manufacturers like Intel Corporation (Santa Clara, California) and National Semiconductor Corporation (Santa Clara, California) is described as "confrontational" or "screaming matches" by those who have been there. Certainly, it is not an environment for overly sensitive individuals. Life in a Silicon Valley company has been described as a pressure–cooker, and perhaps too much has been made of the drug abuse and broken marriages that are the predictable outcomes of a long workweek filled with organizational conflicts and relentless pressures. (See, for example, Mike Malone's *The Big Score.*) In this environment, it is absolutely amazing that products get designed and produced at all; more amazing that they show the typical electronics–industry trend toward increased functionality and performance in a smaller package at a lower cost.

In the electronics industry, unlike many other industries, there is a fairly predictable technology trend toward better performance *and* reduced cost. Within the auto industry, a readily available contrast, the average selling price of a car goes up year after year. The size and weight of the car may decrease, the gas mileage may increase, the styling may get better or worse, but prices always will increase. The electronics and computer industry, in contrast, is one of the few in which the opposite is true. The performance and function-ality go up, the package gets smaller, and the price–per–function goes down.

Most of the advances in electronics and computer technology have been due to semiconductor technology, the ability to pack thousands of transistor switches and dozens of complex circuits onto a tiny piece of silicon. Microminiaturization makes it possible to shrink a transistor without altering the function it performs in any way. Digital counting circuits, for example, make up more than 90% of all modern electronic and computer systems. Transistors in digital circuits have only one function: switching *on* and *off*. They switch *on* to register one mutually exclusive logic state—a logic 1; they switch *off* to register a logic 0. Typically, the size of transistors is dictated by the magnitude of the voltage and current they carry. However, transistors in digital circuits need not be designed to switch any particular voltage or current level; they need only to put that voltage *on* or *off*. Consequently, a microscopic transistor handling a practically unmeasurable voltage still can provide a recognizable logic state. Literally thousands of these microscopic devices can be packed side by side on the same semiconductor substrate.

Looking at the increasing density of semiconductor devices, the chairman of Intel Corporation, Gordon Moore, projected that the degree of semiconductor complexity (measured in the number of transistors per chip) was likely to double every two years. This projection, known as Moore's Law, has been verified each year since the first transistors appeared in 1959 (see Figure 1.1). Current–generation VLSI (very–large–scale integrated) devices like Motorola's (Schaumberg, Illinois) 68020 32–bit microprocessor or Intel's (Santa Clara, California) 80386 provide between 200,000 and 250,000 transistors on one chip. The largest memory devices are coming in with close to a half–million transistors per chip.

This accelerating complexity puts two severe pressures on the electronics industry. First, the outrageous pace at which these new devices appear means that product life cycles are severely shortened. Compared to last year's products, next year's models will have not just a few more bells and whistles, but twice the performance. Why, then, should anyone spend time, energy, and money maintaining last year's models? Second, the increasing complexity of VLSI devices means that the products and systems that take advantage of these components likely will take longer to develop. If, for example, the user expects the power and performance of a PC to double every two years, the manufacturer must assign more engineers to design each product to cope with the increased complexity and still remain within the two–year market window. Marketers can easily envision a danger zone in which products are obsolete almost as soon as they come to market (see Figure 1.2).

Any marketer will understand the difficulty in crystal gazing—attempting to predict what products will be sellable next year, two years, three years, or five years down the road. In the electronics industry, however, the movement toward higher performance in a smaller package is not only a guidepost, but also a drumbeat. No company can stand still, no matter how successful it has been in the past, and every new project becomes a race against the clock.

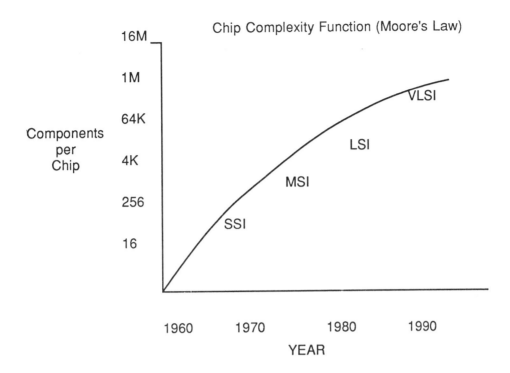

Figure 1.1: Chip Complexity Function (Moore's Law). Gordon Moore's law reveals that the degree of semiconductor complexity (transistors per chip) doubles every two years. Small–scale integration (SSI) developed into medium–scale integration (MSI), then large–scale integration (LSI). Very–large–scale integration is projected for the year 1990.

Within the commercial electronics industry, the most sizable market share frequently goes to the manufacturer *who gets there first*. Consequently, a marketing consideration in this industry always will be time to market. While it is desirable to extract the highest possible price for a product, market elasticity—an increase in the number of buyers—always is responsive to lowered prices, and the presence of competitors always will have a tendency to force prices downward. A second marketing consideration, then, is competitive price per function (or price per performance) for electronic merchandise. Additional considerations include ease of use for an end–user product or ease of integration for an OEM (original equipment manufacturer) product; that is, one that becomes part of a larger system. Finally, the product should be reliable and easy to service.

Consider this well-known example: Engineers had barely learned to rate the performance of Digital Equipment Corporation's (Maynard, Massachusetts) (DEC's) VAX 11/780 supermini—a refrigerator–sized box—as 1 MIPS, when single–chip microprocessors like the Motorola 68010 began to appear in the late

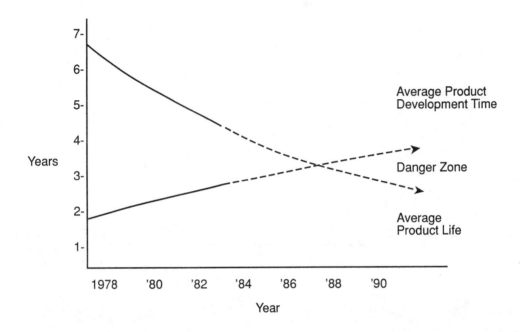

Figure 1.2: The danger zone. Products can become obsolete almost as soon as they reach the customer. Considering average product development time and average product life, a danger zone can be predicted.

1970s and early 1980s. These processors made it possible for manufacturers like Apollo Computer Corporation (Chelmsford, Massachusetts) and Sun Microsystems (Mountain View, California) to pack almost as much power as the VAX 11/780 into a desk–side box no bigger than a two–drawer file cabinet. Now the VAX 11/780 has been replaced by DEC's own desk–side computer, the MicroVAX II. However, in mid–1986, Apollo, Sun, and Intergraph Corporation (Huntsville, Alabama) introduced graphics workstations—powerful single–user computers—with 3 to 5 MIPS of available processing power (up to five times more power than the original VAX 11/780) using 32–bit microprocessor chips.

At this writing, DEC's largest computer, the VAX 8800, takes up the largest portion of an air–conditioned room and delivers about 12 MIPS of processing power. However, there are microprocessor chips based on supercomputer principles like RISC (reduced–instruction set computing) now capable of producing between 8 and 14 MIPS, as well as workstations embodying these chips. By the end of the decade, analysts agree, more than 20 MIPS will be available in desk–side or other single–user packages. This relentless trend toward increased performance in smaller packages at lower cost forces even a market leader like DEC to run very fast to stay ahead of its competitors in the workstation and computer–systems areas.

In this environment, CAE hardware and software tools can be understood as the specialized computational machinery and software needed for an organization to bring its commercial electronic products to market faster.

Resolving Engineering Trade–offs

Engineering circuit design typically is a matter of resolving trade–offs; that is, striking a balance between high performance, low cost, ease of use, ease of manufacture, durability, and—an increasingly important consideration in a competitive market environment—time to market. The trade–offs are easiest to visualize in the construction of a consumer–electronics product, though they apply to other areas of electronics as well: commercial computer systems, industrial controls, and military and aircraft electronics, for example.

For instance, it is possible to build all elements of a PC system on one large PCB (printed circuit board) using commercially available microprocessor chips, single–chip memory, disk drive, communications and graphics controllers, and 7400–series chips as glue logic. Such a circuit would be relatively easy and inexpensive to construct, with most of the engineering work devoted to the PCB layout, rather than to the circuit design. But such a circuit probably would take up large amounts of space on top of someone's desk, and the assembly—though relatively cheap—might not be competitive with that of other manufacturers doing the same thing.

A highly touted solution is to shrink as many of the PC's components as possible down to LSI (large–scale integrated) and VLSI semiconductor elements: that is, to combine the oscillators, data separators, line drivers, motor–control processors, and microcode–storage ROMs (read–only memories) into a single chip for disk–drive control. Similarly, the CPU (central processing unit), instruction cache, and MMUs (memory–management units), as well as much of the main memory and glue logic, can be combined on another large chip. The graphics–processing elements and character generators, similarly, can be combined on another large chip. In sum, an entire IBM–PC/AT computer can be reduced to five or less LSI components. The resulting computer can take up much less space on the desktop (or lend itself readily to other applications where small size and increased reliability due to smaller component count are important), and—in high volumes—cost much less to manufacture. This is the approach taken by manufacturers like Chips and Technologies (Milpitas, California), which designed a five–chip set in conjunction with AT&T Technologies (Sunnyvale, California) to help PC–clone makers get to market quickly, and by Faraday Electronics (Sunnyvale, California), whose chip set and new ruggedized packaging gear the PC toward industrial–control applications.

But such an approach is not without risk. Doing a VLSI shrink can be costly and time–consuming. What companies refer to as NRE (non–recurring engineering) costs can be as much as $50,000 or $100,000 even before the first prototype is delivered, and development time can be a year or more. If demand for the improved product does not attain a certain level, not only the development costs but market share itself may be sacrificed.

While few CAE vendors stress cost factoring as part of the tools they provide to engineers, weighing these factors is, nonetheless, part of the engineering process. Make–or–buy decisions typically are part of an engineering team's charter. Deciding whether a particular circuit function is built with off–the–shelf parts or combined in a custom or semicustom device involves a number of departments within an organization, but the decision–making process, inevitably, is most strongly impacted by engineering.

Engineers and Computers

Historically, the favored engineering tools were slide rules and hand–held calculators. These devices applied some sort of mathematical computation—addition, subtraction, multiplication, division, square root, or some combination of these—to a string of numbers. Mainframes and minicomputers were used for the larger computational jobs, such as simulation (predicting the behavior of a complex circuit) or design–rule checking (verifying that the quantifiable aspects of a design fit within the tolerance of a particular manufacturing process). While the FORTRAN programs would reside on a corporation's large host computer, engineers would spend many hours on an IBM 3270 or DEC VT 100 remote terminal typing a textual description of a particular design, using very clipped sentences and long lists of numbers. From the terminal, the task would be entered into a job queue to be run with other jobs the computer was doing, such as payroll calculations or inventory checking. While the job itself would take several hours to run, its actual completion time would depend on its position in the queue, and results of the computation—in the form of a thick, difficult–to–interpret ream of computer paper—would take days to come back.

Modern computer technology has changed much of this. It is now possible to have the computational resources of a mainframe or minicomputer sitting on (or next to) one's desk. We have long accepted the notion of the automobile as personal transportation, and the fact that computers are becoming cheaper is bringing business professionals to the same level of acceptance.

The engineering workstation is another class of PC with somewhat more computational muscle (measured in the raw *speed* with which calculations can be completed), more memory and storage options, and, in some cases, a more sophisticated data–communications facility. In addition, workstations and PCs provide something that would have been a luxury on even the most powerful mainframes and minis: sophisticated graphics. This graphics capability has confused many software vendors and corporate purchasers, obscuring what it is that electrical engineers actually do with these machines. One problem is the proliferation of very expensive workstation software and turnkey (hardware and software) systems that key too heavily on graphics and become obsolete very quickly.

Another problem is the proliferation of low–cost CAE software for PCs. Because they become cheaper every year, these machines are ubiquitous in many corporations today and are, in fact, used for engineering work. Unfortunately, many vendors of CAE software for PCs have assumed that the market for engineering aids tracks the initially explosive market for PCs.

The early distributors of PCs thought that everyone would use a computer if it was easy and cheap enough. Though the products of Apple Computer Corporation (Cupertino, California) have always occupied the high end of the toy computer market, the Macintosh line deserves enormous credit for promoting a new image—borrowed from the Xerox Star (Palo Alto, California)—of what easy–to–use should be. Unfortunately, the CAE market does not track the PC market. Making a product less costly and easier to use may get more circuit designers to use it, but will not increase the number of electrical engineers in the world or the number of people who have to design circuits for a living. This is not an open–ended market, but a very small, focused one—with very specific requirements.

For example, one of the fastest selling CAD (computer–aided design) software packages, AutoCAD produced by Autodesk (Sausalito, California), allows designers to construct perspective drawings of mechanical parts or architectural layouts on a graphically boosted IBM–PC. This is a mechanical–drafting package that has little to do with electrical–engineering work. Engineers may use the graphics extensions of the IBM–PC to draw and visualize electronic circuits (enter a schematic), but the real value of this process is in the analysis of circuit performance the computerized representation allows you to make.

In principle and practice, engineers will use current–generation computers and workstations in the same way that they once used slide rules and calculators: to manipulate numbers. The computer–graphic screens are used merely as a window on the computational process, a way to display data—not as a tool for drawing pretty pictures. The best engineering tools remain computational devices for manipulating engineering data. Forget pretty pictures: The more data the computational machinery can manipulate in shorter amounts of time, the more useful it is as an engineering tool.

Equipping each computer with its own screen, however, provides an advantage over what can be accomplished with mainframes and minicomputers. By giving the user a window on the computational process, computers are made interactive. That is, the user can insert himself or herself into the computations and carry on a dialogue with the computer. While traditional mainframes and minicomputers would perform all their operations in a batch–processing mode, taking each job as a long task from a queue with other long tasks, new-generation workstations provide much more interaction with a user. It is this *interactivity* that distinguishes workstation technology from previous-generation computers, and has, in fact, transformed the way electrical-engineering work is performed.

Actually, all computers, even workstations, perform tasks in a batch-processing mode. The workstations, however, tend to execute shorter tasks and display the results of these activities on a user's screen. Even with jobs involving long, difficult computations, the response is likely to appear more quickly on a workstation than on a remote terminal on a mainframe. Consequently, new engineering software is being created and long–standing batch–processing software is being rewritten to take advantage of this interactivity. Engineering tasks that require individual knowledge and judgment, such as circuit design or printed–circuit–card layout, now can be combined with those tasks requiring long–winded calculations, such as simulation.

Most computers and workstations in engineering environments will have to perform both interactive and batch–processing tasks. The job of drawing or entering a schematic, for example, is an interactive task that must be performed in conjunction with a human operator. The job of calculating how that circuit will perform, however, may take several hours of computer time and typically will be performed in a batch–processing mode. In many cases, a circuit will be entered on a workstation and the simulation will be computed by a mainframe. The results of the computation, though, could be sent back to the workstation display. The technology trend in CAE is to make everything interactive, to shorten the response time for everything the computer does, so that the results of a simulation appear almost as soon as the schematic is entered. That way, the engineer knows instantly whether a mistake in design has been made and can make the correction immediately.

CAE, CAD/CAM, and CIM

The proliferation of general–purpose engineering workstations and PCs that can be equipped with software for specialized tasks also has made it difficult to distinguish electrical–engineering work from CAD, CAM (computer–aided manufacturing), CIM (computer–integrated manufacturing), electronic publishing, or other disciplines that appear to make good use of workstation technology. In the early stages of workstation automation, corporations referred to CAD and CAM in the same breath. As the software programs that were run on workstations became more sophisticated and more specialized, CAD and CAM became separated, and a new division—CAE—was added. Now the term CAE makes no clear distinction between computer–aided mechanical engineering and computer–aided electrical engineering. Consequently, some manufacturers use CAE to refer to mechanical–engineering activities—the calculation of stresses (forces and heat) on mechanical parts—and EDA—electronic design automation—to refer to electrical engineering. Both EDA and CAE refer to the design of electronic circuits.

The entire electronics industry, however, is hinged on the meaning of these terms. During the past several years, there has been a confusing proliferation of engineering aids—software tools—designed to promote workstation productivity. The problem is that tools for engineering and manufacturing do not complement each other. Just as engineers can appear to be working at cross–purposes with the marketers, the software tools developed for manufacturing layout can be totally incompatible with those used for engineering. All the productivity gains implied in the use of workstations by engineers can go out the window as manufacturing and test experts struggle to decipher the electronic files that engineers provide. In some cases, a file cannot be transferred, and an entire schematic must be entered from scratch onto the system used by manufacturing. This is a net productivity loss. Consequently, the electronics industry now is working toward the integration of these software tools. The terms CAD/CAM and CIM are coming to refer not just to specific disciplines, but rather to a *corporate strategy* for building, using, and integrating these tools.

The future of CAE tools, in fact, will rest on the decisions made by major corporations. Many industry leaders believe that, though they are inexpensive, the proliferation of PCs and individual workstations within the corporate context has created an uncontrollable situation. Not only is it difficult to integrate these very specialized products into a design and manufacturing process, it also is difficult to supervise the labor of individual workstation users. In many corporations, the thinking is that CAE and other workstation activities should be tied to the corporate mainframe, regardless of how inefficient this may seem initially. By tying all individual computers to a central host computer, marketing, engineering, and manufacturing groups all can work from the same database. Accessing this database may be slow for individuals, but the corporation has some assurance that the computerized efforts of different groups will be somewhat compatible and that these groups will function with at least some concern for overall corporate goals. This line of thought is pursued not by the majority of small, aggressive companies ("cowboys") that seem to get so much of the glamour of the electronics industry (if not the revenues), but by the large, vertically integrated electronics–manufacturing firms.

Problems of Vertical Integration

While the most significant European and Japanese manufacturing giants work toward vertical integration—the ability to manufacture all parts of a system under one roof or, more realistically, within the same organization—American electronics manufacturers are much more fragmented. Most American companies are too small to produce all elements of a product in–house. Thus, the responsibility for designing, prototyping, evaluating, and eventually producing a new system is parceled out among sometimes dozens of separate companies. One company is responsible for the VLSI components. Another company—a skunk works—could be responsible just for the design of the electronic circuits that a PCB will contain, not the physical design of the board. Another company might be responsible for the layout and manufacturing of that board. Another company might be responsible for integrating that board into a system, while still another would package and sell the system to an end user.

As a consequence, European and American manufacturers have different philosophies regarding CAE (and its relation to CAD and CAM). The European model calls for large mainframe capabilities and the integration of all types of electronic–circuit and manufacturing data on one large database. The American model parcels the CAE, CAD, and CAM functions among different machines and databases; develops specialized software and computational machinery to serve the needs of just these specialized areas; and then attempts to forge artificial links between design and engineering, engineering and manufacturing, engineering and test, and test and manufacturing.

Among the European manufacturers and the largest American manufacturers such as IBM (Armonk, New York), DEC, and Hewlett–Packard (HP) (Palo Alto,

California), there is a concern for mainframe computational resources; large databases; and improved techniques for organizing, quarrying, and manipulating these databases. Among American manufacturers, there is more interest in high–performance graphics workstations and PCs, as well as specialized software for schematic entry, logic simulation, and layout, but there are few easy ways to get from one function to another. Perhaps the emphasis on workstations and PCs is the electronics industry's incarnation of American individuality, but the penalty is isolation and lack of communication. Even as small American manufacturers go their own way (sometimes at great business peril), there seems to be an increasing interest in standardization and networking.

The CAE Standards Issue

Standardization can be interpreted as movement toward conformity: guarantees that all cars will be black and all flavors vanilla, insurance that any manufacturer can build a sellable product because its hardware and software are compatible with everyone else's sellable product. Standardization also can be much more loosely interpreted to mean that CAE files generated on one manufacturer's workstation at least can be read by another workstation.

Networking refers to the electronic cables and communications system that link workstations with each other, with test equipment, and with larger mainframes. If schematic entry is performed on a workstation, and the more computationally intensive logic simulation is performed on a mainframe or superminicomputer, the electronic network becomes the means (the highway) for shipping CAE data from one computer to another.

Whether it is considered vanilla or not, there is a definite trend among CAE vendors toward segregating CAE software from their hardware platforms. The best known manufacturers catering to the specialized concerns of electronic-design engineers, Daisy Systems Corporation (Mountain View, California), Mentor Graphics Corporation (Beaverton, Oregon), and Valid Logic Systems (San Jose, California)—sometimes jokingly referred to as "the DMV"—initially started as turnkey systems vendors. They would provide proprietary workstation hardware and specialized software bundled together as a single nonbreakable package for $110,000 or $150,000. The strength of these manufacturers was in their highly specialized CAE software, and the need to keep up with new workstation trends—that is, to provide a hardware platform that consistently reflected the state of the art in performance—proved too taxing.

Consequently, Daisy and Valid began to unbundle their software packages and to make them compatible with the most widely used computers and workstations. For Valid, the most popular engineering computers appeared to be those of DEC (particularly the VAX, the MicroVAX II, and the VAX GPX workstation) and of Sun. For Daisy, the choice was the IBM–PC line and newer products using the Intel 80386 microprocessor, since its own proprietary workstations were based on the Intel processor architectures. The software runs on OEM workstations provided by Apollo and probably could be made to run on other workstations using a similar Motorola 68000 microprocessor architecture, such as those of Sun or HP. While Mentor currently is a leader among CAE turnkey systems vendors, the company may be interested in unbundling its software if the popularity of Apollo workstation platforms begins to falter.

The current growth of CAE software vendors depends not just on their ability to provide special features to the engineers that use this package, but also on the software's ability to run on a range of popular computer platforms. The fast growth of Case Technologies (Mountain View, California) was due not only to the low cost of its IBM–PC–based CAE package, but also to the fact that this package would run on Sun workstations and large VAX minicomputers equipped with Tektronix's (Beaverton, Oregon) color graphic terminals. Similarly, Analog Design Tools' (Sunnyvale, California) analog–design software runs on practically all 68000–based workstations (for example, Apollo's, Sun's, and HP's), as well as on coprocessor–equipped IBM–PCs.

If full CAE software compatibility is not available, however, users are demanding at least software file compatibility—the ability to transfer design files from one system to another. Reflecting this demand is a growth of standards committees, like those sponsored by the IEEE (Institute of Electrical and Electronic Engineers). One example is the committee on EDIF (electronic design interchange format) formed by several dozen CAE vendors, responding to requests from users. The EDIF committee is a recognition of the fact that no one software company can provide *all* the tools an electronics manufacturer needs to design and build circuits, but that there should be some standardized way to transfer electronic files. The common principle is that the design data generated by one system should at least be readable on another system. A standardized file format would promote better data communication not just among the specialized packages used for engineering and manufacturing layout, but also among different software packages used for the same application. In other words, a circuit generated on (say) a Daisy system should be able to be manipulated on a competitive and incompatible system, such as one provided by Mentor.

Obviously, one CAE turnkey system vendor might feel uncomfortable with providing the means to allow its software to be run on a competitive system— even the design files the software generates. Consequently, the committee's work—developing a middle ground, a common design file format—is going very slowly, and results are not entirely satisfactory. On the other hand, the smaller CAE vendors recognize that the very life of their products is tied to compatibility with other systems. No one company has the resources to dominate this application area, and the only way to keep a seemingly niche product alive is to ensure that its files will be readable on a number of systems.

As an alternative to standards committees, software skunk works have emerged. These are service organizations that help manufacturers to port software programs or files from one system to another. The most promising of these is EDA Systems (Santa Clara, California), which is receiving support from a dozen of the top CAE software and hardware–platform manufacturers.

In summary, we probably should forget about CAE as an enhancement to individual creativity and look at CIM or CAD/CAM as a way to resolve organizational conflicts by building computerized links among those groups charged with the physical package design, the electronic circuit design, and the manufacturing of a product.

While this book may feel promotional, it is not really an attempt to proselytize or to sell CAE products. The thesis is that the success of CAE tools depends on an understanding of the design–engineering process itself. Understanding how design engineers work, what they do, and how their work fits into the scheme of things in both large and small corporations is the key to understanding CAE. This also includes an understanding of the links between design engineering, manufacturing, and test. It is important to understand what engineers do—where they fit in the process of converting an idea into a sellable product—before it becomes clear how computers can be an aid to that process.

The Design Process Flow

A typical design cycle is shown in Figure 1.3. Frequently, the design process begins with marketing research. The decision to build a new electronic product—an entire system or an element in that system—often comes from marketing. A new product idea may come from many sources: field sales staff reporting on current customer demands, ongoing marketing research, or urgings from higher management. In many organizations, the marketing group is charged with the responsibility for synthesizing these various inputs and building the description of a sellable product.

The engineering department receives the initial product description and is responsible for converting it into an actual product specification; that is, a guideline for a manufacturable product. While the engineering department is sensitive to stated market considerations, it is not governed by them nor by the whims of any other corporate group. It is engineering that typically must perform the impossible: convert a marketer's fantasy into a manufacturable product. It is engineering's job to increase functionality while keeping component costs low.

After reviewing the initial product specification, engineering may decide that the product marketing wants to have is just not manufacturable, or is just not manufacturable at the price that the field sales force says it must be to be competitive. The initial product description will need revision. In many engineering firms, the initial product description is a collaborative effort between marketing and engineering. In other organizations, the initial product description results from an adversarial relationship between engineering and marketing.

The end result of the design–engineering process is a blueprint for manufacturing and testing the finished product. If the product is an IC (integrated circuit), the blueprint is a set of photolithographic plates or masks that are used to define the microscopic interconnection lines between transistors on the surface of a silicon chip. If the product is a PCB, engineering will produce a set of plans for etching the metal interconnection lines or traces on various layers of the board, a drilling guide for putting holes or specialized mountings in

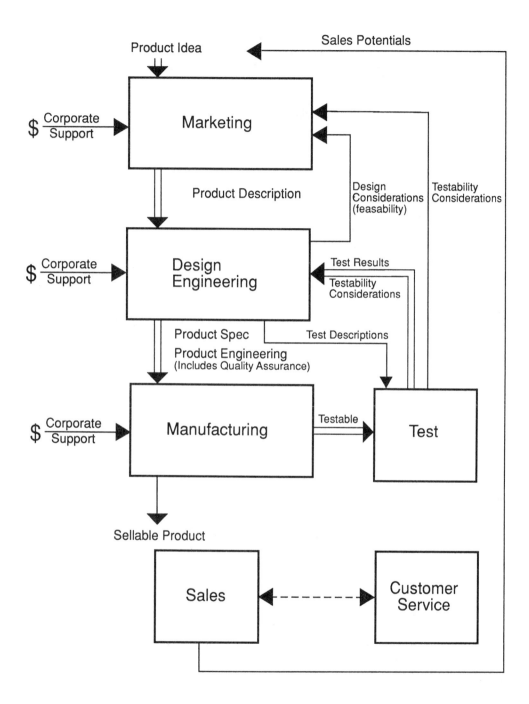

Figure 1.3: Block diagram of a typical design cycle. The design cycle, shown in block diagram form, begins with marketing research, moves into the engineering department, then to manufacturing and sales. It is the engineering department that converts the marketer's fantasy into a marketable product.

the board, and a parts list for the components mounted on the board. If the product is an entire system, the manufacturing plans will include descriptions not just of the IC components and printed circuit cards, but of the backplanes and mechanical assemblies as well.

Engineering work, however, seldom ends with delivery of the manufacturing specifications. Engineering must provide some criteria to verify that the manufactured product is working right; that is, some instructions for debugging the early prototypes, for testing finished goods, and for serving units in the field. Often, the actual design process will require frequent interactions among engineering, manufacturing, and test groups. For a semiconductor-manufacturing operation, prototype testing may reveal faults that could be corrected only by a redesign. For a big computer (or analog) system, prototype debugging is considered part of the actual design process.

Marketing and sales also may be involved in the engineering process at other points besides the beginning or the end. In the effort to get the product working by a certain deadline, engineering may be forced to incorporate another manufacturer's LSI components rather than perfecting its own. The marketing executives may be called in to make a choice between a higher ASP on the finished product or a longer time to market, neither of which the company can afford if its products are to be competitive.

Similarly, engineering is never entirely off the hook, even after the specifications have been released to production. The test–engineering group, for example, could indicate it is not happy with the way a part is testing: Too many units are failing to pass outgoing inspections. The ratios could indicate a fault in the manufacturing process or a fault in the test program. Engineering judgment is needed to determine whether some of the criteria for passing final inspection are too severe or whether perfectly good parts are being rejected by a much–too–stringent test.

• The Plan of This Book •

The flow of engineering work and its relationship to manufacturing and test will be explained in the following chapters. The process of generating a schematic or designing an electronic circuit is discussed in detail in Chapter 3. Graphics workstations make it easy to draw circuit diagrams, but, since the schematics typically must be converted to a textual format before simulation can be performed, manufacturers perpetually are searching for other, more efficient ways to create circuits. The computer's understanding of how components are interconnected in a circuit is the key to understanding the netlist–extraction process, as well as the role of object–oriented database technologies and artificial intelligence. This is covered in Chapter 4.

Harnessing the computer to verify whether or not the circuit will work is discussed in Chapters 5 and 6. The simulation of analog circuits requires different computational resources than does digital–circuit simulation, so a separate chapter is devoted to each.

Similarly, the physical layout of printed circuit cards is a different process from the layout of ICs. The former is discussed in Chapter 7, the latter in Chapter 8. Chapter 9 covers how the manufactured devices are tested, both in the prototype phase and in the production phase, and how CAE can help or hamper this process.

Where it makes sense, the processes described in each chapter are amplified by explanations and projections from acknowledged experts in each field. These individuals and their companies are on the cutting edge of this new field, and their insights are a valuable supplement to the basic structure provided.

The book ends with some projections about the CAE industry, its current state, its future, and its likely impact on the whole American electronics industry. By implication, some far-reaching assertions are made.

In the meantime, it would be difficult to understand what engineers and CAD/CAM strategists are doing with new-generation computer technology without first understanding what workstations are, how they work, and how they differ from mainframes on one side, PCs on the other. This is revealed in the chapter that follows.

CHAPTER 2

TOWARD AN INTELLIGENT DIVISION OF LABOR

• The Quest For More MIPS and MFLOPS •

Now that a word processor and database manager replace the engineering notebook, a spread sheet replaces the slide rule and scientific calculator, a mouse and 1000–line graphics screen replace a drawing board, and a minisupercomputer models the behavior of a complex circuit, it may be hard to understand the continual pressure for more and more computational power. For corporate managers, it may be especially difficult to appreciate the growing need for processing power, when only a small proportion of an engineer's time is actually spent on the computer, and an even smaller proportion is spent designing and analyzing something (see Figure 2.1).

While microprocessor technology has reduced the size and cost of mainframe resources to the point that they now fit on every worker's desk, there still is an enormous differential between the computational power of desktop workstations and that of superminicomputers. It is not just a matter of adding bells and whistles. Modern computers are being asked to juggle more simultaneous tasks, and the tasks themselves are becoming more complex. If you add more horsepower to an automobile engine, somebody will find a use for it.

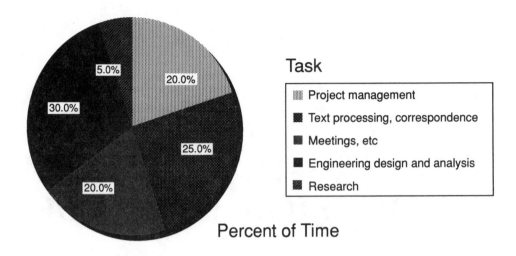

Task

▓ Project management
■ Text processing, correspondence
■ Meetings, etc
■ Engineering design and analysis
▨ Research

Percent of Time

Figure 2.1: Designer's time. Although processing power is a growing concern, this need is hard to visualize when it seems that a designer spends little time at the computer and less time designing and analyzing.

But the automobile analogy is instructive in other ways: Four hundred horsepower and aerodynamic styling buy you very little in bumper–to–bumper traffic. A Volkswagen Beetle does as well as a Porsche in that situation.

In this chapter, the push for more computational resources is explained. Some insight is provided into the ways computers work and ways they can be made to work faster. This paves the way for understanding computer tasks, large and small. It then is possible to begin to make assessments among the kinds of jobs computers are required to perform in an engineering environment and the ways these jobs can be allocated.

• A Primer on Computer Architectures •

With all the tasks that computers are skilled at performing, it is easy to lose sight of the fact that a computer—like Babbage's original arithmetic machines—is really a mechanical counting device, whose gears and latches are emulated by digital–pulse trains and transistor switches. It is not rude to think of a computer as an elaborate Rube Goldberg chain of activity, driven by a monkey working up and down on a pump handle. The difference between a Rube Goldberg cartoon and a modern microcomputer is that the electronic gear train has been reduced to microscopic components, and the pump handle goes up and down 16 or 20 million times each second.

In operation, the computer's CPU controls the activities of several dozen, often hundreds, of these elaborate Rube Goldberg chains. Which chain or combination of chains is put into operation is determined by the microcoded (1s and 0s) portion of a computer's software program called an *instruction*. Most commercial computers in use today are built around what is called a Von Neuman architecture, in which each 400–ns (400 billionths of a second) clock cycle is divided into instruction–fetch/instruction–execute phases. If you extend the pump handle analogy, the instruction is fetched or "sucked–in" on the upward swing of the clock or pump–handle, and pushed out to other elements of the system on the downward swing. The execution phase of the clock cycle includes an instruction–decode operation in which the CPU, functioning like the switchmaster in a complex railroad yard, selects the chains or data pathways.

More often than not, the instruction requires the CPU to find a number in its main memory, bring that number into a central processing area, perform some sort of transforming operation upon it, and return it to main memory. The instruction–decode sequence typically precedes an address–generation sequence, in which the CPU computes or calculates the memory location of the number it needs to act upon and then opens the switches or gates to that location. In the next swing of the clock or pump handle, the number or operand is sucked into the CPU. It then is pushed through to machinery that will transform it, either by adding another number to it (a multiply is typically a successive add operation; for example, 5 x 3 is really 5 + 5 + 5), or by subtracting another number from it.

The power of any computer system, therefore, can be visualized as the complexity of the instructions it can execute and the speed with which it can execute them. Modern computers, in fact, are rated according to the number (in millions) of complex instructions their CPUs can execute each second. A 1–MIPS machine, for example, is capable of executing one million instructions per second. A 5–MIPS machine, in principle, is five times as powerful. Most of the current-generation workstations, based on 32–bit microprocessor technology, currently are performing in the 2– to 5–MIPS range (though the trend is to pack ever more power into these small machines). Modern mainframes and minicomputers now are delivering between 8 and 12 MIPS.

CPUs also are rated according to the MFLOPS they deliver. This number (millions of floating point operations per second) is a measure of the computer's math–processing ability. It is taken seriously in engineering and scientific realms, especially where the computations are long and difficult. It is this measure that distinguishes supercomputers from powerful mainframes. For example, a Cray supercomputer (the X/MP) can sustain about 80 MFLOPS. An IBM mainframe (a 3090 equipped for vector processing) will sustain about 16 MFLOPS. A modern workstation, however, will sustain less than 1.

The power of the computer system also depends on the amount of main memory space available for programs and data, the amount of disk–storage space available, and the ease with which usable/interpretable data can flow between the machinery and its human operators. This relationship can be visualized in a block diagram of a computer system (shown in Figure 2.2).

This suggests that, apart from the MIPS or MFLOPS ratings, the performance of any computer system depends on all elements working together. The activities of all elements of the system must be synchronized. The movement of data and instructions to and from main memory must proceed at rate dictated by the CPU. Similarly, the I/O (input/output) activity—the

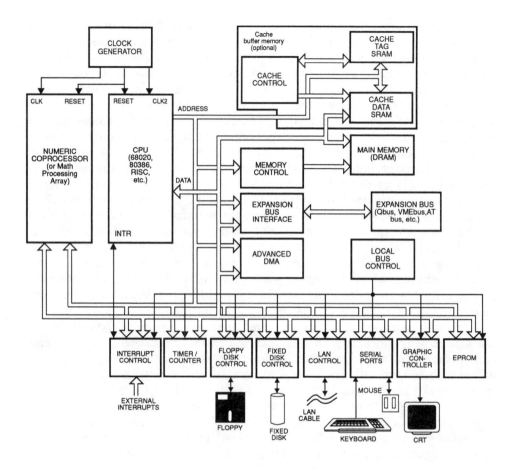

Figure 2.2: Generic computer block diagram. As illustrated, the performance of any computer system depends on all elements working together. CPU and math–processing units are integrated, but do not interfere with each other.

movement of data from disk storage to main memory, from keyboard to memory, or from memory to screen—involves the operation of mechanical devices and necessarily will proceed at much slower rates than CPU–to–memory transfers. But these movements must be coordinated so that they do not interfere with the operation of the CPU or math–processing units.

• Computer Hardware Trends •

Practically all advances in computer hardware are related to semiconductor LSI, but the obvious ones will be discussed first. Modern computer technology is indebted to semiconductor–memory technology even more than to microprocessor CPUs. The more main memory the CPU has to work with, the larger the tasks it can perform. Even with a relatively slow CPU, a large local–memory space will offer performance advantages over a system that continually must swap out data with disk storage to keep its memory banks from being filled.

When all computers occupied air–conditioned rooms and needed armies of technicians to run them, adding 16 KB (kilobytes—one thousand bytes) of memory to a corporate computer required a capital equipment investment decision from the board of directors. Today, that much memory in semiconductor ICs literally can be purchased in a Sunnyvale, California, supermarket for less money than a six–pack of beer.

Just a short time ago, most computer banks were built on 16K memory chips. These were replaced by 64K and then 256K memory chips. Today, most computers are being delivered with 1–Mbit (megabit—one million bits) memory chips, and new designs incorporate an expected wave of 4–Mbit devices. With LSI technology literally quadrupling semiconductor memory capacity every two years (Figure 2.3) and competitive market pressures forcing prices downward, any system can have as much memory as it needs. The only real constraints are physical: the size of the box the memory must fit in, the amount of electrical power available to run it, and the cooling system installed to keep it from overheating.

Similarly, Winchester disk drives and other magnetic storage devices are ways of packing more data onto smaller platters. The capacity leader in small hard disks, Maxtor Corporation (San Jose, California) has demonstrated 5–in. drives with 760 MB (megabyte—one million bytes) of capacity and 3–in. drives with over 170 MB. These drives, like the 380–MB units now being shipped by Maxtor and a half–dozen other companies, are intended for engineering and graphics–workstation use. The larger mainframes and minicomputers make use of Winchester drives with 1 GB (gigabyte—one billion bytes) of capacity in 8– and 10–in. form suitable for rack mounting in a computer room.

The most attention–getting trends in computer systems are advancements designed to shrink the computer's CPU and/or make it run faster. If it is recognized at the outset that VLSI microprocessors represent mainframe and superminicomputer CPUs that have been compressed through semiconductor technology, the large multiuser machines can be examined for clues as to what the next generation of workstations and PCs will look like.

Superminis and Minisupers

Historically, the big uniprocessors—general purpose machines with single, powerful CPUs—have been the preferred vehicles for most engineering activities. Like the children's toys we know as transformers and gobots, these mainframes and minicomputers continually transform themselves, converting themselves into a high–speed number–cruncher for one user, an efficient database manager for another user, a transparent electronic–mail message for yet another. However, to do this job more efficiently, the supermini is becoming a multiprocessor machine, adopting not just a specialized front end for graphics or a specialized back end for floating–point operations, but also multiple CPUs.

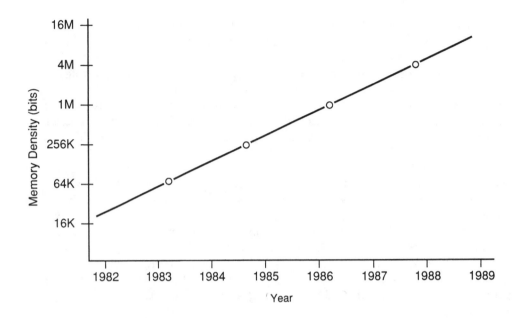

Figure 2.3: Growth of direct RAM (random-access memory) bit densitities. New designs incorporate an expected wave of 4–Mbit devices.

The largest number of these products has come from the Route 128 Circle in Massachusetts, from manufacturers like DEC, Data General Corporation (Westboro), and Prime Computer Corporation (Framingham). DEC products have enjoyed enormous success in the engineering world—more so, in fact, than those of IBM.

Many analysts believe this is due to software consistency: All VAX machines from the largest superminis (the 8800) to the smallest personal workstation engines (the MicroVAX 2000) use the same VMS operating system and the same applications software. This contrasts sharply with IBM, whose high–end mainframes, midrange minicomputers, and low–end PCs each use different operating systems and software and present no clear migration path for the user.

On the other hand, software compatibility can be perceived as a mixed blessing in a competitive and rapidly changing hardware environment. The need to retain software compatibility, for example, may keep DEC from striking out boldly in new architectural directions, though its acknowledged mission is pursue ever higher levels of minicomputer performance.

All minicomputer manufacturers, like DEC, are being pressed from two sides with performance challenges from more specialized processors. On one side, new–generation minisupercomputers perform vector and floating–point math faster than the best superminis. On the other side, parallel processors and high–end workstations based on microprocessor technology offer better interactive response time on a large variety of tasks.

The traditional distinction between superminis and minisupercomputers—between mainframes and supercomputers—has been not in their MIPS or MFLOPS ratings, but in their ability to do vector math. Superminis and mainframes are largely scalar–processing machines; minisupers and full–scale supercomputers are vector–processing engines. Simply stated, vector processing is a method of processing a massive amount of data with one instruction load. For example, a vector *add* operation on 100 numbers would load the *add* instruction once into the CPU and perform one operation on all 100 numbers. A scalar process, in contrast, would force the CPU to fetch, load, and decode the *add* instruction 100 times until all the numbers are summed, a process that eats up clock cycles with repetitive instruction operations (see Figure 2.4). For large volumes of data that are subject to manipulation by the same instruction, a vector processor can outperform a scalar processor by several orders of magnitude.

As a rule of thumb, the need for vector processing will depend on the length of the vector; that is, the amount of data that needs to be manipulated with one instruction. Calculating the trajectory of a space probe as it rounds a corner around Uranus is an application that will benefit from vector processing. Autorouting an IC or printed circuit card, since it involves many different instructions, will not benefit from vector techniques. Computing and printing payroll checks, similarly, are decidedly scalar operations.

Although it has some the fastest scalar–processing engines in the world, the supercomputer products of Cray Research (St. Paul, Minnesota) probably are the best examples of vector processors. New–generation mini–Crays include the products of Floating Point Systems Corporation (Beaverton, Oregon), Convex Computer Systems (Richardson, Texas), Alliant Computer Systems Corporation (Action, Maine) and newcomer Multiflow Computer (Branford, Connecticut). Like the Cray supercomputer, these machines are particularly capable of performing long calculations involving vector and floating–point math operations. Unlike the Cray–2, which needs specialized cooling and power systems and costs about $15 million, the minisupercomputers are air–cooled, run on conventional power systems, and cost about $1 million.

A manufacturer like DEC, which has enjoyed success with a general–purpose computing architecture, will avoid modifying that architecture to serve the specialized needs of vector math. It is more likely that DEC will add on or cluster a vector–processing capability to its general–purpose minicomputers, either by building its own attachment or by entering into a joint–marketing agreement with another hardware vendor like Floating Point Systems.

However, many mini and supermini manufacturers are borrowing supercomputing techniques as a way to make their own general–purpose CPUs run faster. One technique is to build the data–processing and data–transmission engines with specialized semiconductor technologies, such as ECL (emitter–coupled logic) or CMOS (complementary metal oxide silicon), which provide much faster gate responses than do the older but still popular TTL (transistor–to–transistor logic). Another technique is to balance fast CPU performance with other parts of the system: very large physical memories (over 1 GB on many

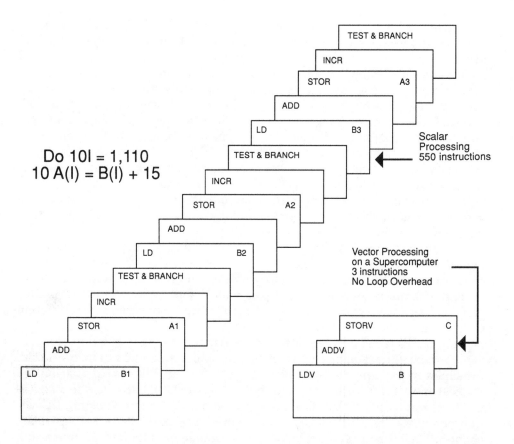

Do 10I = 1,110
10 A(I) = B(I) + 15

Figure 2.4: Scalar and vector instructions for a loop. For large volumes of data, subject to manipulation by the same instruction, a vector processor can outperform a scalar processor by several orders of magnitude.

systems) and high–speed (100 MB/s) CPU–to–memory data paths. Multi-gigabyte disk space also will be available.

Increasing Use of RISC

The most dramatic and far–reaching of the borrowed supercomputer techniques is the use of RISC CPUs. As it now is used, RISC refers to a number of CPU techniques, all embodied in the first supercomputers built by Seymour Cray for Control Data Corporation (CDC) (Minneapolis, Minnesota). First, there typically is a register pipeline or instruction cache that moves program instructions into the CPU at a very high rate of speed.

Second, there typically is a data cache and local MMU that is optimized for fast load–and–store operations. Simply stated, this mechanism minimizes the amount of complicated address calculation the CPU must perform. The new superminicomputers embody the same assumptions as do the Cray and CDC

Cyber machines: Address calculation and main memory access can slow down the system. Consequently, many of their innovations involve fast MMUs, and increasingly large data caches (up to 256 KB on many large systems). This architecture makes it possible for new–generation machines to use cache in the same manner as main memory, to use main memory as if it were a virtual–memory space, and to access relatively slower disk memory less frequently.

The third feature of RISC architectures is a reduction or simplification of the number of instructions the CPU must interpret. There is an assumption that it generally will take the CPU several clock cycles to decode a complex instruction (remember the analogy we used before: a switchmaster in a railroad yard) and establish the necessary data paths for its execution. RISC architects break a single complex instruction into a series of smaller, easier to decode sequences in an effort to minimize the amount of decode hardware and save clock cycles (see Figure 2.5).

The net result is that the tempo of RISC machines is measurably faster than that of a conventional CPU, even with the same clock speed. While the conventional CPU swings like a pendulum between instruction–fetch/instruction–execute, instruction–fetch/instruction–execute phases, the RISC CPU beats out a steady execute, execute, execute, execute. The consensus among computer architects is that RISC provides a much faster computer (see Figure 2.6).

Perhaps the best example of a mainframe/mini manufacturer using supercomputer techniques to increase performance is HP's choice of RISC principles in the design of its new CPUs. The use of RISC CPUs provides the HP–930 and HP–950 computers, introduced in 1986, with roughly 2 to 20 times the performance of previous HP–1000 minis and HP–3000 mainframes. Conservatively, the HP–930 provides about 4 MIPS, while the HP–950 provides about 7. Both machines are equipped with a proprietary MPXL operating system, geared primarily for commercial applications. The HP–9000 Model 840, announced at the Design Automation Conference (DAC)—the annual convention of CAE equipment vendors and users—in July 1986, is an engineering version of the HP–930, equipped with HP–UX (a version of AT&T's UNIX operating system). HP's philosophy in implementing RISC computer architectures (as well as a networking architecture that interconnects many otherwise incompatible mainframes, minicomputers, and workstations) will be discussed later in this chapter.

Despite the performance advantages embodied in RISC, however, the introduction of the HP Precision Architecture was delayed for some substantial period after it was developed, while HP attempted to prove to its customers that the new machines would offer some sort of software compatibility with the previous generation of HP minis and mainframes. Like other supermini manufacturers, DEC and Data General, HP was shackled by its own previous success: It could not introduce a bold, new, high–performance architecture unless it represented a growth path for previous HP computer users. This need for software compatibility (in this case, source–code compatibility) forced the architects to make certain performance compromises in the design of the new machines. While the future shows a clear trend to RISC processing techniques, the need to maintain software continuity with existing computers will keep

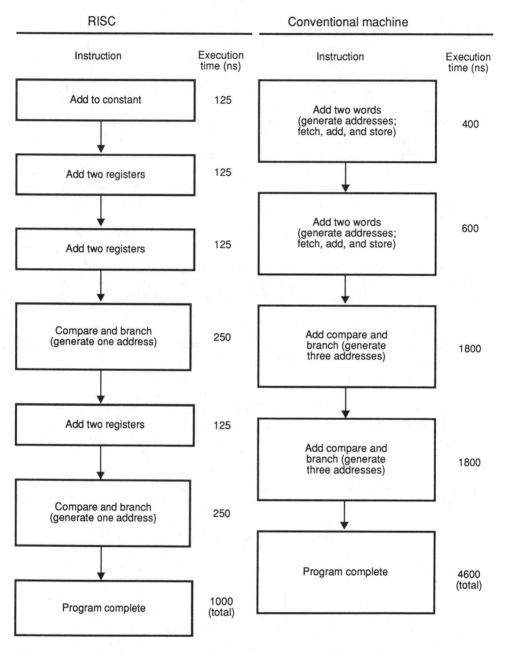

Figure 2.5: RISC machine speed. The tempo of RISC machines is measurably faster than that of a conventional CPU, even with the same clock speed. The block diagram illustrates this by comparing instruction execution times.

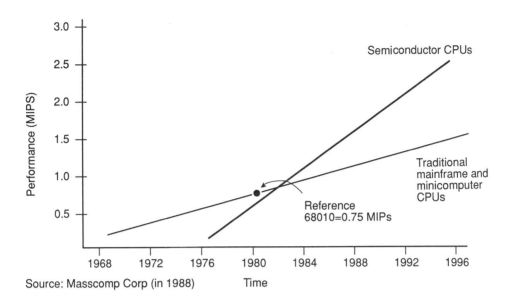

Source: Masscomp Corp (in 1988)

Figure 2.6: Single–CPU performance trends. RISC architects break a single complex instruction into a series of smaller, easier to decode sequences to minimize the amount of decode hardware and save clock cycles.

RISC (and another supercomputer architectural technique, parallel processing) from completely dominating the minicomputer market in the next few years.

With the blessing and burden of software compatibility, supermini manufacturers like DEC will remain wedded to high–speed uniprocessor architectures. The near future, however, shows a clear trend toward increasing overall throughput by putting multiple CPUs on the same high–speed bus and by clustering entire computers on a high–speed transparent network. The VAX 8300, for example, consists of two VAX 8200 CPUs linked together on the 13.3–MB/s VAXBI bus. The current top–of–the line VAX 8800, a 12–MIPS machine, puts two CPUs on a 60–MB memory–to–CPU bus. It would not be outrageous to anticipate a four–processor version of this system in the near term, or an eight–processor system within in the next two years. While the big uniprocessors probably will use 4 or 8 CPUs (16 CPUs on the largest machines in 1991), there is an emerging challenge from start–up minicomputer manufacturers who use microprocessors to comfortably tie together 20 or 30 CPUs.

RISC will be discussed in greater detail later in this chapter.

The Challenge of Parallel Processors

If performance is measured not in the MIPS available for one task, but in the number of tasks or users the system can support sensibly at the same time, the big uniprocessors will continue to be challenged by the parallel–processing engines that put a dozen or more VLSI microprocessor CPUs on the same bus. Manufacturers of parallel–processing engines, such as Sequent Computer Systems (Beaverton, Oregon) and Encore Computer Corporation (Marlboro, Massachusetts), will claim higher performance than that of superminicomputers at a fraction of the cost. Here, performance (or throughput) is the number of tasks or users that can be serviced by a single machine—not necessarily the MIPS available for one user.

With Argonne National Laboratories' (Champaigne, Illinois) Linpack equations, Lawrence Livermore National Laboratories' (Livermore, California) DO Loops, and other math kernels, for example, the existing parallel processors have benchmarked very poorly against VAXs and other big uniprocessors. This is because the programs can measure only the performance of one microprocessor CPU, no matter how many CPUs are configured in the system. Until the benchmark programs and other batch–processing jobs are parallelized—a horrendous software effort—there really is no way to test the assertion that a single task will run faster on a parallel machine.

However, clear evidence is beginning to emerge that the parallel processors will offer much higher throughput per user than will a big uniprocessor on certain types of interactive tasks (such as database queries or transaction processing). While the response time of big uniprocessors becomes uncomfortably long as the number of users increases, primarily because the depth of the queue increases, a parallel–processing machine shows little of this performance degradation. Moreover, the addition of more processors increases its accessibility to the user.

The best examples of bus–based parallel processors, like the Sequent Balance 21000 and the Encore Multimax, are finding use in office automation (word processing, spread sheets, and office file management) and industrial process–control tasks, but have not as yet found permanent use in the CAE environment. Several years ago, a Menlo Park, California, start–up corporation called Shiva Multisystems attempted to partition a SPICE (simulation program with integrated circuit emphasis) for the Sequent machine. The Berkeley–trained company founders had hoped they could get this popular analog–circuit simulator to run faster by running the program on a parallel processor. However, the company experienced only limited success using MOS (metal oxide on silicon) circuit models, and was later absorbed into a simulation–software company called Simucad (Menlo Park, California) (see Chapter 6). The anecdote is worth mentioning as an example of both the promise and the frustration offered by microprocessor–based parallel processors.

Using a new–generation, 32–bit processor, a 30–CPU machine can provide performance in the range of 40 to 80 MIPS. However, because machines of this type depend on performance in a close linkage between software instructions and associated hardware, a strenuous programming effort must be completed before this power can be harnessed for large CAE tasks. Consequently, a computationally intensive task like SPICE simulation likely will be reserved for big mainframes and minicomputers. However, in the quickness of their interactive responses, the parallel processors emulate single–user workstations and PCs in the use they make of 32–bit microprocessors and other VLSI devices.

Coprocessor–Based Workstations

Since VLSI technology makes it possible to miniaturize many functions of minicomputer CPUs through semiconductor technology, there is a perpetual shrinkage or downsizing of computational resources. By integrating many CPU functions on a microprocessor device smaller than a thumbnail, a roomful of computer equipment can be compressed into a small box that fits comfortably on top of (or along side) a desk. To be sure, the minicomputer makers like DEC are constantly expanding the capabilities of their machines to handle larger software programs, to run these programs faster, and to run more of them at the same time; in other words, to handle an ever–increasing number of users.

However, no sooner does DEC or someone else implement a powerful multiuser system than semiconductor manufacturers begin finding ways to shrink board–level systems down to a handful of chips or a number of chips down to one or two semiconductor devices. There are compromises in any single–chip design: Not all the functions of a VAX CPU could be duplicated in a single–chip device. A general–purpose microprocessor cannot respond to the same range of software instructions as can a VAX, nor can it move data as fast or control the same size semiconductor memory. But semiconductor technology is becoming so advanced— that is, the speed of the transistor devices is so fast and the level of integration so high—that the compromises embodied in microprocessor CPUs are becoming smaller with each generation.

The pace of VLSI technology development is so rapid, in fact, that many analysts believe that if the large minicomputer makers were not perpetually trying out new techniques (like RISC, instruction caching, and pipelining), the computational ability of microprocessor–based computers would have surpassed that of the big uniprocessors several years ago (see Figure 2.7). The turning point, officers at Masscomp (Westford, Massachusettes) suggest, was the invention of the Motorola 68000–family microprocessor. Until that time, single–chip microprocessors were limited in the amount of data they could move in any clock cycle (8 or 16 bits) and the amount of memory space they could control (64 KB) without the help of additional processors. The 68000 provided a 32–bit internal architecture (the ability to operate on 8-, 16–, or 32–bit data), controlled a 16–MB local–memory space, and offered a microcode–instruction set with some 56 VAX–like instructions, putting single–chip microprocessors in the same league with large uniprocessors like the VAX. While their ability to handle multiple users was limited, the 68000–family processors could run the same kinds of programs as the large minicomputers and complete them just as quickly.

The 68010 introduced in 1984, for example, provided computer architects with 32–bit internal registers, a 16–bit data path (32–bit numbers could be sucked–in, 16–bits at a time), and a 24–bit address path (allowing up to 16 MB of direct memory addressing). Small computers using 68010 microprocessor technology (supplemented by a sophisticated bit–mapped graphics capability) provided up to 75% of the processing power of a VAX 11/780—in a much smaller package and at a fraction of the cost. The first of these graphics workstations

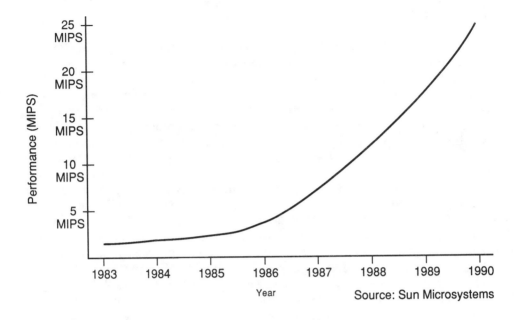

Figure 2.7: The trend in single–user workstation power.

was introduced by Apollo in the early 1980s, followed quickly by workstations from Sun and later by HP. These workstations, especially the products of Apollo and Sun, are among the predominant computers used for electrical engineering.

Because each iteration of the Motorola family of processors seems to embody new features and functions—faster clock rates, wider data paths and address ranges, and on–chip caching—the workstations using these processors show a very clear trend toward increased processing power. The Sun–3/200 workstation, for example, is based on 25–MHz versions of the Motorola 68020 microprocessor and is supported by the 68881 floating–point processor, which provides up to 125 KFLOPS (thousands of floating–point operations per second), or an optional floating–point accelerator board, for up to 865 KFLOPS. These machines are said to perform in the 4–MIPS range.

While 68000–family processors are dominant among OEM workstations, there is competition from other microprocessor devices that deal with 32–bit numbers. The most visible of these is the 32–bit Intel 80386 which provides more than twice the processing power of Intel's 16–bit processor, the 80286. The 80386 offers computer architects a choice between instruction pipelining using on–chip address–translation caches and employing wait states to access main memory. The first choice is closer to a RISC minisupercomputer architecture, while the second offers the versatility of a general–purpose processor. The pipeline mode, for example, allows the 80386 to develop as much instruction processing speed as the 68020—4 MIPS—but at a slower and more economical clock rate (that is, 16 MHz for the 80386, compared to the 25 MHz required for the 68020 to develop 4 MIPS). With on–chip data and instruction caches, the newer 68030 begins to nullify the performance differences between the Motorola and Intel 32–bit processors. Both the Motorola 68020 and 68030 and the Intel 80386, for example, will directly address 4 GB of physical memory.

Because the differences in speed, address range, and data–handling ability of Motorola's and Intel's 32–bit processors are becoming less significant with each generation, the performance differences between these processor types no longer can account for the differences in workstations and PCs. In fact, the distinctions between workstations and PCs never could be attributed only to the differences in the processors used.

For example, Daisy, one of the early leaders in the electrical–CAE business, entered the market with a turnkey CAE system (a graphics workstation with integral software) based on Intel's 16–bit 80286. It provided the same level of performance as the turnkey systems sold by Mentor, another market leader. Mentor's systems were built around the Apollo workstations using the 68010. Similarly, when Daisy introduced the first dedicated workstations based on the Intel 80386 processor (the Logician 386 and the PC/AT–like Personal Logician 386), the company estimated that these machines provided up to 4 MIPS—comparable power to that of Apollo or Sun workstations based on the 68020.

These microprocessor–based machines can be regarded as points along a trend line that shows workstation vendors incorporating ever more mini and superminicomputer muscle into increasingly small deskside or desktop workstations. Many analysts believe that a 100–MIPS workstation using bipolar, ECL, and GaAs (gallium arsenide) device technologies, along with RISC and multiprocessing architectures, conceivably could appear by 1990. A more usual 1990 projection is that workstations with 20 to 40 MIPS will be common in the time frame (see Figure 2.8). Already, workstations with 8 to 10 MIPS of processing power—using RISC processing techniques—are finding their way into the market.

RISC Comes to Microprocessor-Based Workstations

Even as microprocessor technology has reduced a refrigerator–sized computer to a device as small as a thumbnail, the architectural techniques embodied in new–generation minisupercomputers also are subject to LSI and VLSI miniaturization. Consequently, a competition is developing not just between the Motorola and Intel architectural types, but also between the general–purpose processors that put all CPU functions (including some obscure ones) on one chip, and the chip sets that execute a smaller number of instructions but at a much faster rate. By stripping much of the software instruction–decoding mechanisms off the chip, in fact, it is possible to develop a microprocessor that not only runs faster, but (with fewer transistors) is smaller and easier to manufacture.

The architectural trick, with processors of this type, is to hardwire the most frequently executed instructions; that is, to build a circuit that will perform the operation automatically without a software cue. This saves the time ordinarily involved in loading and decoding the software instruction. A

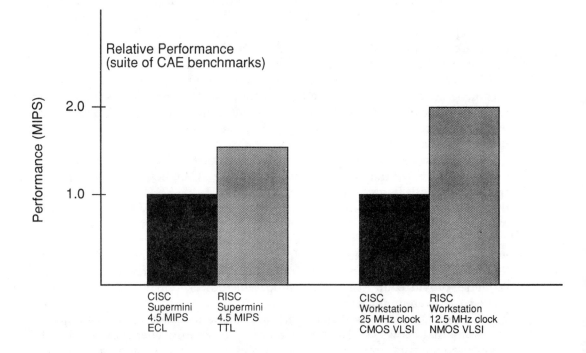

Figure 2.8: Performance comparison, CISC versus RISC architectures. RISC provides performance gains and, in turn, increased real–time capabilities.

second trick is to pick a set of instructions that could be implemented efficiently in software and to identify those infrequently used instructions that it make sense to leave off the chip altogether.

For example, computer scientists believe that the vast majority of CPU operations, even on a general–purpose computer, can be classified as Load and Store operations. That is, the majority of instruction–processing time is devoted to sucking some numbers (instructions or data) into the CPU and putting the result somewhere (a memory location) after the operation is complete. Only a minority of the instructions require the processor to do anything (*Add, Compare, Branch*, etc.) with those numbers. Consequently, a great deal of processing time could be saved if the load–and–store operations were hardwired; that is, performed automatically in hardware rather than by repeated software decoding and interpretation. This can be accomplished by caching, by using a buffer memory as an automatic loading zone for the instructions and data sought by the CPU most often, and by using an automatic address–generation mechanism to identify storage locations for processed data.

This is the thinking embodied in the chip sets developed by Mips Computer Systems Corporation (Sunnyvale, California), and Fairchild Semiconductor Corporation. (Fairchild is a totally owned subsidiary of National Semiconductor, although the marketing and manufacturing rights to the RISC processor—called the Clipper chip set—now belong to Integraph.) The Fairchild–developed Clipper chip set includes a RISC processor embodying a three–stage execution pipeline with overlapped instruction fetch and decode operations and two companion cache and MMU chips. The two integrated 4–KB cache and MMU chips are almost identical, except that one is used for data and one for instructions. In addition to CPU operations, the RISC processor performs floating point–operations. It executes 101 hardwired instructions and only 67 in software. With a 33–MHz clock (a 30–ns—nonosecond, one billionth of a second—cycle time), the Clipper CPU will develop about 5 MIPS and will perform floating–point math at a rate of 690 KFLOPS.

The Mips chip set, the R2065 introduced in March 1986, contains two chips. One includes a fast register pipeline that moves data quickly through on–chip ALU (arithmetic logic unit), multiply/divide, or shifter units; the other performs memory addressing, exception handling, and error recovery. The second chip includes a memory/cache control, with a tag comparator and parity checkers to make sure the right set of data and instructions flow from cache to processor and from processor to memory. Developers of the chip set (including Stanford University professors and engineers once associated with the 68020) believe it can sustain 8 MIPS with a 16 MHz clock, and can provide a peak of 16 MIPS. This is more than twice the processing power of the Intel 80386 (with a 16–MHz clock) and the Motorola 68020 (with a 25–MHz clock).

Advocates of workstations based on RISC processors believe that they are a steeper growth path to processing power. The most noteworthy advocate of this belief is Sun, which, in addition to producing 68020–, 68030–, and 80386–based machines, astounded the world with the introduction of the Sun–4/200 in July 1987. Since all previous generations of Sun workstations were based on the Motorola 68000–family microprocessors, the new machine provided the highest computational power of any workstation product available—about 8 VAX–type MIPS—but little software compatibility with previous–generation machines. The Sun–4 was built around the SPARC (scalable processor architecture) chip set jointly developed by Sun and Fujitsu Microelectronics (San Jose, California). Sun's management had no intention of departing from the use of the popular 68000–family processors and, in fact, announced its intention to use the next–generation Motorola processor, the 68030, in future products. The introduction of the SPARC–based machine was meant to broaden the spectrum of Sun workstation products and to give those users who were willing to develop new software (or to recompile existing source code) for the new machine a higher performance alternative to 68020–based designs. Indeed, SPARC architects felt that the chip set would outperform all existing microprocessors—other RISC types as well as general–purpose types.

Though it offers some of the highest computational performance, the Sun–4 was not the first workstation to use RISC microprocessors. The first workstation to use a RISC processor was the IBM–RT/PC. Despite software support from CAE software vendors like Silvar–Lisco (Menlo Park, California), the inclusion of the UNIX operating system, and IBM's name, the RT/PC was not particularly successful as an OEM workstation. The reason, perhaps, is that the 2 MIPS provided by the RT/PC just was not a dramatic enough performance improvement to justify the effort needed to convert software to the new machine.

A much more dramatic announcement was made by Integraph at the 1986 DAC. The Integraph entry, called the Interpro 32C, was a 5–MIPS workstation based on the Clipper chip set. While the computational work is performed by the Clipper, the I/O channels of the Interpro 32C—all the data movements—are controlled by a separate Intel 80186 processor. Integraph remains insistent that this processor not only outperforms comparably configured computers based on the Motorola 68020 or Intel 80386, but takes up the least PCB real estate to do it.

A few years ago, Cadnetix Corporation (Boulder, Colorado) announced that it would use the R2065 RISC chips manufactured by Mips Computer Systems as an engine for accelerating SPICE circuit simulations and netlist compilation (computationally intensive tasks described in Chapters 4 and 6). What Cadnetix calls their CDX–760 board provides up to 10 MIPS for these tasks.

Workstations Versus Personal Computers

With the exception of Daisy's workstation offerings, there has been a noticeable split between workstations using Motorola–family processors and PCs using Intel processors. The choice had less to do with performance than with cost: While the 80386 resembles the Motorola microprocessors with separate address and data lines, previous–generation Intel devices used multiplexed address and data lines. In addition, it is possible to fold data lines; that is, to suck in a 32–bit number through an 8–bit–wide port by taking 4 clock cycles to bring in the number 8 bits at a time. Earlier Intel processors, like the 16–bit 80286 or the popular 8088 (a microprocessor with a 16–bit internal architecture and an 8–bit external data bus), will tend to give up some clock cycles in switching their external bus lines between memory addressing and data transfer. But because the resulting device requires a package with fewer I/O pins, it is less expensive to manufacture. Moreover, the computer system that uses an Intel device will require fewer processor–to–memory bus lines, and it, too, will be easier to manufacture.

It is for this reason, perhaps, that Intel–type processors have dominated PC architectures. Apart from the microcontrollers used for industrial process control, the earliest PCs were intelligent alpha numeric terminals attached to mainframes and minicomputers in an office environment. These machines were based on the Zilog Z80 processor, a version of the Intel 8080. Much more visible, however, are the IBM–PCs and PC clones, which were built around the 8088. The more powerful 80286 was embodied in the PC/AT, while the 80386 is at the top of IBM's PC line, in the PS/2 (Personal System/2) Model 80.

However, because microprocessors are becoming so powerful, the distinctions between graphics workstations and PCs are becoming more difficult to recognize from the outside. An 80286–based IBM–PC/AT equipped with a Microfield Graphics (Beaverton, Oregon) card and a 15–in. Hitachi America (San Bruno, California) monitor is almost indistinguishable from a Daisy workstation. A high–end PC like the Macintosh II from Apple bears a rather striking resemblance in features, functions, and packaging to Apollo's low–end workstation, the DN3000. Both machines use the Motorola 68020 processor; both offer high–resolution, bit–mapped graphics. Clearly, the distinction between PCs and workstations is not only in the choice of microprocessors.

Rather, the distinctions between the two revolve around costs: No matter how many performance features and functions appear in these machines, PCs are built around manufacturing cost considerations. Semiconductors (processors and memory) are cheap; packaging (cabinetry) is not. If you use a 32–bit processor with a 16– or 8–bit external data bus (like the Motorola 68010 or 68000), 32–bit data and instructions must be brought into the processor in 16– or 8–bit chunks. You still can handle 32–bit numbers. Similarly, if you use a 16–bit processor with an 8–bit external data bus (like the Intel 8088), you give up several clock cycles to suck in each byte, but you still can handle 16–bit numbers; that is, 16–bit software can be run. In either case, you can build a small computer that does the same work as a larger machine, albeit a little slower.

In addition, by using 8 or 16 bus lines instead of 32, a less complicated printed circuit card can be manufactured, and smaller, less–costly connectors can be used. Semiconductor memory is cheap, but every 2 MB requires another insert card and elevates the cost of the backplane, connectors, power supplies, and cooling equipment. By deliberately limiting the amount of main memory, the amount of current needed to power the system, and the size and cost of the power supply can be reduced. By limiting the power consumption, the amount of heat dissipated by the system also is decreased, thus reducing the size and cost of fans, heat sinks, and other cooling equipment. In the graphics arena, it costs an order of magnitude less to implement a 640– x 360–pixel bit map on a 12–in. monochrome CRT screen than to implement a 1280– x 1024–pixel bit map in 16 colors on a 19–in. monitor.

It is expected that multiuser minicomputers will continue to offer more raw processing power, in MIPS and MFLOPS, to each user than will single–user workstations. By the same logic, workstations would be expected to offer more power than PCs. The rapid development and cost reductions apparent with microprocessor CPUs may effectively punch holes in these assumptions. However, you still get what you pay for: Minicomputers will continue to offer more main memory, more disk space, and more network–communications ability than will workstations. Similarly, workstations will offer more memory, more disk space, and better graphics and networking—and will cost more—than PCs.

Operating System Support

Another place where gross distinctions can be made between workstations and PCs is in operating–system support. (An operating system is an internal software task juggler that organizes and schedules the hardware resources of the computer and serves as a glue or knitting that binds the applications program to the computer on which it runs.)

Although the original Apollo workstations used a proprietary Aegis operating system, most contemporary workstations are equipped with some variation of AT&T's UNIX operating system. The most popular revisions of the system developed at AT&T's Bell Laboratories (Murry Hill, New Jersey) include Release 4.2 BSD (Berkeley Software Distribution), a performance–oriented version of UNIX perfected at the University of California at Berkeley, and UNIX System V. While some kind of adjustment or tweaking invariably is required to make the software run smoothly, the UNIX operating system gives application–software developers a reference for programming a wide variety of computers. That is, by writing a single program in (say) the C programming language, a program that uses UNIX calls and subroutines, it is possible to harness that program to practically any computer—workstation, minicomputer, minisupercomputer, or even a PC—that uses UNIX as its internal task juggler.

The IBM–PCs, in contrast, use some version of Microsoft Corporation's (Redmond, Washington) MS–DOS (Microsoft–disk) operating system. While this easy–to–use operating system has formed the foundation of literally thousands of business and office–automation software programs, it has some limitations for engineering programs. Specifically, its most widely used versions (Releases 2.1 and 3.0) limit the address space of the PC to 640 KB. The DOS environment normally has a 16 MB memory address space: The first 640 KB normally exist as local memory in a PC system; the next 128 KB are reserved for low–resolution, bit–mapped screens. An additional 64 KB is reserved for the BIOS. The remaining space (more than 15 MB) exists as a seldom–used DOS extension.

While this presents practically no limitation for word–processing and spread–sheet computations, it does impose limitations on engineering work. A PC, for example, can perform computationally intensive tasks like logic simulation or PCB routing, but the size of the circuit simulated or routed will be very small. Similarly, MS–DOS (or IBM's incarnation, PC–DOS) has few provisions for multitasking. While the machine is cranking away on a logic simulation or autorouting problem, it can be used for nothing else.

New operating systems like OS/2, jointly developed by IBM and Microsoft for 80386–based machines, provide a multitasking capability that allows these PCs to run UNIX and DOS programs simultaneously. However, until OS/2 or Release 5.0 of MS–DOS become widely available, there are only a few ways to get around the 640–KB MS–DOS limitation. One way is port UNIX to the 80286– or 80386–based computer and to run DOS programs as a window within the Unix environment. This was the solution harnessed by Daisy, for example, whose Logician workstations run DNIX, a variation of UNIX 4.2. In operation, the Daisy operating system is booted (put into operation) from the DOS environment. The first 150 KB of the memory space made available by DOS are assigned to the computer's system monitor. The next 750 KB are permanently assigned to DNIX. The remainder of the 16–MB space is dynamically allocatable between DNIX and DOS. This means that DOS programs can be run as a window within the multitasking DNIX environment.

The other methods of overcoming DOS involve hardware add–ons to the PC and PC/AT. One method is to use a hardware implementation of the Lotus, Intel, and Microsoft Expanded Memory Specification (Version 4.0), which allows the PC to access up to 32 MB of local RAM (random–access memory). The specification uses bank switching—or paging 64 KB at a time—to map a memory window into the 32–MB space.

Another frequently used solution is an insert card manufactured by Opus Systems Corporation (Cupertino, California) for the IBM–PC. Using the Fairchild Clipper chip set or a National Semiconductor 32032, the Opus Systems card gives the IBM–PC and compatibles a coprocessor with which to run UNIX software programs. CAE software manufacturers taking advantage of this additional capability on the PC include FutureNet Corporation (Chatsworth, California) and Analog Design Tools (Sunnyvale, California).

Replacing the Intel CPU with a more powerful (and expensive) coprocessor, and partitioning a big (85–MB) hard disk between DOS and UNIX operations may seem like retrofitting a Volkswagen Beetle with a Corvette engine. The cost of adding a coprocessor, larger memory, disk space, power supply, and graphics capability, in fact, is very close to that of a comparably equipped UNIX workstation. Regardless of the costs, many people, both users and software developers, believe that this approach provides a more comfortable CAE solution than does an OEM workstation.

No engineering department manager or corporate purchase agent wants to hear that the $100,000 turnkey CAE system purchased last year now costs $50,000 and soon will cost $20,000. Nor, do they want to hear that the manufacturer of their $100,000 system is now out of business. Software developers do not want to think that they are sinking costly labor into hardware that will be considered next year's boat anchor. There is much fear and suspicion in the CAE arena, which is not unjustified. It is a competitive, fast–paced market that just is not large enough to support all its current participants.

While this book is not intended to predict the winners and losers among the participants in the CAE market, we can shed some light on the trend of user preferences. First, there is safety in numbers. For this reason, CAE is becoming a big–company business, with users and software developers putting their efforts into those hardware platforms that have the largest distribution in corporate and engineering environments. These include the products of DEC, IBM (in the office environment), and HP.

Second, there is an insistence on hardware and software standards that, over time, will make every workstation look and feel like every other workstation, every PC look and feel like every other PC. No software developer wants to port programs to 45 different machines, many of which will disappear. Software development is much easier if there are only a few standard computers. The knotty differences between the 68020–based products of Apollo, Sun, and HP—even some of the RISC–based machines like Integraph's—can be tolerated, as long as they all run UNIX. That way, if one of these hardware manufacturers goes out of business, the software developer still has a product that will run on other machines.

Third, because of price erosion and rapid hardware obsolescence, users tend to avoid turnkey systems. They will buy software separately from hardware and tend to minimize the investment in hardware regardless of the MIPS rating. That way, if the hardware becomes obsolete (and chances are it will), the hardware costs can be depreciated in less than two years, and the software can be moved to another low–cost platform. Because of this strong tendency to buy workstations cheaply, the IBM–PC, though computationally puny, still retains a place for CAE and other engineering activity.

For these reasons, the CAE world increasingly will revolve around three major computer architectures: DEC platforms (like the MicroVAX II and MicroVAX III) using the VMS operating system; graphics workstations using 68000–family processors with the UNIX operating system; and souped–up PCs (like the IBM–PC/AT) employing an Intel processor architecture and the MS–DOS operating system.

Toward an Intelligent Division of Labor

Which hardware makes a better platform for CAE work is a different debate, with the marketers of PC–based CAE software making outrageous claims for PCs in areas that require many MIPS to run efficiently and the marketers of deskside systems insisting that all engineers in every organization need their own $100,000 workstations. The debate has obvious elements of slob appeal versus snob appeal, pitting something like the Honda Civic against a BMW. In reality, there also are a number of tasks that can be performed sensibly on a PC; there are also tasks that must be performed on a mainframe or minicomputer. One purpose of this book, in fact, is to provide enough insight into each of these tasks that a division of labor is obvious: Knowing how a computer performs schematic entry, netlist extraction, simulation, or routing is key to understanding what kind of computers will do these jobs successfully, and what type of human interface is required. All we can do in the remaining pages of this chapter is to offer a flavor for these tasks, so that the seemingly contradictory pulls between more MIPS and cheaper desktop computers can be partially reconciled. In this sense, we are offering an insight into the engineering trade–offs and compromises that the CAE industry is making.

The experience many engineers have gained with PCs, as well as with early turnkey systems, has created an awareness of the types of computational resources required to perform CAE tasks.

High–resolution graphics are needed for schematic entry and for physical–layout tasks, whether for an IC or a PCB. This is an interactive task performed by a person. The engineer makes an entry on a workstation or PC, gets visual feedback from the computer, makes another entry, gets more feedback, and so forth until the job is done. Much larger computational resources are needed for netlist compilation, simulation, layout, and DRC (design rule checking). These are batch–processing jobs that historically have taken hours of run time on a mainframe or big minicomputer. For these applications, obviously, the PC/AT (even an AT with add–ons) is barely adequate, despite a trend toward making these jobs interactive.

In reality, every software program or subroutine can be seen as a batch–processing job for a computer; that is, it will take some predictable amount of time to run through its calculations and give the user an answer. The more difficult the computations and the longer the list of variables the computer must juggle, the longer it will take the computer to come up with an answer. Since autoplacement and routing problems, for example, frequently involve many thousands (sometimes millions) of operations, the software may take several hours to run on a mainframe computer. (In many large corporations, these programs are submitted into a mainframe's batch queue and are run with other jobs like paycheck computation in the middle of the night when user demands on the system are minimal.) These computations can be performed in seconds by a Cray–type supercomputer (albeit with a time–sharing fee of $7000/hour). No matter how many operations are involved, the program can be considered interactive if the computer takes its cue from a person on a terminal (for example, the user hits *Return* on the keyboard), runs through its calculations, and puts the response on the terminal screen before the user's attention begins to flag. The threshold, according to computer ergonomists, is about four seconds.

While CAE tasks like netlist compilation and electrical and physical DRC traditionally have been performed in a batch–processing mode, corporate and market pressures to complete a design quickly are forcing these tasks into an interactive mode. The idea is to simulate a circuit or route a PCB at the same time the schematic is entered on the workstation screen. Instead of creating a schematic on a computer and waiting an hour for the machine to extract a netlist and perhaps a day to complete a logic simulation—only to discover there was an error (say) in the choice of components—the interactive simulator could calculate results and point out errors to the user almost as soon as they are made. This would shorten the design cycle considerably.

There are two ways of doing this. One is to develop specialized software algorithms and to streamline the program so that millions of computer operations can be reduced to several hundred, with approximately the same results. For example, object–oriented databases—software techniques borrowed from the field of artificial intelligence—embed conductivity information (that is, netlists) and design rules in the CAE database. Consequently, these jobs now can be performed on–line—that is, interactively—on workstation CPU (as long as it has a big virtual–memory space).

The other method is simply to run the calculations on bigger, faster computers. For example, the autoplacement and routing of cells for a gate–array IC (or of ICs for a PCB) are massive computational tasks that increase almost exponentially with the size and complexity of the circuit. Several popular routing algorithms are discussed in Chapters 7 and 8, but the increasing size and complexity of these routing projects forces engineering teams to harness ever more powerful machines.

Consider an analogous problem: If, on Christmas Eve, Santa Claus spent just 10 seconds in each of the world's estimated 840 million homes, it would take him 266 years to complete his rounds. Clearly, this is an unacceptable response time. One solution is to parcel out the task among 840 million "microSantas." Another is to harness a blazingly fast "superSanta," which reduces the time spent in each home from 10 seconds to 20 μs (microseconds—millionth of a second). That way, Santa can complete his Christmas rounds within a sensible 5 hours.

The appearance of powerful new workstation platforms (and accelerator boards) means that the user will have more local processing power available for CPU–intensive CAE tasks such as netlist compilation, logic simulation, automated placement and routing, or physical and electrical DRC. But it should be clear that not even the most powerful workstations of the future will be able to provide *all* the computational resources needed for CAE tasks.

The middle–of–the-road position is to find a cost–effective workstation platform; that is, to provide the individual engineers with only as much computational resources, graphics, and disk space as they need to do their jobs, and to transfer the larger computational tasks to a big machine through a communications network. Many corporations feel that if 75% of the user's time seems to be spent on interactive tasks (such as schematic entry), it makes no sense to pay the full price to equip each user with a 4– or 5–MIPS workstation. The Apollo DN3000 (with network interfaces to a VAX or assorted accelerators) still is considered one of the best price–performance breaks.

For this reason, even a workstation power leader like Sun has strategic alliances with minisupercomputer vendors like Convex and Alliant that allow the extended power of these machines to go on–line with a Sun. The NFS (networked file system), developed by Sun, is an increasingly popular way to transfer engineering files.

An additional advantage of network architecture, is that they provide a way to interconnect fundamentally different computer types. HP's networking strategy, for example, interconnects IBM mainframes and PCs, DEC's superminicomputers, and HP's own minicomputers and 68020–based workstations. While Ethernet has come to be the dominant data–transmission method in engineering environments, HP's networking strategy also embraces IBM mainframe protocols such as SNA (system networking architecture) and HDLC.

Windowing and Graphics

One of the advantages provided by big, high–resolution workstation screens is that they allow the user to open and visualize multiple windows—to graphically depict different computational jobs running simultaneously (in multitasking mode) on the workstation or on different computers in the network. In the ideal CAE environment, multiple CAE functions can be displayed in windows on the user's workstation screen: One window can show a user schematic; another can show a simulated waveform and timing–verification diagram; a third can portray part of a layout or additional menu options for the user. In a perfectly interactive environment, for example, a change in the schematic automatically will produce a change in a simulated waveform on the screen.

The majority of 68020–based workstations offer high–resolution controllers and monitor combinations with a 1024– x 840–pixel (or 1280– x 1024–pixel) resolution, up to 256 simultaneous colors with a choice of 15– or 19–in. Hitachi or Mitsubishi monitors. Some manufactures, like HP, have concentrated on increasing the speed at which the 2–D (two–dimensional) screen paints its images; others, like Apollo (with its DN580 graphics accelerator) increased 3–D (three–dimensional) graphics capability.

The majority of electrical engineering work—schematic or text entry and the visualization of waveforms—is performed on 2–D flat screens. While there is an increasing interest in the ability to visualize the dimensions of an electronic design's enclosure (a task requiring 3–D wire–frame capability) or to visually simulate the thermal hot spots on an IC or printed circuit card (requiring 3–D color imaging), the majority of CAE tasks require only 2–D graphics capability.

Most PC platforms use the VGA (video graphics array) as the standard color interface for PC–based systems. The EGA graphics controller and compatible monitor provide 256 colors on a 640– x 480–pixel screen. While there are a variety of graphics controllers on insert cards for the PC and PC/AT that bring the color–pixel resolution closer to 1024 x 800 pixels, like the fast bit–slice devised by Microfield Graphics, there are very few software drivers for these among PC–based CAE packages. (The PCB–layout package from Personal CAD Systems—PCAD—of San Jose, California is the only noteworthy exception.)

This limited resolution can make big schematic–entry projects very tiresome. Using a PC for CAE work is very much like driving a Volkswagen Beetle across the U.S. It is cost efficient: people do it all the time. But there obviously are more comfortable ways to travel. These will be discussed in Chapter 3.

While a very–high–resolution display (1024 x 800 pixels) is a minimum requirement for comfortably visualizing a complex circuit (or dividing the screen into multiple viewing windows), the flat 2–D display requirement means that each pixel need not be very deep. That is, the scanning mechanism on the CRT needs only to turn each pixel on or off as it scans across the screen. A black–and–white image, in fact, will display almost everything an engineer needs to see with electrical CAE. Even where color is used to make the screen easier to read (as, for example, in displaying multiple waveforms for analysis on a single x–y axis), the color pixels merely need to be turned on or off by the scanning mechanism. Usually, three circuit boards, representing red, green, and blue (RGB), are all that is required to produce any color combination. Electrical–CAE work requires that each pixel—whether it is red, green, or blue—merely be turned on or off.

The computational requirements of mechanical CAD, in most cases, will be more difficult to meet than those of electrical–engineering work. To portray a sense of depth with 3–D images, each pixel must reflect a different level of light intensity. The brighter pixels will portray sections of an object in the foreground; the darker pixels will portray sections of an object receding from the viewer into the background. The computer graphic machinery in this case must not just turn each pixel on or off, but must calculate the level of light intensity for each pixel and activate a mechanism capable of scaling the light intensity at that point. For color displays, the computer calculates the light intensity for each of the RGB color planes.

To understand the complexity of this computational work, it is necessary to recognize the number of pixel points the computer must deal with. For a 1280–x

1024–pixel screen, the computer must deal with almost 2 million pixels. To prevent a fatiguing screen flicker, these pixels much be refreshed (totally redrawn) 60 times per second. Even for a 2–D black–and–white drawing, the computer must refresh 120 million pixels each second. For a color screen, merely turning each RGB pixel on or off would force the computer to choose among eight possible colors at each pixel location. The average viewer can distinguish eight–bits of light intensity at each pixel point; that is, the viewer usually can distinguish among 256 distinct intensity levels. If an 8–bit light–intensity level is added to each color board, the computer is forced to choose among approximately 16 million color/light–intensity combinations at each pixel location. This means that the computer that controls the graphics screen must make about (120 million x 16 million) pixel display choices each second.

Consequently, it easily can take hours for a mainframe or small supercomputer to calculate the pixel–display coordinates of an elaborately colored, textured, and shaded object. The degree of complication increases as the user attempts to rotate the object to see a different view or to visualize the relationships among objects as they move in concert or randomly on the computer screen. Calculating all the coordinates can tie up a Cray–type supercomputer for hours at a time. Since a Cray–2 sells for approximately $15 million, and time–sharing can cost more than $7,000 per hour, the depiction of motion on finely shaded and textured objects is required only for the most well–funded projects.

One way to minimize the computational task is to simplify the image, by reducing the number of textures and light sources, settling for a crude surface depiction rather than the smooth surface, or letting a skeletal structure or framework represent the entire object. By reducing the 3–D image down to a wire frame, the number of computations is reduced to something that can be handled by a PC.

Another solution is to pack supercomputer resources into a workstation package. The new–generation superworkstations are single–user systems in which an extremely high computational ability is combined with extremely high–performance graphics. Applications like mechanical stress analysis or thermal imaging, according to analysts, will require 10 to 20 MIPS and 3 to 10 MFLOPS of floating–point support. The graphics engine likely would be a specialized accelerator capable of producing 4096 colors on a 2000– x 2000–pixel screen.

A machine like this now is in development at Stellar Computer (Newton, Massachusetts). This multiprocessor machine should have mixed scalar and vector capabilities, with between 20 and 30 MIPS of scalar performance and 40 MFLOPS of vector performance. Both vectorizing and parallelizing compilers are necessary for the operation of the computational engine, which would produce 100,000 to 200,000 rendered polygons per second from a deep Z–buffer.

This applications area is not just for start–up companies. DEC has designs for high–end interactive graphics applications, as do Tektronix, HP, and other established workstation vendors. One of these vendors, in fact, has produced the highest–performance 3–D graphics engine based on a proprietary RISC architecture. The competition, however, is fierce: Tektronix's Information Display Group is hard at work on the successor to the 4129 graphics workstation.

HP, in fact, already has established a reference point—the machine to beat—for high–performance graphics with the introduction of its HP–9000 Model 320SRX. Called the Renaissance, this graphics engine has hardwired many of the transform algorithms that convert 3–D coordinates into 2–D raster space using NMOS (negative-well metal oxide silicon) VLSI devices. Consequently, the Model 320SRX has up to 20 times the speed of similarly priced machines in rendering a 3–D object on a 1280– x 1024–pixel screen.

How these developments will affect electrical engineering work is a subject for considerable speculation. To integrate a 3–D model into the electrical–CAE environment, the wire-frame or solids model still must share the computer screen with the electrical circuit, the waveform display, and the documentation package. Similarly, the computational resources must be shared with the netlist compiler and the logic simulator. Consequently, the integration of 3–D images with 2–D electrical CAD will require some concerted software efforts. While a workstation that does some of this already has been constructed for wafer test purposes by Schlumberger (San Jose, California), its impact on electrical CAE may not be fully appreciated for some time to come.

Fortunately, because of the computer and workstation advances discussed in this chapter, we can at least start to visualize some of the more imaginative possibilities. One of these is RISC.

• The Effects of RISC on CAE •

Over the past several years, the trend has been toward placing more computational power on the desk of the individual engineer. The trend began with the move from batch–oriented computing to time–shared systems. With a terminal on his or her desk, the engineer could undertake analyses and simulations that previously were beyond the capability of the individual. Engineers no longer were bound by delays through the computing center.

The advent of the engineering workstation furthered this trend. With the workstation, the engineer not only can run analyses and simulations as desired, but also can use graphics to accurately represent the object being designed, or to graphically represent the results of simulations. Since humans work much better with pictures than with numbers, this allows much greater insight into the design process. The result is better designs in a shorter time. The faster simulations run and the more realism in the graphic image, the better the design process will be.

The Need for More Power

Although modern workstations provide greater computational power than many superminicomputers, there is an ever–increasing appetite for computing power. Supercomputer–like power is required to accomplish graphic representations and simulations in real time. Engineers could be much more productive with real–time display of information. Workstations based upon CISC (complex instruction set computing) microprocessors have reached a performance plateau, where gains are coming more slowly.

One approach to increasing computing power is to off–load the workstation through the use of high–performance compute servers. This solves part of the problem, since computational power now is available to any workstation on a network. However, data–intensive tasks may not proceed any faster, due to the speed of the network. Also, graphics performance still is a limiting factor in overall throughput, which puts increasing pressure on the performance of the workstation.

The widespread use of PCs has made network computing resources even more important. While the PC is adequate for many tasks, simulations and complex analyses need greater computational power. High–performance computers fill this need, but at a relatively high price. In addition, users would like to have real–time graphics capabilities on PCs without paying an unreasonable price for the capability.

The trend is toward a distributed computing environment that allows the use of a variety of systems integrated into a network. Each node on the network is tuned to a given task, such as schematic capture, simulation, or board layout. The cost of each node is minimized for the capabilities needed. Specialized servers provide capabilities that are needed by all nodes, but that are too expensive to replicate. Therefore, performance gains are required at all levels of the environment while still retaining cost–effectiveness.

Into this power void comes the RISC–based system. In many cases, RISC allows higher performance at lower cost. It can fill the need for network computing resources and workstations cost effectively. It also can be used as the processor model for a variety of graphics and computation accelerators.

The CISC Model

CISC systems are based the premise that it is most efficient to write software in high–level code and to use an instruction set that closely parallels the high–level code. That is, each source–code statement has a dual in–the–computer instruction set that performs much the same function. Complex instructions then are interpreted into a set of simple instructions (*load, store, move, add, branch,* etc.) that execute directly in the hardware. It is easy to write compilers for CISC systems; there are many ways to accomplish even the most complex tasks. Unfortunately, the optimum path through the system is very difficult to find, even for an experienced programmer. Tuning of the generated code may prove an arduous task.

Generally, a CISC architecture is designed to produce microcode from the compiler. The microcode then is interpreted to simple machine instructions, which are executed on the hardware. The interpretation is invisible to the user. Often, programmers are allowed to write their own microcode routines to speed execution on repetitive tasks.

Implementations of CISC CPUs have been accomplished in VLSI. Many such processors contain over 300,000 transistors. The microcode interpreter is a large part of the silicon involved, and there is little opportunity for adding capabilities, such as on–chip cache.

The RISC Model

RISC designs arose from the realization by computer researchers that the complex instructions in CISC architectures seldom are used in real applications, and that the instructions that are used most are simple. These simple instructions often can be executed in one machine cycle. So, if the simple instructions can be implemented in hardware, the complexity of microcode can be eliminated. The system should be less expensive and run faster.

Thus, RISC requires a reduced number of simple instructions, implemented in hardware, most of which execute in a single machine cycle. Architectures generally limit instruction execution to a register–to–register model to limit memory access, use a Load/Store access for all memory to allow easier optimization of code, and are heavily pipelined.

Assuming that an instruction can be executed with each machine cycle, the average performance of a RISC system (measured in MIPS) should be much greater than that of a comparable CISC implementation. However, if many times more instructions are needed to accomplish the same task, the advantage is lost. The key to limiting this code expansion is the optimizing compiler. Optimizing compilers are the most important software link in the chain of performance improvement. RISC architectures take advantage of the simple instructions, Load/Store memory access, and a very regular instruction set to allow easy implementation of optimizing compilers. Code expansion usually is minimal for most RISC systems.

Instructions on typical RISC systems may execute at an average rate approaching 80% to 90% of the clock rate. This gives MIPS ratings that are a comparable percentage of the system clock rate (see Figure 2.8).

In real systems, large performance gains are possible. For example, RISC systems implemented in slow technologies, such as CMOS, and TTL, often exhibit performance greater than that of a comparable CISC system using ECL, usually considered a fast technology. At the same time, component count is reduced, resulting in lower cost and higher reliability. Lower component counts also mean that there is room in VLSI implementations for various additional features on the chip. On–chip caching will improve performance, for example, by reducing access time. Many RISC architectures are implemented using less than a third the number of components that CISC uses.

Application to CAE Problems

The performance gains possible with RISC will allow a variety of approaches to increasing the real–time capabilities of the engineer. Workstations with high computational capabilities and high–performance graphics will allow simulations and visual realism to be achieved. If, instead, the engineer uses a PC or lower performance workstation, computation may be accomplished at a network computing resource (server) using RISC architecture. This server could cost less than equivalent superminis implemented in CISC architectures.

PC graphics will become more sophisticated. Using compute servers on the network, the PC can be mostly a user interface and graphic engine. RISC concepts applied to graphics–display processors will increase their performance. The cost of the PC will remain nearly constant, while the range of tasks will increase. Real–time displays of data can be achieved with high–performance graphics, and computation may be performed on a remote server.

It is clear that RISC computing concepts can be applied widely to CAE. A distributed network of systems ranging from PCs to large compute servers may be implemented with RISC, adding performance at each node. Cost for a given level of performance is reduced, and reliability is increased. Standard networking, such as X–Window and ARPA/BSD (Advanced Research Projects Agency/Berkeley Software Distribution) services, will allow sharing of the CAE problem over the network. The user can choose the right system for each node on the network to balance cost and performance. Each piece of the application is performed at the node that is best equipped to accomplish the task (see Figure 2.9).

The whole range of systems still will be required. PCs fill the need for low cost, while supercomputers may be needed for very complex simulations. RISC will help to keep the price/performance ratios improving.

Potential Limitations

Many CAE problems can be solved efficiently with parallel, rather than sequential, algorithms. Digital circuit simulation is a good example of this. Because of their inherent simplicity, it often is assumed that RISC architectures cannot accommodate parallel processing. This is not strictly true. While a given architecture may be so designed, it also is possible to design the architecture to allow parallel RISC systems. At least two workstation vendors have announced this capability in a RISC architecture.

Expert software designers may be able to tune code to achieve optimal throughput. Microcode routines often are used in this effort. Since microcode is not used on RISC systems, tuning becomes difficult. In fact, tuning may be less useful on RISC systems, anyway. Researchers have found that the optimizing compilers used with RISC compare favorably with the best hand–tuned code. Hand–tuning may achieve gains of a few percent. In addition, some RISC architectures allow writing of special routines in a microcode–like environment, sometimes called millicode.

This leads to the consideration of special instruction sets designed for a given task. In CISC, this is accomplished easily using microcode. With RISC, these instructions can be implemented by special compilers designed to handle the specific problem. These compilers may be handled as libraries to other language compilers. The resulting instruction stream still may be optimized, and multiprocessors still may be used.

RISC does not inherently lock out the useful capabilities of CISC. It is merely a simpler way of implementing similar systems. The major change is in the interface between hardware and software, not in the theory of computation.

The trend is toward more computational power for the individual user in a CAE environment. Engineers want more simulation, realism, and real–time capabilities in their systems. These capabilities will allow them to produce faster, better optimized designs. They can use human cognitive powers on graphical representations of designs to make better design decisions.

CISC designs in microprocessors and superminicomputers are reaching a performance plateau where gains are coming more slowly and with increasing effort. It is getting more difficult to constantly improve the price/performance ratio.

RISC offers the advantage of improved performance with reduced complexity, which dramatically improves the price/performance ratio while increasing reliability. In addition, RISC may be applied to a wide range of system components covering a modern distributed computing environment. High–performance graphics systems for PCs and workstations may benefit from RISC processors. Workstation computational power may be increased to allow real time simulations using RISC processors. Finally, RISC can be applied to high performance compute servers, offering excellent price/performance ratios.

The marketplace has come to expect dramatic reductions in the cost of computing power over time. RISC presents an opportunity to meet those expectations for the foreseeable future.

• Networking •

Networking also plays a vital role in increasing the productivity of the CAE design team. First, networking facilitates the sharing of CAE databases among team members, so that information can be passed easily from one phase in the design process to the next. Second, networking allows CAE designers to use a wide range of resources. These resources include application programs or data that reside on different computer systems with possibly different operating systems and varying classes of performance. Also, high–performance printers, plotters, and disk drives can be shared. In short, networking allows you to access the resources needed to complete the design process.

This section will examine the characteristics of the CAE design–computer environment that pertain to networking. The networking implementations and concepts that are prevalent in the industry and are designed to meet these needs then will be introduced.

Key Networking Needs in Electrical CAE

Figure 2.9 characterizes the typical CAE networking environment. The computers are connected to a high–speed LAN (local area network) in a bus topology. The computers shown above the LAN are the mini and mainframe

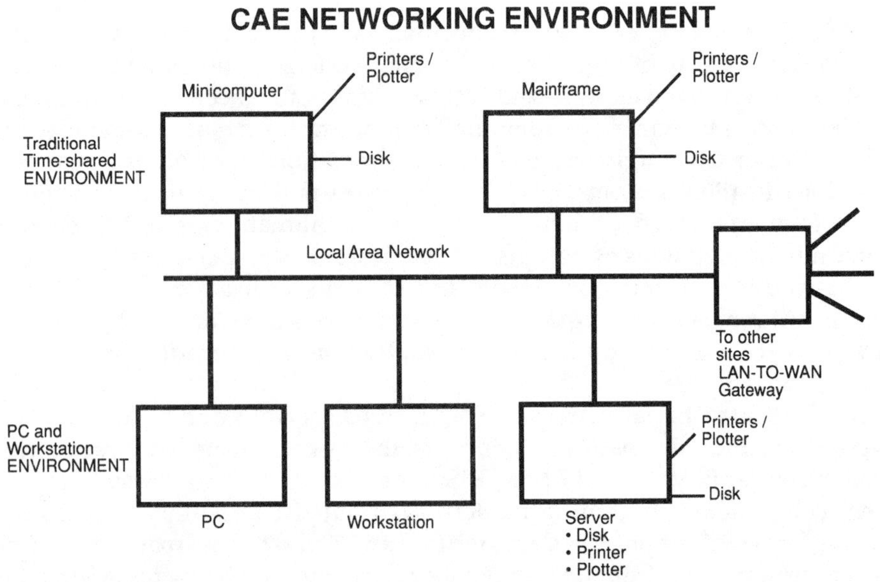

CAE NETWORKING ENVIRONMENT

Figure 2.9: The CAE Networking Environment.

computers. Before the emergence of PCs and workstations, CAE was performed entirely on these classes of machines, with multiple terminals connected to each host computer. This is known as *time–sharing the host computer*. Many CAE applications now are being performed on PCs and workstations and, as a result, networking must provide the integration of the traditional mainframe and minicomputer environment with the new, distributed PC and workstation environment. Also, servers have emerged as a key component, providing the sharing of resources, such as disk files, printers and plotters, and computation, among users on the network.

CAE applications now exist on many classes of computer systems, including PCs, workstations, minicomputers, superminicomputers, mainframe computers, and custom hardware, depending on the computing requirements. For instance, schematics may be captured on PCs or UNIX workstations and passed on to a higher performance computer for simulation, analysis, or routing of the design.

CAE applications exist on a wide range of operating systems, including DOS, UNIX, VMS, MVS, and many others. Networking is required to provide the links and services between computers running different operating systems. File translations must be performed by networking during file transfers to handle the differences among operating system in how data is represented (byte format) and how data is stored; for example, sequential, fixed–, or variable–length record, sequential or indexed file organizations. In addition, networking allows a designer on one computer to log onto another computer system and run applications on that remote computer.

CAE applications exist on many different vendors' computer products. Generally, no one hardware vendor can satisfy the computing requirements for the entire design, analysis, test, and documentation process. In addition, users would like to be able to choose the best price/performance option available for a particular task. Networking protocol standards play a very important role by allowing networking implementations on different vendors, products to communicate. The U.S. Department of Defense (DoDARPA)'s early development work on communications protocols, in combination with later work done by the University of California at Berkeley for its UNIX Release 4.2 BSD, have defined the de facto industry standard for networking protocols on UNIX computers. These protocols have been adopted on many computers and operating systems. These protocols, often collectively referred to as TCP/IP (transmission control protocol/internet protocol), are examined in more detail later.

Designers need to share information and access common information to complete the design, analysis, test, and documentation process. In situations where PCs and workstations are used by CAE designers, networking is essential to provide many of the resource–sharing features of a large multiterminal mainframe computer. However, instead of large central disks attached directly to a multiterminal mainframe computer, file servers on the network service requests for data by workstations. Networking capabilities are necessary to provide this access with satisfactory performance, security, and reliability. In addition, application–program developers need a programmatic interface to the file system so that programs can be written to access data that may be stored either locally on the same system or remotely on a file server on the network. The NFS has emerged as the de facto networking standard for distributed file systems on UNIX computers and has been adopted on many non–UNIX systems as well.

Shared databases that are accessed by CAE designers are very large and include designs, parts libraries, programs and other information. They need to be kept up–to–date, secured against unauthorized access, accessed quickly, easily managed. It is common for designs to be several megabytes per file. As a result, the standard RS–232 cabling with data rates at 19.2 kilobaud or slower is unacceptable. LANs have been developed that are optimized for high performance over limited distances between computer systems.

CAE design teams generally are located in a common facility and occasionally need to work with designers at other physical sites. LANs provide high–performance communications among computers and allow for easy addition and deletion of systems from the network. High–performance LANs serve as the primary network for high frequency traffic between workstations and servers or between workstations and workstations for communication among the design team. For less frequent communications with computers at other sites, there are WANs (wide area networks). In a CAE environment, computers generally are directly attached to a LAN; however, for communication with systems on a WAN, there are specialized computers called gateways that route data from LANs to WANs.

CAE designers need access to high–performance and relatively expensive output peripherals, such as printers and plotters, for high–quality documentation. To amortize the cost of these expensive peripherals by allowing the design team to share printers and plotters, the designer's workstation or PC must be networked to a computer that has the printer or plotter attached locally. Networking implementations allow application programs to send printed output to remote printers on the network. In addition, the end user or programmer uses the same commands to access remote printers or plotters as would be used to access local printers and plotters.

CAE applications use high–performance bit–mapped graphics with easy–to–use windowing interfaces. Networking extends this capability to allow graphics–based applications running on a remote computer to be displayed in windows on a designer's workstation. In fact, several windows can be displayed with application programs running on several different computers on the network. As a result, the designer can be running several applications at once on different computers.

The CAE designer often needs access to computer information in other functional areas including accounting, inventory and manufacturing. Networking provides the links to computers in these other areas. For example, these areas may perform functions like routing the PC board, prototyping and manufacturing the design, or maintaining the manufacturing specifications and parts inventory.

Now that we have examined the networking needs in CAE, we will now describe some networking implementations that address these requirements.

Connecting with the Host Computer

CAE designers working on terminals need access to a host computer running applications written for a time–shared environment. Databases, printers, and plotters are attached locally to the host computer and are shared by the CAE designers.

Traditional Time–sharing Environment. The traditional time-shared environment is shown in Figure 2.10. CAE applications on the host computer are written for alpha and graphics terminals, such as IBM's 5080 or 3270 families of terminals or DEC's VT 100, 200, or 300 families of terminals. These terminals require special escape codes and data streams to display data. Each type of terminal has its own set of escape codes and data streams, and the host computer must be able to send the correct sequence of information to the terminal to make it work properly. Although Figure 2.10 does not show the host computers networked to other computers, this can be done. For instance, networking to computers in other functional areas, such as manufacturing, may be required. The diagram shown in in Figure 2.10 has been simplified, because in the traditional time–shared environment, a single central host computer with attached peripherals is the resource that is being shared by the CAE design team. IBM mainframe computers can communicate with other computers using IBM's SNA. DEC minicomputers can communicate with other computers using DEC's DECnet networking architecture.

These vendor–specific implementations for items such as terminal inter-faces, operating systems, networking protocols, and database formats generally

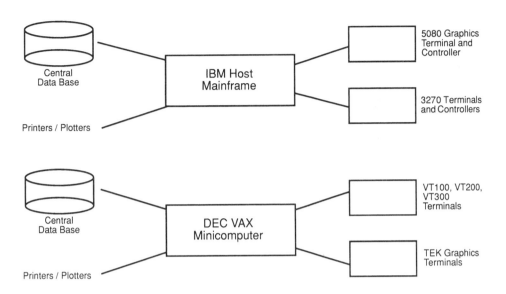

Figure 2.10: Traditional time–shared environment.

make a CAE solution available only on one vendor's hardware. Fortunately, the computer industry is beginning to move toward standards in many areas to provide a well–integrated distributed environment. This will allow CAE managers to choose the appropriate equipment for a task without being locked into a particular computer vendor for all their computing needs.

Distributed Environment. With the emergence of low–cost, local computing on PCs and workstations and the availability of CAE applications on a wide range of computers, many new networking requirements were introduced. Networking standards, new basic connectivity, server communications, and integration of the new distributed environment (see Figure 2.11) with the traditional time–shared host environment have become important networking areas. Each of these areas are examined in more detail.

To ensure that a wide range of computers can communicate with each other, networking standards for data communications have begun to emerge. These are discussed in the following sections.

International Standards Organization OSI Model

The International Standards Organization (ISO) standards body has created an OSI (open systems interconnect) that describes networking functionality. In addition, the model separates different networking functionalities into seven layers: application, presentation, session, transport, network, data link, and physical. The highest layer, application, defines the networking applications

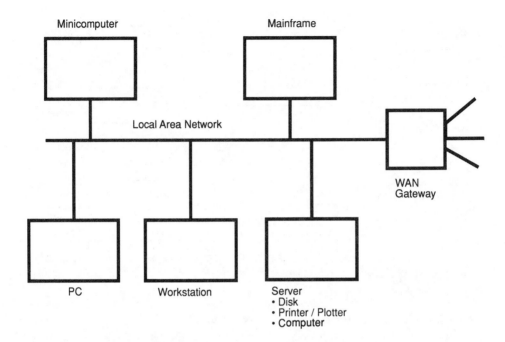

Figure 2.11: CAE distributed environment.

or services that are provided to users of the network, such as file–transfer or virtual–terminal services, and the lowest layer, physical, defines the physical media used to transmit the information, such as coaxial cable. These layers are described below:

Layer 7—Application Layer. Provides the networking services for the end user. Examples include file transfer, virtual terminal, remote command execution, message (mail) handling, and remote file access.

Layer 6—Presentation Layer. Provides transformations of the data to transmit over the network more efficiently. Transformations include compression or encryption of text.

Layer 5—Session Layer. Establishes and maintains network connections between pairs of communicating systems on different computers on the network. Functions performed include mapping symbolic names to network addresses, dialog control, and synchronization between end–user tasks.

Layer 4—Transport Layer. Transports information between end–user machines without knowing the network topology and path to route the information between systems. Functions include end–to–end error detection and recovery and multiplexing of network connections.

Layer 3—Network Layer. Responsible for routing data packets over the network from the source computer to the destination computer. In addition, this layer handles packaging of transport information into efficient packet sizes for transmission over the network.

Layer 2—Data Link Layer. Responsible for sending data reliably and efficiently over the network medium. Checksums are used to check data integrity, and retransmission schemes are used to resend faulty data.

Layer 1—Physical Layer. Responsible for the transmission of the raw bit stream over the network medium. Layer 1 handles voltages and electrical pulses and defines the cable and connection components.

The OSI model helps networking vendors to modularize their networking functions and their associated networking protocols that exist in their products. This allows for easier interchange of alternative networking protocols among vendors, resulting in more flexible networking products to CAE users; for example, a file–transfer service that is supported using several cabling schemes.

For two systems to communicate, they both must use the same networking protocols. Unfortunately, the model does not specify the actual networking protocols that networking vendors should use. For this reason, the OSI model does not address the entire problem. However, it does provide the essential framework for networking vendors and standards bodies to develop networking protocols at each layer of the model. If vendors then can agree to implement the same protocols, multivendor communications can be achieved.

The ISO standards body has been working on the actual networking protocols to allow for multivendor communications. This is the first effort made by a bona fide standards body to provide multivendor networking standards and verification tests. All computer vendors are committed to the networking standards that result from this work. However, the standards probably will not be prevalent until the 1990s due to the development effort required.

UNIX Networking Standards

The predominant nonproprietary operating system in CAE is UNIX. Along with UNIX there is a set of networking protocols that were included in UNIX Release 4.2 BSD. These protocols consist of the ARPA networking services and the Berkeley UNIX networking services.

Distributed File System Standards. Recently the NFS has been adopted widely as the networking–protocol standard for distributed file systems for UNIX. In addition, there are NFS implementations for the IBM–PC and DEC VAX/VMS computers.

A distributed file system provides the capability needed to share central disk files on a file server and to share output peripherals such as printers and plotters. NFS allows a user to extend the local file system to include a file system or part of a file system that exists on a remote computer on the network. Therefore, application programs can run on the CAE designer's computer while the data resides on a remote computer. Also, programs can be located and down-loaded from a central disk when the designer chooses to run the program.

AT&T has included the RFS (remote file system) distributed file system in UNIX System V.3. RFS entered the market after NFS and, as a result, is not as prevalent today as is NFS. RFS provides similar functionality to NFS, but, is designed specifically for UNIX computers.

Local Area Network Standards. LAN standards are used widely in the CAE environment. The IEEE committees have been instrumental in developing these standards. The LAN standards specify layers 1 and 2 of the OSI data–communications model. The most predominant LAN in CAE is Ethernet or IEEE 802.3 using coax cable in a bus topology. The bus serves as a broadcast medium for all systems on the LAN. In this configuration, Ethernet/802.3 LANs transmit data at the rate of 10 Mbit/s.

The IEEE 802.3 standard also specifies an alternative wiring scheme that uses standard twisted–pair telephone wiring. All systems are connected to a central hub box in a star topology. This specification uses a transmission rate of 4 Mbit/s. There currently are several proposals for a 10 Mbit/s option to the specification using twisted–pair cabling in a star topology.

The other IEEE 802 standards also are listed in Figure 2.7. A key difference between IEEE 802.3 and the others is that 802.5 uses a CSMA/CD (carrier sense multi–access with collision detection) protocol to control access to the shared LAN cable, while 802.4 and 802.5 use token–based schemes. The CSMA/CD protocol is similar to the protocol used over a party line for voice communications. A system can broadcast a message if no one else is broadcasting a message. If two or more systems broadcast at the same time, there is a collision on the LAN cable, and each transmitting system uses a backoff scheme to determine when it can retransmit.

With token–based schemes, a system must possess a *token* (a unique string of bits) before broadcasting a message. A single token is passed sequentially to each system on the network. Thus, there never will be collisions on the network because only one system at a time can transmit a message. IEEE 802.4 LANs use a bus topology like Ethernet/IEEE 802.3 LANs. IEEE 802.5 LANs use a ring topology, where each system on the network is physically linked to two other systems, resulting in a circular ring of computers.

There has been a long technical debate over the advantages of CSMA/CD and token–based protocols for LANs. Generally, it is agreed that under light network traffic, CSMA/CD protocols are more efficient and under heavy network traffic, token–based protocols are more efficient. However, Ethernet/IEEE 802.3 LANs are much more prevalent in CAE than are the other LAN standards.

In addition to providing a necessary component for multivendor communications, LAN standards also provide the performance needed for most CAE applications and networking services used today. The LAN link generally is not the performance bottleneck for system response and file throughput. The focus now is on providing faster protocol processing in the upper OSI layers and faster file–system accessing. Today LAN standards have allowed for file–throughput rates of over 800 kbit (thousand bits per second) between workstation–class machines, resulting in the transfer of megabyte files in a matter of seconds.

Basic Communications Capabilities

The CAE distributed environment requires some basic communications capabilities. For instance, a CAE designer on a PC may want to pass a file to another CAE designer on a UNIX workstation or on a DEC VAX minicomputer.

The basic functions needed for communications are file transfer, virtual terminal, remote command execution, and mail and interprocess communications. Examples using the ARPA/Berkeley UNIX networking services follow. The remote system is called *rhost* and the user log–in name and password for the remote system are *guest* and *pass1*.

1. File transfer among minicomputers, workstations, mainframes, and PCs. Example using ARPA FTP (File Transfer Protocol):

System Prompt	Command	Results
>	ftp rhost	Establish a connection to the remote computer *rhost*.
Enter User Name: Enter Password:	guest pass1	Log into the remote computer using the user name *guest* and password *pass1*.
FTP >	send local1 remote1	Send local file *local1* to computer *rhost* and name it *remote1*.
FTP >	bye	Terminate the ftp connection.

Example using Berkeley rcp (Remote computer Protocol):

System Prompt	Command	Results
>	local1 rhost:remote1	Copies local file "local1" to remote computer *rhost* and names it *remote1*. The user name and password for the remote system are contained in a local file and do not have to be entered.

FTP or rcp allows a designer on one computer to pass a design file to another computer. For example, further analysis or archiving of the design could be performed on another computer.

2. Virtual terminal, or the ability of a user on one computer to log onto another computer over the network.
    Example using ARPA Telnet:

System Prompt	Command	Results
>	telnet rhost	Open a connection to the remote computer *rhost*.
Enter User Name:	guest	Log into the remote computer using the user name *guest* and password *pass1* and run applications on the remote computer.
Enter Password:	pass1	

The virtual–terminal capability allows a user to run programs on another computer. This lets the designers use their terminals or workstations as terminals to any other computer on the network. Virtual terminal gives the designer interactive access to remote computers that have more computing power or may run an application program that is not available locally.

3. Execute commands on remote computers on the network and return the results to your computer.

    Example using Berkeley rsh (remote shell):

System Prompt	Command	Results
>	rsh rhost cat remote1	Execute the UNIX command *cat* on the remote system *rhost* using remote file *remote1* and display the results on my local system.

While virtual terminal gives designers interactive access to other computers, remote command execution allows them to set up automated or batch processing on remote computers.

4. Send and receive mail between systems on the network.
    Example using ARPA SMTP(Send Mail Transfer Protocol) and UNIX mail system:

System Prompt	Command	Results
>	mail guest@remote1 < local1	Send mail message in file *local1* to user *guest* on remote system *remote1*.

5. Program–to–program communications for writing distributed application programs.

   Program–to–program communication or interprocess communication (IPC), is performed using networking program calls. Programs must be communicating on a sending and receiving computer. They communicate by establishing a socket, or virtual circuit (software circuit between programs) and transmitting data over this socket. One program waits for requests from the other program (server), and the other program initiates communications with the other program (client). The following example is not syntactically correct, but does show how IPC is performed.

   Example using Berkeley UNIX sockets: (Pseudo–program Code):

Client Computer		Server Computer	
s = socket;	Get a socket	s = socket; bind(s,addr);	Get a socket Set server's socket address so clients can contact the server.
		listen(s);	To set up the queue to wait for requests.
		accept(s);	Wait until a request arrives.
connect(s,addr)	Connect to server socket. Wait if server is not ready yet.		
send(s,data)	Send data	recv(s,data)	Receive data.
close(s)	Close socket		

   IPC provides the low–level tools for developing custom applications. For instance, distributed applications could be written to check to see if there is an inactive plotter on the network.

Server Capabilities

Servers were created to use a wide range of resources on the network such as printers, plotters, computing power, or disk storage. Basically, servers are computers that provide services to the network. Often, vendors package servers as dedicated systems that are used strictly as servers and are not used for normal operation. For instance, PC file and print servers often are dedicated PCs used as servers and sometimes are custom, low–cost hardware. In many cases, a computer does not have to be a dedicated server and can perform server operations and regular application work simultaneously. This often is the case with UNIX workstations, which can have a disk drive that is being used by users on the network and is simultaneously running workstation applications. The most common servers are disk/peripheral (printers and plotters) and compute servers.

Disk and Peripheral Servers (Printers and Plotters) Servers. To share files productively so that application programs can execute using either local or remote data a distributed file system is needed. Like a local file system, where programs and users have a way to organize and manage local data, a distributed file system serves the same purpose for data stored throughout the network. Distributed file systems also provide a flexible interface, so that it is invisible to the user or the programmer whether the data being accessed resides on a local disk or a remote disk. In addition a distributed file system provides the means for spooling to output devices on the network, such as a printer or plotter. Therefore, distributed file systems allow users to share expensive output devices and to use less disk storage for programs and data.

Example Using the Network File System (NFS)

NFS allows users to extend their local file systems to include a file system (or part of a file system) that exists on a remote computer on the network. The linkage to remote files can be set up by the computer or network administrator, and the end user can execute commands without regard for where the data resides.

If the server system had a shared directory of files under the project directory, each client system would execute an NFS *mount* command to add this shared directory. Following the *mount* command each user could execute commands using the files in the remote directory.

Client System

> Mount server:/project /project	Make remote directory *project* and files under *project* available. This command most likely would be run automatic-ally for the user at system powerup.
> ls /project	Display on the client system the remote file names under the remote directory *project* on the remote server system.

Compute Servers

Compute servers provide computing power to users on the network. A typical application of compute server would be to run the analysis and simulation of design on a more powerful minicomputer after finishing the logical design on your workstation. Compute servers also may need to be accessed to run application programs that have been written for a particular machine or operating system.

The two key networking services needed to use a compute server are virtual terminal and remote command execution. (See the previous examples using the Berkeley *rsh* and ARPA *telnet* commands.) The *remote command execution* command provides batch or noninteractive execution on a remote computer. This would be used, for example, when running a long simulation on a remote computer. After initiating the simulation program from the workstation, the user could start work on something else. When the simulation completes and notifies the workstation, the user then could examine an output file with the results of the simulation.

The virtual–terminal capability would allow the user to execute a program on a remote system interactively. For instance, an interactive PCB–routing program could be run on a remote system.

Windows have emerged as an easy–to–use interface for displaying multiple tasks on a display. Windows have been extended in the UNIX environment to run application programs remotely and display the windows on a workstation. This windowing technology, called X–window was developed at MIT (Massachusetts Institute of Technology) and is backed by the major vendors in the CAE market. With X–Window, the designer can execute programs interactively on multiple systems on the network.

Communication to Host Mainframes Over the Network

Host computers from the traditional time–shared environment also need to remain a productive part of the CAE distributed environment. The installed base of CAE applications running on these computers remains high. Some CAE applications require very high computational power and must be run on large host computers.

The designer at a PC or workstation needs interactive terminal access to minicomputers and mainframes. These users need the same access to the host computer as those users who are directly connected to the host computer using a terminal. However, since the host application program is written to use the host computer's terminal, there is a need for a program called an emulator that translates the escape codes and data streams output by the application program for the terminal to a format that is compatible with the workstation or PC display.

A host computer often is accessed by PCs and workstations as a compute server, using the services mentioned in the previous section. In addition, host computers often are used to maintain accounting, inventory, and manufacturing specifications for a company. Designs and documentation must be passed from the design computers to the host computer.

• Future Networking Trends in CAE •

The major networking trend in CAE is the migration to the ISO networking protocols. Movement from the well–entrenched ARPA/Berkeley, DEC DECnet, and IBM SNA will be slow; however, every major computer vendor is committed to making this move. The key benefit of this migration is to provide multivendor–compatible data communications. The U.S. government mandated that computer vendors must provide ISO networking in 1989 to win U.S. government business. The ISO protocols likely will be the dominant networking protocols by the mid–1990s.

Networking vendors will continue to add more resource–sharing capabilities. For instance, computing power will be allocated dynamically using process servers to locate an idle computer to run an application program or subroutine. This is called load balancing—the network is responsible for finding the available computing resource without the end user knowing which system the program is running on. Also, load balancing probably will be extended to provide parallel computing on the network.

Networks will become more and more complex and, as a result, will require better network–administration tools. These will include tools to ease accounting for network usage, monitoring and tuning network performance, installing and configuring the network, securing the network, increasing the reliability of the network, and controlling revisions on the network. Name servers will become prevalent, providing services to end users and network administrators for storing and maintaining the network database of names. Names are used for naming systems, naming files, naming users, etc., and there is a need to map these names into network information such as addresses, locations, security rights, etc.

The standard Ethernet/IEEE 802.3 LAN transmits data at 10 Mbit/s. This rate is acceptable today for most applications and probably will be acceptable for some time for a small group of CAE designers. However, with the increase in network traffic over the main facility network links, higher LAN transmission rates are needed. Fiber optic technology has provided the next jump in high–bandwidth LANs. The FDDI (fiber distributed data interface) is a proposed American National Standard for a 100–Mbit/s token–ring LAN using an optical–fiber medium. FDDI will some day serve as a backbone network for lower speed IEEE 802 LANs.

CHAPTER 3

SCHEMATIC ENTRY

• Top–Down Versus Bottom–Up Approaches •

While a manufacturable electronic circuit is the real product of electrical–engineering work, the engineering community is not yet sure whether the process of drawing circuits should be considered a low–level or high–level engineering activity. Do engineers actually create circuits from scratch, using available components? Or do they merely find the optimum alternatives from already existing circuits? Who actually draws the circuit? Does an engineer draw the circuit creatively, the way a composer tries out notes and chords for a symphony? Or does the engineer map out a circuit topology for a crew of technicians who draw a detailed circuit from broad instructions?

Adding computers into the mix complicates the responsibilities shared by engineers and technicians. For example, there frequently is no clear picture in a corporation as to who is responsible for entering a schematic into a computer system, who is responsible for producing (printing) the schematic drawing, or who is responsible for maintaining a company's library of engineering drawings. The computer–graphics workstation and its software could be considered merely a drafting aid. Or it could open a window, a visual aid, onto much more complicated engineering and computer tasks. What a schematic–entry system will do—the subject of this chapter—depends to a large extent on who uses it.

In the 1950s and 1960s, when transistors and logic gates were relatively new commercial devices, practically all electrical–engineering work concentrated on wiring these devices together. This is called a *bottom–up* approach to circuit design. Now that hundreds of thousands of transistor switches (and tens of thousands of logic gates) have been integrated into commercial IC building blocks, engineering attention has shifted from the construction of circuits to the interplay (or high–level integration) of system elements. The ICs, to be sure, must be electrically connected: Each has its own power and ground lines; each has several ports or electrical trunk lines to other circuits around it. But the designers who pick and choose among these sophisticated components no longer consider themselves circuit designers, but rather system architects. Even those engineers who choose components and building blocks for a new IC seldom operate on the transistor level, but make their selections from some very sophisticated predesigned circuit blocks. This approach to circuit design begins at the block–diagram, or architectural, level, and is referred to as a *top–down* approach.

Because of the increasing emphasis on system architectures, component–level circuit design itself frequently is thought to be a retrograde activity practiced only by junior engineers, hobbyists, or the one– and two–person engineering departments among the machine–tool makers and other small shops in the midwest. Electrical engineering, in this view of the world, is a matter of architecting an electronic system from high–level blocks and using computers and other tools to find the optimum trade–off between high performance and functionality, and low–cost manufacturability. The system is conceived in abstract terms as a series of functional blocks.

In practice, there are an enormous number of tweaks or modifications that engineers will make to existing circuits for specific projects or applications. As electronic sensors and measurement devices used in aircraft, industrial controls, and medical electronics continue to evolve, the amplifier circuits for these sensors must be modified continually to provide a greater dynamic range; that is, the amplifiers must be modified to cope with extremely wide variations between the largest and smallest input signals. Similarly, new–generation amplifiers must provide higher levels of sensitivity to small signals and more precision in their ability to reproduce these signals at higher levels.

In digital–circuit design, the integration of functional blocks onto large microprocessor chips does not guarantee an easy joining to main memories or computer buses. Frequently, engineers must use varying amounts of glue logic around the large chips to ensure that they will work properly with other system elements. These glue–logic circuits may require dozens (sometimes hundreds) of digital–logic gates, as is the case where a processor with separate 32–bit data and 32–bit address lines needs to retrieve data from a multimaster computer bus with multiplexed address and data lines. The glue logic for accomplishing this—for negotiating among competitors on an otherwise narrow bus—can have the same complexity as does a VLSI circuit. At the other extreme, a few inverters may be all the logic that is required for VLSI devices that recognize active low to signal devices that respond to active high.

It is in the area of glue–logic circuits that the systems architect and the circuit designer come together. To use a colloquial expression, this is "where the rubber meets the road." Because of the need to visualize glue–logic circuits, all schematic–entry systems will allow an engineer to describe a circuit as a transistor–to–transistor or gate–to–gate wiring pattern. But because of the emphasis on systems–level thinking, an increasing number of design–entry systems will permit electronic systems to be described and entered into the computer as block diagrams. An individual circuit element then can be depicted and entered into the system as a black box, with its behavior described in textual terms with an English–like high–level language.

Some systems allow or encourage designers to depict the black box as a logic *state machine*. Its inputs and outputs invariably will be an array of logic 1s and 0s. Without drawing or describing the kinds of transistors, switches, or logic gates needed to produce a specific output, the engineer simply describes the 1s and 0s at the input, the 1s and 0s produced at the output, and the number of computer cycles it will take to get from the input to the output state. The CAE program eventually will figure out what sort of logic circuitry is required to produce the desired output with the given inputs and timing considerations—an exercise typically called logic synthesis—and will supply the appropriate circuitry from memory.

The approach to design entry that accommodates both component–level circuit design and black–box descriptions is called the *hierarchical approach* to design. As the latter part of this chapter will make clear, it is becoming the guiding principle for all design–entry systems, whether they are based on PCs, UNIX workstations, or mainframe computers. CAE software, in this light, can be understood not necessarily as a tool for drawing circuits, but as an instrument for managing engineering drawings and data.

For example, the CAE system (software and hardware) that aids bottom–up design must manage a database with user's drawings and a large library of components, in addition to visualizing a gate–level wiring diagram. For top–down design, the system must manage user's drawings, which will consist of block diagrams, a large library of predrawn schematics, and, within that library, a library of components. Because of the smaller database requirements, a bottom–up approach can be managed from a workstation or properly equipped PC. The top–down approach typically requires a mainframe or minicomputer to manage all the design data.

The main thrust of this chapter is to describe the bottom–up and top–down design–entry approaches in enough detail that the reader has a clear picture of both the computer resources required and the relationship of design entry to other aspects of the CAE process.

Schematic–Entry Software

Since the major concern of CAE is to verify the system's performance, manufacturability, and cost goals (activities discussed in detail in later chapters), the best design–entry systems are those that feed simulators and layout systems. Consequently, it does not matter whether schematic entry is considered a high–level or low–level activity. It does not matter that the colorful graphics workstations have been the attention–getters in CAE. Schematic entry is becoming less significant among engineering tasks and frequently is delegated to technicians who are not as well trained as engineers. It follows that the major requirement for computer systems and software that help technicians draw schematics is that they not eat up a lot of an engineer's time or a corporation's money; in other words, that they be cheap and easy to use.

The value of any schematic–entry process today can be seen as its ability to support other aspects of the CAE process, such as simulation and layout. The $100,000 and $150,000 prices once charged by turnkey–system vendors—even the current $30,000 to $50,000—would not seem justified if the same system did not also contribute to much more sophisticated CAE tasks such as IC layout. Consequently, the software packages developed by the early CAE leaders such as Mentor, Daisy, and Valid, and by later entrants such as HP and Integraph, offer front–to–back design capability; that is, the ability to go through most stages of the design process from schematic entry to test–vector generation on the same workstation and with the same user interface.

The PC–based schematic–entry packages have attempted to offer users the same functionality. Typically, they do this by grafting another software program, such as a logic simulator, onto a basic drawing package and scaling it to run with the smaller computational resources of a PC. Software manufac- turers like the FutureNet subsidiary of Data I/O (Redmond, Washington), PCAD, the Case Technologies subsidiary of GenRad Corporation (Mountain View, California), and Viewlogic Corporation (Marlborough, Maine) were the driving forces in the early movement toward PC–based CAE, and their marketing programs went a long way toward convincing engineers to perform schematic entry on an IBM–PC. With the exception of the PCAD software, which, at its heart, is an aid to PCB layout, these software packages are very sophisticated drafting aids, with simulation capabilities borrowed from other software vendors and bundled with the schematic–entry package.

Despite its ubiquity in offices throughout the corporate environment, the IBM–PC has severe limitations as a platform for CAE work. Among them are limited computational resources, limited main memory, and limited disk storage. The memory–address range of PC–DOS is only 640 KB, which either limits the size of the drawings that can be entered (the size of the circuits simulated) or forces the software vendor to resort to tricks like virtual–memory allocation. Virtual memory creates the illusion of a larger memory space by periodically swapping data from memory to disk, but this technique actually slows down system response considerably. In terms of what the user sees, slow response and constricted graphics capability can be most annoying.

Most workstations use flickerless 19–in. monitors capable of displaying with 1280– x 1024–pixels. Unless they are equipped with specialized graphics processors, PC graphics resolution goes up to about 640– x 480–pixels on a 14–in. screen. What this means is that a diagonal line will seldom be portrayed as a straight line, but will resemble instead a step function—a staircase across the screen. More annoying, perhaps, is an inability to visualize big circuits on the same screen: For example, by zooming in, expanding an image in a bus–interface circuit, it is possible to examine all the pin labels on a big, 40– or 68–pin IC component. But zooming out to visualize the larger circuit makes it impossible to read not only the labels, but the separate wiring paths as well. Even without a larger screen size, this visualization can be clarified with better screen resolution.

Consequently, many people view PC–based schematic entry as akin to driving across the United States in a Volkswagen Beetle: It can be done; people do it all the time. But there are better ways to go. It is possible to soup up the PC, to rebuild it by putting in more disk space and more sophisticated graphics capability, but this may seem like installing a Corvette engine into the body of a Volkswagen Beetle. For the expense, many engineers simply would prefer a 68020–based workstation running UNIX.

As if the limitations of the PC weren't enough, vendors of PC–based CAE software are faced with competition from less expensive drawing packages that have no pretensions about supporting other aspects of the CAE process. FutureNet, PCAD, Case, and Viewlogic, whose PC–based software once sold in the $8,000 to $20,000 range, face severe competition from OrCad System Corporation (Beaverton, Oregon) and others with schematic–entry packages under $1,000. PC–based schematic–entry software rapidly is becoming a commodity item, with entry packages almost as full as those once marketed by Mentor and Daisy being sold to electronic hobbyists for $295 each.

What this means for vendors of PC–based schematic–entry packages is that they must either scale down what they do to fit comfortably on a PC or they must move the PC–generated schematics onto larger computer systems. With the emphasis in CAE now on simulation, layout, and other computationally intensive tasks, schematic entry is only the front end, the way to get the circuit into the system. However, unless the engineer could move comfortably from schematic entry to simulation and layout, much of the work on a PC would be lost. Practically all the software packages mentioned will submit to a netlist–extraction process (discussed in detail in Chapter 4), which converts the drawings into something resembling a FORTRAN program, readable by simulation programs running on other workstations and mainframes. Apart from that, the vendors of PC–based schematic–entry packages have developed specialized niches for themselves.

Since Data I/O, for example, is the world leader in programming devices for PROMs (programmable read–only memories), it is gearing its FutureNet subsidiary toward leadership in programmable logic. Its software now accommodates three forms of design entry—schematic entry, high–level design entry, and state–machine entry—with increasing emphasis on high–level design entry (discussed later in this chapter), rather than on schematics. The software is geared toward synthesizing or distilling the glue logic to be embedded on a device called a PLD (programmable logic device) by some, a PAL (programmable array logic) by others, or a PLA (programmable logic array) by still others. Because the number of digital–logic gates that these devices harness is relatively small, PLD design and programming can be sensibly managed from a PC.

Case Technologies offers much more sophisticated schematic–entry software, which runs not just on the IBM–PC, but also on Sun workstations and DEC's VAX computers equipped with graphics terminals from Tektronix. While the acquisition of the company by GenRad positions the Case entry programs as merely the front end to very sophisticated simulation and test–development capabilities, the entry program has a formidable history and capability. An incarnation of the SCALD (structured computer–aided logic design) system developed at Lawrence Livermore Laboratories, the Case schematic–entry program allows the designer to operate on several levels: to use the computer's graphics screen as a scratch pad to draw lines and circles, to pull components from a library and interconnect them, or to manage an arrangement of complex drawings.

Most of the available drawing packages allow users to draw lines, arcs, circles, and boxes. With the Case or PCAD software, for example, a line can be drawn on the screen by first selecting a *draw line* command (in some cases, this may be two commands: *draw* and then *line*); marking the beginning point of the line by moving the cursor to an appropriate spot on the screen and pressing *enter* on the computer keyboard (the *return* key on a keyboard or the button on a mouse pointer device); and marking the end point of the line similarly by moving the cursor and pressing the appropriate button. The drawing program usually will fill in the line between the two points, automatically observing the conventions for electronic circuits. For example, diagonal lines seldom are used on schematics. Therefore, the connection between a point on the upper left–hand side of the screen and one on the lower right–hand side will be represented orthogonally; that is, as a horizontal and vertical line with one or more right–angle bends.

Similarly, the software seldom will draw lines through components and other objects preexisting on the screen, but rather will find a pathway around them. Once the beginning point of the line is staked out, however, the computer generally will show the user the path it intends to take to make the connection to the second point and will continually update this information on the screen as the cursor is moved around. To be sure, it is possible to show a diagonal line on the screen (and in a drawing), though it frequently takes a special command in the drawing process.

Boxes and circles are as easily constructed as lines on the screen. Usually, a *draw box* command is invoked, one corner of the box is selected with the cursor, and the box is drawn automatically when the second (diagonally opposite) corner point is selected. A *draw circle* command will require the user to select the center point first; the second selection will mark the radius, and the circle will be drawn automatically.

This process of drawing lines, circles, and boxes, frankly, is becoming the least significant part of the CAE process. Where it is useful is in defining components that do not exist in a library, but that likely will be used in another drawing. In operation, the user can call upon the line–drawing capability to create a new schematic symbol—a transistor, operational amplifier, logic gate, etc.—and commit this symbol to a library of schematic symbols. Whether this new symbol will be recognized in the netlist–extraction process depends on the sophistication of both the drawing program and the netlist– extraction program. At the very least, the drawing program will recognize the created symbol as an element that can be used in other drawings.

Rather than drawing lines and boxes, the process of creating schematics increasingly is a matter of calling up predrawn components onto the computer–graphics screen and then wiring them together. Frequently, the user will peruse a software component library, make a selection by clicking a button on a mouse pointer device, and, with the next click of the device, place the component into an area on the screen. Perhaps the biggest task here is to bring all the needed components to the screen and to lay them out in an intelligent sequence: Engineering drawings, like words on paper, are read from left to right, from inputs to outputs. In the next step, these components are wired together.

Here is where the line–drawing capability of a program like Case's comes in handy. As with other drawing packages, the user must mark the beginning and end points of a completed line. However, where two components are being interconnected, the program will anticipate the most likely pin by the end point of a line and will mark that point with a small triangle. Even if the cursor resides in a slightly different place on the screen, the user has only to press *return* (or a button on the mouse pointer) to get the program to complete a line to the designated pin.

Making a wiring diagram in this manner is not a difficult process, though it can be tedious. Each program will provide its own series of shortcuts. Parallel data–bus lines in a digital–logic circuit, for example, usually can be represented with a single thick line, rather than with 8 or 16 parallel wires. Additionally, the computer graphics screen can be set up to mimic an A– (8.5– x 11–in.), B–, C–, D–, or E–sized engineering drawing—complete with the engineer's company logo, title of drawing, date of drawing, revision and sheet numbers, and other formal information that is kept by the company on engineering drawings. When the schematic is complete, it can be saved in the disk memory of the computer and output on a printer/plotter device.

Because so much of the engineer's job involves connecting components, a component library becomes perhaps the most valuable part of a CAE schematic–entry package.

Symbol Libraries

Even if an engineer is doing bottom–up design, the work seldom begins at the level of transistors, resistors, and capacitors. More likely, SSI (small–scale integrated) and MSI (medium–scale integrated) logic blocks are being pieced together. While these blocks are composed of transistor switches, the on and off states of these devices—interpreted as mutually exclusive states, logical 1s and 0s—are combined into somewhat more complicated switching machines, whose inputs and outputs conform to Boolean algebra statements. With a specified pattern of logic 1s or 0s at their inputs, in other words, these blocks produce a logical and predictable sequence of 1s or 0s at their outputs.

For example, one of the most simple logic functions is the two–input *and* gate. It can be implemented with four or five switching transistors. This device examines the logical states of each input and produces a single output that is a logical consequence of the inputs. If the inputs of the *and* gate (defined as A and B) are both low, then the output (Y) is low. If either input is low while the other input is high, then the output also will be low. The output Y is high only when inputs A and B are high. That is, the output Y of the *and* gate will never be high, unless *both* inputs A *and* B are high. The logical relationships between input and output are summarized in the following function table (truth table).

And Gate Truth Table

Inputs		Output
A	B	Y
L	L	L
L	H	L
H	L	L
H	H	H

An *or* gate, on the other hand, will produce a data high at its output if either of its inputs—A *or* B—is high. Its truth table is shown below.

Or Gate Truth Table

Inputs		Output
A	B	Y
L	L	L
L	H	H
H	L	H
H	H	H

Other examples of digital–logic blocks include *nand* gates (the logical inversion of the output of an *and* gate), *nor* gates (the logical inversion of the or–gate function), and *xor/xnor* gates (exclusive–*or* gates, in which two high inputs mutually exclude each other, producing an output low). SSI functions also include buffers/inverters and enable latches, in which a single logical input produces a single modified output. More complicated logic functions, which use these simple gates as building blocks, are D–type flip–flops, T–type flip–flops, JK flip–flops, and RS flip–flops. The symbols and logical outputs for these functions are shown in Figure 3.1.

Ignoring for a moment the need to represent analog building blocks in a circuit (operational amplifiers, comparators, data converters, phase–locked loops, etc.), the combinations and variations of digital–logic gates that need to be represented in a circuit can get quite complex. So far, we have been discussing simple *and*, *or*, *nand*, and *nor* gates with two inputs. In use, these logical entities can be asked to provide a logical output with as many as eight or ten different input lines. On top of that, the simple logical functions can be combined to provide more complex logic functions—not just flip–flops, but assorted counters, timers, multiplexers, shift registers, adders, or pulse generators. Many of these devices do not respond to a static input, but rather to a transitional state, low–to–high or high–to–low. Many are packaged together for commercial distribution in sets of four or eight on a single IC. (The simplest two–input *nand* gate, for example, the 7400, is a quad device: four *nand* gates on the same substrate and sold in the same DIP—dual in–line package.) A typical TTL data manual, the catalog from Sunnyvale, California–based Signetics Corporation, a subsidiary of N.V. Philips (Eindhoven, Netherlands), for example, lists more than 280 separate SSI devices.

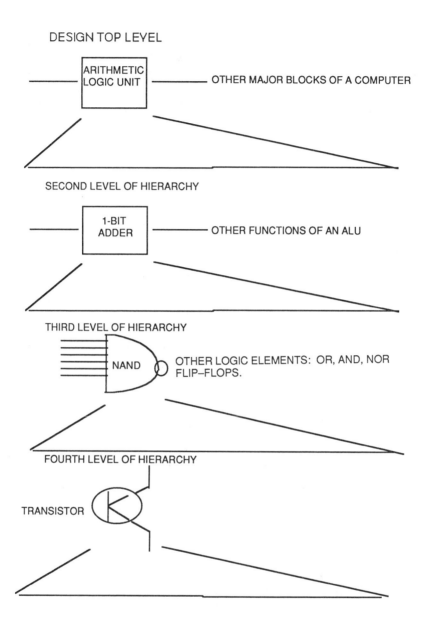

DESIGN TOP LEVEL

ARITHMETIC
LOGIC UNIT —————— OTHER MAJOR BLOCKS OF A COMPUTER

SECOND LEVEL OF HIERARCHY

1-BIT
ADDER ————— OTHER FUNCTIONS OF AN ALU

THIRD LEVEL OF HIERARCHY

NAND OTHER LOGIC ELEMENTS: OR, AND, NOR
FLIP–FLOPS.

FOURTH LEVEL OF HIERARCHY

TRANSISTOR

Figure 3.1: Logic functions. These are the symbols and logical outputs for
D–type: flip–flops, T–type flip–flops, JK flip–flops, and RS flip–flops.

The problem is complicated when the engineer needs to use these same
logical building blocks, but must get the circuits to work at faster speeds. Each
of the SSI elements has a predictable propagation delay; that is, a period of
time in nanoseconds that it will take an output to appear with a given set of
inputs. For a simple 7400–type two–input *nand* gate, this delay is about 9 ns
using standard TTL logic. Nine billionths of a second may seem like a short

period, but in a complex logic circuit containing dozens, sometimes hundreds, of these sequential delays, 9 ns can be uncomfortably long. A faster version of the part, designated 74S00, will bring the typical propagation delay down to 3 ns.

In most circuits, there is a natural trade–off between speed and power consumption. With +5V as a standard supply voltage (that is, the power–supply voltage never changes), increased power requirements will be reflected in increased current consumption. An increase in circuit speed usually will be reflected in increased current requirements. The simple 7400 *nand* gate may take a slow 9 ns to register an output, but it consumes only 8 milliamps (mA) of supply current. The S–series part, 74S00, takes 3 ns consumes but 15 mA. If low power consumption is the designer's major goal, it is possible to obtain a somewhat more expensive part—an LS–series device, 74LS00—that does the job in 9.5 ns, but consumes only 1.6 mA of supply current. An even more expensive part type— a 74F00 built with a semiconductor fabrication process called FAST, developed by Fairchild—provides both high speed and relatively low power consumption: a 3.4–ns propagation delay, with a 4.4–mA typical supply current. The trade–offs continue: a 74HC00, fabricated in the CMOS process, offers an 8–ns propagation delay, but with a supply current of only 20 or 30 microamps (μA). Many CMOS and HCMOS (high–speed CMOS) parts have an additional advantage over TTL in that they frequently can run from supply voltages as low as 2V (although propagation delays will be longer at reduced supply voltages). These trade–offs between TTL and CMOS are summarized in the table below:

Speed–Current Trade–Offs For
7400 Quad Two–Input NAND Gate

Device	Prop. Delay (ns)	Current Consumption (mA)
7400	9	8
74S00	3	15
74LS00	9.5	1.6
74F00	3.4	4.4
74HC00	8	0.020

On the most basic level—the simple two–input *nand* gate—the engineer will be forced to juggle trade–offs, to make a selection from four or five different versions of the same part. These part types are available off–the–shelf, through many sources of distribution—even Radio Shack. It is possible to obtain these SSI logic functions in more exotic semiconductor processes like ECL or GaAs that are optimized for speed. This is the technology used in the supercomputers manufactured by Cray and others. (It also is possible—in fact, it is the goal of many new design projects discussed in this book—to incorporate SSI functions onto a specially made—custom or semicustom—device.) Obviously, there are many engineering choices to be made and many variables to be juggled, even where the simplest SSI logic functions are used in a circuit.

The process becomes even more complicated as the logic becomes more complex. Among SSI and MSI functions, there are literally thousands of devices to choose from. In addition, there are hundreds of LSI and VLSI circuits in various manufacturing technologies from which to choose. These include counters and timers on the most basic level and memory devices on the higher levels of complexity, as well as special–purpose controllers for disk drives, graphics, communications, and other computer–system I/O functions. The most glamorous of the VLSI devices are general–purpose controllers—microprocessor chips—that take in data in 8-, 16-, or 32–bit chunks. There also are bit–slice processors, high–speed devices that operate on data in arbitrary chunks.

While this barely describes the range of digital–logic functions, there is an entire world of analog functions and components the engineer must consider. The most basic of these are transistors and op amps (operational amplifiers), which produce at their output an amplified signal that is directly proportional (analogous) to the small signal voltages that make up their inputs. A low–cost, general–purpose op amp like the 741 will produce an output signal that can swing over a range of ±10V or ±15V at frequencies up to 10 kHz (kilohertz). The typical gain is on the order of 200,000; that is, a signal as small as ±0.05–mV (millivolt) gain can be amplified 200,000 times to produce a ±10V swing.

Here, too, the engineer must consider trade–offs, often more difficult than those involved in the choice among digital–logic circuits. Because transistors make better switches than amplifiers, these switches must be biased in such a way that, though their natural tendency would be to switch on and off, they never turn completely on and never turn completely off. The trick is to apply enough current to the input transistors of the op amp so that the output transistors are forever poised midway between a completely on and a completely off position. But this bias requirement typically extracts a penalty in power consumption and generates a voltage noise that can drown out very small input signals. Consequently, there is a proliferation of op amps that juggle various priorities among high gain, high bandwidth, high linearity, low noise, low–input offset voltages, and low quiescent–current consumption.

In addition to op amps, there are voltage comparators, phase–locked loops, linear–voltage regulators, and switching power–supply controllers. As if that were not enough, there are a range of data–converter parts, whose job is to convert a digital bit stream or number into an analog voltage (a digital–to–analog converter), or an analog voltage into a digital number (an analog–to–digital converter).

Including both digital and analog functions, the electronic–circuit designer is confronted with a choice among literally thousands of functions and part types. It is highly unlikely that the design engineer would be reinventing or redesigning any of these functions for his or her own work, but rather would be picking combinations of these devices for the circuit or system being built. In starting a new design, therefore, the engineers usually study the available TTL, LSI, and analog data manuals—parts catalogs—as the first step in selecting building blocks for their own projects.

If this process is to be duplicated in the CAE environment, the catalog of parts should be available in a software library. With the CAE program running on the workstation, an engineer should be able to peruse a library of available devices on the computer screen, select the ones desired, and copy them onto a worksheet. In picking components for the design, the engineer can go off–line to look at data books and component catalogs, but the process would be greatly simplified if each selected part type were readily available in software and could be pulled up on the computer screen simply by pressing a button, rather than needing to be redrawn from a catalog.

As a result, the importance of large component libraries cannot be understated. The size and fullness of a software component library should be a key criterion in selecting among competing CAE software vendors.

The surface dimension of a component library is a computer–graphic representation of the part or function. It could be a simple *nand* gate or it could be one–fourth of a 7400 device. The graphic representation—even for a 74HC00—would be the same, except that the 7400–series gate would have pin numbers (representing which terminals in a DIP are to be used for inputs and outputs), while the simple *nand*–gate representation probably would not show pin numbers on the screen. Similarly, each op amp could be called to the screen as an op amp, or it could be labeled as a 741 or OP27 or LF352. The screen representation would be the same for each: a triangle with two inputs, an inverting (–) and noninverting (+) input on the flat side of the triangle and a single output on the apex of the triangle opposite the inputs. For op amps packaged in 8–pin miniDIPs (or metal TO–3 cans), all the pin numbers would be the same. Consequently, the screen representation of a 7400 is no different from the screen representation of a 74LS00 or a 74HC00; only the labels are different. The screen representation of a 741 op amp, in the same way, is no different than of an OP27 or LF352. The CAE software vendor, in fact, has the option of saving space in the software library by providing only generic representations of *nand*–gate and op–amp components and letting the engineer label these as desired when entering them into the drawing. It is in the netlist–extraction and performance–simulation processes that the distinctions between generic and special–purpose gates and amplifiers become critical. For drawing purposes, however, it is important to have access to a full symbol library that allows designers to copy part types into a drawing simply by selecting them from the library.

Bypassing the Graphic–Entry Process with High–Level Languages

The process of drawing or entering a schematic into a computer system through a graphics workstation can be extremely time–consuming. In fact, the point of this activity can elude engineers who recognize that the symbols and connections shown on the workstation screen still must be converted into another format—frequently, a text format—in order to feed a logic simulator. As a result, there are many manufacturers who are working toward forms of design entry other than graphics entry.

The schematic–entry process—because it is focused on the interconnection of transistors, logic gates, and small components—typically is geared toward the design of relatively small circuits. The schematic–entry process does not lend itself to a system–level design, in which the engineer or systems architect attempts to describe the interrelationships among large functional blocks or system elements (which are built on a complex configuration of smaller circuits).

These system elements can be represented by block diagrams on a workstation screen, but to simulate the performance of the system, the function of each block must be described by some means other than as a rectangle on a workstation screen. Again, a textual description of the input signals, the transformed output signals, and the timing delays between them is becoming the de facto method for representing complex functional blocks to a simulator.

This textual or high–level–language description of system elements represents a top–down design approach to CAE. With the top–down approach, the behavior and structure of a very large system are described (and simulated) first, before any of its subsystems and components are defined. The behavioral description very often is some derivative of the Pascal programming, and, because there is no need to convert graphical data to text, the simulation program can be run quickly on a mainframe. This design methodology first uses text to describe a system in behavioral and functional terms. The textual program then is converted by the computer—compiled—to a physical (or, in the case of IC design, geometrical) level; that is, a circuit (or IC layout) is generated from the textual description, rather than the reverse.

In sharp contrast to their American counterparts, who rely on interactive graphics for circuit entry, for example, European CAE–system developers are perfecting high–level–language entry for complex system design. In this effort, they may be able to leapfrog American CAE efforts in the ability to describe, simulate, and manufacture very large electronic systems with minimum turnaround. Manufacturers like Siemens AG (Munich, Germany) and British Telecom (UK) are working to build systems in Pascal. Thomson–SGS (Grenoble, France) and the American Microsystems subsidiary of Gould (Santa Clara, California) are attempting to describe systems in an artificial–intelligence language called LISP. (More on this in Chapter 4.)

American cynics may feel that the pursuit of high–level–language inputs is an indication of European inferiority in graphic entry: Certainly, European–developed workstations seldom have been as impressive as those from Apollo, Sun, and HP. And apart from Racal–Redac's (Tewkesbury, UK) IC and PCB workstations, there have been few European turnkey systems that could compete with those of Daisy, Mentor, or Valid. Such criticism overlooks the fact that, rather than showing the American preference toward individual workstations, Europeans typically are more wedded to big mainframes and minicomputers. They need a method of entering system descriptions that will provide consistency in all aspects of a project, from design and simulation through manufacturing.

The top–down design approach insists that the complexity of any system should be expressed in software, rather than in hardware. By building a system in software and managing its objects (software subroutines that describe a complex component or a discrete subsystem), it is possible not only to predict the behavior of the entire system—no matter how complex—before it is actually built, but also to reuse the various modules in different systems. That is, the same functional description can be used to construct a subsystem, a circuit board, or a VLSI component.

The textual description forces the designer to use a structured language that the computer will recognize immediately, rather than a natural language that a computer must be taught to learn. This means that FORTRAN, Pascal, and C are the preferred input languages for design entry. A state machine—a black box that generates a complex sequence of logic 1s and 0s—can be described and compiled from high–level languages such as C or Pascal. Similarly, a high–level–language program can be derived from a state–machine sequence.

The essential challenge facing all CAE software developers, especially with regard to software that generates a physical layout of a circuit (such as silicon compilation), is to bridge the gap between the schematic– or design–entry process and the physical layout of the IC or PCB. In this regard, a Pascal– or C–based reusable software module may provide a better transcription than does a graphical description.

In fact, this sentiment is echoed strongly in this country by advocates of VHDL—VHSIC (very–high–speed integrated circuit) hardware description language—who believe that a high–level language supports silicon compilation much better than does graphical entry. Developed under a mandate from the DoD as part of the government–funded VHSIC program, the VHDL language includes transistor switches as its lowest common denominator. This contrasts with graphic entry, which typically uses the logic gate as its basic building block. VHDL provides the best way, its advocates insist, to move from the high–level language of simulators into the actual descriptions of silicon.

High–level languages are embraced not necessarily as a way to perform silicon compilation, but as a way to simulate complex circuits. In fact, simulating blocks is easier than simulating circuits. Researchers at Siemens AG, for example, have developed a high–level–language structure and methodology for simulating complex systems. This is the same method as behavioral modeling, discussed in detail in Chapter 5. The Siemens simulator, called BORIS (block–oriented interactive system), models an entire system as a network of functional blocks, each capable of passing through a succession of input and output states. The BORIS model segregates function (structure) and behavior. But since BORIS is meant to run interactively on a workstation, a further segregation is made among various system levels.

The basic system model is a series of static blocks (function carriers). Each block is described by the BORIS description language, an extension of Pascal that is used to model inputs, outputs, and internal logic states. Simulation is performed in two steps: First, each functional block is simulated independently. Second, the behavior of the system is depicted by linking the blocks together. The inputs and outputs of the various blocks are linked, while a central run–time coordinator monitors the network for elapsed time and functional compatibilities between connected blocks (are they, for example, receiving expected inputs and generating expected outputs?).

The advantage of first segregating and then linking the system elements is that it allows the blocks to be modeled independently of their use in a system. The functions are broken down into subfunctions that interact by exchanging information. In further design steps, the subfunctions are broken into components, the components are mapped into gates, etc. Each software module can be developed independently.

Boolean Equations for Logic–Circuit Design

Many designers and engineers recognize that, even on the gate level, the schematic–entry process can be totally bypassed using high–level–language constructs. If the circuit behavior can be described as a series of logical Boolean equations—or, on a lower level, as a sequence of 1s and 0s (referred to as a state machine)—the function of the logic circuit can be entered into a computer system without actually drawing it on the screen. A logic–synthesis or optimization program then can find the simplest configuration of gates; the logic patterns can be fed to a larger simulator with little translation; and, as a last resort, the program can draw the simplified circuit on the workstation screen for the designer.

This is the goal of a logic–entry program called FutureDesigner put together by the FutureNet subsidiary of Data I/O. This program is a vehicle for describing circuits in a compact, high–level language. Its promotional material says that it will encourage creativity and experimentation, and it does in fact bypass much of the tedious activity of schematic entry. FutureDesigner, therefore, can be considered among the first PC–based CAE tools to promote a top–down rather than a bottom–up design methodology. The program provides a hierarchical framework for both behavioral and structural elements of a design. In other words, the program allows designers to enter a circuit concept as a behavioral description in a high–level language.

Circuits are described with a series of structural and behavioral representations. Schematics may be used to describe many structural aspects of a design, like the data paths in a memory array. But behavioral descriptions—equations, truth tables, or state–machine diagrams—can be used to enter complicated logic sequencers, decoders, and adders into the CAE system. The FutureDesigner program, in fact, provides on–screen, fill–in–the–blank forms for these. There is a built–in logic–synthesis program that automatically eliminates redundant circuitry and optimizes the trade–offs between circuit size and speed. For those who need to see them, the schematics then can be generated at the end of the process, rather than at the beginning.

Created as an aid to designers of programmable–logic ICs and small gate arrays, FutureDesigner is what IC makers call *technology–independent*: It can be used to create the structural representations—the schematics—for many types of semicustom ICs such as PLDs, gate arrays, or standard cells. Similarly, it works whether the circuit will be fabricated with CMOS or bipolar process technologies or as a series of TTL devices on a large PCB.

FutureDesigner provides what programmers are calling a fourth-generation language, a method for calling routines that manipulate databases. It is a query language, like SQL (Structured Query Language), but specifically targeted for logic designers. In operation, the engineer treats the circuit block like a black box, specifying only the inputs and outputs. As with other high-level–language entry formats, the designer need not worry how the circuit function will be implemented, what it will physically look like, or how many gates it would require for implementation.

The command structure for the FutureDesigner is hierarchical, allowing the designer to specify a variety of fill–in–the–blank forms within the editing mode and then to modify each form according to the requirements of the circuit. To view or edit a form, the designer first initiates an *edit* command and then specifies the type of form to be filled out. In the design–flow process, a *declaration* form is used to define the elements that are used in the design of the circuit. The actual circuit, for example, is specified on an *equation* form, a *truth–table* form, a *state–diagram* form, or some combination of the three. The equations spelled out on these forms may be reduced and factored as necessary to eliminate redundant logic or to fit the equations to the requirements of a particular device type.

At the start of the design process, the *declaration* form is used to specify the kind of circuit being constructed and its input signals, output signals, sets, or specialized macros. Every name used in the design must be declared on this form. The names can include high–level functions such as combinational logic, counters, flip–flops, and latches, as well as gate–level functions. Once named, the actual circuit elements are entered as Boolean equations, state machines, or truth tables.

The *equations* form specifies the combinational or arithmetic operations to be performed on the inputs. For example, the expression $A \mathbin{\&} B$ specifies an *and* gate with inputs A and B, while the expression $A + B$ describes an adder that combines the data at inputs A and B. Meanwhile, the expression $!A \mathbin{\#} !B$ describes an *or* gate with inverted inputs.

In addition to mathematical operations, the system also will construct circuits from relational operators. The relational operators compare two items in an expression to yield a true (all ones) or false (all zeros) value. For example:

$A = = B$ says A equals B,

$A < B$ says A is less than B,

$A <= B$ says A is less than or equal to B.

While the Boolean equations are useful for defining combinational logic, counters, and multiplexers—devices in which several inputs are reduced to a few—truth tables are useful for devices that provide many outputs, such as display drivers and decoders. State diagrams, similarly, are useful for specifying state machines and logic sequencers.

Design information specified in the truth–table form or the state–description form is converted to logic equations before reduction or schematic generation is performed. Truth tables actually are tabular listings of the output states produced by all possible input words. The state diagram is more complicated, resembling a FORTRAN program in which states are described with equations, and transitions are indicated with *go to* statements.

Logic–Synthesis Programs

FutureDesigner and other design–entry programs using high–level–language entry reflect and embody logic synthesis or logic compression. This computer program is employed increasingly not just to eliminate redundant logic from a circuit, but also to gain speedups in system performance by shortening lengthy logic chains and to compress the layout of an IC, making it cheaper to manufacture in volume. For a PLD design, an effective logic–synthesis program can result in compact logic that generates outputs faster and can be implemented in a cheaper device.

In principle, a good logic–synthesis program works like a senior partner— an experienced engineer—looking over the shoulder of a novice and making recommendations based on experience. A junior circuit designer, for example, can draw an elaborate network of logic gates, whose function is to transform a certain pattern of input states into a given pattern of output states within a specified number of clock periods. A senior circuit designer can look at the same pattern of inputs and outputs and come up with a simpler network of logic gates—one that performs the same function with a smaller amount of hardware.

Several logic–synthesis programs are beginning to appear that analyze the logic of a schematic and attempt to come up with an optimum arrangement of logic gates required to perform the specified functions. To do this, the software program must extract the probable logic states produced at each section of the circuit, identify the types of logic devices that can produce that state, and collapse the circuit down to the fewest possible devices required to effect that logic pattern. The program must, in effect, simulate the circuit and then redraw the simplest logic pattern it knows will produce the pattern.

One reason for finding the smallest possible circuit required to implement a series of Boolean equations is to support PLD programming (that is, the construction of programmable logic devices). However, a logic–synthesis program potentially can synthesize the logic for any device in any process technology. When used as the front end for a silicon compiler, for example, the logic–synthesis program will provide a compact chip layout by minimizing the amount of glue logic in the circuit.

One example of this is a program used for the production of gate arrays, called the LSS (logic–synthesis system) by its developers at IBM's Thomas J. Watson Research Center (Yorktown Heights, New York). Another example is a more experimental program, called Socrates by its developers at General Electric's Calma Company (Research Triangle Park, North Carolina). Both programs use artificial–intelligence techniques—specifically, a *smart search algorithm*—to reduce the number of *and/or* gates in a circuit.

The Socrates program is written in C, which typically provides a foundation for fast search algorithms. Running in batch mode on a VAX, Socrates can analyze and reduce 100 gates in several seconds. A graphics terminal is used to monitor the schematics generated by the program from Boolean equations and the degree of area reduction obtained. The program examines all logic in a particular circuit according to two user–defined criteria—area reduction and timing—and replaces logic blocks with smaller blocks from its library.

For example, where area reduction is the prime criterion, two inverters in series can be replaced by a straight wire connection. Where timing is the criterion, a circuit with a two–input *and* gate followed by another two–input *and* gate simply may provide a way to delay the resulting output pulse by one or more clock pulses. The logic–synthesis program, in this case, can eliminate the first first *and* gate from the circuit, identifying its output simply as a slow input to the second gate.

When they first appeared in 1986, logic–synthesis programs Socrates and LSS could analyze only combinational logic—*and* gates and *or* gates. There was no provision for larger circuit blocks. However, new programs now appearing commercially are working toward partitioning large circuits and arranging busing, microcode transfers, and other architectural features. Examples of these new programs are the PLD Design System marketed by HP and the similar PLDesigner created by an HP spin–off, Minc (Colorado Springs, Colorado). Though geared for PLDs, both systems embody a top–down design approach in which a circuit can be entered in almost any form—schematics, graphical state diagrams, truth tables, timing waveforms, or Boolean equations—and later partitioned among various circuit elements and devices and detailed by individual design team members.

In addition to interactive simulation and logic synthesis, these programs will automatically partition a logic circuit and select appropriate PLDs for it. In other words, the system matches the engineer's circuit against the capabilities of PLDs in its library of parts. The software automatically selects the best PLDs for a circuit based on the volume of internal logic and the required pin count (the number of output pins the circuit board can tolerate). The output of the program is a prioritized list of the most efficient PLDs available for this design. (As with symbol libraries, the utility of this program will depend on the vendor's ability to keep the PLD component library up to date with new devices.)

Although the software can partition circuits automatically, the designer always has the option to override the program and specify a preferred PLD. In fact, nonprogrammable devices (for example, 7400–series logic) can be specified for any particular design, since the power consumption of the devices, the availability of the parts, and other factors may impact the design process more than does the partitioning of logic.

The output of these programs is a JEDEC standard fuse–map file that can be transferred to a PLD programmer. Since these systems feature on–line logic simulation, they also are capable of harnessing ATG (automatic test generation) software to provide test vectors. ATG software converts the stimulus input patterns used to simulate the functionality of the hypothetical circuit into a series of test patterns that can be used to verify the functionality of the finished, programmed, and packaged PLD. Since this chapter is concerned largely with the methods by which a circuit, a design, or a schematic is entered into a computer system, the various outputs of this process—PLD fuse–maps, JEDEC files, IC layouts, test vectors, etc.—need not concern us here.

What does concern us is how well the computer system (hardware and software) absorbs the information designers give it. No simulation or layout can be performed unless the computer thoroughly understands the interconnection between components and devices in a circuit. When mainframe computers rather than graphics workstations dominated CAE activity, the connectivity pattern was described in a textual statement called a netlist, which was input word by word, line by line into the computer system on a text–editing terminal. Though CAE activity now takes place on individual graphics workstations, the computer CPU still understands a textual listing (a high–level–language entry) better than it understands a graphical picture. The computer, in other words, must convert the drawing to text before the engineer can move to the next stage of the design process. This process—netlist generation—is the subject of Chapter 4.

• Engineering Revision Management System •

There is a great need to be able to revise existing engineering information to modify existing products or design new products. This information normally is in the form of engineering drawings that are produced on paper, either by a CAD system or by a draftsperson. The ability to easily and quickly modify these engineering drawings electronically instead of having to recreate them has a profound impact on the productivity and timeliness of the design process.

Beyond the ability to modify, revision management requires tools to control the revision process. A control system is needed to ensure that the appropriate procedures are followed and that new drawings go through a release cycle before being allowed into general usage within the organization. The control system should offer a high degree of security to protect information from unauthorized modification. Proper management of the revision process will allow for increased product reliability and ensure that only the most up–to–date information is used within the product–design build and service functions.

The Need for Revision

Quite often, it is necessary to modify a design months or even years after the original design work was done. Often, the original electronic design system, if one were used, is not available or no longer contains the original design data. Usually, however, a hard copy of the design, whether on paper, microfilm, or other media, is available. The hard–copy design data could be reproduced, with some considerable effort, on an electronic design system or by hand on a drafting board. This process is very inefficient, particularly if only a relatively small portion of the original design needs to be modified or subsets of an original design are to be incorporated into a new one. A more efficient and timely approach would be to modify the drawings electronically using revision tools that would receive the data from the drawings, allow modification, and return a new, modified drawing to the user.

Some Typical Examples

A typical example would be the need to redesign a hand–designed PCB to take advantage of some new technology. The majority of the original board layout will remain intact, but a few small areas will need to be changed so that newer parts can be incorporated.

Since the original board was designed by hand, the only available data is a set of hard–copy drawings of the board. To be able to modify the board, a new layout has to be done by hand, the board layout has to be entered into a computerized PCB–layout system, or a method needs to be found to convert the board drawings into an electronic format compatible with electronic revision tools.

A revision system would need to be able to accept the board drawing layout. This can be handled by a document scanner. Scanners are available that allow the scanning of all sizes of paper and microfilm and produce an electronic representation of the original that is compatible with electronic systems. Once the original drawing has been scanned and converted to an electronic format, it is ready for modification on the computerized revision system.

The revision system accepts the scanned data and provides a display of the board layout on the computer workstation. This revision system would allow the editing of any portion of the circuit board, in whatever fashion is appropriate. Lines can be changed, deleted, or moved. Labels for components can be replaced by new designations. Component locations can be modified and changed. New components can be added, and old components can be removed or their locations changed. The entire process can take place on a single workstation, quickly and accurately.

After modification, the electronic system can output a new hard–copy drawing of the PCB, or it can distribute the electronic redesign to compatible systems within the organization for comments or other purposes. The new board can be produced using the drawing created on the electronic editing station, and the finished design is available much more quickly than if it were done by hand or by copying the entire design into an electronic printed–circuit–design tool.

Another example of the need for a revision system would be the need for changing facilities and the management of those facilities. Quite often, the need to move people, equipment, and structures within a building requires that new drawings be done of the facilities. A typical method is either to make notations on existing drawings or to make new drawings by hand. The electronic revision system, by scanning and converting the original facility drawing, will allow easy modification of the layout of people, equipment, and structures. The process can be done on the editing workstation in far less time and at lower cost than could be done by hand. In addition, the final copy is neat and clean, with no notes of modifications scribbled on the drawing.

The above example is very similar to the needs of utility companies, which constantly need to move wires, pipes, poles, etc. The original drawings may have been modified several times, have many notes (some of which may not be legible), and usually are in bad condition due to age or rough usage. The ability to scan the drawing into the editing workstation; modify the drawing; make new notations in legible print; and produce a clean, crisp, high–quality output drawing will allow increased efficiency by producing better information–sharing capabilities. No longer will the user have to guess and interpret which notes on the drawing are the most accurate or recent. The modified drawing will have only the most recent notations, and these can be changed easily and efficiently using an editing workstation. There never will be a need to return to original drawings that contain multiple revision notations and modifications. This will prevent mistaken information from reaching the user.

It is not uncommon to need to modify existing structures, such as bridges, drilling rigs, power plants, or buildings. Original designs were produced many years ago and have all been done by hand on paper. Normally, modification would mean having a draftsperson reproduce the original drawings and make the necessary modifications. With the capability outlined above, it is no longer necessary to make modifications by hand. Converting the original drawing to an electronic format using a scanner that is compatible with the editing system allows the modification to be made on the workstation quickly and accurately. It also allows the existing drawings—which may be in poor condition due to age or use—to be converted, cleaned up, and output without modification. This process ensures that old drawings are not lost due to deterioration over time.

We could find many more examples for the engineering–revision system we have described. The uses—from electrical, mechanical, utilities, facilities management, and other engineering disciplines—are as varied as the end–user needs. The examples above are meant to show a few cases where the ability to convert from an existing drawing to an electronically based modification system greatly improves quality and productivity, while reducing cost and effort.

Revision Management

Managing the level of revision of a particular drawing or set of drawings is required to ensure the highest product quality and production efficiency. This is true whether the end product is a sheet of paper or a sheet of fabricated steel. Ensuring that only the most up–to–date information is used in the process provides maximum quality and profitability.

A typical drawing in a design process might undergo tens or even hundreds of modifications before the end of its life. Each time a change is required, a request must be made to the appropriate regulating authority, the drawing master must be retrieved from the appropriate location, and the revision must be made. The drawing then must be sent out for review to ensure that all groups involved approve of the final changes. Finally, if all groups reviewing the changes agree, the drawing is released and placed into the master file. This revision process must be managed closely if there is to be no interruption in the flow of needed information.

A typical organization has a defined system in place to manage this process. Usually, the organization includes a group whose function is to manage and control drawings and their release cycle. Typically, the group processes the request for change manually, makes the appropriate changes, sends the changes out for review, and releases the drawing.

A much more efficient method would be to use an automated system of document control and release. Such a system would include access to databases describing the location of the master drawings or the drawings themselves in whatever format is necessary. It also would include automatic notification of interested parties that the drawing is undergoing a revision, procedures that must be followed before the drawing is released, and final notification that the drawing has undergone revision and been released.

This electronic control system, when coupled with the electronic modification system mentioned earlier, would allow for a complete revision–management system. A user would enter the system and request a drawing on which to make a change. The system would check to see if that user had access to the particular drawing for revision or merely for viewing. If the user had revision access, the system would retrieve the drawing and allow the user to make the required modifications. At the same time, the system would notify a specified distribution list that the drawing was in process of being modified and would notify anyone trying to access the drawing of this status. Once the user had modified the drawing, using the electronic modification tools mentioned earlier or some other means, the system would notify a distribution list that the modifications were complete and ready to be reviewed and approved and would release the new revised drawing and index it into the database as the latest revision for access.

Additional Capabilities

Beyond the ability to modify and control, the ability to distribute engineering drawings remotely by electronic means will allow a geographically dispersed organization to provide almost instantaneous access to the latest and most up–to–date data for all users. The ability, through a network connection, to call up a drawing from the control system, display the drawing on the local user's workstation or PC, and print locally at a large–format plotter or small–format laser printer will allow all groups within the organization to achieve the highest level of efficiency, instead of having to request a hard copy from a centralized storage area and wait for mail or courier delivery of that drawing.

The localized viewing capability will allow the user to view a large–format drawing on a small screen using panning and zooming functions. In addition, a red–lining feature will allow the user to mark up the drawing and send it to another person on the network. This is particularly useful during the revision review cycle, when comments on drawing changes are solicited. Scaling functions associated with the printing of large formats on laser printers will allow reduced copies of the original to be printed as fast as the local laser printer can operate and also will eliminate the need to have large numbers of relatively expensive plotters available to users.

Additional functionality may be added to the system as required. For example, it is possible to convert a revised drawing that is held in the system in a raster format to a format that can be passed to a vector–based CAD station. This process requires a raster–to–vector conversion routing that processes the drawing into a vectorized format. A simple vector–editing system then is used to optimize the vectorization process and correct any errors that occurred during the computerized vectorization. Once the editing is complete, the vectorized drawing is placed in the proper vector format, such as IGES (initial graphics exchange specification) or an application-specific format, and is either sent directly to the CAD station or placed back into the engineering revision management system for later access.

Likewise, a vector–formatted drawing can be converted to a rasterized format, so that the raster editing and display functions can operate on it. This is handled through a vector–to–raster conversion product. Once converted to raster, the drawing may use all the features of the system.

The engineering revision management system is not limited to large–format engineering drawings. It also can handle other types of documents, such as process sheets, specifications, forms, and data. These other documents may be created on the system or imported from other input systems, such as word–processing or publishing systems. Once placed into the system, these documents can take advantage of all the features of the system that their formats allow.

Conclusion

The engineering revision management system effectively eliminates the possibility of having out–of–date drawings scattered throughout an organization. With one access, a user can tell what the most up–to–date drawing is, whether it is being modified, and who has retrieved the drawing. The user also can look at the revision history. Having this access capability, and being able to distribute electronically and print on demand, will allow an organization to deliver only the most recent information to its users. This will eliminate production problems due to outdated information, provide better quality control and reduced spoilage, and provide a complete standardized control mechanism for the entire organization to follow.

This system can significantly improve the productivity and efficiency of an organization. By substituting automated electronic tools for manual processes, better control of and access to information can be obtained. Information from various sources can be merged and managed, as well as modified easily. The cost saving over manual processes can give a return on investment that is many times the initial cost and provide a payback in a very short period of time (as little as several months).

• Flat, Structured, and Hierarchical Design •

Managing design complexity in increasingly short design cycles represents the greatest challenge to logic designers, whether they implement their end products as an IC or a PCB. An average gate–array or standard–cell design today contains 3000 to 5000 gates, but a significant number of high–end ASIC (applications–specific integrated circuit) designs typically contain up to 50,000 gates. Full custom circuits contain anywhere from 50,000 to 500,000 transistors for designs such as peripheral chips and digital signal processors and up to 1 million transistors for complex microprocessors. Similarly, complex PCB designs can contain as many as 1000 components. Designing such high–density circuits is clearly impossible without tools and methodologies that reduce the complexity of the task.

Hierarchical and structured design have emerged as the key methodologies for creating complex electronic designs. Together, these methodologies manage complexity by allowing designers to approach a design conceptually, at different levels of detail depending on their need, rather than strictly at a detailed level. CAE design tools that support hierarchical and structured design, therefore, enable designers to break a large problem into easily understood conceptual units and free designers from error–prone and tedious detail tasks.

But the abstraction that simplifies the logic designer's task complicates the work of the manufacturing and service departments, which require explicit, hardware–oriented data. This requirement has prompted the emergence of tools that transform the engineer's abstract design into a format that explicitly delineates the design's physical implementation in fully annotated schematics. As a result, designers can work on an abstract level to increase their productivity and the overall quality of their designs, but still obtain the physical design details needed for manufacturing and servicing these designs.

Flat Design

The *flat* design methodology consists of creating the design explicitly from the physical elements that compose it. In the case of a PCB design implemented with LSTTL (large–scale TTL) components, the engineer creates a schematic by specifying connections between specific LSTTL parts, using only these parts as building blocks in the design. The designer draws each component, pin, and net explicitly as the design evolves. This methodology hampers productivity and is prone to errors. It also commits each particular design to a specific technology, so that changing technologies requires a complete redesign.

The major drawback of flat design is that it is a time–consuming process, with most of that time spent on tedious, repetitive, and detail–oriented tasks. For example, to perform a *nand* operation on two 16–bit buses, the engineer must tap off each bit of each bus, join each pair of taps with one of 16 separate 2–input *nand* gates, and tap each output into a 16–bit output bus. In this case and in many others, the designer must draw similar structures numerous times, spending valuable design time performing repetitive tasks rather than tackling design problems.

Creative problem–solving requires the ability to see the problem and the solution on an abstract level. But flat design focuses the designer's attention on how the design is implemented, rather than on the design as a whole. With the constant demand for explicit detail, the designer easily can lose track of the overall design once it is undertaken or fail to envision a whole solution at the beginning of the design. Several designers working on the same design project also can stray from a design concept, thus duplicating effort and, in some cases, working at cross–purposes.

Errors emerge at the conceptual level and at the detail levels of the design. Attention to implementation details, for example, can result in the omission of functions, inefficient interconnection of elements within the system, or awkward configurations of components that implement a function inefficiently. Also, the designer has numerous opportunities to mislabel components, pins, and nets; to connect nets incorrectly; and to leave nets unconnected.

The advantage of flat design is its end product: a set of schematics that can be used to manufacture the design. Flat schematics specify the design explicitly.

Structured Design

The structured computer–aided logic design (SCALD) methodology emerged from an urgent need to meet strict development time constraints. This methodology was developed during the late 1970s by Dr. L. Curtis Widdoes, Jr., and Dr. Thomas M. McWilliams at Stanford University (Palo Alto, California) and Lawrence Livermore National Laboratories. Widdoes and McWilliams developed SCALD to help streamline the design of the complex S–1 computer, a project commissioned by the U.S. Navy.

The SCALD technique increases productivity by enabling engineers to focus on the conceptual, creative aspects of electronic design rather than on the repetitive details. This technique can be used manually or can be incorporated into a CAE system.

Valid Logic Systems was formed in 1981 to design and manufacture CAE systems based on the SCALD approach developed by company founders Widdoes and McWilliams. Because the SCALD methodology was developed under a government contract, it is in the public domain and has been adapted by other CAE manufacturers for use in their systems.

SCALD added a new dimension to design by introducing structure, and it capitalized on the use of hierarchy.

Hierarchical design organizes the design in much the same way that a Chinese box holds increasingly smaller boxes. That is, abstract, higher level hierarchical elements contain increasingly lower level elements that finally provide physical detail at the lowest level. Each hierarchical element contains other elements beneath it that provide additional details of the design.

Hierarchical design allows an engineering team to create an orderly structure for the design process, so that design tasks can be partitioned easily for individual designers. This approach also saves a considerable amount of design time by allowing a designer to create a specific function and reuse it in multiple locations in the design without redrawing that function explicitly.

Structured design manages design complexity by separating logical and physical implementation. To accomplish this, structured design provides a symbolic, shorthand notation for representing detail at a single level of the design hierarchy and relies on the design system to interpret these symbols as their physical equivalents. The shorthand notation and the physical implementation are simply alternative representations of the same design.

Structured notation frees the designer from the tedious work involved in placing and wiring additional elements and results in a simpler, uncluttered graphic representation of the design. Also, the separation between logical and physical design allows the designer to create technology–independent designs, then evaluate a series of different technologies for the final physical implementation.

Structured, Hierarchical Design Tools

An optimum SCALD–based design system consists of design–capture (schematic–capture) tools, verification tools, a tool called a *packager* that maps logical components to physical components, and a tool to create fully annotated schematics. This software generally runs on a stand–alone engineering workstation. However, some software, such as verification tools, might reside on a mainframe for batch processing of very large designs.

Design–capture tools consist of a graphics editor and a set of libraries. The graphics editor allows the logic designer to create (or capture) a schematic on a workstation screen or graphics terminal. A hierarchical graphics editor permits the designer to capture the design at multiple levels of abstraction, from conceptual through concrete levels.

To use a graphics editor, such as the SCALD–based ValidGED editor, the designer selects a component. In the case of ValidGED, an element's graphical representation is called the *body*. The designer then places those bodies and/or library elements on the schematic page represented on the workstation screen. The designer connects the terminals of those symbols with the terminals of the other symbols on the page or specifies how nets connect on another page of the schematic.

The designer can create any element needed, such as a hierarchical block that contains other hierarchical blocks and elements found in the library. When creating a body drawing for an element, the designer specifies the element's properties. Typically, such properties consist of the component name, the pin names, and the bit–width of a fixed–size component (for example, the bit–width of an 8–bit register is 8). The designer also can assign variables to properties such as size so that, when placing the body into a logic drawing, the user can supply a specific value, such as bit–size, for that particular instance of that element. In ValidGED, the designer can create bodies and edit schematics using the some tool; frequently, these tasks must be performed with separate tools on some other design systems.

A typical body drawing for an ALU control block is shown in Figure 3.2. In this drawing, *ALU Ctrl* is the body name, and the pins are named *carryin*, *carryout*, *select*, and *control*.

A design library is a database whose members are logic elements representing components from a technology family such as FAST. Libraries also can exist at other hierarchical levels, such as the transistor level. In conjunction with CAE vendors, ASIC foundries offer libraries of standard cells or gate–array macros that accurately represent the structure and timing characteristics of the specific manufacturing processes.

Each element in the library database can have its own graphical representation, a model used in design verification, and physical information for the packager. For example, Figure 3.3 shows an *and*–gate library element corresponding to VLSI Technology Inc.'s (VTI's) VGT100 gate–array macro *an02d1*. Included in the library are the body drawing and its associated properties, a logical *and* function model for the simulator, timing data specific to the VGT100 technology, and physical implementation information.

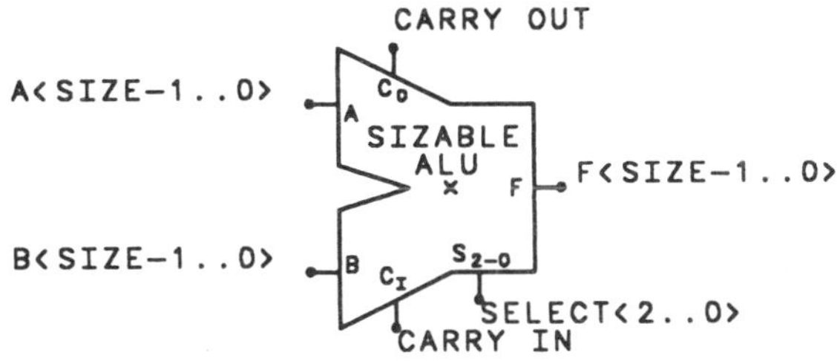

Figure 3.2: Body drawing for an ALU control block. *ALU Ctrl* is the body name. *Carryin, Carryout, Select,* and *Control* are the pin names.

For off–the–shelf components, libraries represent families of components manufactured in a particular technology, such as TTL, ECL, or CMOS. For semicustom IC design, manufacturers supply libraries of standard cells or gate–array macros that support different manufacturing specifications and different technologies. Users such as large systems manufacturers also can build their own libraries for proprietary technologies.

Verification tools check whether a design satisfies the designer's specifications. The functional simulator verifies whether the design performs the function required, given a set of circuit–stimulus patterns. In the case of ValidSIM, the simulator also provides detailed timing information. A timing verifier performs timing checks independently of simulus patterns.

The engineer can verify the design as functional blocks are finished and/or verify the entire hierarchical design at once. To support structured, hierarchical design, verification tools must be able to interpret the structured design notation and expand a design hierarchy.

A packager maps the logical design into physical components, matches signals to physical pins, and labels components and their pins. Essentially, it flattens the design by expanding the design structure. The ValidPACKAGER tool also checks for physical errors, including violations of loading and fan–out constraints, and violations of technology family compatibility.

In other words, it alerts the user if an output pin has too many loads and if ECL and TTL technologies, for example, are mixed incorrectly. After expanding and checking the design, the packager creates a netlist. Finally, using the

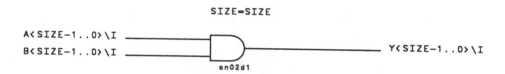

Figure 3.3: *And–gate library element.* Included are the body drawing, a logical *And* function model, timing data, and physical implementation information.

netlist, an automated schematic–generation tool such as Valid's Transcribe creates a flat schematic that can be fully annotated.

Hierarchical Design

Engineers can employ either a top–down or a bottom–up hierarchical methodology, but in most cases they use a combination of both approaches in a single design.

Ideally, the top–down design methodology allows the engineer to begin with a highly abstract representation of the design and end with a highly detailed representation. At the highest level, the designer groups the major functions of the design into functional blocks, then specifies the interconnections between those blocks. In the case of the simple computer design shown in Figure 3.4, the major functional blocks consist of some control logic, the memory, the I/O block, and the ALU. The advantage of top–down design is that the engineer can work from an abstract idea without having to worry about

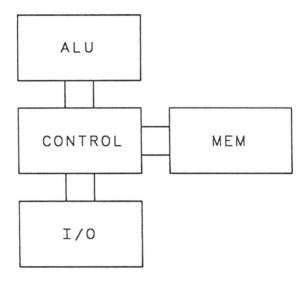

Figure 3.4: Simple computer design. The major functional blocks consist of control logic, the memory, the I/O block, and the ALU.

implementation details. Using top–down design, a design team can partition a complex design and distribute design tasks among the team members.

The engineer selects a functional block and specifies the subfunctions that the specific block contains. The subfunctions then are expanded into greater levels of detail until the lowest level is reached. For a PCB design, the hierarchy ends at the gate level for most digital logic and at the transistor level for analog components. The hierarchy can end either at the gate level or at the transistor level for IC design.

Figures 3.5a–f illustrate a typical hierarchical design. (see pages 91–93).

Bottom–up design is the opposite of top–down design. The engineer creates a bottom–up design by beginning at the lowest level of the hierarchy—in this case, at the full adder (FA) in Figure 3.5f and the ALU–control block in Figure 3.5d—and then moving up the hierarchy. The engineer can create the lowest levels with library elements of a specific technology.

The advantage of bottom–up design is that the engineer can concentrate on critical performance or functionality issues first, to prove whether a certain feature or functionality can be achieved. In the case of a CPU design, the engineer could use bottom–up design to implement critical timing for an instruction–fetching function or to implement hardware–assist for certain instructions. Once completing the lowest level of the design, the engineer then creates higher level blocks by incorporating these bottom–level blocks.

In practice, most engineers use a combination of top–down and bottom–up methodologies. Once a top–level representation of a design or block is complete, the engineer commonly implements the most critical portion of the lowest level of the hierarchy next. Critical design considerations arise from the same requirements for functionality and/or real estate that require bottom–up design. In most cases, the designer specifies one or more levels of the upper hierarchy and then moves to the lowest levels of the hierarchy for critical functions. Then, the designer moves back up to the upper hierarchy to refine the design, adding control logic, reconfiguring logic, or adding function pins, for example, and filling in additional middle levels of the hierarchy.

In hierarchical design, the engineer has a great deal of flexibility in how to debug and verify a design. For example, the designer can verify the design as a whole all at once. But the engineer also can choose to debug the design from the bottom up, one block at a time, to pinpoint sources of errors more easily. After designing a functional block such as this 4–bit ALU, which contains multiple levels of hierarchy, the engineer can verify the function of the lowest level of hierarchy. Clearly, the full adder shown in Figure 3.5f must function properly for the design to function properly as a whole. Once satisfied that the block performs properly, the engineer can then verify the next higher level, the Sizable ALU stage shown in Figure 3.5e. The engineer repeats this process up through the hierarchy.

At any level, the engineer can create a behavioral model of a functional block—a model that includes only high–level timing and functionality data. Behavioral models often are developed before gate–level models to give the engineer a quick way to simulate the functionality of a given level. After the gate–level model is designed and verified, the original behavioral model can replace the block's gate–level model during a simulation of the next higher level of the hierarchy to increase simulation performance.

Because this ALU design operates in a CPU design, the engineer could replace the detailed ALU model with a behavioral model to verify the design function as a whole. Or, the designer could verify the CPU design before the ALU is designed by using a behavioral model. This approach means shorter animation runs in comparison to simulation of an entire large design.

Structured Design

Structured design complements hierarchical design by supporting its intent: to manage design complexity and to free the designer from tedious, error–prone tasks.

ValidGED provides a typical example of the structured–design approach. ValidGED's structured–design methodology relies on the ability to use properties. A property is a name–value pair, where the designer assigns values to an element's properties. The designer can either assign a specific property value, such as a pin name, to a body, or assign a variable to a property such as size. With variable properties, the engineer supplies a specific value for the property only when placing a particular instance of that element in the schematic. This allows the designer to use elements that change as a function of how they are used in the design. This capability is called *context sensitivity*.

The *size* property allows the designer to assign size values to different instances of a generic, or *sizable*, element, depending on the desired bit–width of that element. A sizable element retains the same basic characteristics, but it is replicated as specified by each particular size value. Registers and gates are typical examples of elements that can appear with different bit–widths in different locations in a design.

Context sensitivity allows the designer to create a single sizable element rather than a set of elements in different fixed sizes. The size property also frees logic designers from the details of how to implement the element's bit–size physically, since the design system's packager takes care of replicating a particular instance of the element. For example, a design can use a single graphical body to represent a multiple–bit element, even though the physical implementation of that element in a given technology requires multiple instances of that element.

The *times* property gives the designer a simple way to accommodate different loading characteristics due to fan–out. If a single instance of a typical element in a given technology can drive a certain number of loads optimally, the designer must replicate that element to drive a greater number of loads. Using the times property, the designer simply specifies the maximum number of times the element should be replicated. As a result, the designer does not have to place and wire each instance of the element. The packager flags errors if the fan–out is too great, so the engineer can easily identify a fan–out problem and correct it by changing the times value.

Figures 3.5a and b show how the size and times properties reduce design complexity (see pages 94–95). Figure 3.5a shows ValidGED's structured representation of a clocked 16–bit register. The designer has selected an LS74 register element and an LS04 inverting buffer from the LSTTL library. The designer has supplied a value of 16 bits (16B) for the size property of the LS74 register. An LS74 physically represents a 1–bit register, but the designer does not have to consider this fact. The designer simply supplies the 16–bit size property value. Similarly, the designer uses a vectored notation to specify 16–bit input and output buses.

The designer also has supplied a value of 2 times (2T) for the times property of the LS04 inverter. A single instance of the LS04 inverter would cause the clock edge to rise too slowly, because the 16–bit fan–out exceeds the drive strength of the inverter. As a result, the engineer creates two instances of the inverter simply by specifying the 2T value for the times property.

Figure 3.5b shows an equivalent, flat version of the logic drawing given in Figure 3.5a, created by Valid's Transcribe software. The structured logic drawing has been processed by the packager and the automated schematic generation tool.

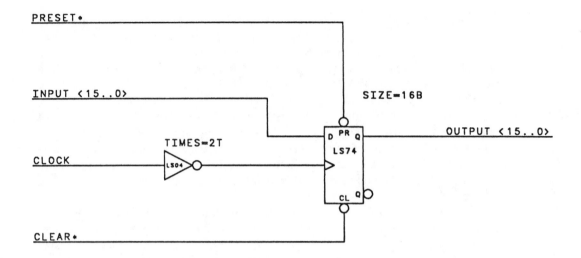

Figure 3.5a: Size and times properties. The structured representation of a 16–bit register is shown.

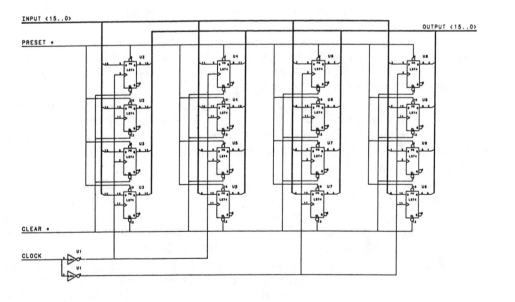

Figure 3.5b: Expanded representation of a 16–bit register.

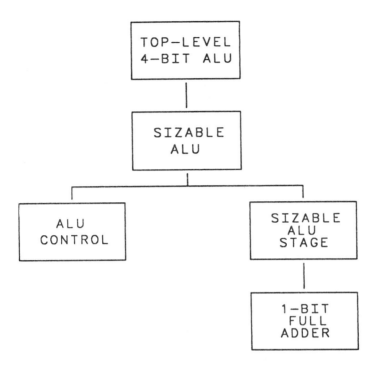

Figure 3.6a: 4–bit ALU design hierarchy.

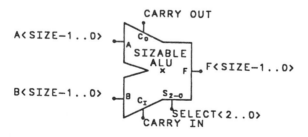

Figure 3.6b: Top–level 4–bit ALU logic drawing.

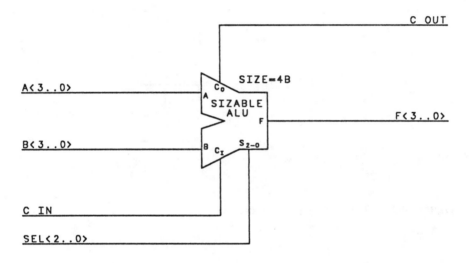

Figure 3.6c: Sizeable ALU.

Using instructions provided by the engineer, the system has expanded the size 16 register representation to a four–by–four matrix of single–bit LS74 registers. Bit 15 through bit 8 appear in the two columns on the left. Bit 7 through bit 0 appear in the two columns on the right. The system automatically taps individual bits from the 16–bit input bus and connects each tap to the appropriate register. Similarly, the system taps register output bits into the 16–bit output bus. All preset pins are wired together automatically, as are all clear pins.

The *times* property of the LS04 inverter has expanded to two instances of that inverter in the lower left corner of the schematic. The upper inverter drives register bits 15 through 8, while the lower inverter drives bits 7 through 0. The system automatically wires the inverter inputs together, so that all LS74s are clocked simultaneously. As a result, each inverter drives an appropriate load.

Technology Independence

Rapidly changing technology places heavy demands on the design engineer. For example, a designer often must redesign a circuit to achieve new system–level objectives such as cost reduction or performance improvement. Frequently, this means changing from one implementation technology to another.

Flat design commits the engineer to a particular technology from the design's inception, but hierarchical design makes no such commitment until the lowest level of the hierarchy. Advanced design systems such as Valid's take advantage of design hierarchy to offer technology–independent design capabilities.

Technology–independent design provides a fast, simple way for engineers to convert a design to a new technology or to compare alternative implementations of the design in different technologies. In general, technology–independent design allows the designer to use generic logic symbols throughout the design and convert the entire design to one technology or another through a single specification at a given level of the hierarchy.

In ValidGED, technology independence starts with the ability to assign variable technology properties to bodies and to assign specific technology values anywhere in the design hierarchy. The design system automatically propagates a technology value down the hierarchy to the lowest level. Then, drawings that assign conditional expressions to library elements allow the system to select particular library elements in a specific technology. For example, in a technology–independent design, if the designer specifies Technology A, then the system would automatically fill in with elements from a Technology A library. Simply by changing a technology value, the design can convert to Technology B or to a Technology C.

The future of hierarchical design lies in maximizing the designer's ability to take advantage of new technologies. Now, design engineers are beginning to employ existing technology–independent techniques in new designs. In addition, CAE vendors are incorporating technology–independent functionality into their

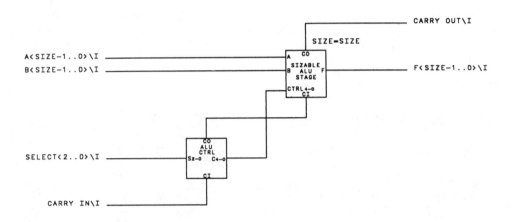

Figure 3.6d: Expanded ALU control block.

systems and exploring new techniques for redesigning technology–specific designs for new technologies.

As increasing design complexity motivates more engineers to adopt structured, hierarchical design techniques, SCALD–based design tools find wider acceptance by the design community. Combined with technology independence, structured and hierarchical design will play an even greater role in improving design quality and reducing time–to–market in a marketplace where managing complexity poses an ever–increasing design problem.

Applying Hierarchical and Structured Techniques in Technology–Independent Design

The following figures show a detailed example of how the designer applies hierarchical and structured design techniques in a top–down, technology–independent ALU design. In this design, the engineer wants to evaluate two different gate–array technologies for implementing an ALU. This example shows how the designer can use a single design and simply change a single global text file (macro) to automatically create two designs implemented with different gate–array libraries: the VTI VGT100 library and the NEC CMOS4 library.

Figure 3.6a illustrates the hierarchy used to represent the ALU design. Each node in the hierarchy has a body drawing, which is a symbol representation, and a corresponding logic drawing, which is a logic–schematic representation. The engineer creates all drawings by using the graphics editor. The designer specifies the function pins based on knowledge of how this element functions in the design. Pin names on the body drawing have corresponding signal names on the logic drawing. The symbol /I is appended to these signal names. Figure 3.6b shows the body drawing for the sizable ALU. This body drawing shows 1–bit *Carryin* and *Carryout* pins, a 3–bit *Select* pin, and three sizable input/output pins. The designer has labeled input pins A and B and function output pin F using a vector notation that takes advantage of the size property. When the designer specifies a size value while placing this body in a schematic, the design system automatically deduces the bit–width of the nets connected to these pins. All other body drawings for the design are created using these same techniques.

Figure 3.6c shows the sizable ALU placed in a logic drawing with connecting nets that could lead to other components and, perhaps, to a higher level of the hierarchy. Here, the designer specifies the ALU size as 4 bits through the *Size=4B* property attached to the body. The engineer has labeled nets A, B, and F as 4 bits.

Next, the designer constructs two functional blocks to represent the ALU at a deeper level of detail. Figure 3.6d shows an ALU–control block with four pins and a sizable ALU stage with seven. The ALU–control logic has been separated from the sizable ALU stage so that it will not be replicated for each bit of the ALU. The *size –size* expression means that the size property value appearing on the upper–level drawing is passed down automatically to this level. In this case of a 4–bit ALU design, the system automatically assigns the value 4 to the sizable–ALU stage size property.

The engineer now expands the ALU–control block because it contains no major functional blocks, only simple logic gates. Note that no technology is specified for these gates (see Figure 3.6e).

Next, the engineer designs the sizable ALU stage, determining that this level requires a 1–bit full–adder functional block and some special nomenclature to cause the 1–bit full adder to be replicated (see Figure 3.6f). The engineer intends for the full adder to be replicated according to the size value assigned in the top–level drawing. Note that the full adder block does not have a size

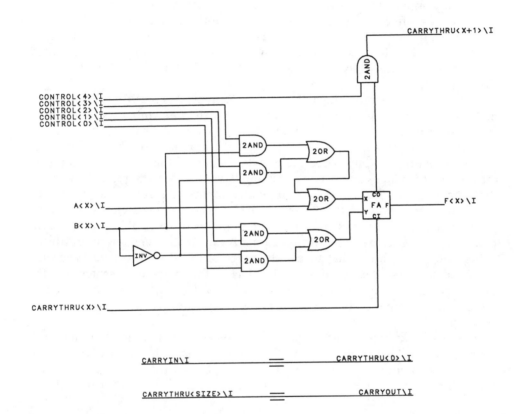

Figure 3.6e: Sizeable ALU stage expansion.

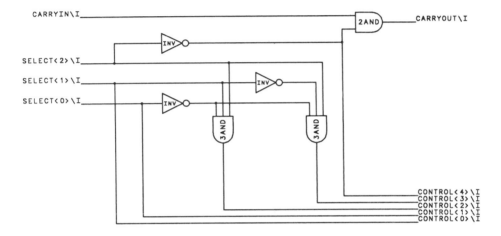

Figure 3.6f: 1–bit full adder expansion.

property assignment. The default method of size expansion would connect all *carryin* pins together and all *carryout* pins together, which would be incorrect in this case. Instead, the text expressions listed in the *define body* and on the drawing itself control the expansion to correctly connect the *carryout* pin of each full adder to the *carryin* pin of the next full–adder instance. This method of specifying the full–adder replication proves more efficient than creating a new drawing every time a different size ALU stage is needed.

The engineer uses generic gates to implement the full adder function. This level of the hierarchy and all higher levels are completely technology independent; the engineer does not need to commit to a specific technology in this drawing (see Figure 3.6g). This permits the engineer to reuse the drawing in numerous other designs using any technology.

Figure 3.6h shows a Body drawing for one of the logic gates used in the full adder and throughout the design. Each type of logic gate in this design requires a *body* drawing so that the gates in the design are generic rather than technology–specific.

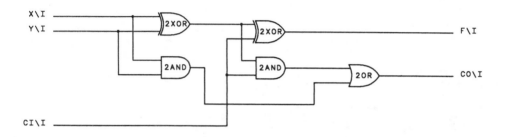

Figure 3.6g: 1–bit full adder logic drawing.

The logic drawing shown in Figure 3.6i correspond to the F312 and gate in the NEC–CMOS4 library, and to the an02d1 and gate in the VTI VGT100 library.

To choose a technology, the engineer includes a three–line text file (macro) that directs the design system's compiler to substitute either the NEC or the VTI technology in the design. Selection expressions appear in the bottom–level drawings that assist the compiler in this process. For example, the expression EXPR=TECH=NEC CMOS4 would appear. This would mean that when the global text macro assigns the NEC CMOS4 value to the TECH property, the design system will use this particular F312 2And gate for each instance of a 2And gate in the design. Similarly, a selection expression would read TECH=VTI VGT100. When this is specified, the design system selects the an02d1 gate for each instance of a 2AND gate.

The F312 and an02d1 gates and all other bottom–level library components have complete verification models particular to their distinct technologies. The engineer can compare the performance of the two gate array implementations of the design by selecting the NEC CMOS4 design in one simulation run and the VTI VGT100 design for another run. The design system uses the identical set of hierarchical drawings for each run, but automatically substitutes bottom–level components appropriate for each technology.

Using this approach, the engineer can quickly and easily convert the design to a new technology once a library becomes available. As a result, technology–independent design techniques allow the engineer to improve design performance and lower engineering costs without having to redesign a circuit completely.

```
PIN_NAME=A<SIZE-1..0>
PIN_NAME=B<SIZE-1..0>  2 AND   PIN_NAME=Y<SIZE-1..0>
```

Figure 3.6h: AND gate body drawing.

Figure 3.6i: NEC CMOS4 F312 AND gate.

• High–Level Logic–Synthesis Tools Reduce Time and Cost of Electronic Design •

Advantages of Behavioral Design Descriptions

Designing with behavioral rather than structural descriptions can be compared to programming in a high–level language instead of a machine language: The design process goes much faster and the results are more accurate and reliable. Behavioral descriptions take a variety of forms. Three typical forms of expression are equations, truth tables, and state descriptions.

Circuits with outputs that are straightforward functions of a set of inputs are best expressed in equations. Equations save the engineer time by allowing the use of high–level operators (addition, greater than, less than, etc.). Developing a schematic of a 12–to–4 multiplexer involves placing 18 gates and routing and connecting 53 lines. In contrast, this same circuit can be described in behavioral terms in just one equation: [Y3..Y0] = (SELECT == 0)& [A3..A0] #(SELECT == 1)& [B3..B0] #(SELECT == 2)& [C3..C0].

This equation specifies the values of the four output wires (Y0 through Y3) as follows: If the combined value of the two SELECT lines is 0, then the values of the output wires are equal to those of A0 through A3; if the combined value of the two SELECT lines is 1, then the values of the output wires are equal to those of B0 through B3; and if the combined value of the two SELECT lines is 2, then the values of the output wires are equal to those of C0 through C3. Writing this equation takes just a few minutes. Design revisions (for example, adding more input lines) also are easy: Instead of placing new gates and routing new lines, all you have to do is to add an expression for the new inputs (for example, D3..D0).

One common form of control logic is the state machine, a circuit capable of storing an internal state reflecting prior events. State–machine logic involves branching to new states. With state machines, the time to be saved by using behavioral descriptions is even more dramatic than with multiplexers and decoders. Because of the complexity of the relationships among internal states, external inputs, and output sequence, an initial manual design of a state machine might take days to develop and, even then, would be likely to contain numerous errors. These errors might require several revisions.

Increasing Complexity

The difficulties involved in expressing logic designs in structural form increase many times over as gate arrays become more complex. When gate arrays had fewer than 1000 gates, schematic designs could be developed with reasonable accuracy. If ASICs are to be a feasible option for a broad range of circuit types, engineers need a set of high–level design–entry and logic–synthesis tools that will accept inputs expressed in behavioral terms.

A number of new systems—for example, FutureDesigner from FutureNet— have been developed specifically to address these problems. Their logic– synthesis capabilities allow engineers to express designs in behavioral as well as structural terms; the software then optimizes the design. To design a circuit with these systems, the engineer begins by working through a screen–oriented editor, using a high–level behavioral–design language to describe the logic circuit in behavioral terms. Features that are particularly helpful in simplifying design development, testing, and debugging include an interactive design editor that provides immediate feedback throughout the design process and a scheduler that tracks which parts of the design have been changed, so that only those parts will be reprocessed. This feature alone saves a significant amount of processing time.

Once the design has been thoroughly tested and debugged, the system automatically applies logic–synthesis algorithms that reduce the design to the minimum number of gates, factor the design to achieve the best trade–offs between speed and circuit size, and produce a schematic (or other output, depending on the technology that will be used to implement the design). The net result is not only substantial savings in the time required to design logic circuits, but also better quality circuits. This is because the ease and speed of revising designs developed with FutureDesigner and other systems allow engineers to experiment.

To demonstrate the system's capabilities, consider the process of designing a classic blackjack machine, based on C. R. Clare's design (*Designing Logic Systems Using State Machines*, McGraw Hill, 1972). The blackjack machine plays the dealer. Behaviorally, the blackjack machine consists of a card reader that reads each card as it is drawn, control logic that tells it how to play each hand (based on the total point value of the cards currently held), and display logic that displays scores. To operate the machine, you insert the dealer's card into the card reader. The machine reads the value and, in the case of later card draws, adds it to the values of previously read cards for that hand. These are the steps involved in using FutureDesigner to develop the blackjack machine design:

Step 1: Develop A Block Diagram. The first step is to develop a block diagram of the circuit, showing a high–level overview of the inputs and outputs. This block diagram does not reflect either the detail level of a schematic or the physical placement of gates and wires.

Step 2: Define Circuit Elements. The next step is to define the input and output signals identified in the block diagram. The blackjack machine design has four inputs: a set of four switches to specify the value of each card drawn, a switch to specify that the card has been entered, a restart–game switch, and a switch to display the score at the end of the hand.

The outputs of the circuit are six lines that drive the decoder/display unit. (In this example, we are assuming that the display driver includes its own seven–segment decoder.)

The system saves time by letting you use set notation (that is, a single variable name) to refer to a set of signals with the same function, as opposed to having to refer to each line individually. Set notation not only saves time in expressing the design initially, but also makes revisions easier. If, for example, you had used the term *bus* to refer to a data bus with six lines, and you later decided it needed seven lines, all you would need to do is change the macros.

Another time–saving feature of FutureDesigner and similar systems is its ability to define macros, allowing a complex expression to be abbreviated by a single symbol. As with set notation, macros save time.

Step 3: Describe the Design. The third step is to describe the design. The system makes this step easier by letting you choose the most natural form of expression for each portion of the circuitry. Equations are used to describe the adder (which adds the newly drawn card to the current hand), the status flags (which light the *hit* and *bust* LEDs—light–emitting diodes), and the card selector (which declares the value of the newly drawn card).

On the other hand, a state description is used to describe the blackjack machine controller. Generating a state description involves two steps: first, creating a bubble diagram that shows the different states and their relationship to one another; second, establishing definitions that express each state in binary terms, specify the actions to be taken at that point, and identify the transition to the next state. Throughout the design–description step, the system processes the design as it is being input. This processing includes parsing the design (checking it for syntax errors) and converting into equations any portions of the design that are expressed.

Step 4: Verify the Design. The fourth step is to verify that the design performs the intended function. To do so, you generate the necessary test vectors; the system then applies them to a behavioral model of the circuit, calculating the outputs that will result from each specification. In the case of Future–Designer, verification functions are performed by the interactive functional verifier, a logic simulator that can work from the original design input. This feature lets you verify the functionality of the design at the earliest possible point. In cases where you know the desired outputs, you can write test vectors to specify both inputs and outputs. The interactive functional verifier then will indicate whether the predicted outputs will, in fact, occur. The interactive nature of the system's verification process means that, once a problem is identified, you can try to resolve it immediately without exiting from the application. You can repeat the verification step after synthesis if you wish, since the verifier works with all forms of the design description.

Step 5: Optimize the Design Synthesis. The fifth step optimizes both the number of gates used by the design and the final size of the circuit. This step involves three operations: converting the design to a sum–of–products form, reducing the logic to eliminate redundancies, and factoring it. The conversion portion of the step converts all equations into a uniform format by expanding any set notation and macros and replacing high–level operators with the four standard Boolean operators (*and, not, or, exclusive–or*). Logic reduction minimizes the size of the circuit by eliminating any redundancies or ambiguities in the design. As part of the reduction process, FutureDesigner resolves any *don't–care* values, setting them to whatever value will result in the lowest gate count. (A *don't–care* value may be assigned to an output whenever its value does not affect the functioning.) Logic reduction has the dual effect of speeding up the design and reducing the number of gates (or gate equivalents) needed for implementation. It can reduce gate count by as much as 50% and design size by as much as 90%. Another benefit of logic reduction is that, by eliminating redundancies, it ensures that the circuit will be fully testable. Testing can verify only that, for a given input, the output will have the desired value. Factoring helps you achieve the optimum trade–offs between speed considerations and space requirements. The system's proprietary factoring algorithm detects and extracts any terms that are used more than once in a set of equations.

Step 6: Implement the Design. The final step in the design process is to implement the design. This step has three parts: partitioning and device fitting, generating the required output, and preparing any documentation that is needed.

There are several reasons to partition the circuitry among more than one device type. For example, you may want to implement a prototype of the circuit in PLDs. All you have to do is to specify which outputs you want in each segment, and FutureDesigner then will automatically partition the inputs. Once you have partitioned the circuit and selected the device type(s), FutureDesigner generates a machine–readable description of the design in the appropriate format. For gate arrays and other semicustom devices, FutureDesigner generates schematics and netlists using JEDEC standard number 12 macrocells.

Gate Arrays from Start to Finish

Before fabrication, a gate array consists of unconnected transistors, or cells. The way these cells are connected determines the type of gate they will form (*and*, *nand*, *nor*, etc.). Gate–array manufacturers provide data books listing all the cell types. Both the gates and the connections between them are formed by a process called metalization. This involves vaporizing layers of aluminum onto the gate array at selected points, so that transistors are connected to form completed gates.

Designing a gate array involves selecting components from the manufacturer's data book and laying them out in the form of a schematic, with lines drawn to show the connections. The schematic then must be translated into a netlist. The next step is to perform a complete simulation of the circuit, including functional verification, fault simulation, and timing, to make sure it works as expected. Next, a layout is developed, with connected gates positioned as close together as possible. A final simulation is performed after this step, to make sure that the circuit, as laid out, will have the desired timing. Finally, the gate array is fabricated.

CHAPTER 4

ENGINEERING DATABASES AND NETLIST GENERATION

• **Netlist Extraction: Converting Graphics to Text** •

We have seen in Chapter 3 how it is possible to draw schematics on a computer–graphics screen and to output these drawings on a printer or plotter so that others can see them. However, the real value of using computers and workstations is not as an aid to drafting, but in the computer's ability to analyze the drawn circuit and verify whether the circuit will do the job it has been designed to do and will do that job within the specified performance (and cost) parameters. Before the computer can verify logic, timing, voltages, and currents, though, it needs a good netlist. How this netlist is created is the subject of this chapter.

The netlist–extraction process is, in fact, very seldom discussed in the literature on CAE: Most texts, papers, and promotional brochures seem to ignore the subject, moving from design entry to simulation without reference to the netlist–extraction, or compilation, process—as if this extremely time–consuming process did not exist or were just too embarrassing to mention. Frankly, devoting a whole chapter in a CAE book to netlist extraction is somewhat like writing a book on men's clothing fashions and inserting a whole chapter on jockey shorts.

But netlists are, in fact, the underwear that supports a great deal of more visible CAE work.

Netlist extraction is so important because schematic entry and logic simulation usually are two entirely different computer programs, even when they are presented by the same software vendor, harness the same menu–driven user interface, and run on the same workstation. The data format for one program (graphics–based schematic entry) is not inherently compatible with the format for the other (logic simulation). While the former makes good use of display technology, the latter takes advantage of the less visible mathematical and computational ability of the computer itself.

The computer, with few exceptions, does not understand the graphic representations of devices. While engineers can recognize the functions of a *nand* gate from a circuit diagram, the computer does not even see the diagram as a D–shaped box with a tiny circle at its apex: It sees it only as a series of shaded and colored dots against a background of similarly shaded and colored dots in a graphics bit map. Consequently, for the computer to see the diagram as a digital–logic function electrically connected to other digital–logic functions, the graphics information must be put into another format.

In most cases, the format is a textual notation compatible with FORTRAN, C, Pascal, or other high–level–language constructs. A software compiler transforms these high–level–language statements into patterns of 1s and 0s that the computer is used to handling. Though the graphics bit map is, in fact, a matrix of 1s and 0s, the electrical–connectivity and digital–logic functions first must be extracted and transformed to text and then recompiled for the various simulation and layout programs.

This change in format from graphics to text is essential to move circuit information not just from program to program, but from PCs to workstations, from one manufacturer's workstation to another's, and from workstations to mainframes. While a large memory space and bit–mapped graphics may equip PCs and workstations for schematic entry, it may take many hours of computation to simulate the functions and timing performance of a complex circuit. Frequently, this is a batch–processing job for a mainframe and minicomputer. While network technology allows files to be transferred electronically between workstations (or between workstations and mainframes), the file format determines whether or not the data generated by one machine can be read and interpreted by the other machine. If the schematics generated on one machine are not readable by the machine that simulates, then the entire schematic–entry effort is wasted. Consequently, the netlist or file–transfer format is an issue that affects the success of the CAE process not just within the context of one project or company, but for the entire CAE industry.

How a Computer Understands Connectivity

A netlist is a network or connectivity description. It is a very structured method of describing a circuit to a simulator or layout program. The structure of the text—the placement of words, numbers, brackets, commas, and punctuation in each line—is critical. A software compiler will convert the textual listing into object code (1s and 0s) for a particular computer and will use the exact structure of the text as a guide to this decoding operation. A misplaced comma or bracket can result in a compilation error and will affect the successful operation of the program.

To generate a simple logic circuit and the netlist to run on a simulator like CADAT from HHB Systems (Mahwah, New Jersey), the following is done. Using what HHB calls the network description language, numbers or names are assigned to reference points (or pins) in the network description. Signal names are assigned to nodes (connections between two or more device leads) and are later used to report the results of the simulation to the user. The netlist here includes three mandatory sections—*header, parts,* and *externals*—and four optional sections—*model, vectors, connections,* and *special info*—followed by an *end* statement.

Of these sections, the most relevant are the *header,* which gives general information such as the circuit name, last update, revision, and comments; the *parts,* which designates the component parts (primitive, elements, macro models, behavioral models) the simulator is to use to create a simulation model for the entire circuit; *connections,* which show show each element is wired into the circuit; and *externals,* which is used to list all primary signal names, such as inputs, outputs, bus lines, and clock signals. The circuit consists of five elements, A1 through A5, comprising a 2–bit shift register whose output (*dout*) becomes active when the input *strobe* is low.

The netlist is easy to interpret. For example, the *or* gate with two inputs is described in the circuit under the *parts* listing as A5 *or/2.* The *connections* section shows A5.Y *dout* as the output of A5, pin Y connected to an external line named *dout.* Similarly, *dout(out)* 6 in the *externals* section says that *dout* is connected to an external pin, with the number 6 assigned as its sensor/driver number.

Although specifically designed for the CADAT simulator, this netlist reflects the same characteristics as those of many other netlist (or pin–list or wire–list) descriptions. All statements the compiler uses, for example, must be bracketed or terminated with another ASCII (American Standard Code for Information Interchange) symbol (like a carriage return). Here, all statements in the network description are terminated with a dollar sign ($). Anything on the line after the dollar sign is considered a comment. Since the CADAT simulator makes no distinction between upper– and lower–case ASCII characters, software statements can be entered either way on a line. Finally, the indentations of the various sections that make up the network description make the netlist easy for designers to read if they have to (and, very frequently, they do).

There are only two ways to extract such a netlist: by hand, or automatically with a netlist– or pinlist–extraction program. In the first case, a user compiles a netlist description from scratch for a particular simulator (or layout program) and enters it into the computer on the keyboard. In the second case, a computer attempts to analyze all the component and wiring data provided by the schematic–entry process and converts these into a textual description that can be used by the simulator.

The success of the conversion process depends on how much intelligence—how much descriptive and functional software information—has been put into the component descriptions and on the schematic–entry program. That is, the utility of the netlist extractor depends on its ability to recognize *nand* gates and *nor* gates and the wires connecting them. Where the process is not successful, where it fails to extract all the components and wiring networks from a schematic, users may as well compile the netlist by hand, since they invariably are forced to make line–by–line edits or tweaks to the netlist file.

Where a schematic–entry program and logic simulator are closely coupled, as in the majority of turnkey CAE systems, the netlist extractor is almost fail–safe. It will compile a netlist that can be used to drive the simulator. Even so, the system typically will allow the netlist to appear within a window on the CAE screen, giving the user a picture of the descriptive files supplied to the simulator and allowing tweaks to be made as required. Where the schematic–entry program and logic simulator are not closely coupled, the success of the netlist–extraction program varies. For example, the netlist extractor may do an excellent job of recognizing all components and wiring nodes, but fail to put the netlist in the specific textual format demanded by its intended simulator.

As discussed in Chapter 3, high–level–language entry has an advantage over graphics entry. Not only is it less tedious and more efficient than entering schematics gate by gate, it also prevents any confusion in the netlist–generation process: A high–level–language description of a logic circuit is a netlist. Since netlist descriptions can be used to describe complex logic blocks or simple transistors, they can preserve the hierarchy of a design. There is no need to flatten a design down to the gate or transistor level in order to run a simulator or layout program.

Often, the component libraries used in design entry contain textual descriptions of the parts along with their graphic representations. Similarly, the schematic–entry program may force the user to identify all nets by labeling all connected outputs and assigning numbers to each distinct node. Many interactive schematic–entry programs have a rudimentary DRC process built into the program to inform the user of inconsistencies and redundancies. Where two separate output pins have the same name, for example, or where two separate nodes have the same number, the user is asked to rename one or the other. Extracting a usable netlist from the program is a relatively simple matter.

There is some effort under way to incorporate artificial intelligence into schematic–entry programs. The computer then could supervise the design work by providing on–line electrical DRC or automatic logic synthesis. The computer in this case would function like a senior partner, looking over the shoulder of the engineer at the terminal, pointing out the mistakes ("You shorted *clock* to *ground*, stupid!"), and indicating better ways of doing things.

In principle, artificial intelligence attempts to give anthropomorphic characteristics to computers in two ways: first, in the area called *expert systems* and second, in I/O responses. With expert–systems technology, the computer is expected to outguess human experts in any subject by learning more facts (and relationships between them) than a human could possibly absorb. With I/O technologies, we are looking for quick and easy ways get information in and out of the computer. Instead of typing on a computer keyboard, for example, we could talk to it or teach it to recognize visual information (in much the same way as did HAL, the talking computer in Stanley Kubrick's *2001: A Space Odyssey*).

Frankly, this research effort offers only a limited payoff in areas like CAE, which are strictly calculated efforts and not greatly dependent on human judgment or intuition. If the goal of this research is to get the computer to respond more quickly, it would be better to construct a faster netlist extractor and simulator than to build artificial–intelligence constructs into a schematic–entry program. Engineers understand the dire consequences of shorting the clock line to ground (that is, making an unintentional electrical connection) and do not need a computer to remind them. This mistake would show up very early in a simulation run.

An intelligent netlist extractor, one that operates in the background of a schematic–entry program, would see this short as a new net created from the combination of two other previously existing nets—*clock* and *ground*—and would prompt the user with a question: "What is the name of the new net?" Alert designers will recognize that a new network has been created mistakenly, instead of an existing one simply having been expanded, and probably will correct the mistake. This is about as close as we need to get to an artificial–intelligence construct, though still very distant from the full interactivity needed in CAE.

However, it is possible to build rule checks into the netlists and related software modules (for example, behavioral descriptions) at the time they are compiled. Consequently, the modules that describe a functional block can have an embedded intelligence. A module generated for one system can be used again in another system design, frequently without translation or recompiling. This is the goal of object–oriented databases.

The Role of Object–Oriented Databases

In principle, an object–oriented database can put schematic entry and simulation on an interactive basis by eliminating (or at least shortening) the netlist–extraction and reformatting operations typically required in moving from one activity (for example, schematic entry) to another (for example, simulation). In principle, the database can be grown to accommodate PCB layout and physical–modeling jobs as well.

The software system is designed so that activities can function almost independently, but remain linked through the common database. A built–in hierarchical database manager functions like an operating system, relieving the applications software of file–management tasks, providing concurrent file access to multiple users (even over a network), and keeping track of files in use (with time stamps and version numbers). In addition to helping an engineer draw circuits and model their behavior, the database can be expanded to include document files or data for cost analysis.

HP's design system is one of the first commercial front–to–back CAE systems built around an object–oriented database. Others include Data General's TEO/electronics software and a system built for internal use at Harris Semiconductor Corporation (Melbourne, Florida). These systems use one database to integrate all the tasks of the design engineer: circuit design, logic design and simulation, electrical DRC, physical DRC, and documentation. By embedding all useful information in the database, a wide variety of CAE software programs and hardware platforms can be supported with only small amounts of tweaking.

In an object–oriented database, an object displayed on a screen, such as a component, actually represents a hierarchical, tree–structured network of information and relations—including its symbol, its function, the electrical states it is capable of cycling through, its physical form, and even its cost. The component object "knows" that the object has graphical representations, pins, labels, connections, and other attributes. In addition, software instructions (that is, intelligence) can be embedded in the software objects. Connecting objects, then, is equivalent to constructing software programs from a variety of subroutines.

Traditional CAE databases, in contrast, are attribute–oriented: A screen object represents only *one* aspect of a component (such as its schematic symbol or footprint). With attribute–oriented CAE systems, a separate data file is required for each attribute and its related processes. In traditional CAE systems, there are schematic editors that deal with graphical representations, design–rule checkers that deal with connectivity attributes, simulators that deal with state attributes, and PCB– or IC–layout systems that deal with physical attributes. Each attribute representation has its own file. Each file contains data that is repeated in some other file. For example, both the DRC file and the simulation file contain connectivity information.

Consequently, attribute–oriented design systems suffer from two major problems: file–conversion time and data management. File–conversion problems appear when a user must switch from one attribute file to another; for example, from the graphical representation used to represent a device to the file that represents the device as a series of high and low states. Data–management problems are caused by having attribute data in more than one place. Usually, data in one location gets changed without the data in other locations being changed. The majority of attribute–driven CAE programs require a separate project–management program just to track the changes to the database made by different users over time.

With object–oriented databases, the graphical representation of a component and its electrical behavior can be specified in the same software object. Attribute–oriented databases, in contrast, make no inherent connection between an object on a screen and its electrical behavior, unless a netlist software program makes a connection between these two attributes.

Object–oriented databases, then, have several obvious advantages over attribute–oriented CAE databases. First, an object–oriented database will provide a run–time improvement on CAE tasks that traditionally have taxed the resources of workstations and larger computer systems. For example, because an object–oriented database allows schematic–capture programs and simulation routines to use the same database structure and information, they can run simultaneously, providing an interactive environment for the user. There is no need for netlist extraction, netlist compilation, or other file conversions to feed a simulator. The time it takes the simulator to show a response to a change on the schematic is greatly reduced.

Second, it possible to grow the object–oriented database—to add additional attributes to it—without changing the structure of the database itself. This feature is especially useful to vertically integrated electronics manufacturers who eventually will build PCBs or design enclosures for their products, in addition to designing the circuits and simulating their performance. The circuit design, PCB layout, and physical design work can be completed using the same integrated database.

Like the abstractions we know as concepts, object–oriented databases serve as a shorthand way to represent a complex of relations with a single object. Concepts provide human workers with the ability to represent and manage very complex information and to expand our knowledge base incrementally; that is, to add new classes, actions, and attributes to our knowledge base without scrapping the whole knowledge structure and rebuilding it. Object–oriented programming allows a computer to mimic this concept–based representation and management of information about the real world.

Generally, there are five features in object–oriented programming: information hiding, data abstraction, inheritance, multiple inheritance, and dynamic binding.

Information hiding allows blocks of data to be defined as independent entities, or objects. A software description of a group of transistors in circuit, for example, can be defined as a VLSI component and can be processed or analyzed independently of its relations or interconnections with other components. Most modern programming languages, in fact, allow the programmer to define self–contained blocks of data that can be manipulated within a routine, without the local operation affecting any procedure or data outside that routine.

With *data abstraction*, an entire class of objects can be treated as one unit. A group of transistors can be treated as a single gate, a group of gates as a standard cell, a group of cells as an IC component, and so forth. The highest level class of objects (the IC) can be processed (in a circuit–analysis program, for example) without reference to the lowest level objects (that is, the transistors).

The attributes associated with a particular device, whether it is a transistor, cell, IC, or system–level component, include its graphical representation, its electrical characteristics, its physical attributes as described by a fabrication process and/or packaging configuration, and even information about its cost from various vendors and distributors. Object–oriented databases support *inheritance* of both attributes and methods. That is, each object includes attribute data that can be entered into the database when the object is created or added to the object as it is put to use over time. Similarly, an entire class can inherit the attributes and methods of many objects. This is called *multiple inheritance*.

Just as spoken language consists of nouns and verbs, programming languages require a segregation between objects (or classes of objects) and the operations that can be performed on them (that is, methods). The ability to treat an operation as a unit regardless of what data actually would be operated on (for example, text, components, grid) is called *dynamic binding* among objects.

Information hiding, data abstraction, and dynamic binding provide a significant advantage over attribute–oriented programming in the ability to represent complex information. The TEO/electronics software builds a robust, sophisticated data structure that represents some complex real–world things in a simple fashion.

In principle, the basic data structure is created by the user during the interactive design process. The database is changed, moved, acted upon, and revealed by a process called message passing. The object–oriented method allows the data structure itself to pass commands to the appropriate data and to hold off interpreting the commands until the data on which it has to operate is known. In other words, instead of shipping data to various procedures as in conventional programming, commands or procedures are given to the entire data structure.

Consequently, graphical display and simulation are not performed as separate tasks on attribute data, but are equivalent to asking the database to reveal or display a different part of itself. In all other systems, the user must extract a netlist, compile it for a specific simulator, create some test vectors, simulate, postprocess, and print or display the timing diagram to see how the circuit functions. With object–oriented software, most of these time–consuming steps are eliminated.

This relational–database feature allows the object–oriented database to serve as the central library–management system for large organizations. For example, the CAE database system can reside on a file server or mainframe computer that is shared by every designer in the organization. Using any combination of networking protocols (NFS, Ethernet, TCP/IP, X.25, IBM's SNA or HDLC, etc.), these file servers can service any remote terminal or workstation, with any combination of central access control and/or transparency to the user.

For example, the database can serve as the central cross–reference for component names that differ across applications, though they refer to the same device. A PCB–layout system may require that a device called 7486 by the engineers be labeled IC86 in the schematic. The manufacturing bill of materials may need yet another name.

An object–oriented database system can keep track of all attribute data, such as company part number, component cost, device temperature range, reliability, and other parameters, in addition to the standard component data. The database also can track related devices that have much of the data set in common—such as SN7486, 74ALS86, and 54LS86–ACN—all relatives of the 7486.

No parts–list extraction program is needed to extract, for example, the total component cost of a design, the number of devices, or the estimated board density. The data is always in the database and is always current—because it is the same database that is being viewed and manipulated. The object–oriented database can be used by vertically integrated electronics manufacturers to track component and design costs.

While the benefit of object–oriented databases seems clear, especially to vertically integrated electronics manufacturers with large mainframe databases, there is a substantial penalty: These databases must be created pretty much from scratch, which will require substantial labor. Creating an object–oriented database requires a large variety of CAE programs, such as schematic entry, simulation, and layout, to be rewritten—partitioned, in effect, among the various components and software objects in the database.

Similarly, all the attribute–oriented data must be rewritten so that the interconnections and interrelations among attributes are clear. In addition, each component or software object must be invested with all the programs—a miniature schematic–entry program, a miniature behavioral simulator, etc.— that it will reveal or display in use. To minimize the person–years of programming required, companies using an object–oriented database must decide on a single schematic–entry routine, a single behavioral model, and a single layout generator that will be embedded in the software objects.

Even then, the process of tying attribute data and program subroutines into one database is a time–consuming (that is, years–long) task. There is enough difficulty now in getting various attribute–oriented libraries to work with separate CAE programs and hardware platforms. Rather than building software objects, a great deal of CAE programming effort is going into translators that will allow various schematic–entry or simulation programs, especially those running on different computers, to use the same component data. The ideal is to get the output of one program (like a schematic–entry package) to serve comfortably as the input to another package (like a simulator) without a lot of tweaking, adjustments, syntax errors, or other failures. The key is a standardized netlist.

• The CAE Standards Issue •

The reality of current CAE work is that it is a nightmare—a Tower of Babel—of incompatible file formats and descriptive languages. Until some kind of file–transfer standard is fixed, netlist converters and translators are required to get the various CAE systems to communicate with each other. In the absence of a standard, the number of file–format translators required is roughly equivalent to the square of the number of different CAE systems in operation. To be precise, N workstations must be supported by $N \times N{-}1$ translators. For example, 12 translators are required if four different workstation types are to communicate fully with each other. And this does not consider the specialized file–format requirements used for semiconductor or PCB manufacturing. This has created an uncomfortable situation for both CAE system users and vendors.

The obvious remedy to this situation is to create some sort of file–transfer standard, a netlist standard. In this way, each CAE system vendor will be responsible for building only *one* translator, one that connects its software or hardware to the standard format, rather than building a translator for every other program and computer. There are two major standardization efforts currently under way: One is an IEEE committee effort, in conjunction with several dozen CAE software vendors, to define EDIF; the other is a DoD–mandated effort intended to support the VHSIC research program. This standard is called VHDL and will be the preferred method for describing electronic components and systems in software to the government.

The structure of EDIF, as defined by Daisy, Motorola, National Semiconductor, Mentor, Texas Instruments (Austin, Texas), and others, has elements similar to an object–oriented database. Particularly, the notion of *views* is built into EDIF: netlist, schematic, logic model, symbols, mask layout, PCB, documents, graphics, and strangers are all just different views of an EDIF file. There is no particular organization (no hierarchy) among these different views, and any of these elements could be missing from a syntactically correct EDIF file.

For file–transfer purposes, a netlist, a schematic, and a logic model should be embedded in the file. The netlist lists parts and their interconnections. A schematic is the graphic representation of logic–circuit design. The logic model, on the other hand, is equivalent to the behavioral description used by a logic simulation to show logic states and timing. The symbolic view shows a symbolic IC layout. This contrasts with the mask layout, which is the actual physical design of the IC. The PCB layout, similarly, is the actual design of the printed circuit. A document includes text descriptions, while graphics are just dumb pictures. Strangers are user–defined extensions to EDIF. Any number of these can be embedded in an EDIF file.

VHDL, in contrast, is a narrower file format that revolves around behavioral descriptions and, therefore, serves as the native language of a simulator. Because of its DoD parent, the basic syntax of VHDL is taken from the Ada programming language. While its strength is on the behavioral level, VHDL can describe a circuit at the gate or transistor levels. As a consequence, many see VHDL as the high–level language to use to support silicon compilation, standard–cell compilation, and other IC design techniques.

There are other standards being developed, although these are of minimal interest to electronics manufacturers. IGES, for example, is useful for exchanging mechanical–CAD data such as wire–frame drawings. The latest version also includes finite–element modeling support and overlaps with EDIF in transferring some electrical data. The importance of IGES to electrical engineers currently is very small, but may increase as the trend toward performing mechanical–engineering and electrical–engineering tasks on the same workstation continues to grow (see Chapter 10).

Standardization and the open–systems concept, while not entirely the same, frequently are mentioned in the same breath. The open–systems concept can be loosely interpreted to mean that CAE files generated on one manufacturer's workstation at least can be read by another workstation.

• Benefits of Standards to CAE Users •

Users of CAE systems, in chorus with ASIC manufacturers, are clamoring for standards. What kinds of standards do they want and why? What particular standards are coming and what will they do? Do the standards overlap in significant ways, and, if so, what should be done about it? This section will cast some light on these issues by explaining what standards can do for CAE users. Also, the three most important standards in CAE will be discussed: EDIF, VHDL, and IGES.

Types of Standards

CAE standards fall into two categories: data–interchange standards and standard tools.

Data–interchange standards, such as EDIF and IGES, are perhaps the best known. These standards allow users to move data from one system to another so that the same design can be processed on more than one tool.

Standard tools are more sophisticated. VHDL is the best example. A designer can use the tool as a part of several packages or on several different hardware platforms, but the same input descriptions can be used and will produce the same output results. Other examples of standard tools are the software packages for ASIC design produced by companies like VLSI Technology and NCR (National Cash Register) (Dayton, Ohio). These packages fit the classification because the same tools run on different platforms.

Why Have Standards?

There are several reasons for users to want products built around standards. There are also reasons, sometimes the same ones, for CAE and ASIC vendors to want standards. Unfortunately, there also are some drawbacks to their use. The benefits will be discussed first.

Better Tools Sooner. The use of data–interchange standards can result in faster development of tools and libraries than otherwise would be possible—users can get better tools sooner and at lower cost. This also means vendors can spend scarce engineering resources on developing tools that meet users' new and future needs, instead of constantly struggling to keep up with the burden of developing many variations of the same old tool.

A good example is the creation of support packages for ASIC design on CAE workstations. Without data–interchange standards, each CAE vendor must create a unique set of symbol and simulation libraries and unique software for netlist and test–vector transfer for each supported ASIC vendor. Furthermore, these packages need to be maintained and updated constantly as new cells are added to the ASIC library and as new versions of the CAE software come out. It is easy to see that this exponential problem can prevent anything new from getting done.

With a data–interchange standard such as EDIF, ASIC vendors can provide libraries and accept information about the finished design in the standard format. The CAE vendor need build only one set of interfaces.

Open Systems—User Freedom. Data–interchange standards and standard tools allow users greater freedom to choose the appropriate tools. If one tool vendor provides the best schematic–capture system and another provides the best PCB–layout system, the user no longer is forced to either use less than the best tool or create and support a link between two systems. In fact, in the absence of standards, it may not even be possible to create such a link, or it may take too long or cost too much to create one with a full set of features.

Another likely scenario is that the customer has used one set of tools for some time, often because those tools were on the market sooner than others or because they cost less. Now the user's needs have grown or the technology has advanced, and the earlier tool set is obsolete. The customer still needs to be able to maintain and improve designs done on the earlier tools, but also would like to move to a better tool set.

With data–interchange standards, the user's designs can be migrated to the new tools automatically. With standard tools, the process is even simpler: Users can run their designs on the new version of the tool with no migration step.

Tool Agreement. One common problem with design environments containing several similar tools is that different tools for the same or similar jobs may not agree in their results. A very common example is a CAE workstation simulator and an ASIC vendor's mainframe simulator. The designer uses the workstation simulator to do a design and, when it is finished, sends it to the ASIC vendor to be fabricated. The ASIC vendor often runs the circuit through its own simulator to verify that it behaves properly. If the results disagree with those obtained on the workstation, it can lead to frustration and delays in producing the circuit.

Standards can help with tool agreement in several ways. Data–interchange standards can prevent errors in workstation simulator libraries, since the process of library translation is done by machine. They also can make the job of tool development enough easier that the workstation and ASIC vendors can afford to do a better job. This means that the capability of the library simulator to model estimated delays, for instance, can be improved.

Standard tools can solve the problem of tool agreement by eliminating it. In the above example, if the workstation and the vendor both use VHDL (even if the implementations are different), agreement is automatic.

Reduce User Relearning. In a world without standards, users conceivably might have to learn an entirely new set of tools every time they did a new design or even part of a design. For instance, each ASIC vendor could have its own set of tools, and anytime users changed vendors, they would have to learn the new tools.

Data–interchange standards make it possible for CAE vendors to support libraries from several ASIC manufacturers on one set of tools. Standard tools go even further by letting the user change CAE vendors without having to learn a completely new tool set.

Drawbacks of Standards

Unfortunately, the benefits of standards are not entirely without cost. Standards can reduce system performance, raise concerns about the loss of proprietary data or customers, and slow the pace of tool innovation.

A tool designed to work with data from a data–interchange standard may be less efficient than a tool for the same job that is tuned for a particular kind of data. A tool that is totally hardwired for some process might be more efficient. A standard tool might be less efficient for a certain narrow range of uses because, to be accepted as a standard, it would have to satisfy a broader range of needs.

Companies that have put a lot of development effort into library data worry that the data could be used without payment if data–interchange standards exist. Companies that have a large customer base worry that design–interchange standards or standard tools may make it too easy for their customers to move to newer, better tools.

The pace of innovation in tools could be slowed by data–interchange standards or standard tools if those standards are not kept up to date. If the standards will not support some new idea or new tool, it will be difficult for that idea to bear fruit.

All these drawbacks can be either lived with or dealt with. Careful (but timely) standards development can ensure that standards do not become inefficient or unwieldy, perhaps by allowing subsets or segments of a standard to be supported. In EDIF, for example, a vendor can support netlist transfer without needing to support schematic transfer. Other efficiency considerations may not be important in light of the other benefits of standardization. If the choice is between having more tools available and having a small increase in efficiency, it may be better to have the tool.

Proprietary data can be protected by simple technical means. It would be simple, for instance, to produce an interface program that checks a status flag and refuses to output data that has the flag set. This would protect data bought from other companies, without keeping users from freely moving data that they created.

Again, standards can avoid inhibiting progress through careful and timely development. Standards should be able to be updated easily to handle new needs without forcing existing users to change. Standards bodies should aggressively pursue timeliness and efficiency in their processes. If these things can be done, the pace of innovation can be speeded by standards, because there will be more resources available to innovate, rather than cranking out yet another link product.

Details of the Standards

In CAE, three standards are most important: EDIF, VHDL, and IGES.

EDIF. EDIF is a data–interchange standard used for all aspects of electronic CAE. EDIF can transfer schematic part libraries, schematic drawings, simulation models, netlists, test vectors, and IC and PCB layouts. An important concept is that an EDIF schematic is an annotated netlist; that is, the emphasis is on the electrical connectivity of the circuit. This does not mean that the graphical aspects are neglected, but rather that the format is tuned to describe electrical circuits as they are depicted graphically, rather than being tuned to describe drawings and then adapted to handle electrical circuits. Simulation models are handled at a low level (gate or low–level functional description). EDIF is targeted to meet the needs of today's CAE users.

EDIF benefits users directly by allowing them to transfer electronic designs from one CAE system to another or from one tool to another. It benefits users indirectly (but substantially) by allowing workstation vendors and ASIC vendors to produce and maintain ASIC support packages quickly and easily.

EDIF was started in 1983 by ASIC and CAE vendors. The founding companies were Texas Instruments, Motorola, National Semiconductor, Tektronix, Mentor, and Daisy. EDIF has been developed by a steering committee, a technical committee, and several technical subcommittees. The steering committee and technical committee include representatives from the founding companies. Technical subcommittee membership is open to all interested parties.

EDIF has been accepted for potential standardization by the EIA (Electronic Industry Association) and the IEEE. Various companies and groups in Europe also have put substantial effort into EDIF.

VHDL. VHDL is the result of a DoD effort to produce a standard for the description of electronic components. It falls into the category of a standard tool, in that there may be various implementations of VHDL simulators, but all should produce identical results given the same input. The basic syntax of VHDL is taken from the Ada programming language. VHDL is the subject of an established IEEE standards committee.

VHDL will benefit CAE users by providing them with a tool for simulation at many levels of abstraction. VHDL can describe a circuit at gate, functional, or behavioral levels. Its major contribution is at the behavioral level.

The standardization of VHDL should induce semiconductor vendors and modeling companies to produce simulation models in VHDL. The result will be more timely availability of models for standard parts, especially more complex parts whose behavior is not well supported by current modeling languages. Eventually, VHDL will be used by semiconductor companies to design both parts and cells for ASICs, and models should be available as soon as the parts are.

The ability to run a simulation on a VHDL simulator from any vendor and expect the same results will free users to choose the best simulator on the basis of performance and features, rather than staying with an older tool because of the investment in models or in user training.

IGES. IGES is a data–interchange standard used primarily for mechanical drawings. Some effort is being put into extending IGES into the electrical realm.

Recent versions of IGES are of limited interest for electronic CAE, since they are used primarily for mechanical CAD. However, many CAE users also are interested in CAD. IGES provides the CAD user with the same benefits of user freedom that are provided to the electronic CAE user by EDIF.

The IGES format uses heavily encoded data in a fixed–column format, reminiscent of punched–card data for FORTRAN programs.

Most CAD vendors support IGES interfaces for mechanical data. There does not appear to be much vendor support for the electrical extensions of IGES.

Relationships Among Standards

Whenever the areas of competence of one or more standards appear to overlap, two questions arise: First, which standard should be used for a particular application? Second, why does the overlap exist? Perhaps an even more fundamental question is whether there should be more than one standard in the CAE field.

On the face of things, it appears that one standard for all areas of CAE, CAD, and CAM would be desirable. In this case, any vendor or user would need to know only one standard no matter what job was being done. There are some practical problems with this approach, however. One is that the establishment of such a standard probably is impossible, simply because of the number of people and the breadth of expertise that would need to be involved. Another problem is that no one person could understand all of such a single standard anyway, so doing a different kind of job with the standard would require nearly as much learning as using another standard.

An alternative is to have one standard for each applications area. This solves the problem of establishing and understanding the standard by using a divide–and–conquer strategy. However, it does raise the problem of areas that fall between applications or that are interfaces between one application and another.

The distinction between data–interchange standards and standard tools should help to explain why standards overlap in the case of EDIF and VHDL. Both standards, for example, include descriptions of circuit behavior. However, EDIF is designed to transfer information that already exists in some form (say, TEGAS simulation models). That information then will be translated out of EDIF into yet another form (for example, HILO simulation models) for use. VHDL models, on the other hand, will be created by a human being and run on (possibly several different) VHDL simulators.

The case of the apparent overlap between EDIF and IGES is more complicated. There are both good and poor reasons for the apparent overlap. The constituencies of the two standards are largely disparate. EDIF is a product of CAE and ASIC vendors, while IGES sprang out of CAD and the DoD. The two communities attend different conferences (DAC versus Autofact, for example) and read different magazines. Thus, the two communities often fail to communicate about their needs and efforts.

There also is a major difference in the styles and schedules of the two groups. IGES has been around longer and has developed more slowly. The IGES community is more concerned with formal standardization, processes, and protocols. EDIF has moved from nonexistence to the threshold of great acceptance in a short time. EDIF developers could best be described as goal–oriented, being primarily concerned with producing a good product in timely fashion.

It is essential that the EDIF and IGES communities make a greater effort to communicate about their needs and efforts. The interface areas, such as wiring harnesses, make a case for better communication between the two communities. A wiring harness has a physical structure and also has electrical behavior (resistance, delay, etc.). Neither EDIF nor IGES alone can describe such an entity adequately and naturally.

The choice of standard for any particular application is clear. For electrical data interchange, EDIF is the choice. For the interchange of mechanical drawings, IGES should be chosen. If the application is a multilevel simulator, VHDL is the best fit.

• Portability •

Everyone has either experienced it or heard about it: the horror of porting code from one platform to another. It starts with a company successfully selling highly functional software, with a sophisticated and satisfied customer base already in place. The same company that was able to develop a complicated set of algorithms and source code on one platform announces that it is beginning to port its software to other industry–standard platforms. The industry eagerly awaits the finished product...and they wait...and they wait.

This scenario is not a unique; in fact, it is commonplace in the electronics arena. However, one start–up company, EDA Systems, successfully ported a complex piece of system–dependent software—an application that involved graphics, low–level disk I/O, and interprocess communication—from DEC's MicroVAX to an Apollo in four weeks. This involved different CPUs and completely different operating systems as well. The key to success was architecting the software for easy portability from its inception.

The software was designed from the beginning with the knowledge that it would have to be ported to multiple hardware platforms. So many viable hardware platforms exist today, with new ones being introduced quite frequently, that it is naive to think the initial development platform will be the only one on which the software eventually will have to run. Since the software will have to be ported eventually, designers should pay attention to portability starting with the system architecture.

Leverage Platform Features

The most important rule for designing systems with portability is to avoid tying the software too closely to unique features of a particular platform. Languages are the most obvious example: The implementation language must be supported on whatever platform the software is going to run on. Other common pitfalls include taking advantage of extremely powerful features of a particular operating system that are not supported by other operating systems or relying on peculiarities of the file system or run–time library.

The way to avoid this trap is to design your own system interface, which can remain the same across machines and operating systems. The system interface should be powerful enough to support any required operation, but also general enough to be implemented on all target machines.

Even when the overall structure of the software has been designed correctly, many potential pitfalls exist in the actual coding process. Languages have dialects, and, frequently, there are enough differences among them to cause problems.

Actually porting the code will be eased by proper preparation, but it still needs to be done. In theory, everything should work immediately; in practice, that will not happen. In a well–designed system, many different components of the code can be ported and tested in parallel, thus dramatically cutting down the time required to port the entire system. In addition, some software is inherently system–dependent. Even here, however, proper design can make it easier to port. For example, in graphics software, assuming as little as possible about the underlying hardware can make life easier when the origin moves from the lower left corner of the screen on one platform to the upper right corner on another.

Finally, not all porting efforts have the advantage of starting from a clean slate. Frequently, the software has been designed and written before any attention has been paid to portability. We will discuss retrofitting portability on existing applications in a later section.

Designing Portable Software

The first step in designing portable software is to identify the universe, the range of systems that need to be supported. This should be done both in terms of hardware platforms—do you plan to support mainframes, minis, workstations, and/or microcomputers?—and operating systems. Overestimating the kinds of platforms to be used makes initial implementation somewhat harder, but attempting to port to a platform not in the initial list may be extremely difficult.

The trade–offs of each platform should be analyzed on a platform–by–platform basis. Even better, restricting the universe to a particular operating system will make life easier. However, any form of UNIX, due to its increasing popularity, is a frequent choice. Even in this situation, dialectal differences between different machines' versions of the same operating system need to be considered at this stage.

It is important that the decision about the platform universe involve technical people as well as the marketing staff. There will be some platforms that will be difficult to support, and decisions must be made as to their long–term value to the company and the market. Again, this decision is not irrevocable, but it should be as firm as possible: It will not be easy to port to platforms outside the initial universe you select.

The next step is to identify all assumptions made about the environment and ensure that they hold true for all machines in the universe. There is some feedback between this step and choosing the universe: It may turn out that some platforms are completely intractable and so have to be given up once the trade–offs are analyzed. Sometimes, these assumptions are extremely subtle. One obvious example is directory structure, which may not even be supported (on IBM mainframes, for example) or may be limited to a fixed depth (such as on VMS). Others are the case–sensitivity of filenames and the naming of files in a network on any platform.

The classic example of an overlooked assumption is the byte–ordering problem. On VAXs and computers based on an Intel 8086–family chip, the least significant byte is stored before the most significant byte; on Motorola 68000–based machines, the order is reversed. In some cases, low–level routines can be written to take advantage of the byte ordering—but when they move to another machine where the bytes are ordered differently, they will not work anymore.

A final implicit assumption to check carefully involves underlying library routines. This is particularly a problem with C, since the library definition is not part of the language. Even a simple routine such as *memcpy*, which copies a specified number of bytes, is not supported on VAX, although the VAX C library in turn contains features not supported on other machines.

In summary, the best way to be sure about a specific assumption is through personal experience or by examining manuals for the machines in question.

Create Assumptions and Stick to Them

What happens when an assumption does not hold true on one of the platforms? Quite simply: That assumption should not be made. For example, if one of the operating systems does not support a directory structure, a program should not assume that it can keep all its data files in a subdirectory. This may seem obvious, and it is, but failing to consider these issues at the very beginning of the design can lead to grave problems later on.

Once the assumptions have been identified and seen to be valid, the design can begin. The first step is to break the design down into manageable pieces, which are called subsystems.

Each subsystem provides an interface to other subsystems. This means that the internal structure of a subsystem can be hidden from the rest of the world, which needs to know only the interface. The interface to a subsystem will remain the same on all platforms, even if the implementation changes.

Circular dependencies between subsystems—A depends on B, B depends on A—should be avoided for two reasons. First, they make it impossible to port one subsystem without porting the other. Second, a change in the interface of A may cause a change in the interface of whatever subsystems depend on it, including B; and that, in turn, may trigger a change in the interface in A, and so on. Keeping a strict hierarchy of subsystems avoids this problem.

A good portable design isolates the system dependencies into only a few subsystems. Ideally, of course, there is *no* system–dependent code, but that will not be the case for any reasonably complicated application. At least, the operating system, graphics, and device interface have to depend on the underlying system.

Only those subsystems that involve system dependencies need to be modified when porting: The interface of these system–dependent subsystems does not change, and that is all the other subsystems care about. Thus, isolating system dependencies decreases the amount of work that needs to be done.

Essentially, specifying the interface of a system–dependent subsystem defines a *virtual machine*. The rest of the software can always talk to the virtual machine, freeing it from understanding the details of the actual machine and operating system being used—virtual machine hides that information.

The virtual machine should concentrate on relatively low–level operations that will be supportable on all platforms. For example, the EDA disk I/O manager supports the operations *read a block from disk* and *write a block to disk*. Higher level, machine–independent routines can use this as a base to build up more complicated functionality. Designing the system in this way may result in an extra layer of software that exists only to separate the rest of the software from the system dependencies. The increased ease of portability more than makes up for the small price in performance.

Care must be taken to keep the virtual machine truly system–independent. In particular, avoid tailoring the data structures to those supported on a single platform. This is easy to do without thinking: Some of the supposedly machine–independent code at EDA used the VMS string format.

There is a constant trade–off between taking advantage of the features of individual operating systems and avoiding reliance on nonportable functionality. In general, the idea is to optimize the system–specific code for individual platforms without changing the interface at all. This requires advance planning, so that the interface supports the needed functionality of any platform architecture.

For instance, some machines (for example, the VAX) support asynchronous disk I/O: reading from the disk at the same time the program is executing. This can make a large difference in execution speed; the I/O may be done by the time the program needs that data, and so it does not have to wait. On the other hand, not all systems support this feature.

The solution, then, is to define a *start–asynchronous–read* operation in such a way that it simply has no effect on systems that do not support asynchronous I/O. This can be done by mandating that programs that call *start–asynchronous–read* also must call the regular *read* procedure when they actually need the data. On a VAX, the *read* procedure will check to see whether the read has already been done asynchronously and, if so, return immediately; on a machine without asynchronous I/O, the read procedure always will read from disk. In both cases, the data is in place by the time the read procedure returns, and the calling program has been shielded from the knowledge of just how it happened.

A final component of portable system design involves the entire programming environment. As above, assumptions need to be identified early in the development process: for example, is there an assumption that each subsystem resides in its own directory? This will lead to problems on machines that do not support directories. Similarly, what is the maximum permissible length for a file name?

In general, automate as much of the development process as possible, to cut down on the amount of information that needs to be shuffled around.

Writing Portable Code

Once the basic structure of the software has been designed, it must be implemented. Since carelessness here can undo the good work on the design, programmers also need to consider portability.

Many of these principles are independent of the implementation language. One obvious example is to identify all system–dependent code clearly at the start. This is code that will have to be rewritten when it is ported; before you can rewrite it, you have to find it.

Paying attention to testability also is important, especially with the lower level or system–dependent functions. Test programs should be written whenever possible to allow problems to be detected and isolated early in the process. Even absurdly simple test programs frequently will find an unexpected system dependence or surprising result; when they do, it is obvious where the problem is.

Similarly, as much run–time checking as possible should be included. This again falls into the category of identifying the root of a problem quickly. The speed–up in debugging more than compensates for the performance loss, especially if the checking can be turned off by a conditional compilation switch.

Care must be taken not to rely too much on error checking from library routines. In one port it was found that several routines were more robust on the VAX than on the Apollo. For example, *tolower*, which converts a character to lower case, would leave a character that was already lower case alone on the VAX, but result in garble on the Apollo. The restriction was documented clearly in the Apollo manual, but it was mistakenly assumed that the VAX implementation was the standard one.

Frequently, performance bottlenecks will require some code to be written in assembly language that is inherently unportable. The best solution to this problem is to write a high–level–language equivalent of each function in assembler. The high–level code should be portable and will provide the same functionality; at the first stages of the port, performance will not be an important issue.

This leads to language–specific coding principles. Some of the traps here are very seductive. Many C and Pascal implementations, for example, support nonstandard extensions. Reliance on these extensions makes the programmer's task easier, but can make porting a nightmare.

The C language leaves the sizes of data types undefined. In particular, since the *int* data type is supposed to be the most efficient on the underlying machine, it may be either 16 or 32 bits. Code should avoid relying on particular sizes for these built-in data types; when an object does have to be a particular size, a type should be defined with the understanding that it may map to different primitive types on different machines.

Another problem in C is procedures that take variable numbers of arguments. This is an inherently system-dependent feature, since it depends on the procedure-calling protocol of the machine and even the particular compiler used. Some portability can be attained by using the UNIX *varargs* macros, but cavalierly passing extra or insufficient arguments and assuming the compiler will do the right thing is a dangerous mistake.

As originally defined, C is a loosely typed language: All pointers are equivalent, and no type-checking is done on procedure calls. The *case* operation can be used to type pointers explicitly, but many C compilers, especially older ones, will allow programmers to get away with almost anything without even a warning. Reliance on loose typing, however, can lead to major problems in portability.

A simple example of this is on a word-addressed machine, such as a Data General Eclipse or DEC MicroVAX, where a pointer to a byte (which may not be word-aligned) is fundamentally different from a pointer to anything else (which must be word-aligned). In this instance, the case operation actually generates some vital run-time code.

A more subtle example interacts with the byte-ordering problem discussed above. When a procedure expects a pointer to a long (16-bit) integer, the results depend on whether the machine is forward-addressed (for example, Apollo) or backward-addressed (for example, VAX). On the VAX, the least significant word of the long integer would occupy the same location in memory as does the short integer. On the Apollo, however, the short integer is in the location of the most significant word of the long integer. Such errors can be extremely difficult to find. These problems would be avoided if C were a strongly typed language. Instead of creating difficult-to-detect run-time errors—which may not even appear until the software is ported—the compiler would detect the problem immediately. Many Pascal and Ada loyalists point to this as one of the major defects of C; in fact, the new ANSI (American National Standards Institute) C standard is strongly typed for just these reasons.

Some C compilers do this kind of checking to a greater or lesser extent. In general, you should use the strictest compiler you can find to perform type-checking (on a UNIX system, LINT also can be used for strict type-checking, although it tends to be slower). This not ease only will initial development, but also will avoid the situation where you port from a laissez-faire compiler to a more rigorous one and suddenly are deluged with surprising warning and error messages.

Porting the Code

The application has been designed and implemented and is running like a charm on the initial platform. Now it is time to actually port it.

There are two goals in porting an application: first, to get a working version on the target machine, and second, to get acceptable performance on the target machine. Getting each subsystem to a working state as soon as possible allows performance improvements to be done on all the subsystems in parallel, and so the basic philosophy is to defer performance issues at first.

Before beginning the port, the order in which subsystems are to be ported needs to be determined. It makes no sense to port a subsystem on the first day when it cannot be tested for a week. Most importantly, any utilities that will be used to help develop the rest of the code should be ported at the very beginning.

Usually, the lowest level subsystems should be ported first, and then the next level up, and so on. This ensures that each subsystem can be tested as it is ported, so that problems can be detected early in the cycle. It also is important to begin the porting of system–dependent subsystems early, because they typically will take longer to port because they have to be totally rewritten on a platform–by–platform basis.

The first, and most fundamental, question is how the files will be transported from machine to machine. A shared network is ideal; many systems support TCP/IP and FTP running on an Ethernet. If the machines do not have some compatible tape medium, a *sneaker net* is the next best option: Load the files to tape on one system, read them back in on the other. For this to work, the two machines must understand the same tape format. Another option is to string an RS–232 cable between the two systems and use a terminal emulator or simple file–transfer protocol such as Kermit to download.

A Case History. The first step at EDA was to port the tool to extract *include* files automatically. This was a relatively small, self–contained program and could be used both as an indication of the likely difficulties and as a development tool through the rest of the porting effort, once it was working. Simultaneously, work began on the system–dependent layers.

The main problems detected at this point were the differences in VAX and Apollo filenames, the varying robustness of library routines, and the different syntax of the *makefiles*. A simple program was written to map VAX filenames into Apollo names; as future subsystems were transferred over, this program could be run on each file. Similarly, another program did the bulk of translation of the *makefile* syntax.

A general rule is that as much translation as possible should be done automatically through subroutines. On the other hand, there are times when it is far more difficult to write a general–purpose translator than to write one that works 98% of the time. At an early stage in the porting process, it is unreasonable to look at this trade–off and decide to do the other 2% manually instead of taking the time to write a full translator. A deeper understanding of the problem may show that the difficult, full translator is not required.

The next step was to port the low–level, system–independent subsystems. These included test routines, so that immediate feedback could be obtained. By this point, some of the system–dependent routines were available; in particular, the disk I/O took less than a day to reimplement. These routines also were tested; a few iterations took out most of the bugs.

As the porting of higher level subsystems began, some subsystems did not have test routines. This meant that several untested subsystems had to be integrated; debugging was much harder, since the bugs were hard to isolate and could be coming from many different places. This difficulty again shows the importance of having test programs already implemented.

Throughout this process, system–dependent code was implemented initially without stressing performance. The key was to get the functionality in place so that other subsystems could be ported and tested. As more and more work went into the system–dependent code, it got more efficient; in the meantime, the porting and testing of other subsystems were not prevented.

Of course, this skeletal description has glossed over a lot of editing, mostly fixing compile–time problems. A few times, bugs were found on the Apollo that also were on the VAX code, so when a problem in the code on the Apollo was fixed, it also would be fixed on the VAX. The code on the VAX was regarded as the canonical version; even the system–dependent code for the Apollo, which would not run on the VAX, was stored there.

Porting does not happen overnight; continuing development on the original platform leads to the problem of porting a moving target. There are two possible solutions: Fix a version to be ported, or attempt to keep the ported versions as up to date as the versions on the original platform. Experience showed that, for the best results, you should commit to one or the other; in this case, efforts were split between the two, which often could be confusing.

When the porting effort was completed, only the system–dependent code had been completely rewritten for the Apollo. The rest of the code, 90%, was exactly the same on the two machines. Much of the success and ease of porting came from paying attention to details and architecture from the start.

Retrofitting Portability

In many cases, an existing application will need to be ported to another platform. The electronic–CAD market has extensive code associated with its applications, which makes retrofitting a challenging and difficult task. In such cases, an already existing application may have been designed without considering portability. It still is possible to apply many of these concepts as an afterthought, although it will be somewhat more difficult than if they had been included initially.

The first step is to list the system dependencies and then attempt to eliminate or isolate them. This may require restructuring and rewriting some of the code. This is an unpleasant task, but the system dependencies will have to be removed from the ported version anyhow—far better to pay the piper now than later!

As much of this restructuring as possible should be done on the original platform, so that it can be tested in an already working system. As mentioned above, it is not fun to port a moving target, so try to have the code in good shape before beginning the port.

The various guidelines discussed in this section should be considered. Wherever possible, the existing code should be made to conform to these standards. At times, this may be too difficult; in this case, the nonconforming code should be thoroughly checked to make sure no bugs have crept in.

In particular, a test program for individual subsystems and modules should be written, and high–level–language equivalents of assembly–language routines also should be tested in the existing environment before being ported.

• EDIF as the Cornerstone of an Interface Strategy •

The ability to interface with a wide variety of systems is an essential need of all CAE companies. This section discusses why EDIF is appropriate for this purpose and how using a standard format and a central, general–purpose database results in a successful interface strategy.

EDIF is a data format for transmitting electronic design information. The goal of EDIF is to facilitate the information transfer among all systems involved in electronic design, test, and fabrication.

Because of EDIF's broad focus, it supports a wide range of interface needs. To maintain an open design environment, a CAE company must provide interfaces in all design areas, including schematic entry, simulation, placement, routing, and back–annotation of results. EDIF also provides a format powerful enough to completely describe a design as viewed from each of these areas.

In planning for the future, a CAE company must be able to accommodate new, unforeseen interface needs. This concern again leads to using EDIF, whose developers already have stated their commitment to evolve as the industry evolves and to meet future needs.

For a standard to facilitate data transfer, it must be used widely among diverse groups to produce and receive information. From its beginning, EDIF's developers intended it to become a standard by use. All major CAE companies have announced support for EDIF, and EDIF is the only standard that has this endorsement. Also, there is a growing number of people interested in EDIF, in attending its workshops, in writing programs for it, and in supporting it.

There are several features of EDIF's design that have resulted in its widespread acceptance at an early stage. These same features make it the appropriate central format for a fully developed interface system.

One EDIF characteristic is its simple, LISP–like syntax. A small group could easily implement a simple parser for testing or for use within the group. Even if these early uses accomplished little practical data exchange, they resulted in a large number of EDIF users within a short time of EDIF's initial release.

Another EDIF characteristic is the *userdata* construct, allowing local, temporary extensions to the format. At first glance, including this construct runs counter to the goal of establishing a standard. In EDIF's early stages, there were data constructs that it could not express satisfactorily. Finding such a data construct is the most common excuse for not using a standard. It also is the most common reason for not using one format for a company's diverse collection of interfaces.

The *userdata* construct partially removes this excuse. A company can create an EDIF form that meets its needs exactly and expresses its data construct accurately. The disadvantage is that any interface using *userdata* constructs must deal with nonstandard features. The decisive advantage is that including *userdata* constructs increases the number of interfaces that can and do use EDIF.

Another advantage of the *userdata* construct is that such constructs are incorporated as standard in future EDIF releases. Informing EDIF committees of various uses of *userdata* is a useful way to inform the committees what standard EDIF is lacking. It also tells the committees which of various proposed constructs would be most needed and used in real–life situations. Because a specific *userdata* construct often is used before its inclusion as a standard construct, constructs are tested extensively before they enter the standard.

Without a general–purpose database, similar functions appear separately in many interfaces. With a central database, all functions can be put into a common area where they are accessed by all interfaces in the system. When grouped in a common area, functions are easier to implement and maintain.

A general–purpose database should follow data structures in EDIF. Although the EDIF manual stresses that it is a format, not a database, an EDIF file describes a data structure. There are several reasons for keeping the database close to EDIF structures. A tremendous effort has gone into making EDIF powerful enough to describe a design fully in all its aspects. This power and this generality also are desirable in a database. Since one company cannot reproduce the efforts of the EDIF committees, it should benefit from the committees' work. Also, translating from the database to EDIF and back occurs frequently. Keeping the database close to the input and output format makes the translation simple, efficient, and accurate.

With the proliferation of design systems, a company devotes more and more of its resources to interfaces. Making full use of EDIF significantly increases interface capabilities offered to customers and reduces the effort required to sustain these capabilities. Ideally, every system would translate in both directions between its own internal database and EDIF.

As the number of EDIF users increases, there is increased pressure on designers and facilities to use EDIF. Designers will demand systems that allow a free flow of information to let their work be used on other systems. This demand will increase the availability of EDIF facilities and the number of EDIF users.

This self–reinforcing growth points to EDIF's acceptance as the standard electronic design–interchange format. Some companies will support EDIF fully and organize interfaces around EDIF and a corresponding database. These companies will be able to decrease the resources needed to develop and maintain interfaces, while providing customers with a wider and more accurate collection of the interface capabilities they demand.

CHAPTER 5

LOGIC SIMULATION

• Toward the Goal of Interactive Simulation •

As has been suggested many times, the real purpose of using a computer as an engineering design aid is to get an understanding of how a finished electronic circuit will look and perform before it is actually made. Hopefully, this will save some of the time and expense ordinarily involved in evaluating and correcting faulty prototypes.

Ideally, computer simulation—that advanced look at performance—should be as interactive as schematic entry. You touch a keyboard or mouse, and something happens on the screen. Almost as soon as you wire together some components in one window of the graphics screen, the simulator should show you the digital waveforms it generates in another window. This works rather well for small circuits, but as complexity increases, reality—in the form of extended run time on the computer—intrudes. First, there is the nasty business of netlist extraction, smoothing, tweaking, and tailoring discussed in Chapter 4. Then, there is the simulation run itself, a process that can take hours (sometimes days). Too often, it produces not those easy–to–interpret graphical waveforms, but reams and reams of almost indecipherable numbers.

With the design of board–level products, it is customary to bypass computer simulations altogether and construct a breadboard of the circuit—a hastily wired prototype—as a predictor of performance and an aid to debugging. Like schematic entry, the wiring of components can be a tedious, detailed, and time–consuming process, although modern wire–wrapping tools have made point–to–point connections fairly easy to complete. A dedicated technician, consequently, can wire a complicated board–level product over a weekend.

Two factors will make breadboarding increasingly difficult, though never entirely obsolete. First, the scale, complexity, and speed of system–level products will make wire–wrap prototypes impractical. You would need a warehouse full of wire to duplicate all the gate–to–gate and point–to–point connections inside a modern minicomputer, and, even then, you would have no idea how fast the thing could run. Because of the dangers of high–frequency cross talk (signals getting tangled), it is impossible to get accurate results from a wire–wrap board running at frequencies of 25 MHz and higher.

Second, even where the same digital logic is used, a breadboard constructed of packaged logic gates cannot entirely predict the performance of a custom–made ASIC. The wire–wrap paths are much longer—orders of magnitude longer—than those encountered on the surface of a semiconductor or, for that matter, on the traces of a multilevel PCB. The logical functions of the ASIC and the breadboard should be the same. But the shorter lead lengths between logic gates and the faster clock speeds of semiconductor devices may provide not just faster timing sequences, but entirely different logical outputs. For example, the inputs to a long chain of sequential logic could change faster than an output could be registered (sometimes referred to as a race condition). Consequently, an ASIC device would appear to behave differently than would an assembled breadboard.

Yet, breadboarding persists in engineering realms. It is not just that the majority of new circuits constructed each year are on PCBs rather than on semiconductor substrates; it also is that breadboards have a concreteness that computer models do not. For simulation—the entire CAE process, in fact—to be successful, it must prove faster and cheaper than breadboarding, it must provide equally accurate results, and, like the breadboard and the test instruments used to evaluate it, it must lend itself to interactive debugging.

Digital–logic simulation is growing in popularity, but what it lacks is full interactivity. Schematic entry, as we have seen, is an interactive process between an engineer and a computer–graphics screen. Simulation, because it requires computational muscle, traditionally is a mainframe activity—a batch–processing job. In the vernacular: You submit a simulation run to the computer, and then you wait.

Reducing the machinery's response time brings us closer to the ultimate goal of closing the loop between front–end design decisions and a full understanding of how the finished product will look and perform. That is, designers should be able to see firsthand on their workstation screens the overall effects of each design change as they enter their schematics. The only way to accomplish this is to speed up the computationally intensive tasks so that answers can be provided in real time, seconds or minutes, rather than in the hours or days it may take for some remote computational resource to do its job. The goal, in other words, is to provide instant feedback, and the only way to accomplish this is to run CAE compute jobs, like digital–logic simulation, so fast that the response to any user input appears to be interactive rather than batch. No matter how many millions of instructions and computations the computer must plow through to get an answer, if it can come up with an answer within four seconds, its response time will be considered interactive. Not an easy task, considering the job the computer must do.

Fortunately, many of the new–generation CAE workstations and workstation engines are architected in a way that lends itself to this simultaneity; that is, they are architected to perform several jobs at once. As discussed in Chapter 2, there is a division of labor that can be harnessed: A workstation networked to a larger minicomputer can perform schematic entry and netlist compilation locally, while a mainframe or minicomputer can crunch simulation data in the background. Schematics or high–level–language entries can appear in one window on the computer screen, while simulation waveforms can be shown in another window.

Similarly, the notions of concurrency and parallelism, as well as high–performance semiconductor CPUs, are affecting workstation architectures. Instead of shipping a simulation task to a mainframe over a network, it is possible to ship the task to a coprocessor card residing within the workstation chassis. Indeed, there is a proliferation of accelerators for PCs and workstations that are intended as speed–up engines for digital–logic simulation.

Simulation becomes interactive as it is speeded up. Yet, high–power computers and accelerator engines represent just one method of speeding up the computations. The other method—like the object–oriented databases discussed in Chapter 4—is to streamline the software to reduce the number of computations the computer must perform to come up with an answer.

There is a great deal of work going on in software algorithm development. An algorithm represents a specialized method of performing a computational task, like simulation. Frequently, it is a shortcut. When you shortcut an otherwise iterative process, there is a persistent danger of coming up not with the right answer, but with an approximation of the right answer. Algorithm development certainly has gone a long way toward minimizing the amount of memory space and computational resources required to produce interactive simulations on a workstation, but whether this solution is more comfortable to engineers than is a breadboard still is an open question.

This chapter will attempt to answer the question by explaining how a digital simulator works, what it needs to be successful, and what efforts are under way to make it both interactive and accurate.

• Function Simulation •

The digital–logic simulator has two jobs: It must predict both the order and the sequence of high–low states—1s and 0s—appearing at the output of the circuit. In short, the simulator must confirm whether the logic of the circuit performs the functions it was intended to perform. A more difficult task, however, is verifying the time it takes, in nanoseconds, for a set of output lines to run high or low after a set of 1s and 0s appears on the input. Functional simulation and timing verification are explained below.

A functional simulator is built on four elements: The first is the interconnectivity pattern provided by the netlist (described in Chapter 4). The second is the behavioral model of various gates and devices used in the circuit. The third is a list of input patterns the circuit is likely to use, and the fourth is a scheduler of events, or *time wheel*. Much of this discussion is based on CADAT, an industry–standard simulator from HHB Systems.

In the execution of the simulation program, the functional simulator will look at the logic state produced at any particular circuit node or net. This will be a high (1), a low (0), an electrically disconnected high impedance (Z), or an unknown state (X). In electrical terms, the output of a logic device must be above or below a certain voltage to be considered high or low. In a 5V system using conventional TTL, any output above 2.4V is considered high (ideally, it should be a full 5V), and anything below 0.8V is considered low (this should be zero). Everything between 0.8V and 2.4V then would be considered an unknown state. However, a functional simulator rarely would examine the actual voltage level (this is more the job of an analog–circuit simulator, discussed in Chapter 6), but rather the mutually exclusive electrical states (that is, high–low states) predicted by the behavioral models used.

Digital circuits usually are simulated at the gate (level–2) or switch (level–1) levels, a simplified transistor model. But as circuits grow, it becomes necessary to simulate a circuit module—say, a whole microprocessor—on a totally different hierarchical level, as a black box. The module is defined by an HDL (hardware description language) and is said to be modeled at the functional or behavioral level. Strictly speaking, the former should describe only function (that is, a state machine), while the latter should be a full description of the module's behavior, including timing. (Sometimes, the term *white box* is used for behavioral models.)

For a simple two–input *nand* gate, the functional or behavioral model is fairly simple: the combination of two inputs produces only four possible outputs. For a 7400–series MSI part, the behavioral models become more complex. A 4–to–16 decoder circuit (for example, the 74154) can produce 16 different outputs with 4 inputs (see Figure 5.1). The behavioral model for a complex VLSI circuit, in turn, can require reams and reams of textual material describing the behavior of the part under most circumstances. In operation, however, most simulators will examine logic primitives—*nand* gates, *nor* gates, and flip–flops—in a circuit.

To run on a computer, simulators depend on mathematical or logical models of components or other circuit elements. As suggested Chapter 4, it is possible to embed the simulation model in the same database that carries a graphical description of a part. When the part is called to the screen, the simulation model is placed automatically into the memory space of a simulation program running as a background task. However, since very few CAE programs use object–oriented databases, the more likely action is to compile all references to a netlist and let the netlist reference cull the appropriate device model from a particular simulator's model library. However, as this discussion makes clear, the variety and type of behavioral models will affect the speed and accuracy of the simulation process.

```
MODEL SNL4154 IS

INTERFACE

TERMINAL

a, b, c, d, g1, g2; IN LOGICAL:   — input pins
o1, o2, o3, o4, o5, o6, o7, o8, o9, o10, o11, o12, o13, o14, o15, o16:
OUT LOGICAL;                      — output pins

END TERMINAL

END INTERFACE:

BEHAVIOR IS TRUTHTABLE:
(g1,g2,d,c,b,a:
o1,o2,o3,o4,o5,o6,o7,o8,o9,o10,o11,o12,o13,o14,o15,o16);
(0   0 00 0 0     0  1  1  1 1  1  1  1  1   1   1   1   1   1   1   1);
(0   0 00 0 1     1  0  1  1 1  1  1  1  1   1   1   1   1   1   1   1);
(0   0 00 1 0     1  1  0  1 1  1  1  1  1   1   1   1   1   1   1   1);
(0   0 00 1 1     1  1  1  0 1  1  1  1  1   1   1   1   1   1   1   1);
(0   0 01 0 0     1  1  1  1 0  1  1  1  1   1   1   1   1   1   1   1);
(0   0 01 0 1     1  1  1  1 1  0  1  1  1   1   1   1   1   1   1   1);
(0   0 01 1 0     1  1  1  1 1  1  0  1  1   1   1   1   1   1   1   1);
(0   0 01 1 1     1  1  1  1 1  1  1  0  1   1   1   1   1   1   1   1);
(0   0 10 0 0     1  1  1  1 1  1  1  1  0   1   1   1   1   1   1   1);
(0   0 10 0 1     1  1  1  1 1  1  1  1  1   0   1   1   1   1   1   1);
(0   0 10 1 0     1  1  1  1 1  1  1  1  1   1   0   1   1   1   1   1);
(0   0 10 1 1     1  1  1  1 1  1  1  1  1   1   1   0   1   1   1   1);
(0   0 11 0 0     1  1  1  1 1  1  1  1  1   1   1   1   0   1   1   1);
(0   0 11 0 1     1  1  1  1 1  1  1  1  1   1   1   1   1   0   1   1);
(0   0 11 1 0     1  1  1  1 1  1  1  1  1   1   1   1   1   1   0   1);
(0   0 11 1 1     1  1  1  1 1  1  1  1  1   1   1   1   1   1   1   0);
(x   1 xx x x     1  1  1  1 1  1  1  1  1   1   1   1   1   1   1   1);
(1   x xx x x     1  1  1  1 1  1  1  1  1   1   1   1   1   1   1   1);

END BEHAVIOR

TIMING IS

TPLH ON ALL FROM a,b,c,d = 24 ns;
TPLH ON ALL FROM a,b,c,d = 22 ns;
TPLH ON ALL FROM g1, g2  = 20 ns;
TPLH ON ALL FROM g1, g2  = 18  ns;
END TIMING

END MODEL SNL4154
```

Figure 5.1: The behavioral model of a 7400–series MSI part. The part becomes more complex because the 74154 can produce 16 different outputs with 4 inputs.

Device Models

These models can exist as primitive logic functions, such as *nand* gates, *nor* gates, inverters, and flip–flops, or they can be elaborate behavioral descriptions of complex microprocessor parts, such as 16– or 32–bit processors. For most of the widely used simulators—GenRad's HILO–3, Teradyne's (Santa Clara, California) LASER–6, GE–Calma's TEGAS 5, or HHB System's CADAT—the library includes both gate–level primitives and behavioral descriptions of SSI and MSI functions, usually 7400–series parts. The behavioral descriptions are created in a high–level programming language, such as C or Pascal, and often may include timing delays, resistive elements, and three–state elements (that is, high, low, and high–impedance states) as part of the device description.

The device models can be very simple, or they can be full and complex— with the penalty of increased run time on a computer. The behavioral description of the 74154 4–to–16 decoder shown in Figure 5.1, for example, required 36 lines of code. But the complexity of this model is significant: Just to evaluate a model, a computer CPU must fetch, decode, and execute an instruction sequence in the same complex sequence as it performs any other mathematical operation. Consequently, when compiled to run with a simulator on a workstation, one gate–level model can require several hundred machine cycles and a substantial chunk of main memory to execute (see Figure 5.2). The problem is complicated with a simulator like CADAT, which distinguishes among a minimum of 4 different logical states for every node, but is, in fact, capable of recognizing up to 21 different states. Simulating the activity of a single gate, therefore, can force the computer to cycle through several thousand machine instructions. This processing requirement increases exponentially with the complexity of the models being called forth. Consequently, there is a demand for software algorithms that simplify processing requirements by stripping down the device models (recognizing only high–low states, for example) and ignoring practically every other condition.

One step in this direction is a package introduced by Gateway Design Automation Corporation (Westford, Maine), called Verilog–XL. Intended as a logic–design tool, like FutureDesigner and other high–level–language entry systems, it nonetheless can match the speed of a minicomputer by reducing the number of instructions processed to about 50 per simple gate. Circuits are defined for Verilog with a proprietary description language that is very close to the binary instruction code actually used by computer CPUs. For example, the output for a *timeout* state machine is defined with a simple *case* statement for five binary values (001, 011, 100, 101, 111):

```
case ({out,in,reset})
'b001 : out = 1;
'b011, 'b100, 'b101, 'b111: out = 0;
```

(The three unnamed inputs have no effect.)

Stimulus Patterns

Behavior descriptions are only one of the elements needed to run a simulator. Another is stimulus vectors—digital words and patterns that will be used to exercise the circuit, to put it through its paces during the simulation run. Here, the user provides a series of logic states that will serve as a stimulus for the gates in the circuit and identifies the clocking sequence for the simulator.

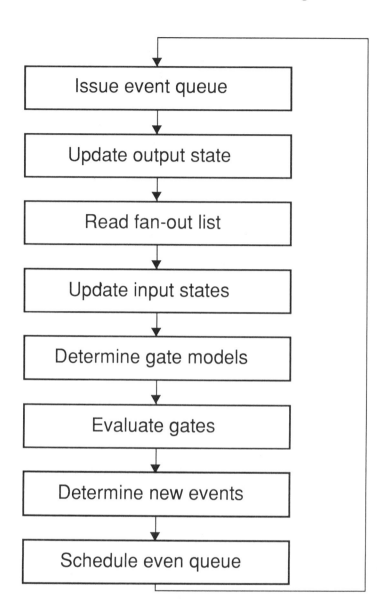

Figure 5.2: Gate–level model flow diagram. When the 74154 decoder shown in Figure 5.1 is compiled to run with a simulator on a workstation, several hundred machine cycles and a substantial chunk of main memory are needed.

For simple circuits, it is possible to put in a small number of logic–input patterns, one at a time, and to inspect the logic outputs produced by each input. For complex circuits, one digital–input word or pattern will "walk through" several successive stages of the circuit before it produces a change in the output states. On top of that, the second digital word can be registered at the input of the circuit on the second clock interval, before the first word actually has produced an output. But by counting all the high–low states at each network or signal node, the simulator can keep a record of the logic produced by each input pattern at each clock interval.

To coordinate the inputs and clocking sequences, most simulators assign two counters to each signal line in a given circuit: One counts the number of times any particular signal line goes to logic 1; the other counts the number of logic 0s. These counters are incremented each time the signal is at a stable 0 or 1 at a time strobe, or sampling interval (usually in nanoseconds), specified by the simulator. Neither counter is incremented when a signal is in a high–impedance (Z) or an unknown (X) state. The counters of the simulator are reset to zero once the first digital word has produced a change at the output of the circuit. The full clocking interval—the number of clock pulses between input and output— sometimes is referred to as a time wheel.

The simulator will provide a digital–output pattern—a sequence of 1s and 0s—that matches the clocking sequence. This pattern can be output from the computer in a number of ways: as a structured file to a disk, screen, or printer, or as a displayable waveform.

Timing Verification

If everything in the chain of logic gates were perfectly sequential, the time delay between inputs and outputs simply would be the sum of specified delays through each gate in the chain. However, since many circuits have combinational logic functions whose inputs themselves are the outputs of long sequential chains, the output of the circuit will depend on the relative timing between these sequential chains. The timing of these circuits, in addition, will depend not just on the estimated propagation delay going through each gate, but also (since we are talking about nanoseconds) on the length of the wiring path between gates. Consequently, timing analysis frequently is very sensitive to the physical layout of the circuit (IC or PCB) and is performed iteratively with layout.

Often, but not always, timing simulation is part of logic simulation. Though an event scheduler is necessary to operate the software program, logic simulators need not be concerned about timing problems in a circuit, because their task is to verify that the state machine implemented in a given circuit functions properly. However, a timing simulator or verifier is required to ensure the absence of race conditions or glitches in the circuit. Timing analysis usually is coupled with logic simulation and performed in the same operation, because both need the same stimulus input file to analyze.

As noted in the behavioral models for the 7400–series parts described in Figure 5.1, timing delays were specified from inputs to ouputs in the behavioral description. These propagation delays can be described, in the simplest terms, as the rise and fall times that represent the time lapse between a change in the input signal and the resulting change in the output of a circuit. In the case of the 74154 4–to–16 decoder, this is a minimum of 22 ns and a maximum of 24 ns from the instant all four inputs (A, B, C, D) are recognized. These timing descriptions are used by the simulator to provide the user with a notion of the cumulative effects of delays through the logic chain.

Most existing methods of timing analysis are based on min–max (minimum–maximum) propagation delays. Also used by the simulator are setup and hold times and pulse widths. A timing verifier like SCALD, a public–domain program developed at Lawrence Livermore Laboratories, recognizes seven timing–related states—0, 1, stable, changing, rising, falling, and unknown. The engineer must specify setup and hold times for each device, in addition to its likely propagation delay.

Most delay–path analysis based on a min–max method actually takes best–case and worst–case timing delays and ignores almost every possibility in between. But this analysis technique still is very useful in visualizing critical paths in a logic chain.

Suppose, as an example of min–max timing considerations, that one gate chain is connected to a flip–flop clock and another gate chain to its D input (see Figure 5.3). For functional–simulation purposes, the 8 inputs will provide 256 different input combinations and, consequently, 256 different outputs. In this example, there are three gate delays leading to a flip–flop D input and three gate delays in the flip–flop clock input. For correct flip–flop outputs, a D transition should come before, not during or after, the clock input. If there is an overlap, the flip–flop output may be incorrect for one or more clock pulses. This is the critical path in the logic circuit.

There is an obvious combination of delays that are worst case—all max on D and all min on clock. That is, the worst–case min–max method assumes max delays for the D chain and min delays for the clock. In this case, the output at Q, never will be the one you would expect based on changes to the input of the D chain. Even if you assume typical values based on TTL data–book inputs (for example, a 15–ns delay for the *and* gate and a 12–ns delay for the *or* gate) for the D chain and max values for the clock chain (for example, 27 ns for each *and* and 22 ns for each *or*), you still get a situation where the D input (39 ns) is changing faster than the clock is (76 ns).

However, this situation is a statistical rarity. Suppose, for simplicity, that each gate has a 15–ns min–max spread; that is, the minimum propagation–delay times for *and* and *or* gates are 5 ns each, and the maximum propagation delays for both types are 20 ns. Make the very conservative assumption that there is a rectangular or equiprobable statistical distribution of delays for each gate. The probability of each gate being within 1 ns of its maximum or minimum delay time (or any other value) then is 1/15. The worst–case min–max probability then is the product of the probabilities for each of the six gates. A more realistic, less conservative delay distribution would make the probability of the worst case even smaller.

One of the obvious problems with min–max timing considerations is that most logic ICs never will be all fast or all slow. Processing, temperature, and geometry variations, for instance, will give these circuits some sort of statistical distribution in their propagation–delay times. This is the principle harnessed by Aldec Corporation (Newbury Park, California) for the design of simulation models. Based on statistical timing analysis, Aldec's software package uses

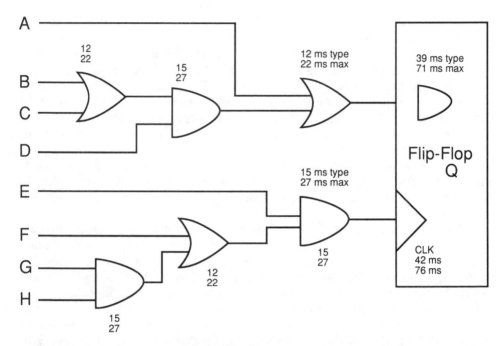

Figure 5.3: Min–max timing considerations.

random–integer delays to predict timing errors. Though the program eventually will run on a workstation—say, an 80386–based PC equipped with a multitasking version of DOS and about 8 MB of RAM—the program is meant to run in batch mode. Apart from the computational power and memory required, the major difficulty in simulating a large chip or circuit board—one with 50,000 to 100,000 gates—is that all the simulated gates have statistically different propagation delays.

Statistical timing analysis has the advantage of being pattern–independent; that is, it provides vital timing information without the need to process huge numbers of stimulus vectors. The stimulus patterns—sometimes, up to 4 million—are included in the statistically validated random numbers used by the simulator for its timing analysis.

Because each circuit has gates with random propagation delays, the simulated model of the circuit also should have randomly selected propagation delays. The next step, therefore, is to build a table of random gate–propagation delays that represent a random circuit. In operating the simulation program, designers must specify the number of random circuits they want to use in their analyses. The more circuits simulated, the greater the accuracy of the statistical simulation, although the trade–off is longer processing time.

Sometimes based on the SCALD algorithm, programs like Aldec's try to find all possible paths through the circuit to determine the effect of incorrect inputs on a circuit—though they cannot exclude false paths. These are paths that could be reached only with impossible combinations of inputs, such as one variable being high and low at the same time. The statistical software will calculate the delay probabilities for a simulated production run, using what physicists and others call a Monte Carlo calculation. It plays the same "game"—a single circuit timing analysis—over and over. But each time, it starts with a new hand—the new set of propagation delays—until there are enough games to build up a statistically valid picture of the most critical timing paths in the circuit.

The Monte Carlo game, of course, is not quite that simple. For one thing, we do not know and may never know the exact shape of the probability distribution of propagation delays for each circuit. For simplicity, we can assign the same equiprobable, rectangular distribution shape to each circuit, with edges set by the min and max propagation times peculiar to each circuit. With such a shape, no weighting of delays is necessary. A set of random integers within the min–max range then suffices for the Monte Carlo delay assignments. But with this assumption, it will not be possible to find the exact probability of failed timing nodes in the real world, only the relative percentage among different nodes. This is sufficient to rank the importance of failed nodes, which is all that is needed to evaluate the circuit design. When absolute failure rates are important, as in a real–world, high–volume production run of products, the user may have to find the actual statistical distribution.

Another Monte Carlo complication is that if we choose random integers for each circuit delay over the full range of propagation delays for that circuit, most of the software run time will be wasted searching for unlikely events. (Remember that in the six–gate example, the min–max probability time was about equal to catastrophic path failure.) The solution is to artificially reduce all ranges by dividing them by some factor greater than unity. It turns out that a reduction to 10% or 20% of the average circuit–delay spread will still find about 90% of all fault nodes above the catastrophic failure rate. To find more failures in a second pass, the range can be increased.

System–Level Simulation

While IC designers have been using computer simulations to evaluate the performance of new chips, only a small percentage of board– and system–level products are simulated. One reason is that it so much easier—so much more concrete—for engineers to build breadboard prototypes and to analyze these with oscilloscopes and logic analyzers. Another reason is that the run–time requirements for gate–level simulation increase exponentially with the number of gates. Simulating a board–level product in this way may be much too time–consuming. For high–gate–count simulations, recent increases in workstation CPU performance and RAM space have cut memory paging and made impressive performance boosts. It still might take 10 hours to simulate 10,000 ns—only 10 millionths of a second—of a superminicomputer's operations.

Consequently, only vertically integrated manufacturers on the order of The Boeing Company (Seattle, Washington), Hughes Aircraft (Los Angeles, California), and General Dynamics (Groton, Connecticut) have the software programmers and computational resources required to simulate anything above 10,000 gates. For the majority of American electronics companies, system–level simulation will not be used widely unless it is faster, more user–friendly, and less error–prone than using real hardware to get the bugs out of a new design.

Simulating entire systems, or even complex board–level products, requires the system to abandon gate–level simulation and move to a different hierarchical plane. It becomes impossible (in terms of computer run time) to simulate every switch and every gate on a large computer board. In this case, the simulator views the system as the interaction between large components and treats these components as black boxes.

Here, too, the availability of behavioral models affects the practicality of board–level simulations. While IC designers need only a relatively focused library of logical structures, system designers typically have to choose from thousands of different IC components—many of them of 1000–gate or more complexity. Each board component needs a software model, or the board cannot be simulated.

As suggested in the discussion of BORIS in Chapter 3, it is possible to model a black–box component as a series of input patterns (1s and 0s), the output patterns they generate (1s and 0s), and the number of clock cycles it will take to get from input to output. Designers, in effect, make up the behavioral descriptions of their black boxes. But what is a satisfactory representation of a complex 32–bit VLSI processor, like Motorola's 68020 or Intel's 80386? How many millions of inputs, outputs, and clock cycles does it take to adequately model these machines in use? Unless there is a usable behavioral model for these machines, functional simulation breaks down and the designer goes back to breadboarding.

There are two ways around this problem. One method is to write a software model for complex microprocessor devices. Companies like Logic Automation (Beaverton, Oregon) and Quadtree (Bridgewater, New Jersey) have gone into business developing software models for these complicated devices. The other method is to fudge it: to extract behavioral patterns from a working device and use these extracted parameters in the simulation of a larger system. This technique is called *hardware modeling*.

The list of available software device models is becoming large and impressive enough to make board– or system–level simulation a practical possibility. Since mid–1985, Logic Automation has been selling behavioral models. There are 800 models in 2400 timing grades commercially available today, and easily twice that number will be in use by 1990. Logic Automation's library includes the newest Motorola processor, the 68030, AMD's 29000 family, many devices in Intel's 80X86 family, popular memories, and even PLDs. The models can be used comfortably with simulators running with Mentor software on an Apollo workstation. Quadtree's models include the Motorola 68000 and the AMD 29000 bit–slice families, as well as 1–Mbit DRAMs and many SRAMs. These models run with Mentor's Quicksim, HHB Systems' CADAT, and the Silvar–Lisco Helix simulators.

Instead of using the gate–interconnection list, Logic Automation bases its models on the internal logic diagram supplied by the manufacturer. An internal register, for example, becomes just a computer variable; an internal multiplier element becomes a software *multiply* instruction; and a *mux*, implying branching, becomes an *if* structure.

To ensure that the models are always up to date, Logic Automation maintains proprietary agreements with the semiconductor manufacturers to receive continually updated functional–stimulus patterns and test vectors for its chip models. The test suite for a state–of–the–art, 32–bit multiplier/ accumulator chip, for example, might include 5000 vectors, where each vector defines the complete I/O for one clock cycle. The models are checked periodically and corrected against the updated test vectors.

In addition, it is important that behavioral models be as free of bugs as possible. This is ensured not only by building a large, reliable database, but also by using built–in intelligence, which make it possible to locate and identify bugs that emerge with each computer run. In operation of the simulator, the model defaults to some acceptable condition and issues an error message whenever it sees a timing or functional violation.

If the user, for example, makes a timing error in setup, hold, pulse width, or frequency, the model will correct it and continue the run while printing an error message. If the user makes a functional error—say, forgetting to initialize a register or creating an undefined interrupt or some other illegal condition—the model will mark the resulting unknowns with "XXXX" on the workstation screen. To avoid shutdown, the run will continue and the unknowns propagate.

The IC models can store 20 or 30 timing–error and 10 to 20 functional–error messages. There is no theoretical upper limit, however. Microprocessor models, for instance, may have several hundred messages.

On a workstation screen, for example, the waveforms and errors generated in a simulation run could appear in different windows of the display, along with the schematics of the circuit being simulated. A *trace* window could show pin waveforms selected by a user as they change over time. A *4. list* window would display the pin values as 1s and 0s.

• Accelerators for Logic Simulation •

As can be seen, the examination of several events and a small number of gates can force the computer to run through several hundred lines of code to come up with an answer. Consequently, the number of computations—as well as the computer run time—will increase exponentially as the complexity of the logic design increases. This rate of increase is even steeper for fault simulation than for logic simulation. A design with 20,000 logic gates can take many hours (if not days) on a mainframe computer. At 50 cents per second for CPU time—the charge many gate–array vendors impose for simulation time on an IBM mainframe—this can be one of the most expensive aspects of evaluating a new design.

To give a feeling for the time involved, assume that a complex digital–logic circuit, meant to run at 20 MHz, consists of 200,000 gates. At any given clock cycle, about 10% of system's gates—20,000 gates—will make some kind of transition. To simulate just one second of the digital circuit, the simulator must evaluate 400 billion events (20,000 gate switches x 20 million cycles/s). Most simulators run through about 500 instructions to process one event. Running on a

0.5–MIPS workstation, it would take about 12 years (over 6 million minutes) to simulate one second in the operation of the digital circuit.

There are two ways to speed up this process: It is possible, as we have seen with Aida's (Santa Clara, California) simulation approach, to reduce run time by streamlining the models used to simulate gate–level primitives; that is, to reduce the number of instructions the computer CPU must process for each gate–level switch. If the number of instructions were reduced from 500 to 50, for example, the same 20–MHz, 200,000–gate design mentioned before can be simulated in a little over one year on a PC–type, 0.5–MIPS workstation.

Robert J. Smith of MCC, the Microelectronics and Computer Technology Corporation (Austin, Texas), has estimated that complex logic simulations will proceed at a rate of 1000 to 5000 evaluations per computer MIPS. Since much of the instruction–processing overhead is in element–routine evaluation (that is, checking and rechecking the behavioral model used) and event–queue management, an average simple gate evaluation will require 200 to 1000 instructions. Smith believes that it is reasonably possible to reduce the number of instructions to 100 to 500 per gate. Consequently, 2000 to 10,000 gate evaluations could be obtained with each computer MIPS.

Using examples of simplified instruction processing provided by Gateway Design for its Verilog–XL simulator, a circuit with 2500 gates normally requires about 4.5 million vectors and 30 minutes on a Sun–3/160. If run in the accelerated (XL) mode—that is, with a very stripped–down instruction set—simulation time drops to 1.4 minutes on the Sun–3 and about 20 seconds on the RISC–based Sun–4. (By comparison, HILO simulation would take about 17 minutes on the Sun–3.)

The other method of speeding the simulation is simply to apply more MIPS by using faster computers: in some cases, machines specifically designed for logic–simulation purposes. The same 20–MHz, 200,000–gate design mentioned before (even with a 500–instruction/gate software overhead) can be simulated in four months on a 20–MIPS computer. This reduction in run time is obtained using a general–purpose computer. But speedups as great as 1000 times can be obtained by the use of special–purpose hardware, called accelerators.

References to accelerators for simulation sometimes reflect a dichotomy between global acceleration and point acceleration. Global acceleration often refers to speedups in all parts of the CAE process, while point acceleration refers to a specific point in the CAE process, such as the simulation run. Frankly, global acceleration typically is a buzz word for the use of a faster general–purpose computer. For example, using a lightly loaded VAX minicomputer instead of a workstation for netlist generation and simulation runs can provide a speedup in the entire CAE process. It represents a global solution.

A point accelerator, as the name implies, is specifically designed to provide a speedup at only one point in the process, specifically at logic or fault simulation. It is designed to do only one job, but it performs that job better than any general–purpose machine. The point accelerators referred to here are built around special–purpose hardware designed to speed up simulation algorithms by factors of 10 to 1000 compared to the capabilities of a general–purpose computer.

The speed capability of the functional–simulation accelerator frequently is described in terms of *gate evaluations/s*. This is the number of gate changes per second that can be evaluated within the simulation run when the inputs do not cause a resulting change in the output; that is, when the inputs are held steady. Usually, this benchmark is computed against a fixed design, with inputs tied together and all outputs open. This method also is a zero– or unit–delay simulation since, with functional simulation, no timing delays are considered in the calculations.

Note that the gate evaluations/s specification is somewhat different from the events/s specification, which is the number of logical state changes that can be scheduled with a simulation run and still produce an accurate result. Events/s multiplied by some sort of equivalency factor—say, 2.5 gates—produces a gate evaluations/s specification.

The companies offering accelerators for simulation include Aida, Cadnetix, Daisy, HHB Systems, Ikos, LSI Logic, Mentor, Silicon Solutions (a subsidiary of Zycad Corporation, St. Paul, Minnesota), Simulog, Teradyne, Valid, Xcat, and Zycad.

The other side of the spectrum are SDEs (system development engines) developed by Zycad, which handle 1,100,000 modeling elements, execute simulations at a rate of 1 billion events/s, and cost $3.3 million. These machines would complete the 20–MHz, 200,000–gate simulation problem mentioned before in a little less than 7 minutes. Zycad's lower priced ($1.1 million) SDEs run with 500,000 modeling elements and 500–million–events/s rates. Further down the scale, a Zycad logic evaluator called the LE 1032 can finish the 20–MHz, 200,000–gate simulation in about seven hours.

Between these two extremes in performance and cost is the Silicon Solutions' Mach 1000, which handles 64,000 elements at a 500,000 event/s rate. High–end products from Aida include the CoSim (cosimulator processor) for Apollo networked workstations. The CoSim products provide capacities from 250,000 to 1 million gates, at 5 million gate evaluations/s. While the machines embody different philosophies—some are geared for IC design, others are for PCBs, and many are meant to couple with specific workstation types—and different levels of user programmability (the faster it runs, the less programmable it is likely to be), there is almost a linear relation between price and capability. However, because the Aida and Zycad simulators describe their performance in entirely different terms, it frequently is necessary to go beyond the raw speed descriptions to get a clear picture of what an accelerator will actually do.

• No Way to Avoid Run–Time Increases •

In CAE, there is debate about whether hardware or software speedups are the best path to pursue. Impressive results have been obtained in the software streamlining provided by Gateway Design Automation in the Verilog–XL simulator. For example, simulation performed on a 30,000–gate circuit using a 68020–based workstation took the Verilog–XL program 847 seconds. A microcoded hardware accelerator performed the same job in 1700 seconds. A high–end, dedicated accelerator took 250 seconds. Perhaps a $1–million accelerator might be worth the 10–minute (almost 600–second) saving: Assuming 50 cents per CPU second, that is a $300 savings. Over time, these savings in run–time charges can mount up. However, the same 30,000–gate simulation could be performed on an IBM 3090 in just 95 seconds. CPU time on a 3090 might go for more than 50 cents per second, but then an IBM mainframe does a lot more than logic and fault simulation.

As a rule, accelerators work only on the gate level and need additional hooks to accommodate higher level behavioral models or the inputs of hardware–modeling systems. This limits their versatility. Also, they must use fixed–time assumptions in their calculations. There is no min–max range that can be accommodated with hardware accelerators. Rather, only one timing value can be embedded in the accelerator as a primitive. Finally, like any special–purpose computer, there are compilation requirements that may cost more in CPU time than does the actual simulation itself.

However, the software streamlines and tweaks also extract their toll. The more any model or simulation routine has been streamlined—the more closely it addresses the CPU, memory, register locations, and other hardware elements for one particular computer—the faster it will run on that computer. However, in optimizing software for one piece of hardware, it becomes more difficult to run that same software on another computer. Software algorithms that have been perfected for Apollo's 68020–based workstations, for example, no longer will run as well on the 68020 platforms of Sun and HP. Consequently, there is an additional sacrifice in portability and versatility.

The faster CAE users want to go, the more they are locked in to special–purpose (limited–function) hardware or software. Users are channeled down a path in which they sacrifice versatility for speed. The $1–million Zycad simulators, as a result, will look like an extravagance to all but the most luxuriously funded CAE departments. The goal of interactive CAE—to have an immediate simulation response to design changes input to the computer—either will be confined to rather small logic circuits or forever put off until the results of week–long simulations can be evaluated.

It is likely that general–purpose—in other words, standardized—solutions will prevail, with their longer run–time requirements, and the CAE user will wind up purchasing ever more CPU time on a VAX, IBM mainframe, or mini-supercomputer (a trend mentioned in Chapter 2). But if the needs of logic and fault simulation seem expensive, the needs of analog–circuit simulation are even more extravagant, as we shall see in Chapter 6.

• Hardware Modeling •

The first commercial CAE systems developed in the early 1980s offered rudimentary functions such as interactive graphics, hierarchical design, and basic verification. These early systems revolutionized the front–end design cycle and enabled the CAE industry to take off.

Verification tools consisted of logic simulation and timing analysis, and these tools made a great impact on the entire electronic design industry, ultimately changing the way designers work. Customers wanted simulation, a tool that mimics a design running through its paces doing a specific task. However, simulation tools required device models in order to work.

Simulation models could be developed easily for gates and flip–flops, but systems designers needed models of complex devices, such as an Intel 8086. Microprocessors were used widely, but no models were available for them. Simulation became quite important to systems designers designing ASICs; they wanted to ensure that their devices would work in the real system environment.

In 1982, Dr. L. Curtis Widdoes, Jr., a cofounder of Valid, solved the problem of a lack of models for complex standard parts by developing a technology called hardware modeling.

What Is Hardware Modeling?

A logic–simulation model of a device is a design tool that accurately mimics the device's logical and timing behavior in normal operation. The model must verify both the logic and the timing behaviors of the operating system containing such a device.

As LSI and VLSI digital devices become more prevalent in system designs, it is difficult to simulate their operation using software. Workstation–based software simulators are too slow and lack sufficient memory to store gate–level models of these complex devices for validation. Therefore, an alternate way to model complex digital circuitry and systems, including those capable of executing instructions under program control, is needed.

Hardware modeling permits designers to use actual devices as simulation models to verify their system designs. Complete accuracy is ensured, since real devices are used as models.

Theory of Hardware Modeling

As complex devices grow in popularity, system–level simulation modeling problems (model development cost, model accuracy, and performance) become acute. Hardware modeling provides a reliable, fast, and accurate way to simulate the operation of these complex digital devices.

With hardware modeling, a simulation model is provided, including both the physical device and a means for controlling the device at normal operating speeds, thus avoiding loss of data of accumulated functions. Specifically, the physical device to be modeled is connected through the hardware modeler to a host that contains a simulator.

The hardware modeler accepts a variety of external devices and provides the control stimulus and sampling necessary to allow the physical device to receive information from the simulator and supply outputs from the device back to the host. Data and logic–state patterns are preserved by effective control of the starting, stopping, cycling, reinitializating, and refreshing of the physical device. In other words, this type of simulation system permits non–real–time simulation of systems, while preserving the real–time characteristics of selected hardware elements of the system. It operates without having to generate a complex software model of each element of the system under test, so the overall performance is high. It also allows the use of software models for other devices in the digital system.

For example, a real physical device being modeled (for example, a dynamic digital circuit such as a microprocessor) is part of a PCB or a system to be tested. The system also includes other logic that must be verified in the system environment. The physical model is coupled through an adapter that provides the necessary electrical and physical configurations to connect device inputs and outputs to the modeler.

The modeler is controlled by a logic simulator running on a workstation or mainframe, which provides the appropriate input signals and samples the resulting output signals in such a way that the user cannot tell if the model is in software or hardware. In fact, a designer may mix software models with physical models in a simulation environment without worry.

There are two types of models: static and dynamic. Static devices hold their own state indefinitely and do not need to be reinitialized. They cannot be shared. Dynamic devices accumulate a pattern history, which is replayed each time the model is evaluated to ensure that the device returns correct outputs. Dynamic devices can be shared among multiple users.

For dynamic devices, the initial input pattern is provided by the simulator and stored in a fast memory. An input pattern is the parallel pattern of bits presented during an interval of time to the inputs of the hardware model. The second pattern comes from the simulator.

Before the dynamic hardware model is evaluated for the second pattern, it first must be reset or restored to a known condition that can be restored identically at any future time. The first, or initial, pattern is retrieved from the fast memory and presented to input pins of the model. Outputs are sampled after a time delay to produce an output pattern. The output values resulting from the input pattern or patterns are returned for use by the simulator.

Using the first output pattern, the logic simulator computes a second input pattern that then is stored in the fast memory along with the first input pattern, creating a sequence. The hardware model is reinitialized by playing both the first and second input patterns. Thereafter, the sequence of all earlier patterns is played back to the model before a new input pattern is presented and outputs sampled.

By using the resulting output pattern, the logic simulator, running on the host computer, can compute the next input pattern. The modeler transparently stores new patterns at the end of the sequence of input patterns previously stored, resets the reference element (either by activating a reset signal line or by applying a reset–pattern sequence to the reference element), and repeats the sequence of input patterns so that the next operational sequence produces one additional input pattern.

The use of the pattern sequence is an important technical contribution, because it allows the reference element's timing requirements to be met without requiring it to stop intermittently during every clock cycle to permit the logic simulator to compute responses at a convenient, non–real–time rate.

Hardware–Modeling Applications

The most familiar application for hardware modeling is system design verification using hardware models of standard parts. Standard parts, such as the 68020 or 80286 microprocessors, usually have less than 128 pins and are modeled as dynamic devices. In some cases, these standard parts are available in a library of behavioral models, but designers prefer to use hardware modeling when accuracy is a priority.

Another important function of a hardware–modeling system is to allow ASIC modeling during the verification of system designs based on these devices. Off–the–shelf behavioral models cannot address this need. If the designer uses a high–level language, it is possible to develop a behavioral model of the ASIC. Typically, ASICs (such as gate arrays or standard cells) have higher pin counts and can be modeled as static devices. This means that there is no pattern sequence required, because the ASICs hold their last state.

Prototype verification often can be done for ASIC parts with hardware–modeling systems. Current modelers can support clock frequencies of 2 to 16 MHz. This approach allows the designer to verify parts functionally, based on the same vectors used in the original design, without the added complexity of translation to a tester format. Outputs from the original simulation can be compared with the simulation using prototypes. This significantly shortens the difficult period after prototypes are available, but the test program is not in final form. Most hardware–modeling systems verify only ASIC functionality; however, there is a trend toward some timing verification.

PCBs can be connected to several hardware–modeling systems available on the market today. This allows system–level simulation based on existing hardware. It also can be instrumental in board debugging since, unlike the typical test–bench setup, complex sequences of patterns can be applied easily from the simulation interface. Results can be compared with previous simulation results.

Hardware–modeling systems allow the designer to evaluate the functionality of complex devices at hardware speeds. Behavioral models can be simulated only at software speeds. Consider the first application category: off–the–shelf devices.

The evaluation speed of dynamic chips in hardware modelers has improved dramatically since the first system came out in 1984. A 16–MHz modeler can replay a history of 256,000 patterns in 16 ms. The time it takes to evaluate a behavioral model varies widely: Generally, the more accurate the software model, the longer it will take to execute. ASIC modeling, the second application category, usually involves static models for the devices. This type of device evaluation can be done almost instantaneously, since only one pattern is presented. An ASIC software model's execution efficiency depends on the skill of the modeler, who is likely to be more interested in the hardware design than in the behavioral description. In many cases, where a hardware modeler is not available, a gate–level description of the chip is used in all subsequent designs based on the chip. Not only is this extremely slow in simulation, but it also is difficult to guarantee the model's continuing integrity.

Hardware Modelers

Valid pioneered the concept of hardware modeling and has developed two application–specific hardware–modeling systems.

The Realchip modeling system addresses the increasingly common problem facing systems design today: the simulation of designs containing VLSI devices such as microprocessors, complex peripheral chips, custom chips, gate arrays, and similar devices. The system uses hardware reference elements as functional models of complex devices; that is, the actual chips. For example, the Realchip model of an 80386 or 68020 microprocessor is the microprocessor itself.

The Realmodel simulation subsystem is specifically designed to operate as tightly coupled hardware–modeling and simulation–acceleration coprocessors, providing both hardware modeling and simulation acceleration in a single application–specific system. The unit can boost simulation speeds of large designs containing VLSI devices, making it possible to develop and debug certain application software for microprocessor–based designs before hardware prototypes are available.

Hardware modeling has been accepted by a majority of electronic designers as the quickest and most reliable way to develop simulation models. For example, TRW (Redondo Beach, California) designed several complex VLSI devices during phase one of the VHSIC program. The chips were so complex that behavioral models would have been very difficult to develop, debug, and maintain. Using hardware–modeling capabilities from Valid, TRW was able to develop the required simulation models in a fraction of the time it would have taken otherwise.

Hardware modeling also improves the overall design turnaround time. For example, DEC used Valid's hardware–modeling techniques to develop behavioral models for C–VAX chips in two weeks; otherwise, using only software, this would have taken approximately seven months. This allowed DEC to verify the design sooner, thereby shortening the design cycle. The product was shipped months sooner than would have been possible using software models.

Hardware Versus Software Modeling

A hardware model is correct by definition. Writing a correct behavioral model is comparable in magnitude to writing a correct operating system (between 5000 and 100,000 lines of code). In addition, a software model is accurate only where it is tested.

A behavioral model of a standard part may be tested by vectors from the model vendor or, increasingly, by a set of vectors provided by the IC vendor. The risk is apparent in the first case: A model vendor is as likely to make errors in test vectors as in the model itself. In the second case, the problem lies in the fact that vector sets used in manufacturing are intended to test for internal faults, not for functionality.

For example, under some conditions, the 68020 chip has a false external-cycle start. This is not documented and would not be reflected in a software model. It is not obvious in normal operation and may not be evident in the IC vendor's test vectors. However, this sort of undocumented, idiosyncratic behavior may result in system design iterations unless correctly simulated with the physical part.

An examination of the modeling process for standard parts shows that the time it takes to develop a new hardware model for a complex part is, conservatively, less than two weeks. Typically, the development of a behavioral model of the same part may take nine months to two years. This disparity continues to widen with the increasing complexity of ICs.

It is a fact that hardware models for new parts are released, on the average, two years earlier than behavioral models. In addition, a user with little training can always develop a hardware model if the vendor does not provide it in a library. With behavioral models from a vendor, the designer is dependent on the model vendor and, as a result, may experience delays.

For modeling ASICs, behavioral models or gate–level models are necessary until the actual prototype exists. However, about 90% of designers use only parts that already exist.

For off–the–shelf models, behavioral models and hardware models are roughly equivalent in ease of use. However, for ASICs, hardware models are significantly easier to develop, use, and support.

The diverse skills of the design team make it difficult to write a correct behavioral model for an ASIC. The chip designer may know the design thoroughly, but lack specialized software knowledge. The system–level designer knows neither the chip's intimate details nor the software language. A software engineer (perhaps in a library group) lacks detailed IC knowledge. In addition, behavioral models are host–dependent, require space in the system, and must be supported.

• The Future of Simulation and Hardware Modeling •

The most important trend that is emerging in the field of simulation and hardware modeling is standardization. At present, it is common for engineering groups to use more than one type of simulator during the design phase or in the process of transferring the design into manufacturing. To be a wise investment, a hardware modeler should be able to support multiple simulators and run in connection with various standard hardware platforms.

The current generation of hardware modelers was designed with standard components in mind. The explosive growth of ASICs in system design means that the next generation of modelers will have to provide the capability to thoroughly address the problems associated with ASIC modeling. Particularly important are the support of high pin counts and making the hardware models easier to develop.

ASIC–prototype verification probably will be another related application for hardware modelers of the future. Then, when prototypes become available from the lab, it should be possible to replace the gate–level description with a hardware model of the part and to verify the device's operation using the same vectors employed in the original simulation. This would allow an earlier determination of whether the device prototype works.

Direct write–on wafers will impact the future of hardware modeling, since they allow ASIC prototypes to be produced earlier in the design process than is presently possible. By cutting links to an array's unused gates using laser micromachining, it is possible to turn out a 2500–gate device in less than an hour and a 5000–gate in slightly more. This procedure allows extremely complex prototypes to be produced in a matter of hours or days, as opposed to weeks. If the actual prototype devices become available earlier, hardware modeling can be made even more effective in the design process, while cutting down on the number of costly prototype iterations.

As workstation technology continues to improve, so must the performance of hardware–modeling systems. As workstations become faster, simulation speed will increase as well. This means that the throughput of the simulation with the hardware modeler should improve dramatically.

Generally, a hardware modeler's performance is thought of in terms of the chip's operational clock frequency. Actually, the time it takes to play vectors through a chip is but a small percentage of the total time required to go from the simulator to the hardware modeler. Software improvements will be of primary importance in optimizing hardware modelers' performance.

The majority of simulation currently takes place at the IC level, and very little at the board or system level. Many ICs come out of fabrication meeting their test vectors, but are not operational when placed in systems. Some IC vendors concede that although functional specifications and pin–level test vectors are met by almost 100% of the devices they manufacture, about 50% cannot be used in systems because the manually generated test vectors did not reflect the correct interaction between the system and the ICs. The solution to this problem will be system–level simulation—a definite trend of the future.

The increased adoption of fault simulation is another trend. As simulation technology develops and those involved with it become more familiar with it, simulation will take place at higher and higher levels. Fault simulation probably will become important not only for ICs, but for boards as well. From its very beginning, the CAE industry has built stronger links between design and testing, design and manufacture. Fault simulation is but another aspect of this. Again, evolution still is necessary in the software and hardware areas, and here, too, standardization will be a key.

CHAPTER 6

ANALOG-CIRCUIT
SIMULATION

• SPICE, SPICE, and More SPICE •

In analog–circuit simulation, designers are not just trying to depict high and low states of an analog—or digital—system, they are trying to get a picture of the changing voltage and current levels at important nodes in the circuit. An analog circuit is expected to manipulate voltages and currents, often at very high frequencies (or rates of change). But even in digital circuits, excessive voltage and current levels will predict hot spots on a board or chip, will determine whether the transistors used are being stressed or overloaded, and will assess the possibilities of latch–up, burnout, or other failures of the circuit in a system.

The distinction between analog and digital circuits, however, does not quite correspond to the distinction between circuit simulators and logic simulators. A circuit simulator can analyze both digital and analog circuits for their changes in voltage and current output. A logic simulator, on the other hand, shows the high and low logic states on a digital circuit's logic gates; obviously, it cannot represent changing voltage or current levels in a circuit, analog or digital.

In analog–circuit simulation, the standard is a program called SPICE, developed at the University of California at Berkeley. Practically all analog–circuit simulators represent improvements and variations on SPICE. Engineers using the program on workstations owe a debt to companies like Electrical Engineering Software (EES) (Santa Clara, California) and Analog Design Tools (now merged with Valid Logic Systems of San Jose, California). These companies have made the input and output of a SPICE run easier to use by converting the original batch program to an interactive format.

A SPICE program, or *deck*, requires all the variables to be stated in a FORTRAN programmer's format. After many hours of run time on a computer (assuming that the computer does not stall or trip over some bad numbers in a string), the results are printed out as long lists of numbers. Often, SPICE jobs submitted into a mainframe's batch queue return incomplete, due to small, easy–to–overlook coding errors. The program has no way to advise users of their mistakes.

In addition, the operation of this program—like the operation of the logic simulators discussed in Chapter 5—depends on the availability of device models. The standard model libraries have serious shortcomings: They include mostly low–level electronic components like transistors, resistors, and capacitors. Only recently have the libraries expanded to include higher level components such as operational amplifiers, phase–locked loops, switching–power–supply controllers, transformers, and other magnetic elements.

Even when modeling switching transistors, the SPICE models typically need extra tweaking. What SPICE attempts to do is to calculate the changes in voltage and current flow with time and temperature. Unlike a logic simulator, the analog–circuit simulator cannot go to a behavioral model to find one of four mutually exclusive logic states (that is, 1, 0, Z, or X). Rather, the circuit simulator must calculate many thousands of points, depicting the voltage rise over time, from a complex network of variables. The voltage rise and fall times, moreover, cannot be described with a simple formula (like Ohm's law, $E=IR$), but require complex differential and integral calculus (like dv/dt).

This calculus usually is performed iteratively: To solve a set of complex equations—say, four equations with five unknowns, the computer arbitrarily picks a value for one of the unknowns out of a range of values and works out a solution for the equations. It repeats the calculation using a different value from the range, noting the difference between the first solution and the results of the next iteration. It keeps repeating the calculation until the range of possible values for the unknowns appears to narrow and the differences in solutions appear to converge by becoming ever smaller and smaller. Unless the device models are well defined, however, this computer calculus can go on forever.

For example, the performance of practically all commercial transistors will change drastically as their case and junction temperatures change. They will be sluggish and likely to latch up in the cool state, improve slightly as they warm up, and increase exponentially in switching speed as they approach maximum junction temperatures. If the junction is heated just a little bit more, the transistors will fail. Depicting these changes in switching performance requires several different sets of equations, one set for each section of the performance curve. Frequently, this creates convergence problems for the computer, since it cannot tell easily where one set of equations leaves off and another begins. The result is that the computer runs through the same computations again and again, coming up with a totally different answer each time and never converging on an acceptable solution. Even where convergence has been obtained and the computations are complete, SPICE by itself does not come with presentation graphics. Users are on their own in interpreting the results of the computation.

The virtue of the new SPICE programs and derivations described here is that they make it easy to input SPICE data into a simulator. Since they report the results of the simulation as a series of waveforms displayable on a workstation screen, they also make it easier to interpret the results of a SPICE computation. While the program still is a batch–processing job for a computer, the easier to use input and output capabilities bring the program closer to the goal of interactive analog simulation.

Butterworth Filter

One example of the complexity in analog simulation is the polynomial equations used to predict the performance of a simple fourth–order high–pass Butterworth filter, constructed with an LF353 op amp as the active element. The filter design has a corner frequency of 1 kHz and a gain of 20; that is, it filters out any signal below 1 kHz in frequency and amplifies anything above that by 20 times.

While the user must specify the bias conditions of the filter and compile the netlist, the relationships defining the basic operating characteristics of the filter are:

$$f_C = \frac{1}{2\pi} \sqrt{\frac{1}{R_1 \cdot R_2 \cdot C_2}}$$

$$A_v = \frac{1}{1 + \dfrac{R_{4A}}{R_{3A}}} \cdot \frac{1}{1 + \dfrac{R_{4B}}{R_{3B}}}$$

where f_c is the high–pass corner frequency and A_v is the gain of the circuit. The high–pass corner frequency (f_c) varies with the squared power of the value of the capacitors C2 and C4. In other words, the corner frequency is quite dependent on capacitor–value changes. The resistance (R) values, though, strongly affect the gain, A_v, of the filter.

The purpose of an analog simulation in this case is to determine the sensitivity of the design to step changes of capacitance and resistance values. This will provide an idea of the tolerances necessary for resistors and capacitors in the finished product. Both parameters are simulated in the same run. To analyze the change in corner frequency with changes in capacitance, the program calculates the response of the output across a range of frequencies and changes the capacitor values during the same simulation. To analyze the gain as a function of the resistances, the program calculates the frequency response to changes resulting from new values of R.

With SPICE, several problems are obvious. First, few SPICE libraries provide the op amp models. SPICE frequently models op amps (like the LF353) as a transistor–level model, which needs a complex circuit description and detailed list of transistor characteristics from designers.

Second, this type of simulation requires a new run for each change in resistor and capacitor value; that is, every small change in R and C requires a new computation.   One way to eliminate repeated runs is to use a statistical–variation analysis, like Monte Carlo, to show the shifting of the corner frequency with changes in component values. Statistical techniques are useful in analyzing the effect of variations in manufactured parts on the reliability of the circuit.   However, this analysis could not be done in SPICE without reworking the program or coordinating batch submissions through an external program.

Finally, to display the result, the user then would have to combine the data points from each run—a rather tedious and time–consuming procedure. Only simple character plots and tabular reports are available in SPICE.

The new analog–simulation tools, however, make this process easier. Instead of starting a new SPICE run for every change in resistance and capacitance, EES's program, for example, allows the simulator to make a sweep over a range of values within the same simulation run.

To carry out a multipoint analysis—one that crosses a range of values—of the filter components, the program uses the *sweep* command. Users can sweep any domain of time, frequency, temperature, or other parameter with high–level–language commands like:

SWEEP TIME FROM 0 TO 100US BY 1US

This is a simple instruction that simulates the circuit in time domain to 100 μs in 1-μs steps.

For the Butterworth circuit, the instruction for the frequency–domain analysis of changes in corner frequency as a result of changes in capacitor values, *cvalue*, is simply:

SWEEP FREQ FROM 10 TO 10 KHZ DEC 100
AND CAP FROM .0005UF TO .0015UF BY .0005UF

The *dec* portion of the command says "calculate 100 points per decade." The *and* clause adds a new analysis domain to this same simulation and defines its range of variation, in this case *cvalue*, in steps set by the *by* clause.

A command construct similar to that of the capacitor analysis determines the variation in gain due to the resistances defined by *rvalue*. The command:

SWEEP FREQ FROM 10 TO 10KHZ DEC 100
AND RVALUE FROM 400K TO 480K BY 40K

tells the simulator to determine the response of the filter to the changing values of *rvalue*.

Toward an Interactive SPICE

EES's program is called PRECISE ASD (for analog system design). It uses syntax similar to that of ISPICE, the popular SPICE derivative, and attempts to make SPICE more interactive by showing the simulator's reaction to each user command. This maximizes the time spent on a workstation, because the results from the simulator are apparent immediately and provoke and influence the next action taken. For example, an engineer can verify an initial selection of circuit biasing voltage before doing a frequency analysis. The designer then can correct any inconsistencies noted immediately, without leaving PRECISE. Designers familiar with SPICE will feel that they have more control over the simulation process.

PRECISE understands simple English commands. For example, *probe nv* tells PRECISE to sample just the node voltages (NV) of the circuit. *Plot vdb (vout)* will graph the output signal on a decibel scale. *Test delay vin vout* will calculate the delay between the signals *vin* and *vout*. The interactive command structure in PRECISE allows engineers to perform analyses that are difficult to breadboard, such as radiation and temperature simulation.

PRECISE links to a library of precharacterized devices, including transistors, diodes, comparators, and op amps. For efficiency, macro models define op amps and simulate all important operating characteristics. The macro model has three stages: The input stage models the differential–mode and common–mode input, the voltage and current offsets, and the second–order effects of slew rate and phase response. The inner stage models differential–mode and common–mode voltage gains. The output stage models the DC (direct current) and AC (alternating current) resistances, the maximum short–circuit current, and the maximum voltage swing.

The results are displayed graphically. Engineers get the key information they need to make design decisions without searching through an entire output listing from a SPICE batch run. Analysis commands like *dc*, for calculating the operating point of a circuit, and *wcase*, for calculating the worst–case operating point based on circuit sensitivities, execute and allow the engineer to analyze the results, make modifications to component values, and rework the design.

PRECISE presents data as connected–line graphs or as formatted tabular reports. The user also has a set of options for titling and scaling the graphs and combining the output with text files. For example, the command *plot vdb(vout)* plots the output response over frequency on a log–frequency scale.

The display overlays all results on the same graph simply by asking PRECISE to overlay *vdb(vout)* from both the first run and the second run. The plot is a concise illustration of the variation in gain with changes in *rvalue* and the variation in corner frequency *fc* with changes in *cvalue*. A study of the plots shows that the designer should set the Butterworth filter values for *rvalue* and *cvalue* at 430 kΩ (kiloohm—one thousand ohms) and 0.001 µf (microfarad—one millionth of a farad), respectively, to achieve the needed filter corner frequency of 1 kHz and gain of 20.

To perform a Monte Carlo analysis, each element is assigned component–value variations that match a distribution representative of the manufacturing process. The distributions can be uniform or Gaussian. To place a three–sigma-point, or 10%, Gaussian distribution from nominal for the resistor values and 15% for the capacitor values, PRECISE uses the commands:

GAUSS 10% R*
GAUSS 15% C*

The following command calculates the AC Monte Carlo:

SWEEP DFREQ FROM 10 TO 10 KHZ DEC 25
AND CASES FROM 1 TO 10 BY 1

For the AC Monte Carlo, PRECISE simulates component variation in a Gaussian distribution for 10–lot cases and then shows the shift in the circuit's frequency response as a result of Gaussian distributions of the lot variations in capacitor and resistor values.

SPICE 3

This is programmers' territory, but the solution to inherent SPICE problems like convergence and speed require revisions in SPICE's algorithms. A few years ago, a Berkeley team made impressive progress by replacing FORTRAN with C– language code and cleaning up some algorithms. The result, SPICE 3, runs more efficiently on UNIX workstations and has become the basis for a number of proprietary SPICE versions.

Perhaps the most dramatic simulator based on SPICE 3, which is gaining ground with CAE–tool vendors, is the SPICE Plus simulator from Analog Design Tools (now merged with Valid Logic Systems). SPICE Plus boasts a model library of more than 2500 devices, including inductors with nonlinear cores.

Thanks to Valid, SPICE Plus runs on Mentor's Idea system—perhaps the most popular turnkey CAE system. While SPICE 3 itself (unlike SPICE 2) includes graphics output, integration in the Idea system provides far more choices. An interface product allows schematics to be moved between the mentor system and Valid's SPICE Plus.

Analog–Component Libraries

Like models of processors and other digital circuits, the advent of affordable SPICE model–parameter libraries for commercial analog components promises to further increase the application of circuit simulators to board–level design. By supplementing their simulation tools with a device library, designers can predict the effects of real component variations on design performance. With a good library, they can use simulation to determine the manufacturability of their designs.

There are two contrasting methodologies for the construction of analog–device libraries. One relies on the data sheet as the primary source of information for the extraction of model parameters. The other (like hardware modeling) relies on measurement of actual devices as the source of data to characterize a device. The latter approach is most frequently espoused by the IC manufacturers, whose engineers are well versed in extracting performance parameters with a wafer probe and, consequently, understand the intricacies of semiconductor–device modeling.

Vendors offer a wide range of products and services—from the libraries themselves to turnkey systems for building such libraries. Their capability encompasses DC characteristics (including the high–current effects of power transistors), junction capacitance, and microwave–frequency AC characterization over temperature. The hardware for such systems costs $100,000 or more.

Vendor services range from characterization of a single component to the development of complete custom libraries that may include BJTs (bipolar–junction transistors), JFETs (junction field–effect transistors), MOSFETs (metal–oxide semiconductor FETs), power–FETs (field–effect transistors), op amps, comparators, voltage regulators, and magnetic materials. Some device models (for example, for power–FETs, op amps, and comparators) most often are macro models composed of discrete elements and controlled sources. Prices for complete libraries range from a few hundred dollars to $20,000.

Some modeling vendors offer very sophisticated software for device measurement and parameter extraction. The software alone ranges in price from $15,000 to $68,000. For many companies, however, the time and cost of becoming deeply involved with device measurements are prohibitive. Simpler tools often suffice, such as the Parts program from Microsim Corporation (Laguna Hills, California), costing several hundred dollars and running on a PC. These tools may be used to estimate model–library parameters primarily from data–sheet information. This approach is more attractive to circuit designers (as opposed to device–modeling engineers), who have no measurement tools at their disposal, but would like to experiment with parameter extraction at their desks.

For security reasons, some vendors encrypt their libraries for use with their proprietary simulators. In other cases, the library is simulator–specific because the parameters are extracted for a model unique to that simulator. The customer seeking generic SPICE models for in–house simulators, therefore, will have to choose from a smaller selection of applicable libraries.

Important simulation features that board–level designers should look for include sensitivity analysis and Monte Carlo simulation. When combined with a good library, these features are invaluable for simulating the effects of real component tolerances on design performance.

Some of the vendors that are demonstrating a significant effort in library construction are Analog Design Tools (now part of Valid), Daisy, Meta–Software (Campbell, California), Silvaco Data Systems, Integraph, EES, Valid, and Cadnetix. Because the model library is spurring development of a new design methodology, it can be expected that every major circuit–simulator and workstation vendor will offer a library before the end of the year.

Today's library parameters consist of a single set of so–called typical values derived from data–sheet information or limited device measurements. However, both design and library–building methodologies probably will continue to evolve rapidly over the next three to five years. More libraries will be based on device measurements, and, ultimately, model libraries will be incorporated in relational databases. From this information, it will be possible to construct multiple sets of parameters; say, for use with a worst–case design methodology.

Trade–Offs in Accuracy and Speed

Analog simulation, like digital–logic simulation, forces the user into a trade–off between accuracy and speed. It is possible to obtain speedups in computer run time by using simpler device models; the trade–off is accuracy. Designers do not get a totally accurate view of how their circuits will perform, but rather a facsimile. Streamlined software algorithms will speed up the computations on a computer, though they will provide only an approximation of the correct answer. While the requirements of digital simulation make it possible to use an accelerator for simulation purposes, no such machinery now exists for SPICE.

Consequently, most of the gains in speed and accuracy result from a wider range of better device models. One example of a circuit simulator that depends on fast device models is the Saber program from Analogy, which provides alternatives to SPICE models for many otherwise complex devices. The program uses full–blown behavioral descriptions (for example, lookup tables) rather than the representational models (for example, mathematical formulas) of SPICE. Saber's model library has over 500 entries, supported by algorithms for matrix solving and integration.

Like SPICE, Saber will simulate any system—electronic, electro-mechanical, mechanical, or optoelectronic—that can be described in terms of mathematical equations. However, Saber claims at least an order–of–magnitude speed improvement over SPICE. The speed gains are due in part to Saber's hierarchical circuit organization and in part to faster sparse–matrix solutions. Rather than the usual exponential increases in CPU time with circuit complexity, the sparse–matrix representations provide linear increases in run time with circuit size.

Even fast convergence is ensured, by allowing the user a choice among three algorithms for finding the DC operating point; moreover, the obtained values are reused whenever possible in successive calculations. Because it depends more on tables than on equations, Saber can tolerate discontinuities in the model equations. The program includes the ability to model discontinuous events, such as the operation of a one–shot pulse generator. It detects the leading and trailing edges of pulses, which can be recognized as logical 1s and 0s—a necessary condition for mixed–mode analog and digital simulation.

Saber's flexibility in modeling goes further: Users can actually feed in their own equations to link the model parameters. As a result, Saber can accommodate not only any IC technology, but even nonelectrical components like motors or drive coils in a disk drive. In addition to the usual DC and AC (transient) analyses, Saber offers sensitivity, noise, distortion, and Fourier analysis, as well as frequency and temperature sweeps. Monte Carlo analysis also will be available.

Users of Saber include military and aerospace companies such as Boeing, Hughes, Martin Marietta (Huntsville, Alabama), Rockwell (Carrogu Park, California), and Westinghouse Electric Corporation (Pittsburgh, Pennsylvania). OEM integrators include Analog Design Tools, Cadnetix, the Computervision subsidiary of Prime Computer (Framingham, Massachusetts), and Racal–Redac.

Other Alternatives to SPICE

One circuit simulator that has become popular for MOS designs is Simon from CADENCE, (San Jose, California). Although developed primarily for the analog analysis of digital circuits, Simon can tackle many analog–MOS circuits that have no feedback. The simulator depends on a Berkeley–developed relaxation algorithm that assumes that certain feedback– and bias–dependent characteristics will have a minimal impact on the circuit. That is, it stream-lines the calculations by relaxing some of the usual constraints at each node of the circuit. ECAD has published a number of benchmarks to demonstrate Simon's speed, but they do not bear out the expected linear relationship between computer run time and circuit size. It turns out that circuit type often is more important than circuit size when it comes to speed gains over SPICE.

One reason is that SPICE spends an average of only 15% of its CPU time on matrix manipulation and 50% to 75% on device modeling (which is Simon's forte only in the MOS–transistor area). Even without feedback contingencies, some circuits (like inverter chains) force SPICE into backtracking and recalculating its solutions with finer time steps. Circuits with wide–ranging feedback, on the other hand, will totally destroy the speed gains offered by relaxation–based circuit simulators.

Because SPICE spends so much time on computing model equations, it obviously can be speeded up substantially if a simpler model suffices in the digital parts of a circuit. Meta–Software is known for its HSPICE, which can tackle such difficult designs as switching power supplies. But HSPICE also gives the user a choice of less accurate models. With the program's Fast Option, benchmarks show a speedup in transient analysis of 85% for a 2–bit adder, with little loss in accuracy. If a larger error—say, 10%—can be tolerated, simulation of the available switch model can run five times faster.

E–logic, another Berkeley brainchild, might hold the best promise for a SPICE replacement. Instead of solving network equations at variable time intervals, E–logic solves them for user–selected voltage steps. So, unless the voltage changes, the simulator consumes no CPU time.

At Silicon Design Labs (now merged into Silicon Compiler Systems—San Jose, California), E–logic evolved into the Adept algorithm. Adept holds a large speed advantage over SPICE—usually two or three orders of magnitude. Furthermore, simulation time grows less than linearly with circuit size. Thus, unified simulation is possible (at least for moderate–size circuits) with the company's Lsim simulator, which mixes the Adept algorithm with a gate–level logic simulator.

Sensitivity to Layout

Just as in a purely digital design, the actual layout configuration of an analog circuit can affect its operation and timing. Long interconnections and multiple fan–outs, for example, can affect an analog signal just as much as a digital one. In the analog world, however, cross talk (the tangling of two otherwise separate signals) represents an additional danger. Because all digital signals have essentially the same magnitude, even a 20–db (decibel) cross–talk figure will have only negligible effects. But in an analog circuit, 20–db cross talk— due, say, to bad routing—can wreak havoc.

As with a purely digital chip, it is necessary to back–annotate the schematics to mark locations particularly sensitive to these factors when the first layout becomes available. There currently is no circuit simulator that can provide such notation to an original design. For digital circuitry, timing analysis usually provides adequate safeguards, but for analog design, a circuit– simulation model is essential. If only a behavioral model were available, designers would have a hard time incorporating the effects of parasitic factors. They would have to estimate the impact of, say, crossover capacitance or inductive coupling on cross talk and modify the model accordingly.

As ICs get smaller, the impact of solid–state effects and geometry (corner discontinuities, channel depth) also must be taken into account. Only a few circuit simulators (like Control Data's ASPEC) are equipped to take secondary technology effects into account. In fact, the day is approaching when simulators even will have to solve Maxwell field equations in critical regions, which will create another exponential increase in the computational resource required.

Because semiconductor geometries will affect the shape of both digital and analog waveforms generated by a circuit, it may be desirable to display both. SPICE, for example, can model the rise and fall of voltages over time, without making any distinction between transistors modeled for analog or digital purposes. The computational resource required for a SPICE run, however, discourages its use for digital–logic simulations—except in particularly stubborn situations.

A somewhat faster program than SPICE is Andi from Silvar–Lisco, which obtains run–time improvements by scaling down some of the device models used in the computations. An MOS–transistor model, for example, provides more detail than does the switch–level model used for digital logic simulation (for example, threshold voltages, channel resistance, on resistance, and gate–to– source and gate–to–drain capacitance). Unlike SPICE, however, it can describe the interaction of these parameters with a simplified set of equations. The program has been used successfully by semiconductor manufacturers such as International Microelectronic Products (San Jose, California), to simulate analog–to–digital and digital–to–analog converters, modems, phase–locked loops, pulse–code modulation circuits, and even switched–capacitor filters. (It has, for example, successfully modeled clock feedthrough in switched–capacitor filter circuits.)

No matter how well tuned, analog–circuit simulators generally do not match the speed of digital simulators. There are software algorithms that attempt to close the gap between the speeds of digital–logic and analog–circuit simulators. For example, Lsim from Silicon Design Labs and Pacsim from Simucad seem to perform analog and digital simulation well. Simucad, for example, has demonstrated considerable speed over SPICE with its Pacsim simulator. Pacsim, which was acquired from Shiva Multisystems when the companies merged, also is believed to be at least an order of magnitude faster than SPICE. Many feel that this represents a feasible candidate for either a core simulator or a unified hybrid—one that simulates both analog– and digital–circuit elements in the same run.

Mixed–Mode Simulation

While some 50% to 60% of current ASIC designs are digital–logic circuits, 10% to 20% are analog circuits, and the remainder—up to 40%—are circuits that must process both analog and digital information. The use of these mixed analog and digital circuits probably will swell to 50% of all ASIC designs by 1990.

The applications for these circuits include telecommunications, test and measurement, and computer interfaces. In telecommunications applications, an analog voice signal must be converted to a digital pulse stream for transmission over telephone lines. Digital test instruments frequently require a changing voltage measured over time to be digitized for storage, analysis, and display. Computer–interface circuitry includes disk drives and other storage–device applications in which the parallel data stream from the computer must be converted to a frequency–modulated analog waveform to drive the magnetic recording heads.

Consequently, there is intense interest in mixed–moded simulations—simulations that represent both digital–logic states and analog voltage levels and waveforms. A digital simulator that can accommodate a number of hierarchical levels (say, switch, gate, and functional) is a mixed–level simulator, though it often is referred to as a mixed–mode simulator. Some experts argue that simulators that can function in both in an analog and a digital environment should be called hybrid simulators, since the term mixed–mode frequently refers to analog simulators that also can model geometry or temperature or even may refer to mechanical components.

However, mixed–mode here refers to simulators that harness both an analog–circuit simulation and a digital–logic simulation in the same computer run and show the results on the same user screen. Even here, there is a distinction between *glued* simulators, whose analog– and digital–analysis software cannot interact with each other, and *core* simulators that use a general–purpose simulator for one domain and enhance it with some limited capabilities in the other. Most core simulators embed a digital–logic simulator into an analog–circuit simulator (like SPICE), rather than vice versa. A unified simulation is one that does not distinguish between digital– and analog–circuit sections.

Creating interfaces between analog and digital tools is not an easy task. Logic levels from the digital domain must be translated into voltage levels for circuit simulation, and vice versa. Hierarchical systems may have to be flattened before simulation. Functional descriptions need to be converted into gates and netlists for digital simulation or into (at least) RC–loaded switches for analog simulation. To do this, outputs from logic simulators may have to be combined with those from timing verifiers.

A hybrid simulator developed by Viewlogic, in cooperation with Microsim, might serve as a model. Both Microsim's PSPICE and Viewlogic's ViewSim run as subprocessors on a MicroVAX, IBM–PC, or similar workstation. The PSPICE circuit simulator, which runs on both the IBM–PC and the DEC VAX, includes GaAs MESFET models, power transformer models, and Monte Carlo analysis. In this marriage of simulators, PSPICE (which is file–compatible with ViewSim, Silos, and Plogic) is used as the core.

Execution switches from one simulator to the other whenever the user–defined domain boundary is passed. Digital circuits can be specified at any ViewSim level from transistor to behavioral. In the latter case, models are described with C routines or in VHDL. State machines can be defined via a PDL interface that accepts state equations.

When simulation switches from digital to analog, state information is converted to voltage values that depend on the technology used. Timing information is translated into an RC–shaped wave, whose capacitance is determined by the fan–out, while the digital technology used (CMOS, ECL, etc.) determines the proper resistance. Three–state levels are treated in the same way. However, user scan define their own interface models in all cases.

Going from PSPICE into ViewSim, threshold voltages determine the logic levels. For example, in the default for TTL, values from –1V to 3.75V are interpreted as low logic levels, and values from 3.4V to 7V are interpreted as high logic levels. The overlap corresponds to trigger hysteresis, so that instability will appear in the simulation only f it also would occur in the real circuit. Voltages outside the specified ranges are interpreted as unknown (X). Because users can override the default values, they have full control over the state transitions. However, the signal strength is always set to driving—a reasonable assumption, because voltages and loads are always known in circuit simulation.

A circuit containing about 2000 digital components (at any level acceptable to ViewSim) and about 200 analog components can be simulated overnight on a MicroVAX. On more powerful workstations (such as the 10–MIPS Sun–4), the simulation consumes less than an hour.

The obvious drawback of the Microsim approach—using a circuit simulator as the core of a mixed–mode simulator—is a speed mismatch between analog and digital simulation. Logic and timing can be simulated quickly at the gate level, and even thousands of gates may take only seconds of run time. Circuit simulation of just a few hundred components using SPICE, on the other hand, can take hours. The only solution to this dilemma is a much faster, yet accurate, circuit simulator.

The problem with mixed–mode simulators that use SPICE or some other circuit simulator as their cores is excessive run time. The other method, less frequently used, is to build a mixed–mode simulator using a versatile digital-logic simulator as the core. Perhaps the most reasonable choice of logic simulators for such a hybrid would be one that has become a de facto industry standard, such as Cadat. With its 21 signal states, this simulator can carry quite a bit of analog information through the digital analysis.

This core is available in a system–level simulator introduced jointly by HHB Systems and Analogy. In operation, the simulator uses the event queue provided by the Cadat simulator and the device models provided by Analogy's Saber simulator. The system accepts EDIF netlist inputs; runs on VAX, Sun, or Apollo platforms; and displays the results on a graphics screen.

The third solution to the interface problem is to segregate analog– and digital–circuit functions and to use separate simulators for different sections of the problem. This method is a *glued* approach; a digital and analog simulator are joined through the same user interface. Special interface programs and software subroutines operate in the places where analog and digital portions of a circuit meet. These subroutines make the transformations between digital-logic states and analog voltage levels (and vice versa) and make some effort to reflect the appropriate timing between these elements.

The Daisy A/D Lab, for example, is one of the first board–level circuit simulators to analyze and display both analog and digital response patterns. The software can display analog waveforms (consisting of varying voltages and currents), along with digital–logic patterns on the same workstation screen.

The A/D Lab joins a logic–simulation program (the Daisy Logic Simulator, DLS) and a SPICE circuit simulator (the Virtual Lab) to the same database and the same user interface. In operation, users enter their analog or mixed analog-digital schematics into the system in the same way they would draw digital-logic circuits. Analog parts like op amps and comparators, for example, are connected with analog–to–digital converters. These components, in turn, frequently are connected with latches, digital counting circuits, microprocessor buses, etc.

Once the circuit is entered, the system compiles a netlist that effectively partitions the entire circuit into analog and digital elements. The Virtual Lab simulator is applied to the analog portion, while the DLS logic simulator is applied to the digital portion. Analog and digital waveforms then are displayed on separate portions of the user's screen.

In the partitioning process, the A/D Lab will account for analog components that interface directly with digital components, by extracting the appropriate I/O impedances of the digital components from a library model for the part and using these impedances in the SPICE circuit simulation. The library of parts includes models for TTL, CMOS, and ECL logic devices, their typical voltage-supply levels, and their typical fan–in/fan–out loads. In addition, the A/D Lab includes a small but expandable library of analog–to–digital and digital–to-analog converters that includes their impedances and timing characteristics.

The software is designed to run on all Daisy platforms, and users have the choice of running simulations locally or remotely on the MicroVAX II or Daisy's Megalogician hardware accelerator. The A/D Lab is available as an option to Daisy's Logician workstation or to the Personal Logician, which uses the IBM-PC/AT.

But programs like this do not represent a core simulator, in which a logic simulator is embedded in a circuit simulator, or vice versa. Where tighter coupling is needed (for example, for an analog–to–digital converter), a core simulator may need to be constructed. Some semiconductor manufacturers, particularly ASIC suppliers, have developed core simulators for their customers, but few of these are available by themselves.

For example, VLSI Technology has developed a cell library that includes behavioral descriptions of both the digital and analog components. To meet the demand for analog designs, the company's digital simulator, VTIsim, has been augmentedby Sierra Semiconductors with analog capabilities in the form of behavioral (more accurately, functional) descriptions. The result is a core–type hybrid simulator.

In the case of digital–to–analog or analog–to–digital converter cells, Sierra provides inputs and outputs in a format that is understandable to VTIsim. (The model is based on SPICE simulations performed on some representative cells.) So, for each digital input value, the behavioral model provides an output voltage and a node impedance.

More precise behavioral modeling for analog circuits has been demonstrated by Harris Semiconductor for use with its proprietary Slice circuit simulator. For example, the 16–channel multiplexer in a digital–to–analog converter with about 1000 transistors could be simulated with the behavioral macro model in minutes, while the original circuit simulation took hours. However, creating the macros is tedious, and simulating a board's worth of circuitry still would require a Cray supercomputer.

Despite its limitations, SPICE represents the cleanest technical solution for circuit simulation. For years to come, therefore, it is bound to remain the standard by which all other analog simulators are measured.

• Analog Simulation Methodologies •

Traditionally, analog design has been performed through a manual process called breadboarding. The process begins with the first idea of what an engineer wants the circuit to accomplish. Engineers may sketch block diagrams and develop transfer functions for various portions of the design. Then, they develop a circuit topology to use as a starting point, find the needed equipment, and gather the components required to build the circuit. The breadboard is fashioned, the test equipment is connected, and an iterative test–and–change process begins. Engineers may build dozens of circuits and spend many weeks at the workbench before they have a circuit that meets their needs.

In addition to the time required for breadboarding, the process is fraught with other difficulties. The working prototype developed works only for the particular components used in it. When the design is manufactured, it will use components that vary through a wide range of tolerances. Will it still work, regardless of the tolerances of the components used? What will be the reliability of the design in the field? Will components be stressed to levels that will cause early failures? In recent years, many computer tools have been developed that can help answer these questions, as well as reduce the time required for a breadboard design.

The first analog–design computer tools concentrated on the computationally intensive job of simulating circuit performance. In circuit simulation, mathematical models of the electronic devices are developed, and the voltage and current relationships at the circuit nodes are used to construct a system of differential equations. Then, iterative techniques are used to solve the equations for node voltages at every point in time. Despite the advantages offered by such simulation, circuit–simulation programs such as SPICE, ASPEC, and SYSCAP have not been used widely until recently, except for semiconductor design. There are three main reasons for this lack of user acceptance.

First, early circuit simulators were developed as batch programs on large computers. Users were required to learn to use a text editor and the job–control language for the computer. Designers would have to draw their circuits, number all the nodes, and type complicated node lists and commands. Typing mistakes were common and not easily found or corrected. A large amount of expensive computer time could be used running simulations on incorrect circuits. When the simulation was completed, users were forced to search through pages of numerical data or primitive line–printer graphs to find the information needed. For analog designers with little previous computer experience, these barriers often were simply too great to be overcome.

Second, an accurate simulation requires accurate models. The models of active circuit devices—diodes and transistors, for example—are based on the complex solid–state physics of the devices. Even when the designer had the training to perform such modeling, the time required for modeling before any simulation could be run often was prohibitive. Large semiconductor companies could afford to maintain staffs of device physicists who could accurately model the processes used on their manufacturing lines, which accounts for the extensive use of batch simulation by IC designers. System designers using off–the–shelf parts were unable to do any meaningful simulation of their designs.

Finally, simply predicting circuit performance is just the beginning of the design problem. Designers need to be sure that their circuits will work through a wide range of component tolerances and operating conditions. Further, the design needs to meet basic requirements of manufacturability, testability, and reliability. Batch circuit–simulation programs do nothing to meet these needs.

By 1985, however, several technological advances had occurred that permitted the development of real CAE tools for analog–circuit design. Low-cost workstations became available, which allowed simulations to be run efficiently on a desktop computer. User interface tools appeared, which allowed the development of workbench environments that would let users take advantage of computer tools without becoming computer experts. The Analog Workbench developed by Analog Design Tools (now merged with Valid) will be used as an example of what can be done with analog CAE tools today.

The Analog Workbench

The Analog Workbench is an engineering–workstation–based tool for designing analog circuits. It can perform the circuit design and testing tasks normally done at a conventional hardware–type engineering workbench. Users are presented with a design environment on the face of a CRT that emulates their familiar manual environment. Separate display windows are used for the circuit editor (breadboard) and various pieces of test equipment.

In the circuit–design process, the Analog Workbench offers groups of related choices referred to as menus. Some menus list commands, telling the system to take specified actions; others offer component choices—a list of transistors, for example, available for use in a circuit.

The menus are presented in a hierarchy that follows a logical work flow typical of analog design. Selecting the top–level menu automatically leads to a menu at a more detailed level. For example, choosing the item *op amp* from the circuit–element menu automatically generates a menu of the specific op–amp configurations available for use in the circuit. This menu–hand–along process continues until the menu with the finest details needed is reached.

The designer selects menu items by moving a mouse across the system's tablet until the cursor is positioned over the desired menu item on the screen, then pressing the *select* button. Sometimes, the menu asks for fill–in information. It may, for example, ask for the name the designer has chosen for a circuit, or it may ask for a value, such as the number of megohms of a specific resistor. The operator supplies information by typing the data at the keyboard. Thus, the menu hierarchy leads the user through the steps with a series of prompts and command choices. The designer can add, delete, move, or copy single elements, lines, or even entire areas of a schematic just by pushing a button.

Entering the Schematic. With the Analog Workbench, the designer can draw a schematic quickly and easily. The user first tells the Workbench what to do in general. That is a top–level (main) choice, so the top–level menu is used. The main menu always is displayed at the top of the screen when the system is on. The choices are Circuit, Shell, Library, Preferences, Utility, and Logout. The designer next uses the mouse to select Circuit from the main menu, which causes a new menu to appear containing a list of the circuits available.

To modify or copy a previously designed circuit, the designer uses the mouse to select the last saved version of the circuit, which then appears in the circuit–display window. The designer selects New Circuit, and a fill–in menu appears that requests the name the designer wishes to assign. The designer then types in the name of the circuit.

The Circuit Editor window then appears on the screen. To draw the schematic, the designer begins by placing the circuit elements and connecting them with lines. To place a resistor at the left side of the schematic, for instance, requires selecting Add from the top–line menu in the Circuit Editor. A pop–down menu then appears, listing the choices available. From this pop–down menu, the user selects Resistor. The selection causes an element–placement menu to appear that shows the resistor and allows a value to be assigned to the component. The user can assign a definite value, like 30K, or can assign a variable name, like *res*, to the value. Variables can be used by other tools to perform advanced analyses on the circuit. Once the value is assigned, the designer simply holds down the right mouse button and drags the resistor to the desired location in the circuit, then releases the mouse button to snap the resistor into place. All the resistors may be placed in a similar fashion (see Figure 6.1).

Probes and Sources. Once a breadboard is completed on a traditional workbench, the user connects signal sources to drive the circuit and probes the circuit with various instruments to determine its performance. Exactly the same thing is done on the Analog Workbench. The user may select current and voltage sources and connect them to the appropriate locations in the circuit. Current and voltage probes then are selected and placed to measure the output values.

Instruments. The schematic drawn in the Circuit Editor now can be tested just as a breadboard would be tested on a traditional workbench. The user may call upon the same equipment that would be used for manual design. Each of the six available instruments—DC meter, function generator, oscilloscope, frequency sweeper, network analyzer, and spectrum analyzer—is displayed in its own window. The designer has the same functionality available in these virtual instruments as is available in the real instruments on a workbench, and the instruments work the same way. Instead of using buttons and knobs, the user selects settings by clicking the mouse on a series of menus.

Instruments are selected from the Instruments menu in the Circuit Editor. When an instrument is selected, a new window for that instrument appears on the display. Selecting Time Domain causes two instruments—a function generator and an oscilloscope—to appear. Selecting Frequency Domain causes a frequency sweeper and a network analyzer to appear. The instruments are connected to points in the circuit by entering a probe or source identifier through a menu selection.

The instrument windows can be placed anywhere on the screen and popped to the top—made visible—or hidden at any time. When instruments are not in use, they may be collapsed into symbolic icons and placed at the edge of the display. A click of the mouse button will cause the icon to redisplay as a window.

The DC Meter. The DC Meter (see Figure 6.2) works like a four–channel laboratory DC multimeter. It contains a top–line Utility option and four DC Meter setting lines. The Utility commands allow the user to redraw, print, or exit the instrument. To use the DC Meter, the user first clicks the mouse button on one of the four channels. A fill–in menu is presented, and the user types in the probe identifier for the point of interest in the circuit. The probe identifier entered then is displayed in the Probes column of the instrument. The value at that probe location is displayed in the Reading column. The user also may enter a formula in the Probes column. If so, the Workbench will display the proper units in the Reading column.

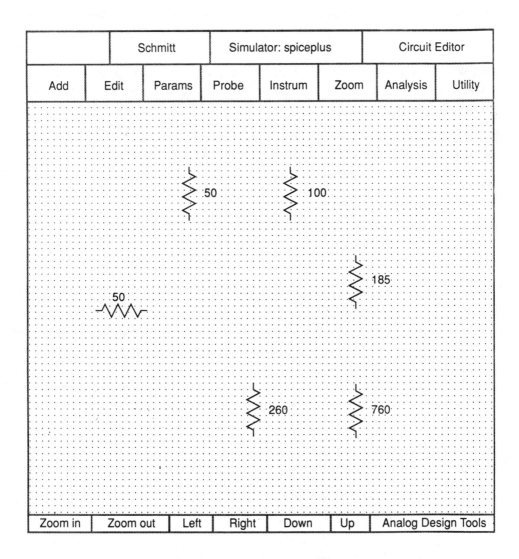

Figure 6.1: Analog Workbench screen. A schematic like the Schmitt trigger using Analog Workbench. Placement of resistors is input in this screen.

The Frequency Sweeper. The Frequency Sweeper (see Figure 6.3) works like a four–channel bench instrument. The top–line menu commands select the frequency range for the analysis. The values selected are displayed in the center of the instrument. The user has the option of selecting logarithmic or linear spacing and the total number of frequency steps to be used. When a particular channel is selected by a mouse click, the user is prompted for a source

dc meter		Instrument : DC Meter	
		Utility	
#	Channel	Probes	Reading
1	DC Settings	B	19.96 V
2	DC Settings	B/A	1.00 KOh (Resistance Calc)
3	DC Settings	(D+A)*4	159.68 mA
4	DC Settings	PR2	398.40 mWt (Do Auto Power Calc)

Figure 6.2: The DC Meter. The DC Meter works like a four–channel laboratory DC multimeter. It contains a top–line Utility option and four DC Meter setting lines.

connection, signal amplitude, and relative phase. The selections then are displayed in the instrument. Channels can be toggled on or off by a mouse click. As in the DC Meter, a Utility selection allows the user to redraw, print, or exit the instrument.

The Network Analyzer. The Network Analyzer window emulates a four–channel laboratory network analyzer. The window contains a top–line menu, a display area, a status line, and setting lines. The Log–Axis menu allows the designer to select a linear or log–decade frequency display. The X–Axis menu is used to select the mode of display for the horizontal axis. If frequency is selected, a display results. The instrument also can be placed in X–Y mode by connecting a vertical channel to the X–Axis. For example, in Figure 6.4, Channel 1 has been set as magnitude of gain in decibels, Channel 2 has been set as phase, and the X–Axis has been set as Vertical Channel 2. Turning off Channel 2 results in a Nichol's plot of magnitude of gain in decibels as a function of phase in degrees. The Freq menu works like the frequency–span knob on a laboratory instrument. It allows the designer to regulate the frequency range of the analysis data displayed—expand, contract, or center, for example.

The Markers menu activates two vertical lines that can be used to take measurements along the horizontal axis. Either of the two markers can be dragged to a particular location and the value at that point read in the status line. In addition to the normal redraw, print, and quit options, the Utility menu allows the user to display or hide a grid and to display intermediate results while a simulation is running.

The Channel Settings area of the window allows the user to select channels and toggle them on or off, just as in the Frequency Sweeper, and to connect

lowpass	Instrument : Frequency Sweeper		
Frequency Range	Linear/Log (Now Log)		Utility
Present Frequency Range 50 Hz to 5 KHZ No. of steps: 200			
#			Source	Amplitude	Phase
1	Sweep Set	ON	A	1.0 Volts	0.0 deg.
2	Sweep Set	ON	F	1.0 Volts	0.0 deg.
3	Sweep Set	OFF			
4	Sweep Set	OFF			

Figure 6.3: The Frequency Sweeper. The Frequency Sweeper works like a four–channel bench instrument. The top–line menu commands select the frequency range for the analysis. The values selected are displayed in the center of the instrument.

channels to probes, as in the DC Meter. Additionally, the user can select a number of other display options. The real part, imaginary part, magnitude, or phase of a signal can be displayed. The vertical scale can be manipulated, and a scale–per–grid division can be selected. In conjunction with appropriate placement of the markers, a number of predefined functions can be selected and their values displayed. For example, direct computation can be made of 3–db bandwidth, 10–db bandwidth, gain–bandwidth product, and signal maxima and minima. Finally, options are provided to let the designer save and label instrument traces.

The Function Generator. The Function Generator window works like a four–channel laboratory function generator. The instrument window has three sections: a top–line menu, a display area, and setting lines. The Simulation–Time entry in the top–line menu allows the user to select the simulation time period. The Utility entry permits the window to be redrawn, printed, or exited.

The setting lines may be used to connect the instrument to a source in the circuit and to select and display a signal waveform. Selecting a channel results in a pop–down menu with selections for source connection, vertical–scale control, and waveform definition. Source connections are made in the same way as in the Frequency Sweeper described above, except that amplitude and phase

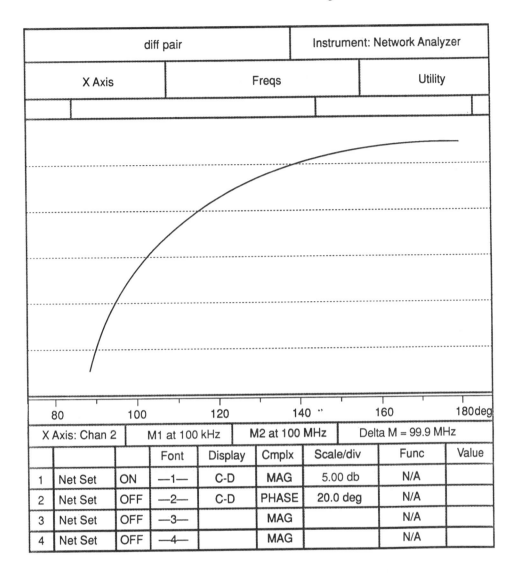

Figure 6.4: A Nichol's Plot on the Network Analyzer.

information is not required. Waveforms are picked from a menu of choices, including square wave, sine wave, pulse, step, sawtooth wave, exponential, single–frequency FM, and piecewise linear. In each case, the designer is prompted for the information needed to fully describe the waveform. Once displayed, the vertical scale can be adjusted as desired. Waveforms may be saved and recalled for future use.

The Oscilloscope. The Oscilloscope window emulates a four–channel laboratory oscilloscope. The window contains a top–line menu, a display area, a status line, and four channel–setting lines. The X–Axis menu in the top line can be used to control horizontal axis display. Normally, time is displayed; however, as in the Network Analyzer window, the user may select a vertical channel. Making such a selection will cause the instrument to function like a lab oscilloscope in horizontal–amplifier (or X–Y) mode. Marker and Utility functions just like those in the Network Analyzer window also may be selected from the top–line menu.

The channel settings are controlled just as in the Network Analyzer. Menu selections are available to label and save traces and set the vertical scale. Also as in the Network Analyzer window, a selection of predefined functions can be used in conjunction with the markers to compute design parameters. The available functions include 10% time, 90% time, 10%-90% time, overshoot, RMS (root mean square), integral, maximum, and minimum. The Oscilloscope also allows the user to apply vender–supplied or user–defined filters to trace data.

The Spectrum Analyzer. The Spectrum Analyzer window performs a DFT (discrete Fourier transform) of the data in the Oscilloscope window, using the Cooley–Tukey algorithm; that is, a fast Fourier transform. The power distribution of the input waveform is displayed as a function of frequency in the Spectrum Analyzer window.

The Spectrum Analyzer looks much like the Network Analyzer, having a top–line menu, a display area, a status line, and channel–setting lines. The top–line menu allows the designer to select a linear or log–decade display for the horizontal axis, set parameters for the DFT, control the frequency display, activate the markers, and perform Utility functions. The channel settings are controlled much as in the Network Analyzer window, except that the available functions include band–center, 10–db band–pass, and 3–db band–pass measurements, in addition to computation of maxima and minima.

Testing Circuits. As an example of how the Analog Workbench can be used to analyze circuits, a differential pair will be considered. First, the DC Meter will be used to check voltage, current, and power dissipation. Then, the Frequency Sweeper and Network Analyzer will find the gain and phase responses and the 3–db bandwidth.

The process starts by entering the Instruments menu in the Circuit Editor. Selecting DC Meter and Frequency Domain results in three new windows being displayed. All that is required to make DC measurements is to select the Analysis menu in the Circuit Editor. Then, from the resulting pop–down menu, Start Analysis is selected. A New Analysis Underway message will display in the DC Meter window to indicate that the simulation of the circuit has begun. When the analysis is complete, the DC Meter is used as described above to obtain the readings at the desired locations. Figure 6.5 shows the measurements obtained for the voltage at probe C, the current through probe F, and the power dissipated in transistor Q2.

To look at the gain and phase responses, the Frequency Sweeper first is connected to the two sources, A and B. Selecting Channel 1 in the Frequency Sweeper window produces a fill–in menu that requests the probe connection,

diff pair			Instrument: DC Meter
			Utility
#	Channel	Probes	Reading
1	DC Settings	C	7.87 V
2	DC Settings	F	712.53 uA
3	DC Settings	F*(C-E)	6.05 mW
4	DC Settings		

Figure 6.5: DC Meter screen showing measurements of the differential pair circuit. This window contains a top–line menu, a display area, a status line, and settings lines. The Log–Axis menu allows the designer to select a linear or log decade frequency display. The X–Axis menu is used to select the mode of display for the horizontal axis. If frequency is selected, this display is shown.

signal amplitude, and relative phase. To allow gain to be read directly, a 1V signal will be applied to the amplifier—half through source A and half through source B. Source B will be given a phase shift of 180 deg. To complete the instrument setup, Frequency–Range is chosen from the Instrument top–line menu, and a range of 100 kHz to 100 MHz is selected. Figure 6.6 shows the instrument with the completed settings.

To start the analog circuit analysis, the Analysis menu in the Circuit Editor is entered and the Start Analysis button is selected. The Network Analyzer window then displays a *New Analysis Underway* message, followed by updates on the progress of the simulation. In this case, the circuit is so simple that the analysis is completed in a very few seconds. To examine the gain and phase responses, Channel 1 is selected and the instrument is asked to display the difference between probe C and probe D. The Scale–Division then is set at a convenient 3 db, the trace is centered, and a label—gain —— is attached to the trace for easy reference (see Figure 6.7). Then, Channel 2 is selected and menu selections are made to display the phase of the signal. Finally, Marker 1 is positioned on the flat part of the gain trace, and the 3 db bandwidth function is selected for Channel 1. This selection causes the instrument to search for the point on the trace that is 3 db lower than the intersection of the marker with the trace. The result, 5.56 MHz, is displayed in the Value column of Channel 1.

diff pair	Instrument: Frequency Sweeper		
Frequncy Range	Linear/Log (now Log)		Utility
Present Frequency Range 100 KHz to 100 MHZ No. of Steps: 100			
			Source	Amplitude	Phase
1	Sweep Set	ON	A	.50 V	0.0 deg
2	Sweep Set	ON	B	.50 V	180 deg
3	Sweep Set	OFF			
4	Sweep Set	OFF			

Figure 6.6: Frequency Sweeper setup screen. Channel 1 has been set to be magnitude of gain in db, Channel 2 has been set as phase, and the X–Axis has been set as Vertical Channel 2.

A Schmitt trigger circuit will be used to show how the Workbench can perform time–domain analyses. A voltage source, A, is added to drive the circuit, and the output will be examined at probe B. The first step is to select the time–domain instruments, using the Instrument entry in the Circuit Editor top–line menu. This selection causes windows for a Function Generator and an Oscilloscope to be opened.

Next, the Function Generator is set up to drive the circuit. The Simulation–Time menu is used to select a 2–µs time scale for the analysis. Channel 1 is connected to source A, and a pulse waveform is selected. The instrument then prompts the user for the information required to describe the pulse. For this simulation, the parameters are: DC offset, 3.4V; amplitude, 0.4V; delay time, 100 ns; rise time, 400 ns; fall time, 400 ns; pulse width, 100 ns; and period, 1 s. The resulting waveform is displayed as shown in Figure 6.8.

To begin the simulation, the user selects the Analysis menu in the Circuit Editor and clicks the mouse over the Start Analysis button in the resulting pop–down menu. The simulation results can be viewed in the Oscilloscope window. For comparison, the input pulse is displayed in Channel 1 of the Oscilloscope. The user simply selects Channel 1, specifies connection to source A, and places the label *Input A* for reference. Next, Channel 2 is connected to probe B in the same way. The user probably will want to measure the Schmitt trigger's hysteresis. To do so, Marker 1 is positioned on the leading edge of the output, and Marker 2 is positioned on the trailing edge. The hysteresis can be read

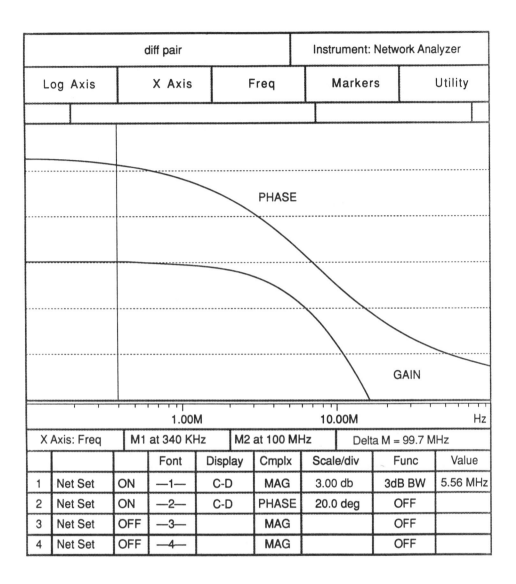

diff pair			Instrument: Network Analyzer	
Log Axis	X Axis	Freq	Markers	Utility

X Axis: Freq	M1 at 340 KHz	M2 at 100 MHz	Delta M = 99.7 MHz			

			Font	Display	Cmplx	Scale/div	Func	Value
1	Net Set	ON	—1—	C-D	MAG	3.00 db	3dB BW	5.56 MHz
2	Net Set	ON	—2—	C-D	PHASE	20.0 deg	OFF	
3	Net Set	OFF	—3—		MAG		OFF	
4	Net Set	OFF	—4—		MAG		OFF	

Figure 6.7: Frequency response for differential–pair amplifier shown on the Network Analyzer screen. This window works like a four–channel laboratory function generator. The instrument window has three sections: a top–line menu, a display area, and setting lines. The Simulation–Time entry in the top–line menu allows the user to select the simulation time period. The Utility entry permits the window to be redrawn, printed, or exited.

easily by the built–in function M2–M1 on the input signal displayed in Channel 1. The result, 24 mV, is sufficient for most ECL applications.

As a final example of the use of the basic Analog Workbench for CAE, the rejection characteristics of the 1–kHz low–pass filter shown in Figure 6.9 will be

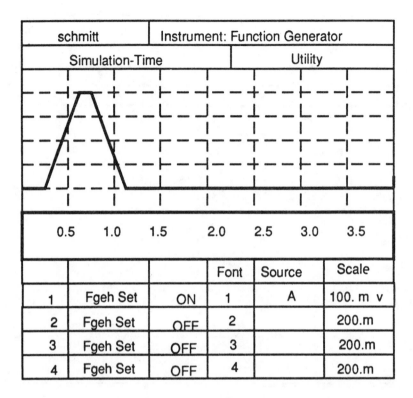

			Font	Source	Scale
1	Fgeh Set	ON	1	A	100. m v
2	Fgeh Set	OFF	2		200.m
3	Fgeh Set	OFF	3		200.m
4	Fgeh Set	OFF	4		200.m

Figure 6.8: Waveform displayed when Function Generator screen is set up to drive the circuit. This window emulates a four–channel laboratory oscilloscope. The window contains a top–line menu, a display area, a status line, and four channel–setting lines. The X–Axis menu in the top–line can be used to control horizontal–axis display.

examined. The approach will be to drive the filter with a 1–kHz square wave and to capture the output in the Oscilloscope. Then, a DFT will be run on the output waveform to check the distortion.

First, the time–domain instruments are selected from the Instruments menu in the Circuit Editor. The Function Generator is set up to supply a 5V, 1–kHz square wave. Next, the analysis is run and results are displayed in the Oscilloscope window (see Figure 6.10). The markers have been set to bracket a 5–ms segment well into the simulation. The DFT will be run on this segment.

The Spectrum Analyzer window is opened from the Instrument menu in the Circuit Editor. To run the DFT, it is necessary only to specify the interpolation method—in this case, cubic spline—and start the computation by selecting the Perform DFT menu button. The result is shown in Figure 6.11. The spectrum appears as expected. Some components of the input signal make it through the filter; everything else falls below the noise floor. The markers can be used to measure the levels of the third, fifth, and seventh harmonics—68, 73.1, and

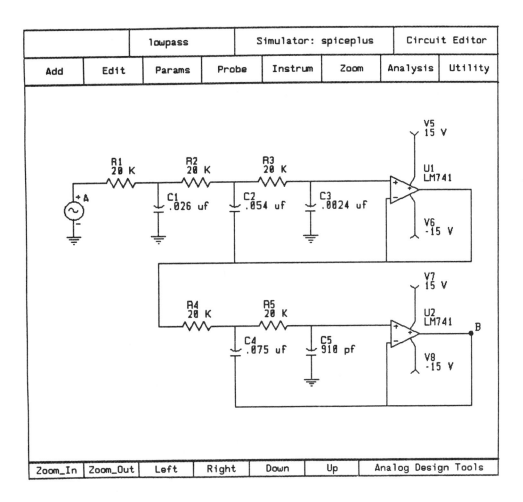

Figure 6.9: 1–kHz low–pass filter circuit screen. This window performs a Discrete Fourier Transform of the data in the Oscilloscope window using the Cooley–Tukey algorithm; that is, a Fast Fourier Transform. The power distribution of the input waveform is displayed as a function of frequency in the Spectrum Analyzer window.

72.9 db below the primary. The filter has the rejection characteristics required for the application.

Advanced CAE Tools. The techniques and tools described so far offer the designer the same functionality as would be found on traditional, manual workbench. The Analog Workbench offers many powerful features, however, that have no bench counterparts. Three of these tools are the Parametric Plotter, the Statistics Module, and the Smoke Alarm module.

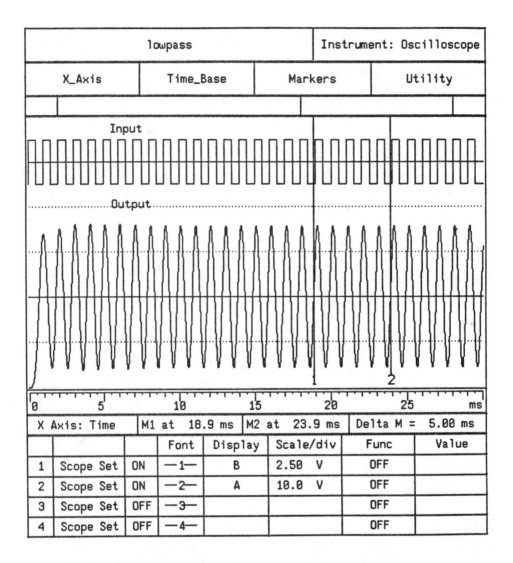

lowpass						Instrument: Oscilloscope

X_Axis	Time_Base	Markers	Utility

Input

Output

0	5	10	15	20	25	ms

X Axis: Time	M1 at 10.9 ms	M2 at 23.9 ms	Delta M = 5.00 ms

			Font	Display	Scale/div	Func	Value
1	Scope Set	ON	—1—	B	2.50 V	OFF	
2	Scope Set	ON	—2—	A	10.0 V	OFF	
3	Scope Set	OFF	—3—			OFF	
4	Scope Set	OFF	—4—			OFF	

Figure 6.10: Transient response for 1–kHz low–pass filter screen. This window shows the measurements obtained for the voltage at probe C, the current through probe F, and the power dissipated in transistor Q2.

The Parametric Plotter. The Parametric Plotter allows the designer to assign ranges of values to components, to semiconductor parameters, and to other parameters in a circuit; analyze the circuit over the ranges of values specified; and then display the results of the analyses in different types of plots. The user is free to assign any desired parameter to either axis of the plot.

To obtain Parametric Plotter results, the Analog Workbench first is set up to make the desired analysis using the procedures described above. Next, the components or parameters to be varied are specified by assigning variables to

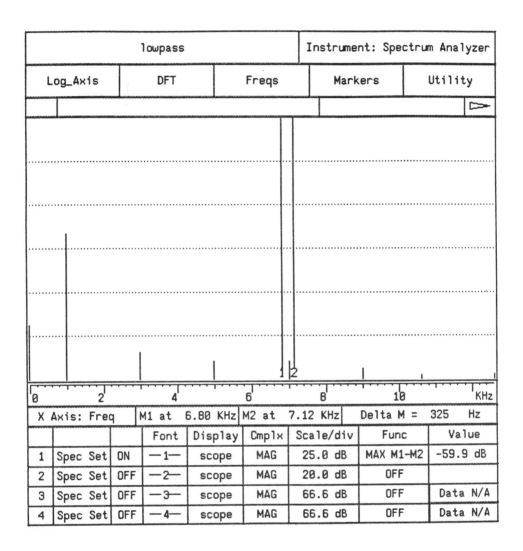

		Font	Display	Cmplx	Scale/div	Func	Value
1	Spec Set	ON	—1—	scope	MAG	25.0 dB	MAX M1-M2	-59.9 dB
2	Spec Set	OFF	—2—	scope	MAG	20.0 dB	OFF	
3	Spec Set	OFF	—3—	scope	MAG	66.6 dB	OFF	Data N/A
4	Spec Set	OFF	—4—	scope	MAG	66.6 dB	OFF	Data N/A

Figure 6.11: Spectral analysis of 1–KHz low–pass filter screen. This window shows the instrument with the completed settings.

their values. Then, the Parametric Plotter window is opened from the Instruments menu in the Circuit Editor. Finally, the Parametric Plotter is used to define ranges of values for the variables and to specify how the results of the multiple analyses are to be displayed. All settings are accomplished by using menu selections.

As an example of Parametric Plotter use, the effect on the 3–db bandwidth of varying a resistor (R5) and a capacitor (C5) in the low–pass filter circuit (see Figure 6.12) will be investigated. To start, the Frequency Sweeper and Network Analyzer are set up to measure the 3–db bandwidth, as described previously. Next, the values of R5 and C5 are replaced with the variables *res* and *cap*.

Then, the Parametric Plotter window is opened from the Instrument window in the Circuit Editor.

The menus in the Parametric Plotter lead the user through the instrument setup. Selecting Setup in the Instrument top–line menu allows the user to select *res* as the outer variable and *cap* as the inner variable and to specify the range of each. The status lines in the lower portion of the Instrument menu show that *res* will range from 18K to 22K in 1K steps and *cap* will range from 890 pf (picofarad) to 930 pf in 10–pf steps.

Next, the Plot Set menu at the bottom of the Parametric Plotter is entered to specify how the analyses will be run and displayed. The X–axis is set to be *res*,; the Y–axis is set to be read from the bandwidth value determined by the Network Analyzer, and the parameter varied is set to be *cap*. Finally, the Control menu in the Instrument top–line menu is used to start the analyses. The Parametric Plotter causes 25 analyses to be run one for each combination of *cap* and *res*. When completed, the results are displayed as shown in Figure 6.12. Among other things, the data show that a 920–pf capacitor and a 19.8K resistor would provide the 3–db bandwidth of 1 kHz that is required.

Predicting Manufacturing Yield. On a traditional workbench, or on the Analog Workbench with the techniques described so far, designs are developed with nominal component values. When circuits are built in manufacturing, however, the components used have tolerance ranges. Generally, the wider the tolerance range, the less expensive the component. Thus, a major challenge for the analog–design engineer is to develop designs that will work over the widest possible variation in component tolerances.

The Statistics module of the Analog Workbench allows engineers to predict performance variations in advance and modify their designs to account for them. The Statistics module is really two tools. The first is a Monte Carlo tool that allows the random variations in tolerances to be modeled and full production runs to be simulated. The second is a Sensitivity/Worst Case tool that assists in pinpointing the exact components that contribute most to performance degradation.

All values of components in the Analog Workbench can have tolerance values associated with them. These include values of passive components— resistance, capacitance, or inductance—and active components—op–amp open – loop gain, transistor beta, or diode–breakdown voltage—for example. Tolerances can be set on individual components, or default tolerances can be set for whole classes of components. For example, all resistors can be made +5%, –5%. Several distribution types—flat or Gaussian, for example—are available through menu picks, or users can define their own. Quality–assurance or incoming inspection data can be used to specify the distribution, if desired.

As an example of the use of the Monte Carlo tool, a 50–circuit manufacturing run for the 1–kHz low–pass filter circuit shown in Figure 6.13 will be simulated. Default tolerances will be set for passive components, using the Parameters menu in the top line of the Circuit Editor. Resistors will be made ±5%, capacitors ±10%, and voltage supplies ±10%. Only two parameters in the LM741 op amps

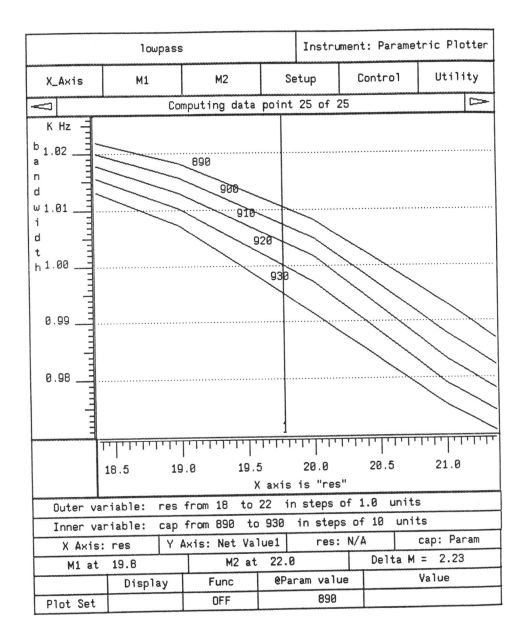

Figure 6.12: Parametric Plotter data screen. This window displays a *New Analysis Underway* message, followed by updates on the progress of the simulation.

will be toleranced. The offset voltage will be toleranced ±50%, and the open–loop gain ±20%.

First, the Frequency Sweeper and Network Analyzer are set up to measure 3–db bandwidth, as described above. Then, to run the Monte Carlo simulation,

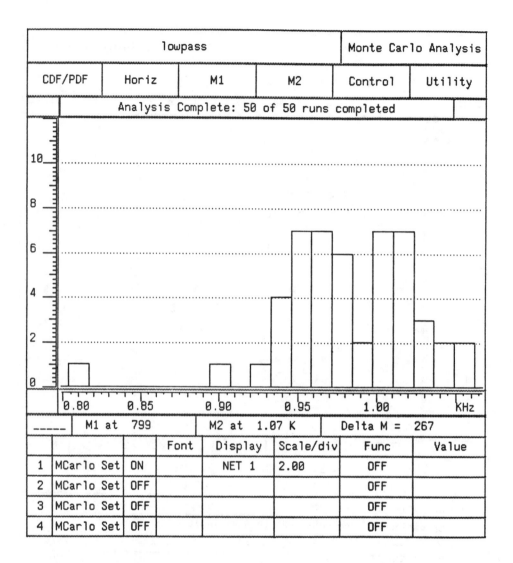

Figure 6.13: Monte Carlo analysis screen showing 1–kHz low–pass filter. The Schmitt trigger circuit shown here will be used to show how the Workbench can perform time domain analyses. A voltage source, A, has been added to drive the circuit, and the output will be examined at probe B. The first step is to select the time–domain instruments using the Instrument entry in the Circuit Editor top–line menu. This selection causes windows for a Function Generator and Oscilloscope to be opened.

Statistics is selected from the Instrument pop–down menu in the Circuit Editor. This results in a second pop–down menu, from which Monte Carlo is selected. The Settings portion of the instrument is used to select the 3–db measurement from the Network Analyzer as the parameter of interest. Finally, the Control menu from the Monte Carlo top–line menu is used to set the number of analyses, 50, and start the simulation.

The Analog Workbench now will run 50 separate simulations. For each simulation run, a random value of each toleranced parameter will be selected from its specified range. When all the runs have been completed, the data are collected and displayed as a histogram of different values for the 3–db bandwidth. The results for the low–pass filter are shown in Figure 6.14. Displaying the data as a cumulative distribution function, instead of as a histogram or probability–density function, allows the predicted failure rate to be measured directly. In this case, if the minimum acceptable bandwidth is 0.95 kHz, a 19.5% rejection rate is predicted.

Once the designer becomes aware that there is a yield problem, the Sensitivity/Worst Case instrument can be used to pinpoint the particular components that contribute to the problem most. To run a sensitivity analysis on the low–pass filter circuit, the Sensitivity/Worst Case window is opened from the Instruments menu in the Circuit Editor top–line menu. Then, the Settings menus are used to select the 3–db bandwidth reading from the Network Analyzer. Finally, the analyses are started from the Control window in the Instrument top–line menu.

The Sensitivity tool starts by performing an analysis with all components set to their nominal values. Then, it performs one analysis for each circuit parameter that has a tolerance assigned. For each of these runs, it increases one parameter value by 40% of its positive tolerance, to determine the ratio of change in the output function to change in the parameter and to determine the relative direction of change. If the output function, in this case 3–db bandwidth, goes up as the parameter value goes up, the sign of the sensitivity number is positive; otherwise, it is negative. In this way, a relative sensitivity, or the change in performance caused by a 1% change in parameter value, is determined. The relative sensitivities calculated for the low–pass filter example are shown in Figure 6.15. As a final step, the instrument uses the information on the relative direction of change and the component tolerance values to compute predicted best– and worst–case values for the bandwidth.

The Sensitivity/Worst Case output shows that R3, R4, R5, C2, C3, C4, and C5 contribute most to variations in the bandwidth. As a quick fix, the tolerances on these devices will be tightened to ±1% for the resistors and ±5% for the capacitors. Running another Monte Carlo simulation shows that all circuits now can be expected to meet the 0.95–kHz specification (see Figure 6.16).

Safe–Operating–Area Analysis. Each component used in a design has a safe operating area (SOA). Worst–case conditions of power–supply voltage, ambient temperature, loading, or signal input can cause components to operate in regions outside this SOA. The results of operating a component outside its SOA sometimes can be spectacular: smoke, flame, or even an explosion. More common than a catastrophic failure, and perhaps more insidious, is the lowered reliability of components stressed beyond their acceptable limits. Mean times between failure (MTBFs) shrink, performance degrades quickly, and mortality rates soar. Ideally, a designer would analyze each circuit under worst–case

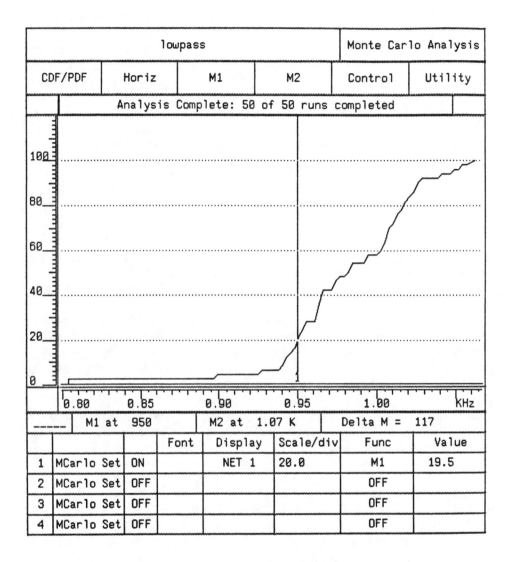

Figure 6.14: Low–pass filter failure–rate screen. This window displays the waveform resulting from the calculation of the filter failure rate.

operating conditions and check to see that all components are operating within their SOAs.

Performing such an analysis can be extremely difficult. The SOA is bounded by a number of limiting factors. For example, Figure 6.17 shows the SOA for a bipolar transistor bounded by maximum collector current, maximum power dissipation, secondary breakdown, and maximum collector–emitter voltage. Different effects predominate at different operating points. To perform an SOA analysis, the interaction among all these factors must be known. The Smoke

lowpass						Sensitivity/Worst Case Analysis	
Display			Order		Control		Utility
Comp	Parameter	Nom	Min	Max	Relative Sensitivity		
C5	Capacitance	910p	1n	819p	-5.951	————————	
R4	Resistance	20K	21K	19K	-5.019	———————	
R5	Resistance	20K	21K	19K	-4.975	———————	
C4	Capacitance	75n	82.5n	67.5n	-4.142	——————	
C3	Capacitance	2.4n	2.64n	2.16n	-4.101	——————	
C2	Capacitance	54n	59.4n	48.6n	-3.286	—————	
R3	Resistance	20K	21K	19K	-2.899	————	
R2	Resistance	20K	21K	19K	-1.773	——	
R1	Resistance	20K	21K	19K	-1.375	—	
C1	Capacitance	26n	28.6n	23.4n	-1.178	—	
Analysis Complete: 22 of 22 runs completed							Next Page
			Display	Min	Nom	Max	
1	Sens Set	ON	NET 1	860.95 Hz	1.00 KHz	1.17 KHz	
2	Sens Set	OFF					
3	Sens Set	OFF					
4	Sens Set	OFF					

Figure 6.15: Sensitivity analysis for low–pass filter screen. To begin the simulation, the user selects the Analysis menu in the Circuit Editor and clicks the mouse over the Start Analysis button in the resulting popdown menu. Now, the simulation results can be viewed in the Oscilloscope window. For comparison, the input pulse is displayed in Channel 1 of the Oscilloscope.

Alarm module checks many parameters for each device. For example, for a bipolar transistor, the following values are checked:

- Maximum base current
- Maximum collector current
- Maximum collector–base voltage
- Maximum collector–emitter voltage
- Maximum power dissipation
- Maximum junction temperature
- Secondary breakdown effects

The Smoke Alarm takes the junction–case and case–ambient thermal resistances into account in making the computations.

The maximum operating conditions are specified on the manufacturer's data sheets and are included in the library information provided with the Analog Workbench. Most users, however, derate the manufacturer's values to provide a design safety factor. Many times, the customer will provide specified derating values for use in the design. This is especially true when the customer is the military. Also, different customers or different applications may demand different derating factors. To accommodate these varying requirements, the Analog Workbench allows users to specify their own derating files. In fact,

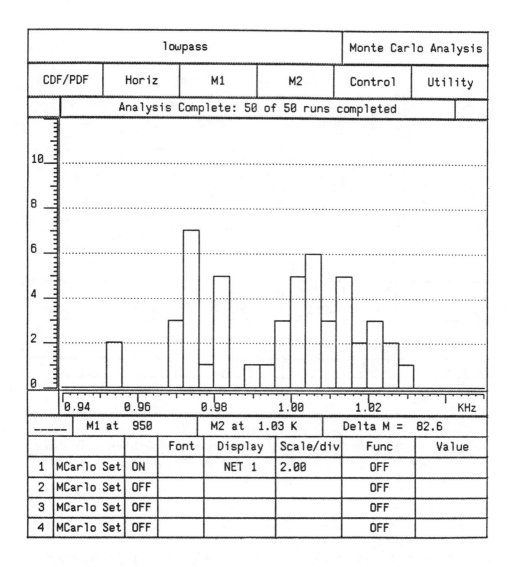

Figure 6.16: Monte Carlo Analysis screen for revised low–pass filter design revisions. This screen shows another example of the use of the basic Analog Workbench for CAE: the rejection characteristics of the 1–KHz low–pass filter.

different derating files can be used on the same design, depending on the customer or application.

As an example of SOA analysis with the Analog Workbench Smoke Alarm module, the current amplifier shown in Figure 6.18 will be checked. The analysis begins by opening the Smoke Alarm window from the Instruments menu in the Circuit Editor window. This action alerts the simulator that additional analysis data must be saved. Next, the Function Generator and Oscilloscope are used to simulate the normal performance of the circuit. Finally, menus in the

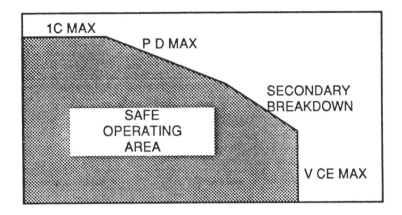

Figure 6.17: Safe operating area for a bipolar transistor. First, the time–domain instruments are selected from the Instruments menu in the Circuit Editor. The Function Generator is set up to supply a 5V, 1–kHz square wave. Next, the analysis is run, and the results are displayed in the Oscilloscope window shown here.

Smoke Alarm window are used to select a derating file and perform the SOA analysis.

The results are displayed quickly in the Smoke Alarm window (see Figure 6.19). The analysis shows that the maximum junction temperature has been exceeded in one diode, and that three transistors have exceeded their maximum collector–emitter voltages. For ease of reference, *smoke icons* are displayed next to the offending components in the Circuit Editor (see Figure 6.20). The designer now could use the Sensitivity tool to determine which circuit parameters contribute most to the excessive values and the Parametric Plotter to help select more suitable component values.

The Importance of Model Libraries

Throughout the previous discussions, circuits have been entered and tests performed just as if laboratory instruments were being used to test real circuits. For the simulated tests to have validity, the mathematical models of the circuit components must be extremely accurate over their full operating ranges. There are two parts to providing accurate models for circuit simulators. The first is to ensure that the models for the basic types of circuit components—BJTs, JFETs, zener diodes, and nonlinear magnetic cores—are accurate. The second part of the problem is to ensure that the parameters for particular parts are accurate. For example, for BJTs, the literature of device physics contains several models

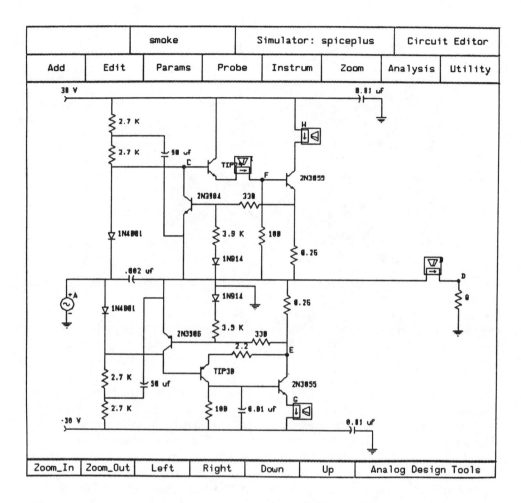

Figure 6.18 : Current amplifier screen. The Spectrum Analyzer window is opened from the Instrument menu in the Circuit Editor. To run the DFT, it is necessary only to specify the interpolation method—in this case, cubic spline—and start the computation by selecting the *Perform DFT* menu button. The result is shown in this screen.

that can be used to predict performance. One of the most common and widely used is the Ebers–Moll 1 model. But, as Figure 6.21 shows, this model gives less accurate results than does the Gummel–Poon model used in the Analog Workbench. The equations of the Gummel–Poon model use 40 different parameters, only a few of which can be obtained from the device data sheets. The SPICE simulator supplies default values for all the parameters, but to predict the behavior of a particular part—the 2N2222, for example—more precise values are needed.

smoke					Instrument: Smoke Alarm
Display		Order		Control	Utility

Comp	Param	Derate%	Derate Max	Peak	% of Derated Maximum	
D2	TJ	100.0	175.000	122.767K	70.2K	⋙⋙⋙⋙⋙⋙⋙⋙⋙⋙<
Q3	VCE	50.0	20.000	38.416	192.1	⋙⋙⋙⋙⋙⋙⋙⋙⋙⋙<
Q6	VCE	50.0	30.000	38.511	128.4	⋙⋙⋙⋙⋙⋙⋙⋙⋙⋙<
Q5	VCE	50.0	30.000	38.056	126.9	⋙⋙⋙⋙⋙⋙⋙⋙⋙⋙<
R3	PDM	55.0	137.500m	135.922m	98.9	————————
Q3	VCB	100.0	40.000	37.886	94.7	————————
R4	PDM	55.0	137.500m	129.923m	94.5	————————
Q5	TJ	62.5	125.000	96.714	77.4	——————
C5	CV	100.0	50.000	19.359	38.7	———
C4	CV	100.0	50.000	19.271	38.5	———
Q6	VCB	100.0	100.000	38.416	38.4	———
Q5	VCB	100.0	100.000	38.056	38.1	———
Q3	TJ	83.3	125.000	41.365	33.1	——
Q6	TJ	62.5	125.000	29.294	23.4	——
Q4 ·	TJ	83.3	125.000	27.000	21.6	—

Next Page	16 Elements Analyzed	
	Ta = 27.0 C	Derate File: project

Figure 6.19: Results of safe–operating–area analysis (shown on Smoke Alarm screen). As an example of Parametric Plotter use, the effect on 3–db bandwidth of varying a resistor (R5) and a capacitor (C5) in the low–pass filter circuit shown here will be investigated.

Two approaches can be used to obtain device parameters. The first employs sophisticated measuring equipment to gather data that can be used to derive the parameters. This approach gives quite good values for the particular device measured, but, since parts—even those from the same manufacturer—vary widely, such models generally are not useful for designing circuits using off–the–shelf components. The second method involves optimizing model parameters to match device performance to the data–sheet curves provided by the manufacturer. This approach has the advantage of providing a generic model, but the process is quite complicated and time–consuming. The best approach is a combination of the two methods. Measurements are made to obtain good approximations that can be used as starting points in optimizing the parameters to match manufacturers' data–sheet curves.

The most common simulator used for circuit design is SPICE. In its standard (or public–domain) form, it contains models for many basic components, including BJTs, JFET, and diodes. Users, however, design with components like operational amplifiers, comparators, analog switches, opto–couplers, sample–

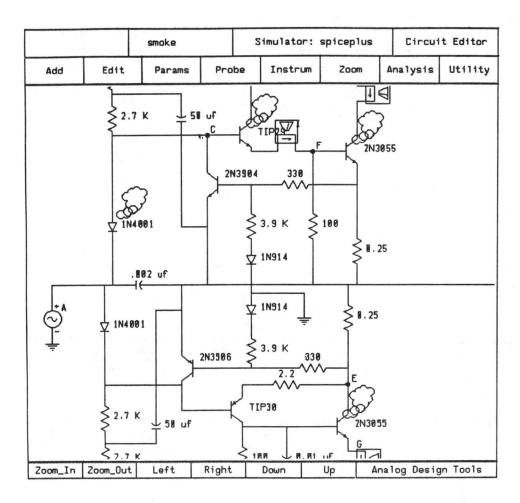

Figure 6.20: Smoke icons displayed on components (in the Circuit Editor screen). This is an example of the use of the Monte Carlo tool, a 50–circuit manufacturing run for the 1–kHz low–pass filter circuit shown here.

and–hold amplifiers, pulse–width modulators, and SCRs (silicon–controlled rectifiers). Designers must either model these complicated devices themselves or obtain the models from vendors that are in the business of modeling such components. Valid, for example, offers a full range of complex device models and a selection of nearly 2000 parameter sets for particular components.

One area that has always posed particular difficulty for the designer using circuit simulation is power design. Most available simulation tools fall short in two areas. First, the power designer needs complex component models like pulse–width modulator and current–mode–controller ICs. Second, the magnetic components used in power circuits are complex nonlinear devices, not the simple linear devices modeled by basic SPICE.

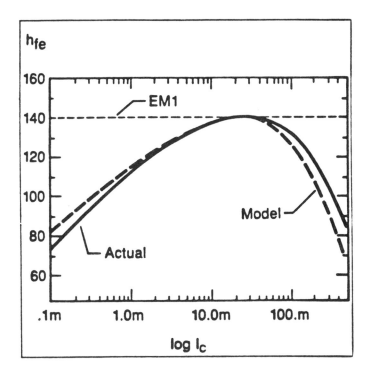

Figure 6.21: Comparison of Ebbers–Moll 1, Gummel–Poon, and actual values for 2N2222 transistor. The results for the low–pass filter are shown here. This screen displays the data as a cumulative distribution function, instead of a histogram or probability density function, which allows the predicted failure rate to be measured directly.

Integrating the Simulator into a Design Environment

The need for simulation of both IC and board–level circuits has contributed to a growing need for a versatile analog–circuit simulator that can be used by several departments within an organization. Because many engineers are involved in the design of a typical board or system, many people must share the same information—including circuit descriptions, simulation models, the stimulus patterns that drive the simulation, and the simulation results. Sharing this information requires the use of a common language for analog– and digital– circuit simulation or at least the ability to translate easily between the two formats. EES refers to PRECISE as a corporate circuit simulator, because it is designed to work in a shared–resource environment that includes several design groups within a large organization.

An important issue that relates to the concept of a corporate–wide simulator is the ability to run the simulator on a variety of hardware platforms. Even though the departments within an organization have different computers, all the departments need to share the same simulation data. Data is shared through a network that links computer resources.

Simulation programs that are designed for portability among a number of popular computers help to ease the data–transfer problem. To ensure that the simulator works precisely the same across all hardware platforms, it is important that the same program—not just a look–alike program designed for the idiosyncrasies of a specific machine—be run on each computer. By writing programs in a standard high–level language, simulator designers can achieve straightforward portability across operating systems as well as across hardware platforms. PRECISE, for example, is written in FORTRAN 77 code and runs on machines such as the DEC VAX and MicroVAX under either VMS or UNIX operating systems; the IBM–PC and Sun, Apollo, and Valid workstations under UNIX; Cray supercomputers under COS and UNICOS; Elxsi (San Jose, California) supercomputers under EMBOS; and IBM–compatible mainframes under VM/CMS.

In working with all these hardware platforms, it also is important for a simulator to work with the various other design tools that run on those machines. The most basic form of interaction is for the simulator to receive circuit descriptions from a schematic–capture database. Because SPICE is an industry–standard tool, its data format is supported by most design–automation vendors; thus, SPICE files can be generated by programs associated with the schematic–capture program. Although the PRECISE data format is not identical to that of SPICE (SPICE's functions essentially constitute a subset of PRECISE's), EES provides a utility program that converts SPICE files into PRECISE format.

It also is useful to pass simulation results back to the schematic–capture database and display them on screen to make it easy for users to view both the simulation waveforms and the circuit that produced them. Figure 6.22 shows the display of information between a CAE workstation screen used by an analog–design engineer and a circuit simulator. The simulator uses the schematic netlist to perform the analyses requested by the design engineer. The engineer can place visual probes on nodes in the schematic and view output waveforms during a simulation. Element values altered during the simulation can be back–annotated to the schematic database.

With some CAE packages, users can place probes in their on–screen schematics to indicate where they want to read simulated voltage and/or current values. The system then passes information about the probes and the analysis to be performed to the simulation package, which simulates the circuit as needed and displays the results on the screen. It is possible to implement this same capability with any schematic capture program and any database that provides access to its data. The extent of data access is an important qualification to keep in mind when choosing design software, because some design automation vendors keep their databases wholly or partially closed.

Another issue related to sharing simulation data is the ability to share data with individuals outside an organization. This is especially evident when dealing with model libraries. Each ASIC vendor develops device models that

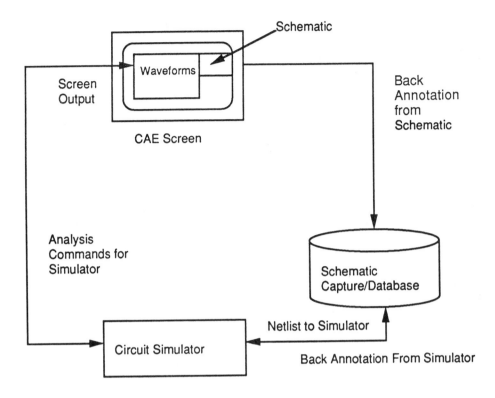

Figure 6.22: CAE workstation screen. The screenshows the display of information between a CAE workstation screen used by an analog–design engineer and a circuit simulator.

match the performance of the devices in its ASICs, for example; ASIC designers, therefore, must gain access to these models to make sure that the correct performance is being simulated. Similarly, users will have to gain access to models for off–the–shelf ICs. At this writing, such models are available only from simulator companies such as EES.

• Digital and Analog Simulation Meet •

The latest requirement for analog–circuit simulators is that they work with digital simulators to simulate circuits that contain both analog and digital components. The first steps have been taken toward this capability by running analog and digital simulators concurrently in a multitasking environment such as UNIX. The programs can pass data back and forth as required to simulate the circuit. Further refinements will smooth this process to provide efficient interaction, so that designers can simulate the increasing number of ICs and boards that contain both analog and digital components.

An analog–circuit simulator can, of course, simulate digital circuits. But the time required to simulate every gate in a complex digital design is enormous, and the results would not be worth the effort. Analog–circuit simulators do have a role in simulating digital circuits, however. By performing an analog simulation of just the critical paths through a complex digital ASIC, the user can be assured that signals will propagate as expected—taking all transistor and parasitic factors into account.

A Basic Set of Analysis Functions

SPICE allows the use of several simulation approaches that fall into three main categories: DC analysis, transient analysis and AC analysis. Within these categories, SPICE can provide DC transfer curves, sensitivity analysis, noise analysis, distortion analysis, and Fourier analysis. Some versions of SPICE add other functions: PRECISE, for instance, offers radiation simulation, worst–case analysis, and Monte Carlo analysis.

DC analysis furnishes the most basic information about a circuit. This mode can be used to determine a circuit's operating point. SPICE considers a circuit to be in an equilibrium state for this analysis, with capacitors open and inductors shorted. DC voltages and currents are simulated. Within the DC–analysis mode, a DC transfer curve can be obtained and a sensitivity analysis performed. SPICE computes the transfer curve by incrementing input voltage values automatically. For each input value, SPICE gives the ratio of the output voltage to the input voltage, as well as the values of the equivalent input and output resistors.

Also within DC–analysis mode, sensitivity analysis helps the user to anticipate the effects of typical variances in component values due to the components' tolerances. The analysis presents a report on the effect of each component parameter on a node's voltage at the quiescent–bias point. This information allows the user to determine which components must have small tolerances, which ensures that these components do not undermine the circuit's operating characteristics. If specifying components with small tolerances is not an adequate prevention measure, the user also can determine which design parameters should be changed to achieve the intended operating point.

In the second major analysis mode, transient analysis, SPICE calculates a circuit's time–domain response for small and large signals. In this mode, SPICE allows the user to measure phase shift or delay time, compare the shapes of output and input waveforms, view spikes, and determine switching characteristics (including rise and fall times). Transient–analysis mode includes Fourier analysis. SPICE decomposes a periodic signal into a DC component and harmonics of the given fundamental frequency.

AC analysis is the third main analysis mode in SPICE. In this mode, SPICE calculates a circuit's frequency response across a range of user–defined frequencies. SPICE automatically increments the frequency of one or more input signals and computes the signals' amplitude gain and phase shift as they pass through the circuit. Results are presented as Bode plots.

AC analysis includes noise and distortion analysis. In noise analysis, SPICE computes the noise that a circuit generates, based on the noise produced by each component. SPICE can display the total output noise and the equivalent input noise for each frequency in an AC analysis. In distortion analysis, SPICE calculates the distortion introduced when the input signal mixes two close frequencies, as in an intermodulation between signals. The distortion is measured at a specific output node and is calculated for every frequency covered by the AC analysis.

How to Simulate Radiation Effects

As an example of how an analog–circuit simulator's analysis capabilities can be used, consider a radiation simulation that is applicable to aerospace applications. This example involves a single semiconductor P–N junction in a nonvolatile SOS (silicon on sapphire) RAM. In this case, an analysis of just one junction is quite useful, because it shows the radiation dosage and duration required to change the state of the RAM cell. In a satellite, a change of one cell in such a RAM due to cosmic rays could mean complete failure of the satellite. For other types of devices and circuits, the procedure given here for one junction can be extended to simulating whole circuits consisting of many semiconductor junctions and other components.

Radiation effects can be modeled as a photocurrent pulse through the P–N junction (see Figure 6.23). The equation describing this effect includes variables for the junction's area and diffusion length, the radiation–dose rate (*gam*), the minority current lifetime (*tau*), the pulse width of the photocurrent pulse (*pw*), and the time delay of the photocurrent pulse (*delay*). Because these types of specialized parameters typically are not available from a device–model library, they must be entered by the user. Some of the variables should be varied to obtain the junction's performance limits, too. Parameters are entered using the notation:

. *SET TAU=0.3U GAM=1.75E6 DELAY=.1U PW=.4U

where U represents a microsecond. To get the junction's response over time, the time is swept using the instruction:

*SWEEP TIME FROM 0 TO 1U BY .02U

The simulated values for the photocurrent and the resulting current through the junction then are plotted according to the command:

*PLOT I(IPHOTO) I(DJUNCTN)

The graph shown in Figure 6.24 is the final result of the simulation process. Armed with this information, a designer could take the appropriate steps to either install shielding around the nonvolatile RAM or make changes to the

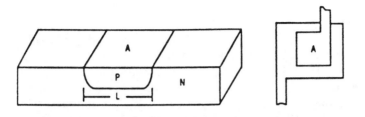

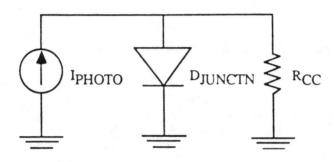

PHOTOCURRENT EQUATION

$I_{PP}=GAM(QGAL)[ERR[SQRT(T/TAU)]-U(T-PW)ERF[SQRT((T-PW)/TAU]$

A	=	Area of the junction
L	=	Diffusion length
Gam	=	Dose rate
Tau	=	Minority current life time
PW	=	The pulse width of the photocurrent pulse
Delay	=	Time delay of the photocurrent pulse

Figure 6.23: Radiation effects. Radiation effects can be modeled as a photocurrent pulse through the P–N junction.

process by which the RAM is fabricated to make it resistant to the anticipated radiation levels.

Vary Parameters for a Good Look at Performance

SPICE includes a temperature–variation feature that can be used in any of the major analysis modes. For any given analysis, SPICE automatically performs successive evaluations while iterating the temperature value.

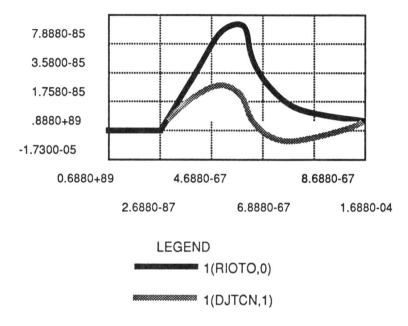

7.8880-85

3.5800-85

1.7580-85

.8880+89

-1.7300-05

0.6880+89   4.6880-67   8.6880-67

2.6880-87   6.8880-67   1.6880-04

LEGEND

1(RIOTO,0)

1(DJTCN,1)

Figure 6.24: Current responses in the P–N junction. This graph shows the final result of the simulation process.

The ability to vary a parameter, such as temperature, while an analysis is performed is an important aspect of an analog–circuit simulator. SPICE is limited to iterating one variable at a time. For example, SPICE calculates a circuit's performance over a range of temperatures by setting a temperature value and varying time or frequency as in a basic analysis procedure. SPICE then iterates the temperature value and reruns the analysis. In this way, a picture of the circuit's behavior over a range of temperatures is created. SPICE also allows the user to alter element values and calculate different operating points for a circuit.

This procedure of iterating one variable (such as temperature) against one other variable (such as time) is called single–domain analysis. SPICE provides this ability, but in a limited form. Specifically, each domain remains separate, so there is little flexibility in how the variables change in relation to each other. PRECISE not only adds the ability to vary time, frequency, temperature, and device–parameter values against each other, but also permits the user to vary them in any combination (see Figure 6.25). Thus, SPICE provides analysis options that allow a circuit to be optimized in ways that are virtually impossible with prototypes.

A simple example of mixed–domain analysis can be seen in simulating a circuit that controls the tone in an audio amplifier. The tone–control circuit is

Inner Variable \ Outer Variable	Temperature	Parametric	Statistical	Frequency
Temperature		Parameter variation with temperature	Monte Carlo temperature analysis	Circuit response with frequency over temperature
Parametric	Parameter variation with temperature		Monte Carlo with parameter changes fixed	Circuit response with frequency over parameters
Statistical	Monte Carlo temperature analysis frequency	Monte Carlo with varying statistics	parameter	Circuit response with changes fixed
Frequency	AC temperature response	AC parametric response	AC Monte Carlo response	
Time	Transient response with temperature	Transient response with	Transient Monte Carlo parameters	

Figure 6.25: Mixed–domain analyses. PRECISE not only adds the ability to vary time, frequency, temperature, and device–parameter values against each other, but also permits the user to vary them in any combination.

based on two operational amplifiers whose function is governed by three potentiometers for setting treble, bass, and midrange. The requirement in this case is to ensure that the circuit will perform as expected for all possible settings of the pots at all possible input frequencies.

Two of the variables—the midrange pot setting and the input frequency—can be varied with respect to each other. The pot is varied by setting the percentage of the total resistance desired; thus it ranges from 0% to 100% and is varied in increments of 25% for this example. The frequency is swept from 10 Hz to 100 kHz. By making it easy to implement the necessary variations in pot values versus frequency, PRECISE provides a straightforward way to get a complete picture of how the circuit performs without running SPICE many times over.

This example shows a histogram of the voltage at node 16 as a result of VIN varying between -.005V and .005V.

```
PRECISE  : >
PRECISE  : >option device = 3
PRECISE  : >sim amp
PRECISE  : >sweep cases from 1 to 200
PRECISE  : >gauss .005 vin
PRECISE  : >histo v (16)
PRECISE  : >go
```

DC MULTIPOINT ANALYSIS COMPLETED TO : 2.0000E+02

HIT RETURN FOR OUTPUT

```
                          AMP                                                      27.0 DEG
MIN  4.851D+00      MAX       8.337D+00AVG   6.449D00  STD DV 5.668D-01 V(16)
4.851D+00           1         ----
5.026D+00           2         --------
5.200D+00           2         ---------
5.374D+00           4         ------------
5.549S+00           11        ------------------
5.723D+00           15        -----------------------
5.897D+00           18        ---------------------------
6.072D+00           23        ------------------------------------------
6.246D+00           21        -------------------------------------
6.420D+00           24        ---------------------------------------------
6.594D+00           22        -------------------------------------------
6.769D+00           19        ------------------------------
6.943D+00           15        -----------------------
7.117D+00           10        ----------------
7.292D+00           6         --------------
7.466D+00           3         -----------
7.640D+00           1         ----
7.814D+00           2         --------
7.989D+00           0
8.163D+00           1         ---
```

Figure 6.26: Monte Carlo analyses shown in histogram form. This example shows a histogram of the voltage at node 16 as a result of *vin* varying between –0.005V and 0.005V.

Statistical Analysis Accounts for Device Tolerances

The ability to compute statistical variations also is available in PRECISE in the form of Monte Carlo analysis, which can help predict product yield. Monte Carlo analysis randomly varies parameter values within their tolerance limits to show how tolerance variations are likely to interact in the actual circuit. The information obtained from Monte Carlo analysis can be shown in histogram form (see Figure 6.26). A related function available in PRECISE is worst–case, or tolerance, analysis. Component values are assigned symmetric or asymmetric distributions, and PRECISE calculates the worst–case maximum and minimum of a target output, based on the distribution and the sensitivity. An analysis of the circuit for these extremes shows a set of upper and lower circuit–response limits.

Monte Carlo analysis could be applied to a tone–control circuit by giving resistors and capacitors uniformly distributed random values within 25% of their nominal settings. PRECISE then combines the functions from the frequency and statistical domains to generate the AC Monte Carlo response; the circuit's frequency response is computed for each random setting of the resistor and capacitor values.

For all the available simulation options, SPICE accepts an input file containing both circuit descriptions and commands that tell SPICE what the user wants. After getting this file, SPICE runs in batch mode; users cannot change any parameters or see any results until the run is finished. Then, if changes must be made, another batch run is necessary. One of the most significant differences between PRECISE and SPICE is that PRECISE is interactive rather than batch–oriented. That is, partial results can be obtained and alterations made to the analysis to get what the user wants without waiting for another run. SPICE's internal structure had to be modified extensively to permit PRECISE to run interactively, but PRECISE still works just as SPICE does in calculating a circuit response.

Simulation of a Board–Level Circuit

To see how an analog–circuit simulator works from beginning to end on a board–level circuit, consider an analysis of a Butterworth filter based on two op amps. The first consideration, as with the tone–control circuit presented earlier, is to model the components involved. With SPICE, the user can develop either a transistor–level model or a macro model that relies on internal SPICE characteristics. Because neither of these approaches is easy, EES provides a library of precharacterized components, such as transistors, comparators, and op amps. In selecting or developing such models, it is good to bear in mind that macro models take less time to simulate than do transistor models.

The circuit–topology description that the simulator will use could be listed by hand or by a schematic–capture system used to draw the circuit. Some of the capacitors may be designated as *cvalue* in the topology, which designates them as variables. These capacitors influence the filter's high–pass corner frequency. By making the capacitors' values variable, the user can direct PRECISE to determine the sensitivity of the filter to different component values.

The flowchart in Figure 6.27 shows some of the steps that can be used to analyze the Butterworth filter. Having created the schematic and defined the topology, PRECISE is ready to check the topology for errors. PRECISE flags errors before beginning to simulate, while SPICE simply aborts or ignores the part of the analysis containing the error.

Once the topology is correct, the user can verify the filter's bias conditions. Then, the real analysis of the circuit begins. PRECISE can be used to simulate two domains in the same simulation to determine the filter's sensitivity to changing capacitance values. To analyze the change in corner frequency with changes in *cvalue*, the program must calculate the response of the output across a

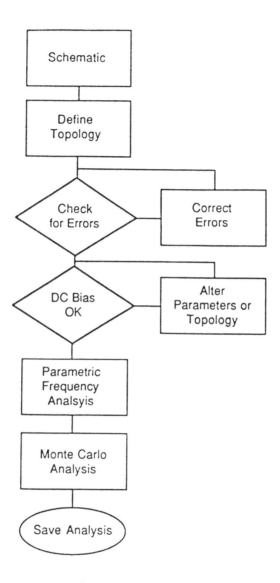

Figure 6.27: The Butterworth filter. This flowchart shows some of the steps that can be used to analyze the Butterworth filter.

range of frequencies and change the capacitor values during the same simulation. (A similar procedure can be used to analyze gain as a function of resistance values.)

Capabilities such as Monte Carlo analysis are especially useful for helping designers to tailor circuits to harsh environments, such as those found in space, at sea, or in automobiles. For a large variety of design tasks, a good analog–circuit simulator can save many hours of tinkering with a breadboard. In addition, the simulator provides information that is practically impossible to obtain from testing a breadboard. The analog–circuit simulator promises to become increasingly valuable as circuits get more complex and run at higher frequencies.

CHAPTER 7

PHYSICAL LAYOUT— PRINTED CIRCUIT BOARDS

• Layout as the Job of a Specialist •

As in the process of schematic entry, there is confusion as to where PCB layout actually fits in the design cycle and who is responsible for this task. The placement of components and component blocks on the PCB, and the routing of wire paths between these blocks, could be considered either the back end of the design phase or the front end of the manufacturing process.

The result of the physical–layout process, in fact, is a manufacturing plan— a physical plot (or wiring map of the board) and PG tapes that could be used to drive automated (computer–controlled) drilling and milling machines. The wiring plot, showing the location of components, the mounting holes for their pins and leads, the surrounding solder pads, and the wiring paths between them, typically is plotted on a transparent plastic acetate. In the manufacturing process, a copper–covered phenolic board is coated with a photosensitive resist material and is exposed to a light shining through the photoplot. When (say) a positive resist is developed, it forms a hard crust that duplicates the desired wiring pattern; other areas of the resist layer are dissolved, exposing the copper metal underneath. The board is placed in a chemical bath that etches away the exposed copper in all areas except those protected by the hardened resist. This remaining resist material is dissolved in the final manufacturing steps, exposing the copper wiring pattern underneath. The through–holes for component leads are drilled, the components are mounted, and their leads are soldered to the pads (and sometimes trimmed afterward). In the last step, the metal side of the board (all the exposed copper, in particular) is coated with a plastic material (like nail polish), which prevents further etching or oxidation.

This basic process becomes more complicated as the density of a circuit—especially a digital circuit—increases. Rather than placing wiring channels on just one or two sides of board, it now is customary to build multilayer boards by etching a number of very thin circuit boards and sandwiching them together. This requires a higher degree of precision in the etching and drilling processes, since through–holes and vias (electrical paths between various wiring layers) must line up exactly when the final product is assembled. Multilayer boards with up to eight layers are common throughout the electronics industry, although precision manufacturing techniques allow even more. Many ultra–high–density, performance–driven electronic systems—supercomputers and defense electronics—will use circuit boards with up to 48 wiring layers.

Other manufacturing complications include the methods by which the components are mounted and soldered to the board. If they are stuffed and soldered by hand, the spacings between components and the size of the solder pads must be large enough to allow the human operators to get their fingers in. If components are stuffed into the board by automatic insertion equipment, the location of pads and holes must be much more precise—along precisely controlled axes—but still large enough for the fingers of the insertion machinery to move in and out. Spacings also are influenced by the soldering method, whether the component leads go through the board and consequently are available for soldering on just one side, or whether the leads will rest on the surface of the board, forcing solder to be applied to both sides of the board. Finally, there are new circuit–board materials—plastic flex circuits, used in space– and weight–sensitive applications such as aircraft controls and hand–held 35–mm (millimeter—one thousandth of a meter) cameras—that force entirely new requirements on the physical layout process.

As a consequence, PCB layout traditionally has been the job of manufacturing specialists, who typically were concerned less with the performance and operation of the electronic circuit than with the requirements of the manufacturing process. Layout specialists figure out (usually by trial and error) how to arrange all of a circuit's components so that they fit onto a PCB of a certain size. Then, with even more trial and error, they decide how to route the board's traces so that all the components are interconnected properly. It is possible, as with semiconductor manufacturing, to make perfectly valid electrical interconnections between components using microscopically thin lines, or traces. But such lines are practically impossible to create with PCB–etching techniques, and layout specialists would wire a board in ways that would allow uniform, relatively thick trace widths.

In this area of design, as in others, a scenario in which the criteria mapped out in the schematic–entry process are tossed out the window just to get a usable netlist into a simulator can have discouraging results. With many users today working with a schematic–capture package from one company, a logic simulator from another, and board–layout tools from yet a third, much of the productivity gains can be lost as designers attempt to move from one activity to another. Because the integrated solutions may involve several third–party design tools, a highly integrated system like Mentor's, for example, tends to be a rarity. The Mentor Board Station lets a designer look at the schematic in one window and the board layout in another. Without the benefit of this integrated user interface, not only are layout specialists forced to reenter a netlist by hand, but the layout–sensitive performance characteristics of a circuit frequently are ignored in the effort to make everything fit the manufacturing criteria.

Consequently, the circuit–design and physical–layout processes need to be joined more tightly. There are a growing number of programs, as will be seen in this chapter, that allow engineers to become more actively involved in the layout process. To be sure, there is some resistance in engineering realms to using PCB–layout tools. As one pundit quipped: "Real engineers don't lay out PCBs." But engineers can become more actively involved in the layout process, not just by generating more usable netlists, but also by specifying layout–sensitive performance parameters during the design–entry phase. Another method of bringing engineers and layout specialists together is to hold design engineers responsible for preliminary layouts and to provide software tools that allow engineers to visualize a layout as they enter a circuit into the computer. Both of these possibilities will be explored .

Bridges Between Engineering and Layout

In their initial stages, automated design tools actually were mainframe–based CAD and CAM software provided by companies like Applicon (Billenca, Maine) and Computervision. However, the same graphics–workstation technology that enabled companies such as Daisy, Mentor, and Valid to create an entire market—and an engineering discipline, called CAE—by integrating schematic–capture and logic–simulation tools was accessible to circuit–board–layout experts as well.

Because they often are graphical aids, many PCB placement and routing tools have been integrated with workstations and harnessed to the same windowed user interface. In principle, this should allow a closer coupling among layout, simulation, and schematic entry. For example, where the performance of a circuit is sensitive to layout, engineers can attempt a tentative layout before they run a simulator. They then can adjust the layout and/or the circuit based on what the simulation is telling them. There are problems in this scenario, however. One is that neither engineers nor their layout systems will know all the manufacturing design rules as well as layout experts do. It is possible to build manufacturing design rules and automatic DRCs into layout–software databases, but, unless a company is vertically integrated or has a single source for PCBs, whose design rules should be embedded? The system cannot juggle all possible manufacturing databases. Manufacturability, then, will remain an open question, subject to more detailed answers by layout specialists.

The second problem is that layout—like simulation—can be run–time intensive. It may take hours to autoplace, route, and check a complex circuit board, and, even then, layout specialists are needed to tweak the layout or hand–wire the connections for which the computer could not find a path. In fact, placement and routing, like interpreting the results of a SPICE run, are computer jobs that still need a lot of human intervention to be successful, even though they run in batch mode. Consequently, layout specialists may insist that they can lay out a board faster by hand than on a computer, and, where this is true, the utility of automated layout tools can be questionable.

One important consideration is that the design tools used by engineers should supply a forward annotation path; that is, they should provide a way to tell layout specialists some of the things the circuit–design engineers had in mind. With the Mentor Board Station, for example, engineers can enter into the design database special considerations such as component placement for proper cooling, and the PCB–design tools will retrieve such data automatically. In this way, the design engineer has an automatic communication path to the layout specialist.

A design system like Allegro provides communication between circuit designers and layout specialists. Allegro, called a rules–driven design system, is the product of a merger between CAE–oriented Valid and Telesis Systems (Chelmsford, Massachusetts), a company with broad experience in PCB layout. Using Allegro on Sun workstation platforms, circuit designers can directly influence gate assignment, physical component placement, and subsequent routing operations to ensure that the finished PCB reflects the schematic's performance characteristics. These what–goes–where–and–how instructions are conveyed to the board designer through the netlist, and Allegro's automatic placement and routing routines obey these engineering rules.

Whether a designer lays out a PCB manually or uses computer–aided tools, the basic steps in the process are the same. The automated design tools, however, should speed up the cycle by allowing each step to be performed faster, more easily, and more accurately. Basically, the design cycle falls into three major phases. The first phase involves transforming the conceptual design into a schematic and deriving a netlist and bill of materials. Then, the design is verified and the schematic updated if changes are necessary. The second phase involves placement, routing, verifying connectivity, and checking design rules. The final phase covers postprocessing the PCB design data to generate both the artwork needed to fabricate the board and the files needed to pass data to NC (numerically controlled) drilling, automatic–insertion, and automatic–testing equipment.

For parts placement, PCB–design packages offer alternatives ranging from manual, to interactive, to fully automatic placement. In some cases, one system may offer all three choices. Many of the existing layout tools—especially those geared toward PCs and workstations—are intended primarily as graphic aids for layout specialists. These tools allow specialists to do a manual placement of parts on a board and to visualize a "rat's nest"; that is, to see on the screen which pins are electrically connected and where the largest, most difficult–to–

route concentration of wires (or nets) is occurring on the board. The rat's nest shows all the interconnections between the various components as vectors. With experience, a PCB designer can look at a rat's nest and pick out where components should be moved or reshuffled to avoid interconnection difficulties when the board is routed. By shifting components around, designers frequently can untangle the rat's nest; they can effectively reduce the concentration of wiring paths in one area and spread the wires more evenly over the surface of the board. In some cases, a colored histogram at the edges of the screen will help the designers to get another view of the wiring concentrations and to spread these evenly across the board .

After the parts are placed, the traces between components must be routed. As with parts placement, routing can be accomplished either by hand or automatically by the computer. Once the board has been designed, connectivity verification and DRC usually are performed. Connectivity verification is a process of checking the printed–circuit routing pattern against the netlist for the circuit. DRC is a process of checking the PCB layout against the criteria of a specific manufacturing process. DRC may be implemented as a batch–process run after routing is completed or as an interactive process. With interactive DRC, the system alerts users whenever they attempt to route a trace that violates a predetermined condition, such as the spacing between traces. In either case, though, it is necessary that the design rules for a particular manufacturing process be available (or specifiable) in software for the program to use as a reference (like a behavior model in a simulator or a device parameter in SPICE).

Unlike schematic entry, which is strictly an interactive process, or simulation, which runs as a batch–processing job, layout typically requires both graphics and computational resources. The graphics are required to help the engineer and/or layout specialist to enter the constraints into the system and to visualize the resulting layout. In many cases, the layout specialist will move components about on the screen, finding optimum arrangements for them. The computational resources are called into play when the computer is asked to find routing paths for all the wires that run between these components—routing paths that are consistent with the netlist, the manufacturing constraints, and the performance goals of the circuit. The computer often can crunch for many hours on a complex routing problem and still find a path for only 96% or 98% of the wires. The specialist will be called in to complete the last 2%—a job that could take an additional 15 or 20 hours of the PCB designer's time.

Computer Requirements for Printed–Circuit Layout

With both interactive layout and batch autorouting, the heart of the layout system usually is a matrix or grid that helps locate components in relation to each other. With an interactive layout system, for example, layout specialists pull a part from a software parts library, find a grid location with a cursor on the computer screen, and snap the component into place with a button on a mouse pointer device. (Alternatively, they can perform this activity from the computer keyboard, typing in the name of the parts they wish to place and their intended locations on the screen grid and then hitting the *Enter* key.) But this task puts a premium on the graphics capability of the system.

In the first phase of layout, a usable netlist must be generated from the schematics. As with simulation, there is the problem of converting one database to another. In the component–placement stage, the interconnections or wiring between components are less significant than the graphical representation of the component itself. Here, the generic part type indicated in the schematics must be identified with a more specific part type and with a specific package outline. In effect, the package outline provides an entirely different graphical representation of the part—one that makes sense to the layout specialist rather than to the circuit designer. This graphic must show not only the outline of the package, but also its pin–outs with proportional spacings and dimensions.

For example, a *nand* gate identified on a schematic or netlist may not be the functional equivalent of a 7400 part. The 7400, to be precise, includes four *nand* gates in one package, and it is the pin–outs and dimensions of the package that must be understood, rather than the logical functions of the *nand* gate.

An additional complication here, as in other areas of the electronics industry, is the constant revision in the way parts are packaged. The 7400–series logic devices invariably are available in DIPs with fixed dimensions. However, the availability of 7400–series logic devices in surface–mount packages creates new problems for automated–layout programs. The SMDs (surface–mounted devices) frequently use the same semiconductor die as do the DIP parts (and provide the same electrical functions), but the package dimensions and pin spacings are half those of the DIP.

In addition, not all the package dimensions and pin spacings for SMDs have been standardized. While a majority of SMDs, especially the 7400–series TTL logic families, provide 50–mil (0.050–in.) pin spacings (half those of ordinary DIPs), there are SMD package outlines for DIP devices that provide even tighter pin spacings than 50 mils and even four–sided, leaded chip carriers from Japanese manufacturers with metric pin spacings of approximately 28 and 22 mils.

Another complication is that while the DIPs have long leads that are inserted into through–holes in the PCB and soldered from the bottom, the SMDs have leads that are bent to rest directly on wiring traces and are soldered to the board from the top.

Large PCBs—those with hundreds of ICs—traditionally have taxed the resources of PCs and other small workstations. There seldom has been enough graphics resolution or memory to lay out a large board, nor enough processing power to automatically place and route all a board's components. Boards populated with the newer SMDs are even more difficult to depict graphically, because of the finer pin spacings of the small–outline components.

To accommodate these devices graphically, there are a number of requirements. First is a library of parts that provides graphic models of the most dominant SMDs from American and European manufacturers. Where the models do not currently exist, such as for devices with unusual pin spacings, layout specialists must have the software tools and sample pads to create them.

At the very least, the user must be able to create models and footprints for devices not covered in the available libraries.

A second requirement is within the layout program itself: Because of confusion between Japanese and American SMD pin spacings, users should be able to specify grid–pin spacings in English (thousandth of an inch) or metric (millimeter) units in their layout grids. The layout screen must display spacings as tight as 25 mils. (In addition to an interactive layout editor, these finer grid–pin spacings also should be available to the autoplacement and routing software—though with predictable increases in run time.)

A third requirement is that, because SMT (surface–mount technology) allows components to be located on both sides of a PCB, the graphical models must be able to represent devices on either side of the board. To meet this requirement, a mirror image of each part in the library is used to represent the part on the far side of the board from the viewport.

Surface–mount packaging represents only one type of packaging consideration. The trend toward VLSI creates microprocessors and other complex logic parts with sometimes hundreds of I/O pins. Typically, these devices are packaged in two ways: With less than 100 I/O lines, they can be packaged as LCCs (leadless chip carriers); with more than 100 I/O lines, they can be packaged in 128– or 256–line PGAs (pin–grid arrays).

New package configurations, such as SMT and high–level logic in LCCs or PGAs, force both PCB designers and the programs that automate some of their work to learn new dimensions, to visualize new images on a layout screen, and to build extra criteria into automatic routers. In addition to SMD, a layout program must be able to recognize user–created polygons or odd shapes as electrically sensitive layout areas. This feature is especially useful to analog-circuit designers, who typically must draw large ground planes to shield small signals operating at high frequencies.

Because of these requirements, PCB–layout systems have used both mainframe hosts with graphics terminals and engineering workstations. It is only recently that successful PC–based layout packages have emerged to deal with the problems presented by SMT. The combination of high–resolution graphics hardware and parts libraries in software makes it possible for layout specialists to perform hand placement and routing of components on IBM–PC/AT–type workstations. With Release 2.0 of PC–CARDS, for example, PCAD became the first CAE vendor to bring SMT to PC–based CAE systems.

The PCAD program is a good example of an interactive printed–circuit layout program. Like many layout systems, it can display multiple layers: Some are used to depict wiring patterns for a multilayered PCB; others are used to record manufacturing data. For example, the device footprints and electrical connectivity can be represented on two layers. Successive layers can represent a drilling guide for through–holes, a solder mask or paste for wave soldering, a milling guide for keyholes, a silk–screen guide for board labeling, etc.

The PC–CARDS program, in fact, provides a menu selection (*layr*) that allows users to define layers in any manner. They can be electrically active or inactive and enabled for display on the screen or disabled to remain invisible.

The enabled layers, in turn, can be highlighted with different colors to aid PCB designers in their work on–screen.

The pins on this multilayer map, similarly, can be defined by the user as through–holes, vias, stitches, hidden vias, or simple surface pins (for SMDs). The new PC–CARDS program allows the user to define up to 64 different layers and pin types—a growth path to the future, since 64 layers currently are beyond the capabilities of even the most sophisticated, cost–no–object board makers.

For example, a later incarnation of PCAD's PCB–design system, Master Designer 386, is meant to run on new–generation PCs using the Intel 80386 as its CPU. While the Master Designer software runs on 80286 machines as well as on 80386–based platforms, it handles boards two to three times larger (and routes up to twice as fast) as systems tailored for the 80286–based IBM–PC/AT. The system, which includes multilayer automatic routing, handles designs with 1300 components, 2500 nets, and 32,000 pins.

Other companies implementing PCB–layout software on the IBM–PC include OrCad and Visionics (Sunnyvale, California). OrCad's PCB software includes automatic routing, which allows the user to mix track and via widths. Routing is entirely interactive, and connections that are routed manually are taken into account automatically.

As discussed in Chapter 2, PCs are regarded as underpowered cousins of 68020–based workstations. As a rule, PC–based systems can handle small, uncomplicated board designs, while large, complex boards call for the power of the high–end workstations. There are two limitations of PCs in the layout environment: One is main memory (the PC–DOS operating system has a 640–KB ceiling); the other is graphics.

By increasing the main memory space available, it is possible for large circuit boards to be laid out on PCs. Release 3.2 of Case Technology Vanguard PCB–layout system, for example, takes advantage of the Expanded Memory Interface devised by Intel, Lotus, and Microsoft. This takes the form of an add–in card that allows 8088– and 80286–based machines to address up to 16 MB of memory. With the use of this card, the Vanguard system can lay out boards with 225 to 300 ICs. The EE Designer III software from Visionics is another system that attempts to overcome the traditional 640–KB memory barrier of PC–DOS by using the Lotus–Intel–Microsoft expanded–memory specification.

Similarly, while these PC–based systems use standard EGA graphics adapters that provide 640– x 480–pixel resolution in 8 or 16 colors, it is possible to obtain higher resolutions using graphics insert cards and VDI (virtual device interface) as the software–to–hardware interface for printed–circuit layout programs. While the screen paints used may not proceed as fast as those of CAE programs using a hardware–specific interface like EGA, the use of VDI enables PCAD users to move up to high–resolution graphics.

For example, an IBM–PC/AT graphics controller provided by Microfield Graphics and 15– or 19–in. monitors built by Hitachi provide a resolution of 1024 x 800 pixels, with more than 256 displayable colors. SMDs then could be presented on the same screen with normal DIP devices with no loss in clarity.

Much of the interactive layout work is performed on fully equipped workstations, such as those provided by Apollo, Sun, and HP. Case Technology, for example, provides its Vanguard Stellar CAE Design System on a variety of platforms, including Sun workstations and DEC MicroVAX machines, in addition to the IBM–PC/AT extensions mentioned before. While its programs typically have been geared toward mainframe hosts, Computervision offers a Professional PCB Designer program for the Sun–3/60. Cadnetix and Calay also provide PCB–design software for use on Sun platforms. The PCB Engineer, a software offering of Integraph, is a set of PCB–design tools for a VAX rewritten to run on Integraph's own Interpro 32C workstation, based on the Fairchild Clipper chip set.

While graphics may seem to be an easy problem to resolve, problems within the inherent intelligence of the program, such as recognizing electrical connectivity, are more imposing. Netlist compilation and parts placement and routing programs depend on a full understanding of connectivity.

Many PCB–layout programs (including PCAD's first release of PC–CARDS) use a pin or node to denote the electrical inputs or outputs of a device. Since DIPs and other leaded devices are mounted on one side of a PCB and electrically connected (soldered) on the other, any reference to a device's electrical pin automatically would connote a through–hole on the PCB. To accommodate SMDs, however, the model of electrical pins—the data structure—needs to be revised.

In PCAD's implementation, the electrical connectivity of SMDs is referenced with surface pins; that is, pins that are connected to only one layer of the PCB—the layer on which the component is mounted. This allows a number of capabilities that can be used by the most sophisticated PCB manufacturers.

One example is interstitial or hidden vias on a multilevel board. The interstitial via will connect one layer of a multilevel board with another, without breaking through to the outer layers. Because the surface–pin representation pertains to only one layer of the board, it is possible to place the interstitial via directly underneath the SMD's mounting pads.

In addition to interstitial vias, the system can recognize simple stitches—electrical threads—between one surface and another. While only the most vertically integrated board manufacturers—American aerospace companies or European consumer–electronics firms—will be able to produce boards with interstitial vias, the majority of PCB layouts still will make use of the stitching capability to recognize electrical connectivity between two or more PCB layers. Even those manufacturers whose efforts are confined to two–layer boards will need a multilayered connectivity model to set an autorouter in motion.

Autoplacement and Routing Techniques

The placement of components can be done manually on the layout systems just discussed. The wiring paths between these components also can be selected manually on such systems. But this effort would tend to duplicate much of the manual labor involved in entering components and wires onto a schematic diagram. A more practical solution is to use the netlist generated in the schematic–entry phase and use the computer to select an optimum placement of components and an optimum wiring path between them.

Because of the changes in circuit density and in the way devices are packaged, PCB placement and routing software constantly is being rewritten with new algorithms—mostly with a view to reducing the amount of run time on a mainframe or workstation. While manual placement and routing require a graphics workstation or graphics–enhanced PC, the computational resources required to perform large circuit autoplacement and routing mean it will be some time before these mainframe tools filter down to PCs.

There are programs like Scientific Calculation's ÊCARDS, for example, which is a PCB–design system for the VAXstation 2000. This actually is a scaled–down version of a VAX minicomputer program. Aimed at medium–density boards, the software theoretically can place up to 600 components and route interconnections on 20 board layers. It is likely, though, that run time would be overly long on a PC, unless the number of components, interconnections, and wiring layers were substantially reduced.

There are a number of programs that will perform a semiautomatic placement of components: Based on the netlist (or pinlist) available, the program first will display a rat's nest and/or a histogram on the screen. This will show the concentration of trace wires running through each section of the circuit board. The autoplacement routine then will juggle the order of components (or component clusters), attempting to find the arrangement of components that provides the lowest concentration (density) of trace wires on the board. The placement program will observe performance criteria, such as critical timing paths and thermal distributions, specified by the user.

Like a chess program, the placement program can run for hours (sometimes days) attempting to find an optimum component placement. The larger the number of components, criteria, and wire nets, the more complicated the placement task will be and the longer the computer will take with it. Whether this process results in better parts placement than could be accomplished by hand (using computer–graphic tools) is subject to debate. Similarly, the degree of human intervention required to get an optimum layout also is subject to debate. Some manufacturers let a computer run for a given amount of time on the problem and then let a human operator finish the job. Other manufacturers let layout specialists arrange component clusters based on their knowledge and experience and then let the autoplacement program take over. Some PCB layouts will require constant interaction between human and machine.

Because of the run time involved, and because the best placement of components likely will depend on the routing of wires between them, it is probable that most organizations will use the experience of layout specialists to place components on a board, but will let the computer select the wiring paths. It is hard to specify the crossover point, but the more complex circuit–board layouts become, the more inevitable it is that autorouting will be called into operation.

Grid Routers

Most of the existing autorouting programs operate as grid routers, building a trace or wiring path between device pins by moving from point to point on a wiring grid. Acting as a road map over the board's routable area, the grid determines the possible route segments. The PCB–design products developed by the Omnicad Corporation, subsidiary of ECAD, make use of grid–routing techniques. The Omniroute II software uses the Lee–Mor algorithm for its autorouting system.

Two main characteristics distinguish the Lee–Mor, or costed–maze, algorithm. First, the board is mapped as a grid, and each physical location on the PCB is represented in a bit map. Second, a cost function controls the routing procedure. This function allows variables, such as adding a via, to have a cost associated with them. There may be up to 30 costed variables. Moreover, various routers based on Lee's algorithm can produce quite different results, depending on how the cost functions are implemented.

The Lee–Mor autorouting algorithm determines trace paths across a grid pattern by calculating the least–cost path between a single source pin and up to nine surrounding grid–point locations. In effect, the program adds temporary traces in nine possible directions: forward, backward, left, right, four diagonals, and vertical (a via). This approach permits 90– and 45–deg bends in the connection paths.

On a computer screen, this movement would resemble a wave front of possible trace paths emanating from the source pin and moving toward the target pin. This flooding routine considers all possible paths to the target pin, working around obstacles in its path. As the wave front progresses, it leaves temporary trace segments between grid points in every possible direction. The flood is complete when the wave front reaches the target pin.

Grid points are occupied if an obstacle—such as a via or another trace—covers the grid point. The wave front does not add a temporary trace where it would interfere with one of these obstacles, but instead moves around them. As the wave front works its way around the obstacles, it also shapes itself according to a system that (in advance) assigns a cost to each move from a grid pin. For example, adding a via typically costs more than a move that allows the trace to stay on the same layer of the board.

Any point along the wave front represents a partial net whose total cost is equal to the sum of the cost of each move along the grid. For instance, a partial net may include one diagonal segment (cost value 15) and one horizontal segment (cost value 5), for a total cost value of 20. A second partial net, along the same flood line, could include four horizontal grid segments, at a total cost value of 20. A third partial net might be simply a via, also at a cost value of 20. After the connection to the target is made, the cost values of different paths are compared, and only the lowest cost path is used. The path chosen will be the one whose temporary traces reach the target pin at the lowest cost value. All others are erased, and the computer will route another net.

When the flood routine is finished, the program performs a walk–back, which creates a representation of the actual copper trace. The autorouter applies the design rules as the width of each trace becomes known. For instance, the program considers a path to be available if the distance to the nearest obstacle is at least one–half of the trace width plus the clearance required between traces. The result is a layout that correctly follows the design rules, rather than one that is just an estimate based on grid–point locations.

A usable assignment of cost values is critical to the operation of the Lee–Mor algorithm. For the Omniroute II software, the cost values represent a statistic derived from more than 2000 PCBs routed since 1983. Designers fine-tuned the cost values by testing each change in value on a large sample of old and new boards. In addition, they developed a series of cost values for specific routing problems, such as memory arrays, ground nets, and SMDs. For example, regular patterns in C or S shapes are the most efficient paths for connecting memory arrays.

There are two types of problems: One is run time; the other is the degree of completion. (The manufacturing specialist might have another criterion for evaluating routers; for example, the number of vias created by the router. These tend to elevate the manufacturing cost and decrease the reliability of the board.)

Grid routing is very time–consuming, and there is no consistency from program to program. Put several different routers to work on the same board design, and quite different route times may result. In addition, SMT (with its narrow pin spacings) and fine–line routing techniques (which send several trace lines between pins of a device) will call for a finer grid pattern. By raising the number of grid points exponentially, a finer grid pattern can further stretch out the amount of time the computer needs to complete a routing job.

Because of the fine grid–point spacing needed, 0.010 and 0.020 in., programs based on the Lee–Mor algorithm require both a large computer memory space and a fairly long run time. But the memory requirement is greatly reduced by the use of nonuniform grids—locating some component pads off the grid—which eliminates thousands of grid points. That is, instead of using a finer grid to accommodate SMDs, the router uses a normal mesh with additional points indicated for surface pins or extra–fine traces. On fine–line boards with two or three traces between component pins, for example, nonuniform grids achieve completion figures equal to those of uniform grids, but with up to 40% less memory usage. This solution makes the router act like a nongrid system.

Gridless Routers

One problem with grid–based routers is that today's boards often contain an assortment of device packages, pin–grid arrays, connectors, and so on, each with very different pad spacings. As a result, it is getting harder to achieve satisfactory routes using a fixed grid size. Efforts to solve this problem led to the development of gridless and plastic–grid algorithms.

A grid–free router is basically a grid–based router with an exceptionally fine grid, perhaps on the order of 1 mil. This approach is particularly useful for fine–line autorouting of two or three tracks between component leads. While no grid is displayed, all grid points are used in the computations. This feature lets the program recognize pin patterns for SMDs, LCCs, Eurocard connectors, edge-finger connectors, and other components whose pin patterns do not correspond to an English 10–mil grid.

The amount of memory and run time needed to accommodate this mesh can be reduced by calculating only those grid points that will contain printed–circuit traces. A nonuniform grid with grid lines spaced optimally for the specific components employed can reduce the number of grid points by up to 40%. Designers also can locate off–grid pins by establishing additional grid points wherever these pins occur. The plastic–grid technique divides a board into cells like a maze router, except that each cell may differ in size from the one next to it. Consequently, the grid pattern varies dynamically over the surface of the board. Cadnetix, for example, has developed a flexible–field router that relies on the plastic–grid algorithm. With this approach, Cadnetix claims an improvement not only in run time, but also in board quality: Boards routed with this technique typically have fewer vias or perhaps even fewer layers.

There are routing algorithms—variations on the Lee–Mor algorithm—specifically designed to provide run–time improvements. One variation is to run the Lee–Mor algorithm with a specific set of constraints. For example, the router can ignore all vias and between–layer stitches and confine its flood pattern to just one surface. Similarly, the autorouter can be directed to use the inner layers or the outer layers of the board. Another technique is to confine movements of the router to the horizontal direction on one layer of the board and the vertical direction on another layer.

Other approaches to routing include pattern–fitting algorithms and the Hightower algorithm. Pattern–fitting algorithms make use of artificial–intelligence techniques. The Hightower algorithm, for example, uses a grid–layout pattern. Instead of proceeding in all possible directions from a source point, the router will send the trace in only one direction (horizontally or vertically) across the board. The trace will continue in that direction until it either hits an obstacle or reaches the edge of the board. It then will walk–back one or more grid points and change direction (by 90 deg). It will repeat this process until the target point is reached. While this algorithm tends to be much faster than a flood–routing technique, the routing pattern may not be as efficient, and there always is the danger that 100% routing completion cannot be obtained.

Percentage Completed

After run time, the major concern is what percentage of the routing is completed. According to Charles J. Simon in *Computer–Aided Design of Printed Circuits*, for a board routed to 85% completion, it would take almost as much work to route the remaining 15% of the traces as to route the whole board from scratch.

Each new trace routed requires that at least one of the existing traces be rerouted. As a result, an 85% completion rate means that a minimum of 30% of the traces must be rerouted—and these typically are the most difficult ones. At completion rates above 90%, the job is a little easier, and real productivity gains can be realized.

The 100% routing completion of a complex PCB frequently will require the use of a rip–up–and–retry routine or algorithm. This is a way to look back and modify the connections already made in order to help locate the final connections. Typically, this requires an artificial–intelligence technique in which the program analyzes a partly completed board to learn where improvements might be made during rip–up and retry. During the analysis, the program finds out which areas of the board are congested, where the blocked channels are, and where trace density is high. Combining this information with the design rules, the autorouter moves traces from congested areas to areas with more open channels. The Omniroute II software, for example, can take complex PCBs that are 91% to 93% complete after sequential routing and complete them to 100% with rip–up–and–retry routing.

In operation, the router proceeds in several stages, examining one section of the board at a time, wiring sections together, and then fine–tuning the entire wiring pattern. For example, in the first stage—a *memory pass*—pins on a memory board or section are connected in straight lines. A second *initial pass* limits routing to a small area and does not insert vias. A third *comprehensive pass* routes over a larger area than the initial pass and inserts up to one via per net. Fourth, an *exhaustive pass* considers the entire board and does not restrict the number of vias. Fifth, a *rip–up–and–retry pass* relocates existing traces to open channels for additional connections. Finally, a *manufacturing pass* modifies traces to shorten them, eliminate vias, and generally optimize the layout.

Special Considerations

There are special considerations in layout and routing. One is speed. The Insight router, for example, part of Valid's Allegro system, includes design rules for high–speed transmission lines. A transmission line is a wiring trace whose length must be a specific multiple of the wavelength of the signal being propagated (that is, the higher the frequency or speed, the smaller the wavelength and the more precise the trace length).

In operation, the router might understand that a high–speed net requiring transmission lines should be given priority and routed first. The router automatically places sources and terminators at opposite ends of the transmission line, while a terminator–assignment program searches a list of resistors to select and assigns terminators to minimize signal reflection. Insight also takes care of routing high–frequency nets as daisy chains. If the design allows stubs (T–connections), the router generates only stubs that do not exceed a maximum length defined by the user. Insight automatically routes corners using 45–deg angles, because these gradual changes in signal paths (rather than abrupt 90–deg changes) minimize signal reflection.

Other special considerations are the thermal characteristics of a PCB that may emerge during layout. There are a number of programs based on finite–element and finite–difference techniques that determine steady–state temperatures over a regularly spaced grid of nodes. The computation time depends primarily on the number of components and the number of nodes for which temperatures are calculated. The results can show the hot spots and heat–conduction patterns across the surface of a PCB. This information is useful in predicting the reliability of a board in use.

One example of a thermal–analysis program is Valid's Thermo–STAT. The program uses three types of information: the placement of components on a board, descriptions of the components' thermal characteristics, and a description of the board's operating environment. Information in the first category, component placement, is taken directly from Valid's Allegro PCB–layout database. Placement data from Scientific Calculation's SCICARDS PCB–layout system or from a Computervision system also can be imported into Thermo–STAT.

The components' thermal characteristics also are readily available to the program in a library of models. The library currently provides thermal data on more than 2000 devices. For devices that are not covered by the library, Thermo–STAT includes intelligent default values.

The final type of information Thermo–STAT needs is a parametric description of the board's operating environment. These parameters include the adjacent board temperature, board–to–board spacing, altitude (to account for the effects of atmospheric density), gravitational orientation (to determine the effects of natural convection), forced air–flow velocity, and inlet–air temperature. Both natural and forced–convection heat–transfer mechanisms are modeled, allowing the engineer to simulate the natural rising of the dissipated heat, as well as the additional cooling factors provided by fans.

Temperature is a major factor in most reliability formulas, such as those defined in MIL–HDBK–217, the commonly accepted source of formulas and algorithms for predicting MTBF. A difference of 1 °C in temperature calculation results in a 5% change in reliability predictions for a typical PCB. Still, programs that help predict MTBF based on a thermal analysis are a rarity in PCB layout.

Back Annotation

A back–annotation path from the PCB–design tools to the schematic–capture system is one final consideration. With back annotation, a designer feeds pin assignments and reference designators back to the design database. Maximum routing flexibility suffers, for instance, if the pins of a quad op amp are assigned on a schematic before placement and routing are done. Also, if revisions are made to the PCB, back annotation supplies an easy way to update the schematic. Back annotation, though important, is not included in all placement and routing packages, since it depends on the degree of integration between the layout program and the schematic–entry software. An integrated system like the Mentor Board Station, for example, lets a designer transfer information about the routed board (such as trace lengths) back to the design database. Then, engineers working on a high–speed design, for instance, can rerun their simulation and note the effect of the traces on signal propagation through the circuit.

• PCB Design Tools •

A PCB CAD system does not exist in isolation: It often is part of an integrated design environment that extends all the way from front–end CAE circuit–capture and analysis applications to back–end CAD/CAM applications. Protecting an investment in a PCB/CAD system involves much more than the quality and support of the PCB/CAD application itself. It centers on the degree of integration and flexibility of the database within the total CIM environment and the ability to relate diverse types of user–defined data to the design database.

Database Structure

A database structure should be arranged so that it can accommodate additional database elements that may not even be imagined at present. That database should work at a semantic level that is as high as possible and should not descend to detail too rapidly. For example, the relational structure should indicate a component's location, rather than begin by representing the component as a series of line elements. The semantic content of the databases should conform to good database–design practice, being properly normalized and nonredundant. It should be structured to be relevant in an application sense rather than in a software sense. It should reflect the eccentricities of the software. The types of fields should be thought about in terms of their meaningfulness to someone who understands the application, not only to a software engineer. In short, the database schema should be designed without consideration of its software implementation, only with concern for describing PCBs in meaningful PCB terms.

The database should recognize a number of entities, such as the logical world of circuit elements, the physical world of paths, and the bridge between them—their mapping. The logic elements, in turn, must be mapped into models for simulation. In the analysis phase, the database structure must take into account the possibility that more than one simulator will be used, requiring different models. One solution is to have a relational system that relates the appropriate model to its respective simulator, depending on the simulator selected. The database also has to consider physical artifacts, such as pad stacks and layers, which are application artifacts, not some software abstraction.

Logic elements, of course, must map to packages, but the graphical appearance of the logic elements and their interconnections also must be mapped into the database. In this context, a graphical representation is a side effect of a model. A database should be concerned with artifacts that are really modeling elements. In fact, an excessive concentration on how a system looks graphically is an abiding fault of most PCB/CAD systems, which treat a captured design as if they were just drawing pictures of it. A database that handles all artifacts, including graphics, as models can tell the designer at any given time what the overall model looks like.

Database Accessibility

There are two major circumstances for which the database must be accessible to the PCB/CAD user in order to link to another application: to replace an existing application within that vendor's suite of applications, or to add an entirely new application. In the first case, designers might replace a piece of the application supplied by the vendor because they are not satisfied with the vendor's approach. But, more likely, they will be adding functionality, adding, for example, a thermal–analysis package to a system that lacks one. In either case, designers must be able to add to the schema sensibly and to interrelate the added structure with the data that is in the preexisting schema. So, for the case of thermal analysis, it would be necessary to add the relations that have thermal characteristics for the devices. The schema should be extensible and should use common key fields, such as component part numbers. The extraction of data then becomes relatively straightforward, because it is only a matter of correlating the key fields that contain the part number of the extended schema with the common fields in the existing part of the database.

Putting data back into the database requires more care. The external applications need to ensure that after they put data back in, the database is still coherent. The biggest problem occurs when the database artifact expression uses high–level semantic statements that relate records in one area of the database to subsidiary records in another area. The external application must obey a similar set of relational rules, or an incoherent database will result.

If the database does not have some sort of report–generation facility, it is not complete. Report generation implies that one is producing printed reports that can be read, but it involves much more. It enables the designer to restructure data in the database and output it in a variety of forms, to produce formatted data for a variety of other programs. Racal–Redac's PCB/CAD program, VISULA, for example, works by using a report generator to create file structures that will be read by other programs, not by people. Such an expandable system safely protects the CAD database while linking its new relation.

Database Expandability

Relational databases are very useful when they can relate a new set of data structures to a preexisting set. For example, it may prove helpful for design engineers to have part price and availability information at their fingertips during the design process. In this way, costs can be controlled and parts can be used that are already in inventory, thereby reducing the number and variety of parts that need be stocked. In a conventional CAD system, it is difficult to place such data in an area where it is available to design engineers. With a relational database, the user can create another relation in the database that has the stock numbers, as well as information from the main corporate database, such as price and availability.

The engineering team may wish to add nominal MTBF as a relation. The report writer can be used to join the MTBF to the rest of the database and perform a simple calculation to determine the nominal MTBF for the complete board (ignoring temperature effects). This could lead to a determination early in the design process to use MIL–SPEC parts.

Racal–Redac's VISULA Release 4, running on an Apollo workstation, provides a good example of how a database can be configured with the ability to add and extract user–defined information. Consider adding a schema (added database structure), with filename *cos.s*, that relates information about part number, part type, manufacturer, cost per device, and reliability (MTBF) to a central database where a design database also resides.

First, the schema is defined and added to the database (see Figure 7.1). Next, a form is created (see Figure 7.2), which permits the designer to begin entering data into the new schema. The form then is compiled and data is entered. To extract data, a report is created and compiled (see Figure 7.3) that produces an output in the desired format.

ASCII data for applications such as cost relation can be loaded and unloaded from a separate ASCII library into VISULA'S central database. A script is used to extract the total cost of the board. The script writes to the screen to tell the operator what is occurring in real time.

Industry–Standard Hardware Platforms

The advantages of porting software to industry–standard hardware platforms are well understood, but the porting process itself is not merely a matter of simply selecting a common operating system and high–level language, particularly with complex interactive programs. Simple recompilation of the program is not going to meet the need for portability. The architectural differences between the platforms have to be taken into account. Designers have to structure their software internally to protect the majority of it from depending on its hardware environment. They must accept the fact that some users transport the software from one machine to another to compensate for differences not only in language, but also in the graphics environment and the method by which keyboard input is available to the program.

Software designers should deliberately structure the software package so that the majority of it is insulated from the vagaries of a shifting industry–standard environment. VISULA'S software addresses this problem by using buffer modules that are platform–dependent and can be rewritten as the need arises. This allows more than 90% of the existing code to be reused for each software porting.

There are interface–graphics standards like PHIGS or GKS that permit the exchange of graphic data between platforms. However, if the application is to exploit the total capabilities of a particular platform, the designers almost always will be better off tailoring the software to the platform, rather than accepting the limitations of the interface standards. Often, the use of the interface standard to hide the differences between the platforms results in a surprising degradation in performance from one workstation platform to another.

```
The schema cos.s is shown below:

database central

file costrelib

field cos part number  type  char  length 24  index dups
field cos part type  type  char  length 22
field cos manufact  type  char  length 7
field cost key  type composite  cos part number, cos manufact
                              index pri
field cos part  type  float
field cos relib  type  float
```

Figure 7.1: Schema drawing is defined and added to the database.

Interestingly, a list of industry–standard platforms for a CAE/CAD–only workstation environment is different from that for a CIM factory–automation environment. The tools used in the design office of an engineering service group are going to be different from those used on the factory floor. For professional engineering workstations, the list, in priority order, would include: VAXstation GPX, Apollo and Sun, and, perhaps (eventually), IBM's RT–PC. For CIM, the list also would have to include HP, with its installed base of HP–3000–series computers in factory environments, as well as IBM for its mainframes.

Choice of High–Level Programming Language

The selection of a high–level programming language is critical to the application's performance and its ability to be migrated among different computing platforms. A key issue is the availability of compatible compilers for each of the platforms. The language chosen also should allow a good deal of structure to be imposed upon the code. On that basis, Racal–Redac chose not to use FORTRAN. Although FORTRAN compiler compatibility is very good, there is no capability for structuring complex databases.

Pascal, in many respects, is a good language except for the fact that it is somewhat incomplete. One major shortcoming is its requirement for separate compilation of each module, which then must be compiled into the next level of module hierarchy. A number of vendors, including Apollo, have enhanced Pascal to overcome this limitation. Unfortunately, everyone who has cured this problem has approached its solution quite differently, so the compilers are incompatible in moving from one platform to another.

```
database central
screen
{
                Cost and Reliability Information Per Manufacturer

                Part number         [f000                        ]
                Part type           [f001        ]
                Manufacturer        [f002        ]
                Cost per device     [f003    ] in cents
                Reliability (MTBF)  [f004    ] failures per second



]
end

attributes
f000  =  cos part number,
             required,
             reverse,
             nonupdate,
             comments  =  "Enter part number";
f001  =  cos part type,
             required,
             comments  =  "Enter part type";
f002  =  cos manufact,
             required,
             comments  =  "Enter manufacturer";
f003  =  cos part,
             required
             comments  =  "Enter cost of device in cents";
f004  =  cos relib,
             required,
             comments  =  "Enter reliability of device in
                               failures/second";
end
```

Figure 7.2: Form drawings are defined and added to the database.

Racal–Redac finally settled on C, not because it is the best high–level language, but because it allows you to do some compilation that other languages cannot do and is highly structured. In fact, the pointer manipulation allowed in C is quite dangerous to the database and error–prone in programming. Although C is not so much a standard as it is an ANSI specification, almost everyone who supplies C compilers has done so in compatible ways, thus avoiding the need to customize extensions to the language, which often are incompatible. C–compilers, then, are much more compatible than are FORTRAN compilers.

```
The report costinfo is shown below:

database central end

define
            variable  totcost  type  integer
            variable  part type  type  character  length 22
            function   expform
end

input
            prompt for part type using
            "Enter part type:"
end

output
            report to "costinfo.out"
end

read into x
            cos part number
            cost part type
            cos manufact
            cos part
            cos relib
            where cos part type matches part type
end
sort by cos part type end
format
first page header
let totcost = 0
before group of cos part type
            skip 1 line
print "part type:", cos part type
print "+------------------",--------------------------
print "I    part number", 7 spaces
"I Manufacturer", 2 spaces
"I Cost in cents", 2 spaces
"I Reliability  I"
print "+------------------",--------------------------
on every record
let totcost = totcost + cos part
print "I ", cos part number, "I   ",
cos manufact, "   I",
cos part, "  I ",
expform (cos relib), "   I"
after group of cos part type
print "+------------------",--------------------------
skip 1 line
print "The total cost is  :", totcost using "#,###"
end
```

Figure 7.3: Reports extract data and compile it in the desired output format.

Dedicated Links to Front–End Tools

Links to schematic capture and simulation should operate at a relatively high semantic level and should be as simple as possible. Such links should allow not only full descriptions of the circuit, but also partial descriptions to permit incremental recompilation of the circuit as the design proceeds.

There rarely will be effective communication between two sets of applications packages unless there is active willingness on the part of both vendors to cooperate on the interface. If one vendor insists on keeping its database–package coding secret, then one end of the link will remain opaque. This may continue until pressure from customers forces the issue.

In mapping from one system to another, there has to be some common point of reference, because there is likely to be some mismatch between the semantics of the data structures. Bridging this mismatch is the biggest problem in converting from one database representation to another. The problem arises from the different sets of entities that exist in the databases. In going from a lower semantic level to a higher one, data synthesis must take place to extract higher level meanings from lower level entities. For example, if the lower level description views the entities as gates, this data will need to be distilled upward. In going from a higher semantic level with more intelligence to a lower semantic level, information is discarded. For example, in going from a highly intelligent description of a PCB to 2–D drafting, information is thrown away furiously.

Intermediate Format Interfaces

EDIF is moving slowly, steadily forward. The biggest danger in standards development is that those selected become a convoy solution; that is, moving at the speed of the slowest. This does not appear to be happening with EDIF, however. Instead of reducing performance to the lowest common denominator, EDIF, in a sense, is reducing it to the least common factor. Its success depends totally on the demands to be placed on vendors that it be available, that it be adhered to, and that its standards be good ones.

Within EDIF, some data types now are transportable through EDIF, while some still need a good deal of work. EDIF is not too bad at handling logic data or silicon–structure data. Its major deficiency (which is being resolved) is that it does not properly represent the layers and other application artifacts within PCBs.

EDIF already conveys two–dimensional information, such as part location. There are ways of extending EDIF to add height or some other property, but this is an extension, not part of EDIF's standard definition. Users wishing to exchange data in this way would have to agree upon the nature of the extension used.

A new version of EDIF, Version 2, was released in July 1987. For PCB designs, Version 2 will handle netlist transfer and schematic transfer, including back annotation. Still, it does not cover the physical aspects of board layout.

The PCB Technical Subcommittee of EDIF is working on this area. One of the main issues is the modeling of layers. Another issue is the modeling of pad stacks—putting pads on different layers without having to repeat the pad specification each time. One other area that should be mentioned is transfer for incremental design changes. EDIF needs the ability to transfer an incrementally updated partial netlist instead of transferring the entire one. Later releases of EDIF are expected to address all these issues.

There are two types of linkage of PCB/CAD to CAD/CAM tooling that should be considered. First is the linkage to manufacturing–fabrication tools such as drills, profilers, pick–and–place machines, and automatic component–insertion machines. Second is taking a subset of the data and linking it to mechanical design; for example, laying out a PCB for equipment–packaging purposes. This may not require electrical–connectivity data, but will require component–placement and board–outline information. Alternatively, designers might do mechanical–packaging work before they start board layout, because there may be components whose position will be determined by mechanical–packaging constraints, not by electrical–performance requirements. The issue, then, is to provide linkages that allow the use of the mechanical design system both before and after board layout.

There are two ways to meet postprocess requirements for manufacturing. One option is to write a program that extracts data from the database and formats it for every type of plotter, drill, and profiler on the market, a very expensive and time–consuming process. Or, one program could be provided for each class of device that has to be driven with CAD data: one for CNC drilling, one for plotting, etc. Then, the machine parameters could be input through a menu–driven data–entry process, since there are relatively minor differences between the data needed by each vendor's version of the machine. (Incidentally, it is not clear to what extent manufacturing engineers should interact with these postprocessing facilities to optimize them.)

In mechanical CAD, the IGES standard has been around for a long time. It is only recently, in the latest version of the specifications, that IGES has become particularly useful for PCBs. Before this, it was far too heavily oriented toward mechanical design problems in 2–D drafting and 3–D solids modeling. It did not represent electrical connectivity properly; it dealt with lines and solid modeling artifacts. The latest version of IGES is much improved and could become an effective standard.

Expandability to New Packaging Technologies

In most PCB/CAD systems, the physical design rules for the board are an imbedded set of rules whose parameters are contained in a technology file where each parameter (for example, minimum trace and pad spacing) is a fixed value. In a future enhancement, VISULA may handle high–speed logic, such as GaAs and ECL, by defining the design rules more flexibly. The design rules still would be oriented toward a particular technology–based rule set, but also would be able to include rules such as min/max timing delays on nets and relative timing between nets. One possible strategy is to make the inputting of rules totally arbitrary, but the implications of this strategy for performance degradation are considerable, since rules checking typically is performed interactively. A compute–intensive, on–line rules check would slow the entire design process. Although not possible at this time, efficient on–line rules checking using an arbitrary user–defined set of rules is a worthwhile long–term goal.

• PC–Based CAE Software •

PCB Design Process

The process of designing and laying out a PCB product starts with an engineering–schematic sketch of a circuit that is given to a layout specialist who does a manual layout. This method requires the layout person to interpret the schematic, draw the corresponding PCB layout with a pencil, and then perform hand taping. Artwork is produced from the tape layout photographically, and formal product documentation is produced by the drafting department using the engineering–schematic sketch and the layout drawings.

The part of the product–design process being reviewed starts with the capture of the circuit information, continues with the physical design, and concludes with the physical implementation.

PC–Based CAE/CAD. International competition has created the need to develop more complex, reliable, cost–effective products in a shorter period of time, at less cost, with smaller staffs. This situation has forced engineers, PCB designers, and management to seek new solutions, tools, and design methodologies. The problem of how to design and produce PCBs most quickly and economically is a major issue facing companies that sell electronic products.

Many engineers and PCB designers still use manual methods. Some have been using mainframe CAE/CAD systems and engineering workstations to assist them with their tasks. These users most often are at large companies that can afford the large initial capital outlay.

The integrated capabilities that are available on PC–based systems are changing the roles of the engineer and PCB designer. The traditional process takes a long time, is very iterative, and requires lots of communication to prevent errors. With the tools now available, engineers can communicate information more easily to documentation and PCB–design groups and be involved in all aspects of the design process from start to finish. PC–based CAE/CAD systems for PCB design are becoming the standard for electrical engineers and PCB designers and are changing the traditional definition of the design–and–layout process. The low cost of these systems has made design tools that previously existed only in large companies on a shared–capacity basis available to everyone.

PC–based tools are approaching their larger counterparts in capability. Data taken from "A Study of the Low Cost PCB CAD Market" by H. G. Marsh in the November 1986 issue of *Printed Circuit Design* magazine, and a 1987 Dataquest CAD/CAM Industry Service report, show the design methods used for

PCB layout in 1986. Thirty–four percent of the designs were done on workstations or mainframes, 31% were done on PC–based CAD systems, and 35% still were done manually (see Figure 7.4). Other studies indicate that up to 75% of the PCBs being designed today can be done on a PC, and the price–performance ratio definitely favors the PC.

The role of PC–based CAE/CAD software in the product–design process includes design entry or schematic capture of the circuit information, engineering analysis, packaging of the schematic symbols into physical parts, placement of those parts during physical design entry, routing of the traces, physical analysis of the layout, generation of artwork, obtaining drilling–machine and insertion–machine information for manufacturing, and documentation of the product. Figure 7.5 shows this overall process. Several examples will be used to illustrate how a PC–based CAE/CAD system fits into various research, design, and manufacturing environments. These applications involve the use of the system in both small and large organizations. Products containing both digital and analog circuitry are included.

Application of CAE/CAD Tools. Schematic capture is more than electronic drafting. An intelligent database is needed to capture all the information related to a schematic, so that the circuit can be analyzed and physically implemented with computer assistance. The electrical attributes, characteristics, and interconnections of the components must be stored, as well as the graphical information.

Physical design, or layout, is the last step in a product's design cycle. It is during this process that schematic symbols are converted or packaged into their physical equivalents. These packaged parts then are placed and the wiring paths between them defined.

After component placement, the wiring paths or traces need to be routed. This also can be done either interactively with manual methods or automatically. In the interactive method, the rat's–nest display is turned off, and a specific pin is selected for wiring. The individual net associated with that pin then is shown as a guide. A sophisticated autorouter with window routing, priority, and 45–deg capability also can be used for boards that have both analog and digital circuitry. When the layout is completed, a design–rule check is performed, and a file containing *was–is* change information is fed back to the schematic database. These changes occur due to the process of layout–placement optimization and the swapping of pins or reference designators. The schematic then is updated with the final packaging assignments. This process is known as back annotation and is used to keep the schematic and the physical design consistent.

Film or artwork is required to manufacture the board. To complete the end–to–end process, a link from the CAD system to the CAM system is needed. Plotting utilities take layout information from the PCB database and generate plotter commands that are used with pen plotters to produce either inked drawings that can be photographed or photoplotter files for photoplotting. Other utilities generate NC drilling data for transfer to a paper–tape punch and positional information for automatic–insertion machines. Other interfaces

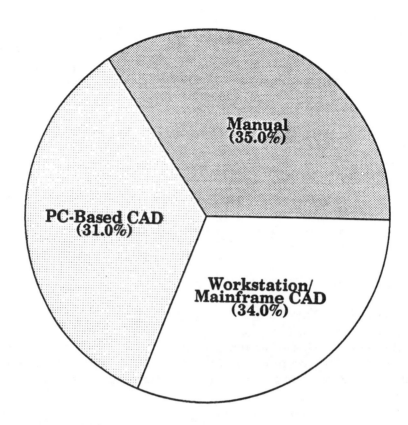

Figure 7.4: Design methods for PCB layout.

provide a data path from the CAD system to wire–wrap machines and PCB prototyping equipment.

Case Studies. Four different experiences with a PC–based CAE/CAD system, PCAD, will be used to illustrate how an automated PCB–design system fits into the design and manufacturing environment. These case studies involve the use of the system for both digital and analog designs and show significant savings in person–hours and design–cycle time, with fewer design errors and higher quality designs. Users of CAE/CAD systems typically save 40% to 60% in design hours and the length of the design cycle. Actual case–by–case savings are a function of designer experience and the size, complexity, density, and digital/analog mixture of components.

The first case study involves a problem faced by most service bureaus— severe time constraints. Typically, a customer brings in an engineering– schematic sketch of a circuit for a new product and says that the board must be laid out and the job completed in a specified period of time. In this case, the designer was allowed 150 hours. A sketch of an all–digital design was given to a layout specialist, who started drawing a manual layout with a pencil. (This

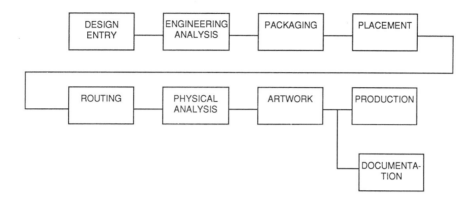

Figure 7.5: Product design process.

pencil drawing then would be digitized to obtain the artwork.) It soon became apparent that the manual layout times were unacceptable. The job then was changed to the CAD system, where the powerful interactive– graphics PCB–layout capability was used, and completed on time. The finished board contained 201 20–pin IC equivalents and was implemented as a six–layer board with a density of 0.42. (The density is calculated by dividing the usable board area in square inches by the number of 20–pin IC equivalents, where the usable board area is determined by subtracting 0.25 in. from each side and then multiplying the resulting height and width.)

The second case study illustrates the end–to–end capabilities of a PC–based system and the CAE/CAD interface. This board was a high–density digital design. Six sheets of schematics were created in 56 hours; this circuitry translated into 105 20–pin IC equivalents. The board design took 105 hours and was implemented as a four–layer board with a density of 0.36. Having the design information in a CAE/CAD database paid off when it came time to do the first revision. One sheet of the schematic, affecting 12 ICs, was redrawn and the layout was edited. This revision was accomplished in 28 hours.

The limits of a PC–based system and the PCB designer's creativity are illustrated by the third case study. An engineering sketch of a video board that was half digital and half analog was given to the designer for layout.

Analog PCB design is different from digital design and has unique requirements. The use of a large number of components with different sizes and shapes and with irregular footprints makes placement more difficult and creates irregular routing channels. Certain components have fixed locations. High–frequency signals, RFI (radio–frequency interference) considerations, power demands, and heat–dissipation problems contribute to design complexity. Trace location and length, signal isolation, and the use of ground planes for shielding are very important.

The interactive capability of the CAD system proved to be very helpful in exploring various placement and routing alternatives. When completed, the board had four layers and constrained 900 components. Due to the number of components, the board design was split into two databases, and the artwork for the board was produced by a photographic–merging technique. Although the initial CAD layout took the same amount of time as was estimated to do the job manually, it paid off in the time saved performing continuing product changes.

The fourth case study further illustrates the value of a PC–based CAE/CAD system for analog design. The data was taken from a project done by a service bureau for a large company. Schematic databases for 33 D–size and 3 C–size sheets were provided to the service bureau. Twelve PCBs ranging in size from 2.5 x 6.5 in. to 18 x 18 in. were laid out. The six boards with the greatest complexity were selected for this case study. One board was 33% analog, one was 75% analog, and the rest were 100% analog. The estimated time to do the six boards manually was 1177 hours. Using the PCAD system, the actual time was 314 hours. This resulted in a time saving of 863 hours, or 73% of the estimated time using traditional manual methods. Additionally, all boards were completed on time.

PCB Design–Requirement Trends

The changes in technology, complexity, and density of PCBs are placing ever tougher requirements on engineers and designers and the CAE/CAD tools they use. Technology has moved from simple SSI and MSI TTL circuits to ECL, PLD, ASIC, analog, RF (radio–frequency), and hybrid circuitry. Packaging density has grown from one transistor per package in 1960 to more than 100,000 transistors per package in the 1980s. Standard DIP packages are being complemented with PGA and SMD parts. Multilayer boards and fine–line geometries are commonplace. The nature of the electronics business and the products produced makes it very probable that this trend will continue and may even accelerate.

The hardware considerations for tools that can meet these design requirements involve the PC or workstation microprocessor (normally a 80286, 80386, or 68020), the amount of RAM required, the disk storage used, the graphics display, the communications capability, and the input and output devices.

The CAE/CAD software from PCAD runs on off–the–shelf PCs such as the IBM–PC/AT and clones. Typical configurations include 640 KB of main memory, a hard disk drive, enhanced color–graphics capability, a serial communications port, a mouse, and a printer or plotter.

Business Considerations

As stated earlier, the need to develop more complex, reliable, cost–effective products in a shorter period of time, at less cost, and with smaller staffs is the driving force behind the acquisition of CAE/CAD systems. Since this is basically a business issue, several questions arise with respect to productivity, return on investment (ROI), time to market, and product–design methodology. To paraphrase a famous quote, "To buy or not to buy CAE/CAD, that is the question." What will be the impact on your company if you do or you do not? What if your competitors have CAE/CAD and you do not? Tough questions, when everybody is competing for resources and budget dollars.

How well does the CAE/CAD system meet the established expectations and objectives? What are the resulting benefits? The case studies discussed show a significant savings in person–hours and design–cycle time, with fewer design errors and higher quality designs. As pointed out, users of PC–based CAE/CAD systems typically save 40% to 60% in design hours and the length of the design cycle.

An example of payback analysis and ROI can be constructed from our first case–study. Nine PC boards that would have taken 1867 hours using manual methods were designed in 849 hours using a CAE/CAD system. This equates to 207 hours per board and 94 hours per board, respectively. If we assume that an engineer or designer spends 75% of his or her time in some design activity, or 1500 hours per year, at an annual salary of $30,000, and a CAE/CAD system costs $15,000, then we find that for each engineer or designer and CAE/CAD system:

The total number of boards that can be designed manually per year is:
$$\frac{1500 \text{ hours/year}}{207 \text{ hours/design}} = 7.2 \text{ boards}$$

The total number of boards that can be designed with CAE/CAD per year is:
$$\frac{1500 \text{ hours/year}}{94 \text{ hours/design}} = 16.0 \text{ boards}$$

The cost per board designed manually is:
$$\frac{\$30,000/\text{year}}{7.2 \text{ boards/year}} = \$4167 \text{ per board}$$

The cost per board designed with CAE/CAD is:
$$\frac{\$30,000/\text{year}}{16.0 \text{ boards/year}} = \$1875 \text{ per board}$$

The cost savings per board is:

$$\$4167 - \$1875 = \$2292 \text{ per board}$$

The number of boards that need to be designed to pay for the CAE/CAD system is:
$$\frac{\$15,000 \text{ system cost}}{\$2292 \text{ saving/board}} = 6.5 \text{ boards}$$

The payback period for the CAE/CAD system is:
$$\frac{6.5 \text{ boards}}{16.0 \text{ boards/year}} = 0.41 \text{ years, or 4.5 months.}$$

The saving per year is:

$$16.0 \text{ boards/year} \times \$2292 \text{ per board} = \$36,672$$

The ROI is:
$$\frac{\$36,672 \text{ savings/year}}{\$15,000 \text{ system cost}} = 2.44 \times 244\% \text{ per year}$$

To fully realize the benefits of a CAE/CAD system, changes need to be made in the product–design methodology and the organizational structure. Management must plan the direction and objectives clearly when automating the design process. A CAE/CAD manager or administrator should be assigned to implement the new systems and the associated policies, procedures, standards, disciplines, libraries, revision control, data control, and archiving that will be required. Like the corporate MIS group, the use of CAE/CAD affects the entire organization throughout the processing of design data and the distribution of information.

• Rules–Driven Design •

In the typical design environment, there is a clear distinction among the electrical, logical, and physical implementations of a design (see Figure 7.6). The successful design of ICs and electronic systems requires the skills of both design engineers and physical–design specialists. However, these design–team members often have different goals for a design's physical layout, which can jeopardize design integrity.

Design engineers want a layout that is logically and electrically correct, with related functions grouped together to obtain the shortest critical–connection paths. High–frequency signals should be routed without stubs to reduce ringing and signal delays. Also, design engineers prefer routing with 45–degree angles to reduce reflections.

On the other hand, layout designers want components placed so that signal traces are easily routable; the length of the trace is not a prime consideration. For layout specialists, the use of stubs and 90–degree angles is a reality of routing.

Design engineers could prevent many physical–design discrepancies if they explained to layout specialists how to circumvent trouble areas. Once the schematic entry and design verification processes are completed, the design engineer normally hands off the design, in the form of a netlist, to a specialist for physical layout.

Herein lies the problem: The netlist defines only the functional components and their connectivity; it does not identify the functional groupings of components nor indicate which nets are critical paths that should receive special consideration in placement and routing. Without direction from the design engineer, the design specialist responsible for layout will strive for tight component placement and 100% routability without considering the design's electrical requirements. Often, the result is a design that does not meet performance requirements.

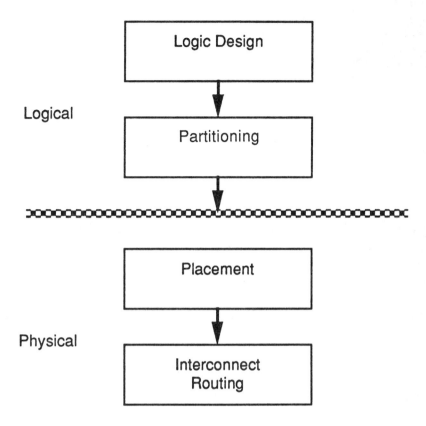

Figure 7.6: Design process.

To improve communications between front–end and back–end engineers, introduced the concept of rules–driven design. Rules–driven design permits engineers to include physical implementation rules in the schematic environment, along with component and connectivity values, to guide the physical design of ICs and PCBs.

To be effective, rules–driven design requires the tight integration of schematic capture, simulation, and verification tools with CAD tools that implement the physical design. A design example will illustrate the importance of integration for successful rules–driven design.

PCB–Design Example

Suppose that marketing has asked a design team to develop a single–board computer with the power of a small mainframe. To meet performance goals, the design must incorporate a high–speed clock circuit (see Figure 7.7), which means that the board should be implemented in ECL, rather than in TTL. To achieve

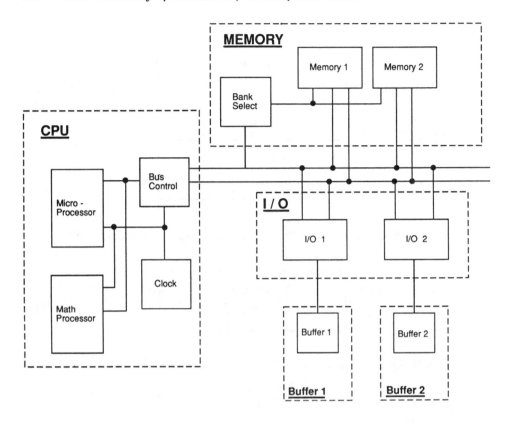

Figure 7.7: Rules–driven design. This block diagram shows a typical single–board computer. Dashed boxes identify related functions that should be grouped together on the finished PCB.

size requirements, the board must use SMT, which will further complicate the design process.

While technological advances aid the development of high–performance, high–speed, compact designs, they introduce new design rules that impact physical layout and manufacturing. For example, while ECL yields exceptionally fast designs, it is more sensitive to cross talk and heat; while SMT allows for dense packaging, it impedes layout efforts. Rules–driven design permits the design team to manage new design methodologies easily.

Implementing Rules–Driven Design. Using ValidGED, a hierarchical schematic editor, the design team captures the board design, defines the floor–plan (groups related functions together), identifies critical nets, and assigns priorities to component connections. To verify the board's circuitry, the design team simulates the logic with ValidSIM and checks the timing analysis with ValidTIME. When the optimal design has been achieved, the design is transmitted to the PCB designers for physical layout using Valid's Allegro design system for PCBs.

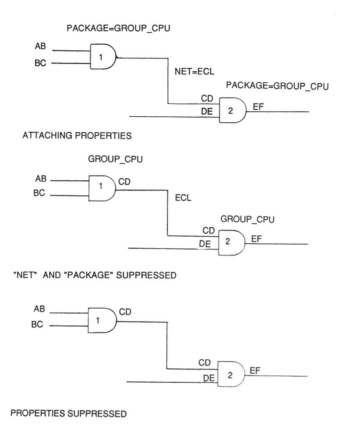

Figure 7.8: Rules are attached to components and nets as "properties" which become part of the design database.

Allegro, the first commercial expert–system available for PCB design and layout, recognizes and observes the properties assigned to components and signal nets in the schematic. Traditional PCBCAD tools follow only design rules governing spacing: line–width, line–to–line, line–to–shape, line–to–pad, shape–to–pad, shape–to–shape, and pad–to–pad. While these rules are important, they do not address specific electrical requirements. Allegro observes several classes of engineering–generated rules. Each rule has a prefix, *package* or *net*, that identifies the property assigned to the component or net and a suffix that identifies the specific rule applied.

Allegro is easy to use (see Figure 7.8). While in the schematic environment, the design engineer selects the *property* command from the menu, then points at the component or net where the property is to be attached and types the directive. Gate 1 has the property *package=group–cpu*. This means that gate 1 should be a part of a larger group called *cpu*. Allegro will place this component in the room identified as *cpu* for layout.

Signal *cd*, the net that attaches gate 1 to gate 2, has the property *net=ecl*. This identifies the net as an ECL net and tells Allegro to give it special treatment during physical layout. Note that gate 2 also is labeled as a part of *group–cpu*. It is not necessary to retype the directives each time; properties can be copied using the *copy* command in the ValidGED package.

Since properties can clutter the schematic, experienced design engineers usually display only the suffix. When design engineers are working on the schematic for logical functions and are not concerned with properties, all directives can be suppressed: The properties can be recalled with the press of a button.

Controlling the Floorplan. Floorplanning is the assignment of logical functions to specific areas of the design. Most PCB automatic–placement systems are based on algorithms that are not sophisticated enough to recognize and observe logical groupings of components. However, the rules–driven–design concept permits design engineers to identify in the schematic related functions that should be grouped when the design is laid out. Allegro understands the directives specified by the design engineer and incorporates these in the design's physical layout.

Managing a design's floorplan is desirable for several reasons. First, logical groupings speed the placement process. Since general grouping decisions have been made, the number of possible layout patterns is reduced.

Second, grouping logical components assists the autorouter to achieve the optimal routing strategy. Since the components that need to be connected are physically closer, critical paths (as defined by the engineer) are shorter. Therefore, cross talk and line reflections can be eliminated. Also, grouping logical functions makes the completed design easier to test and repair.

To create a design's floorplan, the design engineer includes a diagram of the board's divisions with the netlist given to the layout specialist. Each division, called a room, is assigned a name based on the components that will occupy the room.

Priority Nets

In addition to grouping logical functions, rules–driven design allows engineers to specify the priority of component placement within each room. Using the *weight* property in ValidGED, the design engineer can specify the relative importance of components that need to be placed.

For example, if the bus between the microprocessor and the math coprocessor in the CPU room is given the highest priority, Allegro first will position the microprocessor and the math coprocessor to optimize the net. If the design engineer has assigned secondary priorities, to other nets, Allegro will place these next. If other nets are not assigned weights, Allegro will place the remaining components with consideration of their affinity (number of actual connections) to other already–placed components.

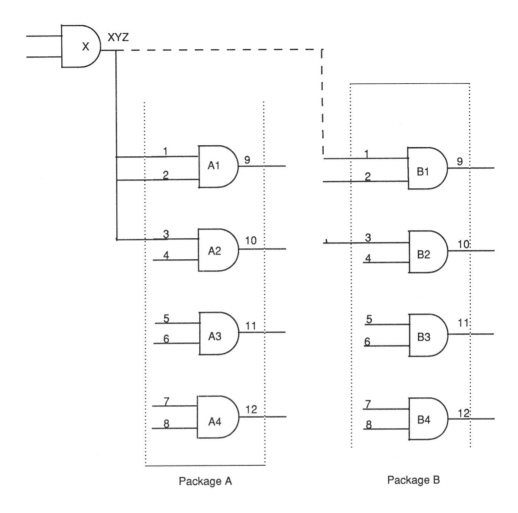

Figure 7.9: Diagram of Allegro PCB routers. Allegro, like most PCB routers, employs swapping techniques to assist routing.

The PCB designer can optimize the layout using the floorplan and the assigned priorities. Rooms can be treated like individual PCBs. The designer can establish the optimal placement grid for each room based on the components to be housed (axial, DIP, SMDs, etc.), define boundaries between rooms as hard or soft, and indicate component location (pin 1 or body center) to accommodate downstream CAM equipment.

Routing Control: High–Frequency Nets

Allegro, like most PCB routers, employs swapping techniques to assist routing. If package A and package B are identical, but are located on different parts of

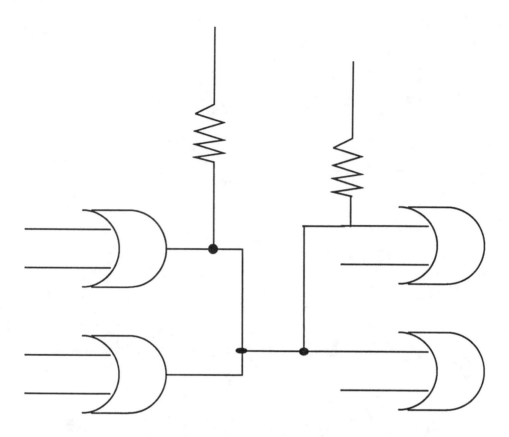

Figure 7.10: Diagram of a typical ECL net.

the board, it is possible to simplify routing by swapping the input pins on individual gates, gates within a package, gates between packages, or complete packages (see Figure 7.9).

With TTL, swapping is an acceptable technique to alter routing, but with ECL, swapping can cause problems if gates are part of critical high–frequency circuits. Swapping may make a critical trace too long, causing reflections that could result in unstable circuit operation.

To prevent swapping of high–frequency nets, design engineers can indicate on the schematic where swapping is permissible. A variety of directives control swapping. For example, *fix–all* prevents all swapping for the specified package; *no–swap–comp* prohibits swapping of complete components, but allows gate and pin swapping. With rules–driven design, engineers can modify the floor plan to accommodate swapping. They can indicate where swapping is and is not allowed: within a package, within a room, or from room to room.

Once packages and gates are defined, the next step is to rout the traces. Figure 7.10 shows a typical ECL net as it would appear on a schematic. Since ECL outputs can be wired *Or*ed, there are multiple sources as well as multiple loads. There are two ways that an ECL net could be routed. First, routing typical of TTL nets could be used: 90–deg corners, vias that change levels on the board, and stubs to connect multiple loads. While this routing is acceptable for TTL, it will result in excessive reflection in high–speed ECL nets.

Second, ECL routing could be used: 45–deg angles, no vias, no stubs, and daisy–chain routing. Since Allegro understands sources and loads, it routes all sources first, then all loads, and places the terminator at the end of the daisy chain. Allegro will handle all nets identified as ECL in this manner.

The label *net=ecl* imposes specific rules on the autorouter. Individual routing functions can be controlled with a variety of directives. *No–route* tells Allegro that a specific net will be routed manually; *route–line–width–(value)* specifies a line width greater than the standard—power lines and some analog lines may be wider than signal lines; *route–priority–(value)* identifies the order in which traces are to be routed; and *stub–length–(value)* is used to limit the length of stubs.

To achieve 100% routing, rip–up–and–reroute techniques often are used by autorouters. However, when a trace is ripped up, the new trace usually is longer than the original. This may be acceptable in TTL designs, but with ECL, the design's performance could suffer. To control this function, Allegro has a directive, *no–ripup*, that protects previously routed critical nets.

Conclusion

Rules–driven design allows engineers to communicate with layout designers to produce high–performance ICs and PCBs that are logically and electrically correct, as well as easier to test and repair. The key to rules–driven design is an integrated set of tools that permits front–end design functions to direct back–end design functions.

Properties assigned in the schematic drive the downstream layout functions of placement and routing to produce the optimal design. With rules–driven design, the schematic contains the implementation rules, as well as the functional definition of the design. These rules become part of the design database.

Rules–driven design is the keystone needed to link the design cycle with the product life cycle. With rules–driven design, test engineers can work with design engineers to specify signal accessibility in multilayer boards for automatic test equipment (ATE); rules to prioritize components for automatic insertion can be included to aid CAM efforts; and, chip design can be expanded to include hybrids.

Valid Logic Systems believes rules–driven design in the next major advancement in design methodology, perhaps matching structured, hierarchical design in its impact on electronic design.

CHAPTER 8

PHYSICAL LAYOUT— INTEGRATED

• The New World of ASICs •

The proliferation of CAE tools, including those for schematic entry, netlist extraction, and logic simulation, has greatly shortened the logic–circuit design cycle. The immediate beneficiaries are the semiconductor manufacturers, who have been the first to use these tools to compress circuits with hundreds of thousands of switching transistors and tens of thousands of logic gates into VLSI semiconductors. But while these tools have produced standard products like new–generation microprocessors (the Intel 80386 or the Motorola 68020, for example) and very–high–density memories, they can be used efficiently for custom products as well. Major electronics system users and manufacturers—the large automobile manufacturers, for example—increasingly have petitioned the semiconductor manufacturers to build specialized parts for them.

Consequently, there is a movement toward improving these automated tools, to decrease the time involved in designing and building a new semiconductor and to lower the manufacturing cost of the finished product. There also is a movement among semiconductor manufacturers to lock in new business by putting these design tools in the hands of their potential customers and encouraging them to design their own chips. Hence, there is a strong promotional effort on behalf of customer–designed ASICs.

While ASIC technologies like gate arrays and PLDs have made it increasingly easy for experienced logic designers to convert board–level circuits to compact MSI and LSI components, there frequently is little correspondence between a packaged component function (a two–input *nand* gate, for example) and the version of that function that is integrated with the other functions on a single chip.

Like PCB manufacturing, the making of ICs involves photoresist layers and chemical etching. Unlike PCB manufacturing, this chemical etching takes place on a microscopic level and frequently alternates with the process of making chemical implants and growing electrically active layers from these implants in diffusion furnaces with temperatures on the order of 1500°C. Making an IC is like duplicating the architectural complexity of New York City—with its skyscrapers, alleys, bridges, and roadways—on the head of a pin. Keep in mind that if only one transistor on a big chip with 100,000 or more transistors does not work, the entire chip is lost.

Manufacturing ICs might be seen as akin to baking cookies, in that the economy of the process depends on the proportion of perfect cookies or chips that comes out of the oven. The higher the proportion of perfect ICs on each cookie tray or wafer (that is, the higher the yield), the more economical the process and the cheaper the manufactured parts become. But making semiconductors still has elements of black magic, in that very few people know how many perfect parts the oven will produce in each cycle. Increasing the density and complexity of the manufactured circuits only increases the probability that something will go wrong. Few engineers understand the capabilities of a semiconductor–manufacturing process as well as do the semiconductor manufacturers themselves.

Consequently, this chapter makes a sharp distinction between the semiconductor–layout tools that semiconductor manufacturers offer their customers, and those they keep exclusively for their own use. Along with the tools that IC makers release to their potential customers, there often is a promotional message that says, in effect, "We make it easy and cheap for you to design your own IC." While such a statement is not entirely untrue (and is, in fact, becoming more true each day), it needs to be measured against the realities of semiconductor manufacturing. CPU time for fault simulation, as suggested in Chapter 6, can cost $9,000 to $15,000. NRE costs for a new part—even a semicustom IC—frequently run as high as $50,000. And the first prototype of a new IC, complete with a package of vectors for production testing, may cost a total of $100,000. Few electronics manufacturers are in a position to invest this kind of money in a new VLSI part, and those that do hope to recover their investment either with a cost–no–object government contract or with the volumes available in the consumer–electronics market.

Regardless of whether the part becomes a standard offering of the semiconductor maker or is sold as an ASIC to a customer, there is a trade–off between layout efficiency and time to market. While the computer programs are improving, a hand–packed IC layout will offer the highest performance (because of the short interconnection paths) and, ironically, the lowest manufacturing cost (because the small die size produces or yields many more chips with each wafer). Still, handcrafting can take six months of individual effort just on layout.

In contrast, a thoroughly automated effort—an automatically laid–out gate array, for example—can turn out working silicon within six weeks of netlist submission, but the resulting chip is likely to be big, compromised in performance, and expensive to manufacture. The new standard–cell libraries— software versions of earlier SSI and MSI logic components—coupled with sophisticated placement and routing tools, promise even greater silicon efficiency than do gate arrays or PLDs. Standard–cell libraries make it possible to build smaller chips that are less costly to manufacture or to embody even more LSI or VLSI functions on the same chip.

There also is silicon–compilation technology, which promises to generate efficient chip layouts from high–level–language entries, but so far this has been largely an experimental tool for research organizations, big vertically integrated electronics systems manufacturers, or the semiconductor makers themselves.

The largest proportion of new ASIC devices built in the next few years probably will be gate arrays and PLDs. The differences among these products, full–custom ICs, and standard products—especially differences in the way they are laid out—will be examined in this chapter.

Manufacturing Process Technology

In principle, the process for manufacturing ICs should be invisible to customers: They are, after all, buying packaged and tested ICs. But there are many kinds of semiconductor–manufacturing processes that offer special capabilities to and impose trade–offs on the user. This section summarizes some of the semiconductor manufacturing processes and the trade–offs they impose on the IC user.

The biggest trade–off is the speed–power product. There is a natural trade–off between switching speed (in megahertz) and power consumption (in fractions of a watt). The faster a circuit goes, the more power it consumes and the hotter it is likely to get. In the operation of an electronic circuit, not all the energy applied to turning a transistor switch on and off will come out as a voltage or current. A good deal of it will appear as heat. When 100,000 microscopic heat generators are crowded together in an area smaller than a fingernail, there is enough concentrated energy to start fires. Typically, there is an investment in heat sinks, special packaging and cooling equipment (for example, special plumbing, as in the Cray supercomputer) to keep the largest and fastest VLSI circuits cool. Even if the device does not burn itself up, the charges imposed by the utility company for power consumption must be figured into the speed–power balance.

A second trade–off is in density and speed. In principle, the tighter the transistors are packed, the shorter the interconnection paths between them. In practice, the manufacturing processes that produce the fastest transistors also are stuck with large transistors, which makes it difficult to obtain high packing densities. The GaAs process, for example, will produce transistors capable of switching at gigahertz (GHz) rates—billions of cycles per second—but, in addition to consuming extravagant amounts of power, this process allows only small levels of integration.   A 4–kbit RAM is about the highest density obtainable these days for GaAs; MOS, in contrast, currently is producing 4–Mbit RAMs—an order of magnitude more dense.

CMOS is the current darling of semiconductor manufacturing, since it offers users the best balance among speed, packing density, power consumption, and cost. Because of the popularity of the process, it is perpetually being revised to offer even higher speeds, larger packing densities, and less power consumption. This is accomplished by reducing the feature size in microns (μm) of the manufactured transistors. Three–micron CMOS currently is considered run–of–the–mill, while 2-μm CMOS is a more desirable choice for performance. While many semiconductor manufacturers can provide 1.25-μm CMOS, this still is considered a high–end process to be exploited only by handsomely funded projects like the DoD's VHSIC program.

Despite its utility for digital circuits, however, CMOS has its drawbacks. MOS transistors make natural switches, but terrible amplifiers.   They frequently have difficulty driving a signal large enough to be measured at the metal pins of the transistor package. The smaller the feature size, in addition, the more likely it is that the transistor will break down under excessive voltage, current, or heat conditions. Even excessive speed will cause an MOS transistor to freeze or latch up—a stuck–at–one or stuck–at–zero condition.

Consequently, bipolar processes generally are used for analog circuits that must amplify or transmit some sort of controlled voltage or current. ECL is an example of a bipolar process that typically is used for very–high–speed digital–logic circuits. Bipolar processes produce larger transistors, consume more power, and allow less packing density than do MOS circuits.   Some manufacturers are trading on their ability to embed bipolar transistors within a layout of a CMOS circuit—a process that offers the packing density of CMOS with the signal–driving and speed capability of bipolar processes. The layout of these BiMOS (bipolar metal oxide silicon) or BiCMOS (bipolar complementary metal oxide silicon) circuits becomes more complicated, however, and the cost of the manufactured parts goes up.

Because the choice of manufacturing process figures so heavily into the design of semiconductor (whether it is a standard part or an ASIC), the physical layout of the IC is practically dictated by process. The physical layout is, after all, a manufacturing plan—a photolithographic mask set—for the finished IC. Each transistor and each logic gate must be sized and arranged on the chip in conformance with the requirements of the manufacturing process. This must be reflected in the automated layout tools. While there is a strong movement to make these physical layout tools what manufacturers call technology independent, the physical design rules of the manufacturing process somehow must be entered into the system and checked meticulously.

If the layout of an IC is performed automatically by a computer (or by a human operator on a computer), the layout must be checked against the design rules of a particular manufacturing process. The layout produced in one technology will not be suitable for, or easily convertible to, another technology. Even where a 3-μm CMOS layout is intended for use on a 1.25-μm CMOS manufacturing line, the compaction is so drastic that critical paths are affected.

The IC must be simulated again to reveal the effects of timing on critical paths, and, frequently, the layout must be redone.

Building an automated layout system for each particular manufacturing process requires many person–years of programming effort. Rather than expend the labor required for each process, especially as the processes are being revised and changed constantly, manufacturers will try to adopt a versatile layout methodology, one that is compatible with a variety of technologies. The design rules frequently are entered into the system after some tentative layout has been obtained. But the results are never perfect, and some sort of hand–tweaking— the rearrangement of transistors and logic gates by someone who knows the manufacturing process—usually is required. The only way to guarantee conformity with a process, to ensure that each transistor is manufacturable by that process, is to use a layout system specifically designed for that process or to draw each transistor by hand.

Polygon Editing and Other Handcrafting Techniques

Until relatively recently, handcrafting was the only reliable method for laying out an IC. Computer–graphic systems, like the GDS–II system sold by Calma, were based on Data General workstations and intended as a graphic aid to the IC designer who would draw all the elements of an IC by hand. The base, collector, and emitter connections of a silicon transistor on the surface of a semiconductor IC would be represented on the screen as a crosshatch of squares and rectangles (that is, the polygons). Although entered by hand, the output of this process would be a computer–graphics file—in Calma's Stream (GDS–II) format or Calpoly's intermediate file (CIF) format—that could be used to generate the ultraprecise photolithographic masks used to manufacture the ICs.

The masks generated by this process would be geared to a specific semiconductor manufacturing process, such as bipolar, NMOS (negative–well metal oxide silicon), PMOS (positive–well metal oxide silicon), CMOS, or some variation. For each of these processes, the dimensions and placement of the polygons are absolutely critical, since the photolithographic masks generated by the process are used to build devices on a submicroscopic level. The misplacement or incorrect sizing of a polygon at this stage could result in an inoperative transistor in the final IC. And even one nonfunctional transistor out of 100,000 could destroy the functionality of the entire chip.

This methodology—polygon editing—forces the IC designer to either memorize or frequently reference an elaborate set of process design rules (the appropriate spacings for the transistors and contacts) and to draw the diffusion, polysilicon, and metal contact areas for each transistor by hand with meticulous reference to these rules.

Even in an age of higher levels of automation—symbolic editing, precharacterized cell blocks, and automated block–placement and routing programs to handle hundreds of thousands of transistors for each IC—polygon editing is not likely to disappear. As this chapter makes clear, ensuring the functionality of an IC remains an art form that typically requires an experienced IC designer to visually inspect and sometimes hand–tweak each transistor. Since IC designers construct each transistor by hand, based on their knowledge of the manufacturing process, this method ensures the most compact IC layout and is one of the best chances for getting working silicon on the first pass.

A symbolic layout methodology, in which the IC designer builds a layout from predrawn and precharacterized blocks (say, entire transistors), still is a handcrafting technique. Instead of hand–drawing diffusion and contact areas for each device, the IC–layout designer operates on the device level, picking each transistor and laying it down like an element in a tightly woven jigsaw puzzle. On the layout editor's screen, circuit elements with fixed sizes (such as transistors and contacts) are depicted with their true geometric representations to give the user visual feedback of their physical relationships. Transistors are selected and placed by the user at a terminal and then interconnected with stretchable wires that can be depicted by their true width or, as a shorthand, by their centerlines.

Layouts using this technique may not be as precise as those constructed with polygons. Moreover, the feasibility of the technique depends on the availability of large software libraries of transistor devices: Separate libraries are required for every manufacturing process at the semiconductor vendor's disposal. Nonetheless, this is a methodology being perfected for the semiconductor manufacturers by automated–layout specialists like Calma and ECAD.

ECAD's thinking is that by working on the device level rather than the polygon level, IC designers can increase their throughput—regardless of process technology. A symbolic layout editor, like ECAD's Symbad, will speed up a complex IC layout by allowing a designer to place and wire transistors on an IC in the same way that a circuit designer draws and wires components on a schematic diagram. By itself, symbolic layout will speed up the IC–layout process by enabling designers (at a workstation or computer terminal) to place and wire many more transistors each day than they could with conventional polygon–editing techniques. Consequently, experienced IC designers can increase their output from two to ten times: from 10 or 15 hand–drawn transistors per day with conventional polygon–editing techniques to more than 50 transistors per day with Symbad.

The problem with using a symbolic layout editor like Symbad is that its efficiency depends on the availability of a large library of transistors, one that includes all possible transistors for all the semiconductor–manufacturing processes used. Without a full symbol library, the IC designer is forced to go back to polygon editing.

However, tools like ECAD's do allow IC manufacturers to build library parts in a bottom–up manner from the assembled polygons. That is, a designer first uses transistors to build cells, then uses cells to build blocks, then uses blocks to build an IC. With Symbad, for example, users create a library of transistors and other semiconductor devices using a template provided by Symbad and their own process design rules. The process design rules, which are incorporated into the transistor models, contain definitions of the various process and metallization layers, device construction and spacing rules, and measurement and scaling references for every device. These rules can be entered in a textual format with a relatively simple syntax or imported into Symbad in bulk through a user technology file. (For example, the statement EXT POLY DIFFUSION GE 2.0 means that the minimum external spacing between polysilicon and diffusion areas is 2 microns.)

After the technology file is coded, the Symbad file compiler will translate the ASCII design rules for specific processes—NMOS, negative–well and positive–well CMOS, bipolar, and even exotic processes like GaAs—into an internal binary format that can be referenced by all Symbad application tools. The design rules primarily are used for on–line DRC during the interactive editing process. Since the process design rules are built into each transistor compacted by the Symbad system, the designer can function with correct–by–construction tools. The accuracy achieved by DRCs frequently is as good as or better than that of hand–drawn transistors.

The key to success is a common, integrated, and intelligent database—one similar to the object–oriented structures discussed in Chapter 4. This database records the topology of circuit—what connects with what—rather than its physical attributes and dimensions. Though the transistors and their wiring patterns are represented graphically on the workstation or computer–terminal screen, their representations in the database reflect the topology of the circuit more than its physical or geometric data.

The program understands connectivity, for example, and arranges devices and components in the database according to shared wire nets and other electrical interconnections. Each transistor is represented by its functional attributes in the database: These include generic structures with minimum feature sizes (for example, an MOS transistor with 2-μm geometries), plus electrical attributes specified by the user.

Many IC designers feel that polygon editing yields better silicon efficiency than does symbolic methodology. It is possible, however, to further compact the layout using an automatic compactor (with design constraints specified by the user). The compaction is a batch process: Once the elements are selected, placed, and routed, a compactor finds the smallest area consistent with the user–supplied design rules. In the case of ECAD's Symbad cell compactor, the software uses a constraint–graph algorithm that offers the best trade–off between small silicon area and speed. With the constraint–graph algorithm, a layout is modeled by a graph depicting the groups of elements as vertices and the spacing constraints between groups as edges. Groups of elements are formed based on connectivity to prevent them from drifting apart during compaction. For instance, an MOS transistor and the polysilicon wire connecting to its gate form a group and are moved together to preserve the connectivity.

The spacing constraints are dictated primarily by the design rules. For example, the minimum spacing between two wires on a metal layer translates into a *greater than or equal to* software statement. In operation, the compaction software attempts to calculate the shortest paths between connected elements, without violating the design–rule constraints.

The compactor takes a single–direction, multiple–pass approach in compacting a layout. A layout first is compacted in one direction (for instance, in the x–direction, where all objects move horizontally) and then in the y–direction. Users can choose to compact in only one direction when they are confident that there are no violations in the other direction. The order of compaction (x first or y first), similarly, can be determined by the user.

This compaction scheme differs from the virtual–grid approach, a once–promising algorithm in which the relative positions of all objects on one horizontal or vertical grid line remain fixed throughout the compaction. The Symbad compactor, in contrast, is gridless and allows many more degrees of freedom. The position of each element is determined solely by the connectivity and spacing constraints, independent of its grid position in the original layout.

Symbad is meant to run on VAX minicomputers (including the MicroVAX II) under VMS. It requires 5 MB of main memory to run efficiently, and the symbolic editor and associated libraries may require up to 400 MB of disk space. The user interface is a Tektronix 4111 or 4125 graphics terminal (or the Tektronix–compatible Seiko—San Jose, California 1104, 1105 terminals) equipped with a mouse or graphics tablet. Other versions of Symbad will allow the use of VAX GPX and Apollo workstations.

The Symbad compactor, using this algorithm, will take five minutes to compact a 2000–transistor design on a VAX 11/750. There is, in fact, a linear relationship between speed and design complexity. A design with twice the number of objects will take just a little more than twice the time to compact. The resulting IC comes very close in silicon area to hand–drawn and hand–packed designs. Evidence seems to indicate that the silicon efficiency of symbolic layout—with compaction—is well within 10% to 15% of a highly polished manual design.

Gate Arrays

Despite the efficiencies that can be obtained, hand–packed layout—even handcrafting with compaction—becomes increasingly impractical as the level of integration increases. It no longer may make sense to handcraft a VLSI IC with 50,000 or 80,000 logic gates and 280,000 transistors—transistor by transistor. Increasingly, time to market rather than manufacturing cost drives both the semiconductor manufacturers and their customers. They will settle for the somewhat less efficient layouts obtained with automated–layout tools, in favor of a shorter design time.

The manufacturers of a new microprocessor part—Intel, Motorola, or National Semiconductor, for instance—frequently will introduce a VLSI part as a configuration of preexisting blocks and then hand–tweak the layout for manufacturing efficiencies over a period of years. Because of their size and complexity, 32–bit processors like the Intel 80386, the Motorola 68030, or the Sun SPARC RISC processor could not have come to market without the aid of automated–layout tools. Each of these parts, however, will go through a revision—somewhat invisible to the user—in which the layout is compacted to provide the same functionality, but with a higher speed and a reduced manufacturing cost. In a viciously competitive market, the semiconductor makers may not even get a chance to compact the layout of one processor before a competitive next–generation microprocessor makes its appearance.

In the case of a custom or semicustom part, the user may be interested in rapid turnaround and the shrinkage in PCB real estate that a VLSI semiconductor makes possible, but the production runs may be so small that compaction or hand–packing will never be justified.

In many of these cases, a gate array will satisfy the requirements. Next to user–programmable logic devices, gate arrays account for the largest proportion of ASIC designs. A gate array is a semiconductor that is manufactured as a series of general–purpose logic cells and later configured (or wired) to perform specific functions according to the user's specifications. The semiconductor manufacturer configures the arrays by wiring the cells together—metallizing the chip—in the final stages of manufacture.

Most gate arrays are manufactured as a series of general–purpose cells laid out in rows across the surface of a chip. In most cases, the cells are uniform in size, as are the channels between the rows. But in the initial stages of manufacture, these general–purpose logic cells have no assigned function. The cells contain transistor switches that can be configured as simple logic gates, performing *and, or, xor, nand,* and *nor* functions. Several of these cells can be wired together to create more complex logic functions such as flip–flops, counters, latches, and memories. The parts first are manufactured in this general–purpose format and then set aside. Later, after the customer has decided how the cells are to be configured, the parts are metallized, packaged, tested, and shipped.

Because gate–array circuits really are built on the surfaces of preexisting parts, the turnaround for a new design is extremely short—usually weeks. A complex design might take six months to complete, but this still is several times faster than the two years it generally takes to design and build a new microprocessor. The mechanical problems include translating a netlist into a physical layout, choosing the logic cells required to execute the circuit functions, deciding upon their optimum physical arrangement, picking a path for the wiring between the cells, and deciding how the finished parts will be tested (a subject discussed in the next chapter).

Most of the layout programs for gate arrays include an import utility that will compile a simulator netlist—say, from TEGAS—for use by a layout package. In some cases, completely laid–out cell blocks in a GDS–II Stream or CIF format can be imported. If the logic components identified in the netlist can be translated into the cells of a gate array, then the arrangement of cells and the wiring paths between them—a procedure known as placement and routing— usually can be completed automatically by the computer.

Block Placement and Routing

In principle, the block–placement and routing software works like a manual operator, placing component blocks (in this case, layout cells consisting of simple or complex logic), wiring them together, and, in some cases, rearranging the blocks to obtain an optimum (that is, a minimally congested) wiring pattern. While different programs will offer various degrees of user control and interactivity, the same general procedure holds whether the block–placement software operates automatically or interactively. While they are highly interdependent (a good placement program will work to shorten critical wiring paths, while relieving wire–path congestion), placement and routing are two separate programs.

The most efficient placement and routing systems, at least in terms of computer run time, are those that segregate topological data (how things are connected with each other) from physical design rules (what these things actually look like). The initial placement and routing of blocks are performed without reference to design rules, using only connectivity information. Later, a specific set of design rules is applied to the layout process.

In operation, the placement program first makes an initial placement in a floor–planning phase. In this phase, only the connections identified by the netlist, the physical outlines of the block, and the location and layers of the pin–outs are used. The most densely connected blocks are clustered and arranged in a row structure; often, the software will assume that the channel widths between the rows can vary according to the density of the interconnection paths. The routing area between blocks can be estimated by a global path–assignment algorithm, frequently included in the placement–optimization software.

Though this process runs automatically, the user can intervene at any time to optimize by hand the place–and–route decisions made by the machine. On an interactive screen, the user will see a rat's nest with flylines—straight lines drawn on the screen between pin–outs on the same net. Before autorouting, the user can work toward a better placement by moving individual blocks.

The routing areas initially shown on the screen do not accurately reflect the actual space required for physical routing, since it is very difficult for either the system or the user to predict the exact dimensions of the routing areas in the block–placement phase (without reference to specific design rules). However, the positions of the blocks will be adjusted automatically in successive iterations to accommodate the actual physical routing paths.

For gate arrays, the autorouter frequently relies on a combination of channel–routing and switchbox–routing algorithms. The channel router is used for regions between two neighboring blocks in a single row where the pin–outs of the blocks are fixed on the boundaries that form the banks of the channel. Here, two cells can be connected by extending a single wire in one direction down the channel. The switchbox router is used for those regions where the channels intersect each other and where wires typically must establish a junction to effect a bend or right turn.

In normal channel–routing practice, a wire is stretchable in only one direction, lengthwise. A jog is the point along the wire where it can be stretched in another direction. For example, under the direction of the router, a wire can appear to take a 90–deg turn. Within the software, however, the single wire is made up of two segments at right angles to each other. The point at which they intersect is called a jog and usually is specified by the user. The 90–deg jog, however, can be quite costly in terms of silicon real estate, since it frequently forces the routing channels between cells to be wider than they have to be.

When the router reads in the physical design rules, it must calculate the physical coordinates of each individual interconnection line, to generate a final layout. If the routing space allocated during placement is different from that required for the actual routing, the router must either shift the blocks or rows of blocks to expand the routing area to accommodate the physical wire widths, or shrink the routing area to reduce the slack. These time–consuming computations preclude the possibility of interactive routing and force most routers to operate in batch mode only.

In theory, the placement–and–routing system has many degrees of freedom. A sea–of–gates array would allow any general–purpose cell on the array to be configured for any purpose and would accommodate a wide variety of block placements. (This also is true for standard cells.) Many gate arrays, however, include cells whose transistors are laid out in a pattern that lends itself more to one type of logic function than to another. For example, some transistor arrangements lend themselves well to two–input *nand* and *nor* gates and more complex functions such as flip–flops and memories, but not to counters and latches. Such a system would impose layout constraints. In operation, there are a number of such constraints under which the system must operate.

One problem is the number of metallization layers the gate array will allow. While some sophisticated arrays allow triple–level metal (three wiring layers), the majority of gate–array suppliers are offering only two metallization layers. The entire array must be wired on two surfaces.

A related problem is the width of the channels between the rows of logic cells. A narrow channel would tend to limit the complexity of the wiring between the cells of each row.

A third problem (discussed in detail in Chapter 9) is the amount of space on the chip that must be devoted to self–test logic. Many complex–logic ICs include their own test–pattern generators that facilitate testing of the completed chip. These test–pattern generators can take up a good deal of the available logic cells.

The constraints of placement and routing, in addition to absorbing considerable run time on a computer, may force designers into using a much larger array than they had in mind. A design with 4000 logic gates may be forced into a 10,000–gate array, simply because the placement–and–routing software could not find comfortable patterns for the design on a more economical 6000–gate array. While this software typically provides the fastest turnaround for a semicustom IC design, it remains the most costly in terms of silicon use.

Analog Arrays

Practically all semicustom IC applications are geared toward digital–logic gates. Despite the enormous market opportunity, the field of analog semicustom circuits is not as fully developed as is the field of digital circuits. While most of the customizable analog functions now can be satisfied with standardized, prepackaged parts, it certainly is possible to reduce PCB real estate by integrating a variety of linear functions onto a single chip.

There are analog arrays available from manufacturers like Exar Corporation (Sunnyvale, California), Micro Linear Corporation (San Jose,

California), and Ferranti Interdesign (Scotts Valley, California) that, like digital arrays, are metallized according to customer specifications. The design is in the metallization paths between components on the surface of the chip, and this, too, can be automated with CAE software.

However, analog–array technology does not enjoy the same popularity among analog engineers as gate arrays do among digital–logic designers. The reason is that analog arrays tend to be overly large and, consequently, expensive to manufacture. Unlike the completely uniform switching transistors used in digital–logic circuits, the transistors in analog circuits must include a variety of sizes proportional to the magnitude of the voltages and currents they must handle. An amplifier circuit, for example, typically will reflect a scaling of transistors from small to large at each stage from input to output. While a big digital circuit typically will include 100,000 to 250,000 switching transistors, a big analog circuit may use only 32 (not 32,000—just 32!) carefully matched transistors.

A versatile analog array will provide a variety of transistors and other components—resistors and capacitors—that an analog designer might use to build amplifiers, comparators, phase–locked loops, or other analog functions. But just as digital designers find it impossible to use everything available on the array, analog–array users never will use all the components on the chip. If they fail to use some big output transistors, for example, a good third of the surface area of the chip could be wasted. This can be far more costly than the use of standardized, prepackaged building blocks.

Even where analog–circuit elements are combined with digital elements on a semicustom part, the placement and routing of analog blocks typically are done by hand. Analog circuits pose a difficult problem for automated IC layout, for several reasons. First, unlike digital–logic circuits, which use uniformly sized transistor switches, analog circuits require odd–sized transistors. Amplifier circuits, in particular, frequently use a variety of scaled transistors in a chain between inputs and outputs: A small transistor drives a larger one, which drives a still larger one, and so forth. The second problem is that the higher voltages and currents produced by analog circuits will produce hot spots on the surface of the semiconductor. The part must be laid out in such a way that heat will not affect other parts of the circuit and can be conducted away from the device easily. Third, even where the transistors do not contain hot spots and are uniform in size (as in CMOS circuits), an analog circuit frequently consists of odd–shaped blocks. For example, considerable ingenuity is required to arrange the thin–film resistor networks, data latches and registers, and amplifiers and voltage references that are required to make a typical data–converter part.

Consequently, the only block–placement and routing programs to handle analog circuits actually grew from an ability to juggle odd–sized digital cell blocks (such as L–shaped and U–shaped blocks). The first was developed at the Thomson–SGS Microelectronics facility in Agrate, Italy. This place–and–route package works from the outlines and pin–out information provided for predefined digital cell blocks (such as standard logic cells, special–function cells called macros, or hand–packed cells). Since the Thomson–SGS block router is insensitive to what is inside the blocks, it can place and route analog as well as digital cell blocks—even mixed analog and digital cells (such as data-converter parts). The software package performs 100% placement and routing and generates interconnection path lengths and capacitive–loading data for use by a simulator. (Capacitance obviously will have different effects on an analog circuit than on a digital one.) The package runs on a VAX using Tektronix 4109 terminals and is intended to replace the manual routing tasks now performed on a Daisy ChipMaster.

The production version of Thomson–SGS's placement–and–routing software, for example, is intended for use with the Zodiac family of predefined cells. The block–routing software will handle more than 80 different bipolar and IIL (integrated injection logic) cell blocks, including op amps and switched-capacitor filters, as well as digital–logic gates.

Dimensional constraints usually are specified when building a family of cells of the same height or width, which many IC manufacturers call standard cells. By placing constraints on the location of cell pin–outs, the pin–outs of one cell can be matched with those of other cells to ensure easy abutment or easy connection with an external bus. However, the standard–cell approach also can be used to place and route odd–sized cells.

Standard Cells

The major difference between gate–array and standard–cell designs is that gate arrays consist of prefabricated, general–purpose logic blocks, and standard cells exist as general–purpose building blocks only in software. Like the gate–array cell libraries, the standard–cell libraries—digitized versions of earlier SSI and MSI logic components—are coupled with placement and routing tools to build a hypothetical chip. The layout is used not just to metallize an existing chip, but to build an entire chip from scratch. The advantage of this approach is that it provides greater silicon efficiency than do gate arrays. Unused cells never appear in the finished layout or take up space on the manufactured parts.

With many standard–cell libraries, each of the cells is the same height, which simplifies placement and routing, but often creates confusion between gate–array and standard–cell layouts. A standard–cell layout from IMP, International Microelectronic Products (San Jose, California), or AMI, the American Microcircuits Inc. subsidiary of Gould (Santa Clara, California), does not look significantly different from a gate–array layout. But since there are no unused cells on the chip, this process is a very efficient use of silicon area.

Standard–cell libraries make it possible to build smaller chips that are less costly to manufacture. In principle, they make it possible to embody larger LSI or VLSI functions on the same chip. That is, complex logic blocks like ALUs, RAMs, and ROMs, which are difficult to implement with the uniform row structure of a gate array, in principle can be added to the layout of a standard-cell IC (as long as the model of the odd–sized component exists in the standard-cell library). Standard cells, in fact, most often refer to layouts with these odd-sized blocks.

National Semiconductor believes that the largest proportion of new semiconductors built in the next few years probably will be standard–cell designs. Because the chip is designed and built in software, rather than in hardware, the success of a standard–cell design depends on the availability of software models for the logic functions that designers are likely to use.

National's microCMOS Standard Cell Library, for example, is typical of the software models needed to support standard–cell design. The microCMOS Standard Cell family is constructed with 2–μm geometries, using silicon–gate and two–layer metal interconnects. The library contains virtually every digital–logic function used by ASIC designers: *and, or, nand,* and *nor* gates; exclusive *ors*; inverters; D and JK flip–flops; and input and output buffers. In addition to the simple logic gates, the National library includes larger macros, such as counters and memory functions, that can be the building blocks for more complex circuit functions. Future additions to the Macro Cell Library will include complete 8– and 16–bit CMOS microcontrollers, as well as parts with the functionality of the 32000–series 32–bit microprocessors.

National's Standard Cell Library is distributed as a Design Kit consisting of data books, floppy disks describing standard–cell functions, and a netlist extractor. The Design Kit is compatible with Daisy's hardware, although future versions will offer compatibility with the Apollo hardware platforms used by Mentor, as well as IBM PCs such as the PC/XT and PC/AT. Even now, National Semiconductor will accept designs in the popular FutureNet pin–list format.

While the placement of predefined blocks can be performed either manually or automatically, physical layout of a standard–cell design typically is performed on a mainframe or minicomputer. National Semiconductor's own automated design system harnesses mainframe–computer resources—the Hitachi–made NAS 9080 (a National Advanced Systems—Santa Clara, California—computer that is software– and operating–system–compatible with IBM mainframes). Physical layout is performed automatically on the mainframe using VR cell–placement and routing software. Although it requires an extensive amount of computer run time, the VR software (Merlin S) guarantees maximum silicon efficiency with 100% placement and routing.

The placement–and–routing programs that guarantee 100% success without human intervention, like Merlin S, are intended to implement the physical interconnections with minimum wire length and routing area. In principle, the placer can accommodate blocks of any height or width. The placer arranges the position and orientation of the blocks according to their geometry, their pin–outs, and their interconnections, attempting to minimize the chip area. The user, however, must identify any wire nets whose length is critical for a part's performance. This critical path becomes a criterion of the placement activity.

The router, similarly, functions with rectangular blocks of arbitrary shapes and sizes and imposes no artificial restrictions on the locations and layers of the terminals. The system guarantees 100% routing completion, regardless of the initial block placement. Besides individual net routing, the router will provide bus routing (several lines in parallel), where the nets can be bundled together without creating a difference in capacitive loading between any of the wires on the bus (that is, the capacitance on each wire of the bus must remain the same in order for them to be bundled).

In addition to wire length, the router also is sensitive to local congestions. In operation, the router will avoid locally congested channels for noncritical nets. However, it has a tendency to widen the routing channels and to prevent the block positions from being drastically different after compaction than they were at the original placement. The trade–offs between minimum wire length and large channel congestion, consequently, must be weighed by the user before setting the router in gear.

Once the layout has been completed and the critical wiring paths determined, the performance of the IC is simulated once to ensure that all the performance goals have been met. There are several ways to accomplish this. In many semiconductor–manufacturing facilities, for example, a circuit is extracted from the finished layout, and a new performance estimate is compiled from this circuit. In the postroute simulation performed at National, an ECAD LVS (layout versus schematic) program is used to extract a circuit netlist from the layout. This extracted circuit can be compared with the original circuit. The performance of this extracted circuit, however, is simulated again with the HILO simulation software. Once again, the simulator provides a statement of the probable nodes exercised and a general assessment of risks, before the layout is turned over to manufacturing.

As with gate arrays, handcrafted layouts, or any other IC layout, the final product is checked by an IC design engineer on a Calma GDS–II workstation. IC masks are generated from the finished layout, and these are transferred to fabrication facilities for the construction of prototype IC wafers. A wafer probe verifies the integrity of the fabrication process by identifying functional ICs on the first wafer. In the next step, the engineering prototypes are packaged and marked according to specifications. In the final step, the packaged prototype is tested with a Fairchild Sentry IC tester, using vectors (test patterns) supplied with the original design.

The success of the standard–cell program depends not only on the availability of a large library of cell models, but also on the placement–and–routing software used to come up with a layout. To justify the use of standard cells, with their more expensive simulation and longer preparation and layout times, the standard–cell programs consistently must offer better silicon efficiency than can be obtained with gate–array designs.

Consequently, there is a great deal of ongoing research and development in the area of placement–and–routing algorithms. Daisy, for example, probably deserves credit for a fast, reasonably efficient method of arranging gates on a sea–of–gates array. It is called *simulated annealing*, because it is analogous to the process for hardening metals with successive heating–and–quenching cycles. Simulated annealing obtains fairly compact chip layouts by iteratively juggling logic cells. The same process is used with good results to metallize channel–less gate arrays; that is, gate arrays with stretchable channel widths.

As an example of the run–time efficiency obtained with simulated annealing, Daisy used its MegaGatemaster accelerator to metallize a 10,000–gate sea–of–gates array manufactured by California Devices (San Jose,

California). With 85% gate utilization and 1800 nets, the placement and routing of logic cells took a little less than 10 hours.

Another placement algorithm, called *cluster placement*, is said to be somewhat faster than simulated annealing, although its layouts seldom are as compact. Exploited by SDA Systems (now part of ECAD) in a standard–cell placement program called MacroEdge, cluster placement frequently beats simulated annealing by a factor of 10. In operation, the algorithm first groups related cells into clusters, then sorts the clusters according to user–defined priorities (such as gate speed or die size), and finally breaks down the clusters into component cells.

Silicon–Compilation Techniques

Silicon compilation takes standard cells one step further: Instead of placing and routing previously described cells to form a new chip, the silicon– compilation approach allows the designer to build a new cell or series of cells directly from a high–level–language description of the part. In principle, a designer enters a circuit using the same kind of schematic–capture tools as described in Chapter 3. Instead of generating a netlist or a simulation waveform, the silicon–compilation program converts the entry into the layout for a new chip.

Theorists of silicon compilation predict that some day the users of silicon–compilation systems will not have to be electrical engineers, nor know all that much about circuit design. They can be computer scientists or systems architects. All they need is to be able to describe a part in functional terms: its inputs, its outputs, and the number of clocks in between. The compilation system will decide automatically what logic blocks will perform those functions most efficiently, will optimize and configure the internal circuits, will wire the blocks together, and will present a manufacturable layout to the user.

In practice, silicon–compilation technology has a way to go before it reaches this level of capability. While it is being used increasingly in commercial applications—the Genesil system from Silicon Compiler Systems, for example, was used to create Motorola's own RISC computer chip, the 88000— silicon compilation must overcome its image as an experimental tool for university research or DoD–funded projects. Just as standard–cell programs will depend on the availability of software models that depict the physical layout of logic cells, silicon compilation will depend on similar software–development effort.

Among the existing commercial silicon compilers, there are two types. One type relies on a topological description of a circuit— a sort of stick–figure representation—and performs all its manipulations on this topological representation. The design rules are read in toward the end of the process, before the final layout is generated. While this approach provides a high degree of technology independence, enabling one topological description to generate layouts in several different process technologies, and also uses reasonable run time on a minicomputer or workstation, the use of silicon area in the finished layout is never as efficient as in handcrafted layouts, and the layout frequently must be tweaked by a layout specialist.

A good number of compilers using this topological approach have not been commercialized. Gould AMI, for example, has put together an experimental compiler based on this approach to layout, using an artificial–intelligence language—LISP—as a way to teach the compiler new design rules. The French SYCOMORE project, a silicon compiler written in LISP, also embodies artificial–intelligence principles and constructs.

While early credit goes to John Vuillemin, a French researcher at Xerox PARC (Palo Alto Research Center) in California who did much of the work on the Dragon experimental workstation, and to Francois Anceau at Bull Systems Research Labs (Les Clayes, France), work on the SYCOMORE compiler was completed jointly by Bull Systems, Thomson Semiconductors (Grenoble, France), and INRIA—the National Institute for Research in Computer Science and Automation (Rocquencourt, France). Thomson's contribution was logic synthesis and the symbolic layout editor. Bull's contribution was behavioral simulation and autorouting. The actual silicon compiler, however, was built at INRIA in a variation of LISP called LE LISP, which runs on an artificial–intelligence engine marketed by Symbolics (Chatsworth, California).

The French researchers believe that the LISP–based compiler solves autorouting problems faster than other systems do. For example, the autorouting of an entire system consisting of 15 chips, with 15,000 to 20,000 transistors per chip, built in 2-μm CMOS with two–layer metal standard cells on a VTI workstation took almost three weeks (15 working days). The software problem that slowed the routing process was sizing the variable channel widths for multiple PLA blocks and data paths. A Symbolics machine, the French claim, completed the same project with 100% routing in a half hour, using interpretive LISP.

Apart from these experimental efforts, the best–known commercial vendor for this type of compiler is Seattle Silicon Technology (Bellevue, Washington), which also serves as a brokerage for up to 20 different silicon foundries.

The other approach to silicon compilation is closer to a standard– cell approach, in which a layout is built by pulling cells from a library of preconstructed cells with specific design rules and wiring them together. The best–known advocate of this approach is Silicon Compiler Systems. The major advantage is that the compiler can be used by system designers who have little knowledge of circuit design or layout considerations and, therefore, should not be required to tweak a layout.

The Genesil compilation system is based on a library of cells that is developed by Silicon Compiler Systems' customers. In fact, the major product of this company is the GDT (generator development tool), which allows code–writers to integrate their own custom compilers into Genesil—a compiler for compilers. Since functional blocks compiled in the Genesil environment are based on a set of fully characterized primitives, employing a controlled structural design methodology rather than a free–form approach, blocks generated using Genesil also can be used for standard–cell designs.

Release 7.0 of Genesil includes the LogicCompiler for automatic logic synthesis and minimization. This optional program converts high–level functional specifications created by Genesil into a single block of standard cells.

Users can synthesize these layouts with a variety of aspect ratios to improve the chip's floor plan. The LogicCompiler reduces overall chip size by allowing designers to merge several small blocks into a dense, cell–based block. The compiler can accommodate some fairly large logic blocks—RAMs, ROMs, and PLAs, for example.

In principle, these compilers allow a degree of portability between manufacturing technologies. The design for the large logic blocks can be specified using Silicon Compiler Systems' procedural L language. A separate technology file then can be used to define width and spacing rules; this lets manufacturers add new process rules to the program. The LogicCompiler will combine the logic–block description with the technology file to generate the new cell layout. The LogicCompiler intelligently minimizes the logic and automatically maps selected functions into a tight block of random logic.

For the most part, this approach lets the designer concentrate on architecture and lets the physical design tools optimize the results. While the program is useful in merging a number of small blocks together to shrink the layout, it cannot rework large array structures once they have been compiled and committed to the library of structures. It also absorbs more run time on the computer: The experimental SYCOMORE compiler, for example, offers a full order of magnitude improvement in run time for designs built on L–language descriptions.

A third type of layout generator, which represents a hybrid between the topological approach of Seattle Silicon and the cell generator of Silicon Compiler Systems, is a layout–synthesis program developed by by Caeco. Layout synthesis does not use previously compiled cells, but rather creates layouts on the fly from fairly low–level silicon structures. These structures include transistors, vias and contact areas, polysilicon layers, and metal layers. In operation, the system combines a circuit description with a technology file describing the silicon structures for each process.

In principle, the Caeco layout–synthesis system works like an ideal silicon compiler, generating manufacturable layouts from high–level–language descriptions. Since it is closely harnessed to specific design rules, it will generate fairly tight layouts—within 10% or 15% of handcrafted layouts. It builds structures using only lateral FETs. This includes MOS and related manufacturing technologies—CMOS, NMOS, PMOS, and even GaAs—but not bipolar technologies.

PLD Design

At the other end of the spectrum from silicon compilation, PLDs represent the highest percentage of custom or semicustom IC usage. The reason is that—unlike gate arrays, standard cells, or silicon compilers, which must be metallized or programmed to do a particular job by the IC manufacturer—PLDs are programmed by users themselves in the field.

For example, in examining the predominant applications of PLDs, Daisy concluded that glue logic or "garbage collection" was only a small part (less than 10%) of the uses to which PLDs typically were put. More predominant applications were state machines (30%) and encoding/decoding functions (up to 30%). While glue logic can be described in a schematic form, the more demanding applications require a more direct form of logic entry: state machine as well as high–level–language descriptions. Daisy's research revealed that typical PLD usage was not one–step/two–step, but frequently harnessed up to 100 devices to a single system.

There are several names for these types of field–programmable arrays: Some manufacturers call them PAL (programmable array logic), the brand name provided by Monolithic Memories (Santa Clara, California); some call them PLAs (programmable logic arrays), the term used by the Signetics subsidiary of N.V. Philips. One manufacturer, who makes a large PLD with the equivalent of 9000 gates, Xilinx (Santa Clara, California), refers to its part as a field–programmable gate array. In any case, the attraction of these devices is their low entry cost and the fact that the partitioning and programming tools are not controlled by the semiconductor manufacturers, but are in the hands of users. The PLDs rely on fuse–blowing structure to select a pattern of logic functions like *nand* and *nor*. Some manufacturers have vertical fuses; others have horizontal fuse types. But here, too, technology independence is a feature demanded in the partitioning and programming tools.

Users of a PLD design system like FutureNet's FutureDesigner, HP's PLD Design System, Minc's PLDesigner, or the Daisy PLD Master can enter their logic in any form they choose, compile the logic patterns or fuse–maps in any convenient language, and simulate the behavior of the PLD in circuit. Once users are comfortable with the predicted performance, they can download the logic program into the device of their choice. Most of these design systems combine a top–down hierarchical design philosophy and design–file–management tools with an almost interactive simulation capability. They still allow the user freedom of choice in devices, compilers, and programming inputs.

Rather than create a new programming language, for example, Daisy made a contribution in the ability to manage projects using hundreds of PLDs. Its design system will control separate design files for an almost limitless number of PLDs. In operation, the system will manage each PLD by its IC number in a drawing file, a feature that conveniently supports hierarchical design.

In addition, the functions of each PLD can be tried out in Daisy's mixed–mode simulated environment before any of its fuses are blown. In operation, the simulator runs in the background, allowing the user to manipulate circuit inputs (in this case, a state machine) in one window and display the resulting simulation waveforms in another window. Daisy's multiwindowed DNIX environment, in fact, also will show the compiler source file (ABEL is shown) and the programming logic (a JEDEC file) in still another window. In this manner, the user has almost continual feedback on the performance of the PLD in circuit.

While the PLD Master is among the first to allow programmers to work from state–machine inputs—either flow charts or tables—the system actually allows users to enter a logic pattern in any form in which they feel comfortable: as a schematic diagram (with patterns of gates), as a state–machine input, or as a textual high–level–language description. No other PLD programming system allows as many inputs.

In addition, the Daisy PLD Master will support a number of universal compilers—software that converts high–level–language descriptions into PLD fuse–maps—as well as a large variety of dedicated compilers for particular PLD types. The universal compilers include Data I/O's ABEL, while specific semiconductor compilers include Monolithic Memories' PALASM and Signetics' AMAZE. Designs can be compiled for virtually all PLDs, including some of the newest devices from these manufacturers as well as from Altera, AMD, Intel, Texas Instruments, Cypress, and Lattice Semiconductor.

The compilers convert the high–level–language description into a JEDEC file that can be used to program the target device. In the actual design flow, the state machine, schematics, or high–level–language inputs are compiled down to a JEDEC file, which is a description of a specific logic component. The JEDEC file will feed a simulator, as well as a PLD programming machine. A byproduct of the JEDEC file is a test pattern that can be used to test the finished PLD on a Sentry tester.

• Physical IC Design Methodologies •

The Basics of Handcrafted Layout

Handcrafted layout is the art of manually constructing the topology of an IC. Each mask layer is drawn by hand, and devices are formed by intersecting these layers. Handcrafting on a CAD system differs from handcrafting with a pencil, in that the designer may use computer–aided shortcuts to create and edit devices and interconnect layers.

For example, consider the creation of a metal–interconnect run. Using a pencil, the designer must draw the complete shape of the run, carefully drawing the width and the direction of the interconnect. On a CAD system, the designer may make use of a path component. A path is simply a line with a specified width attached to it. In this case, the designer inputs a single line, either the center or an edge, and the system automatically expands the line to its correct width.

Figure 8.1 compares the inputs and results of these two types of design (hand–drawn and CAD input). As can be seen, the use of a CAD system significantly reduces the amount of work required from the designer. Thus, as ICs become larger and the time–to–market requirement becomes shorter, it is imperative that designers make use of whatever automated tools are available to reduce their workload while accomplishing the desired result: an IC that works the first time.

Handcrafting is used as a design methodology where maximum circuit density is required; that is, where the maximum amount of data must be packed into the minimum amount of space or silicon real estate. Highly automated tools, such as block–place–and–route packages and silicon compilers, have not yet met these criteria. While it is true that they reduce the work of the

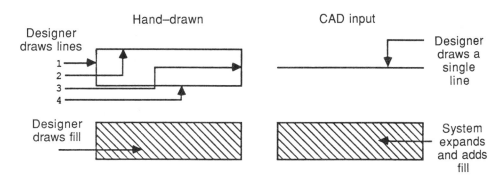

Figure 8.1: Comparing hand–drawn to CAD input. This figure compares the inputs and results of these two types of design.

designer, they are not optimized to produce the most tightly packed areas. To meet this goal, the skill and expertise of an IC layout designer are needed.

The trend in the IC industry today is to mix and match methodologies (for example, handcrafting, automatic place and route, cell generators, silicon compilers, or layout synthesis) to achieve the most efficient use of the designer's time and automated–tool capabilities. This approach is known as *composite IC design.* Each area of the chip is created using the best tool available and the methodology best suited for its needs. Then, the designer puts all the individual pieces together, creating the composite IC.

Handcrafting, although the most time–consuming method, always will play a key role in the design of highly complex ICs. Until such capabilities as the automatic synthesis of layout can duplicate the designer's mind and skill, the art of handcrafting will continue to command a significant role in the implementation of composite ICs.

Building Blocks: Polygons and Devices

There are two levels of building blocks used to create functional elements in handcrafted layout: polygons and devices. Polygons consist of a set of multivertex, closed, noncrossing lines assigned to a mask layer that represents a particular processing material. They are added together (for example, intersected, overlapped, or abutted) to form a complete device or transistor. Each polygon exists independently in the database, so that when designers want to edit or change a device, they must select all pertinent polygons and perform the appropriate edit on each of them. This is an error–prone process, as it is easy to miss a polygon or to make a mistake in one of the edits. Figure 8.2 shows four separate polygons that, when placed together, would form a simple transistor.

As edits become increasingly complex, the opportunity for error increases as well. In addition, when working with individual polygons, there is no device

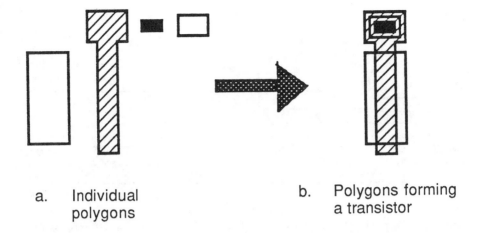

a.   Individual   b.   Polygons forming
     polygons   a transistor

Figure 8.2: Polygons. This figure shows four separate polygons (a) that, when placed together (b), would form a simple transistor.

information associated with the layout (for example, gate size, nodal connectivity, or design–rule requirements). To speed the design process and to reduce the opportunities for error, some CAD systems have introduced the concept of *device–level editing*.

Devices are complete descriptions of transistors composed of polygons, which are treated by the CAD system as a database entity. It is possible to associate parametric information, as well as their topological configurations, with these devices.

When an edit is made to a device, all polygons that make up that device are affected with one edit. If the CAD system provides for design–rule information, the device maintains its correctness, even when edited. Figure 8.3 shows a device—including the gate areas, contacts, and layer–to–layer design–rule constraints—edited to stretch and bend its shape and to add contacts.

If the device were not a database entity, but individual polygons instead, the steps required to achieve the same edits and ensure that they are done correctly would increase by orders of magnitude. Working with device–level entities, instead of with polygons, significantly increases the designer's productivity and reduces the overall design time by eliminating a large percentage of common design–rule violations.

Device–Level Layout: What Is Involved

The layout designer starts from a logic or schematic diagram. The schematic is broken into small and (hopefully) repetitive parts that can be laid out in cells. A cell is a collection of polygons and/or devices that represents a logic function or functions. It can be placed many times in a design, saving the designer from duplicate work.

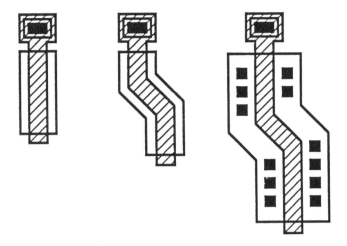

Figure 8.3: Devices. This figure shows a device—including the gate areas, contacts, and layer-to-layer design-rule constraints—edited to stretch and bend its shape and to add contacts.

After the relative sizes of the schematic parts or blocks are established, the layout designer creates a floor plan or block diagram of the entire circuit. The floor plan shows where individual blocks are to be located, as well as how to interconnect them, in accordance with the schematic diagram. Figure 8.4 is a simplified view of the IC design flow.

Each step in the IC design flow is iterative and provides information necessary to the successful completion of the other steps. When errors are discovered through analysis, or when the design of the circuit must change to meet new functional and/or performance criteria, the process begins again. The complete design cycle for a complex IC is a lengthy one, often taking person-years of effort.

When the floor plan is complete, actual layout of the circuit begins. The layout designer completes any necessary cell detail and begins to place and interconnect cells, following the map laid out in the floor plan. Sections of logic that do not lend themselves to the cell approach are laid out as random logic. Random logic includes logic that is used only once and may have to fit into an irregularly shaped area of the chip.

As the layout of the design progresses, the layout designer marks off the completed sections of the schematic and performs incremental checks to help ensure the accuracy (both design rule and logic to layout) of the design. When the layout is complete, it is ready for final verification.

Methodologies: Row-Based Standard Cells

The desire to automate the design of increasingly complex ICs motivated the inception of the row-based standard-cell methodology. This was one of the

The Logic Design Phase	The Physical Design Phase	
Schematic diagram	Mask layout	• Floor plan • Block diagram • Cell design • Composite design
Logic simulation	Mask verification	• Design rule checks • Electrical rule checks • Logic to layout checks • Parameter checks • Circuit simulation
Circuit simulation	Mask production	

Figure 8.4: IC design flow. This is a is a simplified view of the IC design flow.

first IC layout–automation methods, developed in the late 1960s at Bell Laboratories and at RCA. In the late 1970s, commercial products such as APAR and RCA's MP2D emerged.

The only methodology available at the time was handcrafting. This traditional methodology yielded dense, small designs, but took long periods of time to develop and resulted in high NRE costs. These are costs associated with the development of the circuit that occur only once, not each time the circuit is fabricated (as in manufacturing costs).

The row–based cell methodology provides shorter design cycles than does handcrafting, at the expense of electrical performance and die size. Row–based cells also are used to implement certain sections of custom–IC designs, particularly in prototypes, to shorten development time.

The row–based standard–cell methodology is an IC design approach that uses a predefined library of standard functions, called cells. These functions are each designed by hand, characterized, and tested. Cells typically are designed to form rows, connecting power and ground through abutment.

As the engineer creates a logic schematic, the circuit is created by selecting functions from this predefined, precharacterized library, much as a PCB is created by combining standard components. Often, the design system will accept the schematic as input and choose the cells automatically. Automatic placement–and–routing tools arrange the cells in rows, with each cell abutting the next. The cells are of uniform height (pitch) and variable width. Inputs are located on the upper and lower edges of each cell. This differs from handcrafting, where functional blocks can be any size and shape and can have ports on all sides.

Early standard–cell designs were manual methods to connect cells. Now, cells are connected automatically, based on the connectivity indicated in the schematic. Routing generally is restricted to the channel between the rows. This differs from handcrafting, where routing can run through unrestricted parts of any functional block.

The row–based standard–cell design process requires little knowledge of the transistor–level details of IC design, so systems designers, rather than circuit specialists, can create circuits.

The Standard–Cell Library. A cell library is created by an expert IC designer at a semiconductor foundry or at a large corporate design group. The end user is not involved in this process. A library is based on a set of design rules, which are restrictions on the size, shape, and spacing of transistor layouts based on a particular manufacturing process. For example, metal–to–metal spacing is based on how precisely the metal lines can be manufactured. No automatic method now exists for creating standard–cell libraries. All cells in the library are created by hand.

The library designer must take systems–design factors into consideration when designing cells. Each cell must have the ability to function in different areas of the circuit and to connect to a variety of other cells. For example, a *nand*–gate cell could be placed in the far lower left corner of the circuit and be required to drive a cell in the upper right corner. On the other hand, this same cell could merely drive the cell next to it.

For the cells to operate in these various conditions, they generally are overdesigned. This means that the expert designer sizes the cell's transistors for worst–case drive conditions. In a handcrafted design, the function would be implemented differently, using smaller transistors. In addition, the row–based aspect of the cells restricts the designer to placing input and output ports on only two ends of the cell. For these reasons, a function implemented in a row–based cell can be two to three times larger than the same function implemented with handcrafting.

If a semiconductor foundry supplies the library, each cell is designed according to the manufacturing capabilities of that foundry. Although two different foundries may offer a four–input *nand* gate, for example, the cells from those foundries will vary in nearly all respects, including electrical characteristics, timing, and footprint. A standard–cell design implemented with one foundry's library cannot migrate easily to another foundry.

One major difficulty with row–based cell design is library maintenance. Whenever a manufacturing process changes, the cell library must be redesigned. For example, a library designed with 2 μm design rules (where the minimum spacing between objects is 2 μm) must be redesigned to accommodate 1.5–μm design rules.

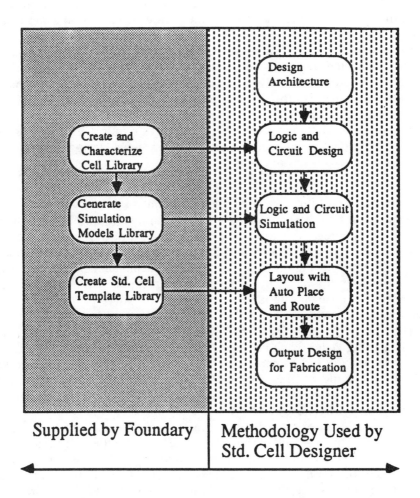

Figure 8.5: A typical standard–cell design methodology. This figure shows the steps used in creating a standard–cell design.

The Standard–Cell Design Process. Figure 8.5 shows the steps used in creating a standard–cell design.

Part of the appeal of standard–cell design is that the foundry shields the end user from the nitty–gritty aspects of designing and characterizing the cells. The foundry is responsible for handcrafting and characterizing the cell library, for generating a library of simulation models, and for creating standard–cell templates that include the cell footprint and pin locations for use in placement and routing.

The user creates the design architecture and a logic design. A schematic is used as input to the standard–cell CAD system and is simulated. The schematic is input to the standard–cell software, which automatically chooses the appropriate cells from the library. A block–place–and–route program places the cells in rows and automatically routes them. The end product is a completed design for fabrication.

Industry analysts had high hopes for row–based cell design when it first emerged commercially in the 1970s. The line of thinking was that as tools become more sophisticated, row–based cell design should become as attractive a methodology as gate arrays in terms of turnaround, but much more attractive in price. But the use of row–based standard cells has not become as widespread as some might have thought. Only about 25% of all ASIC designs are implemented entirely with row–based standard cells.

The biggest problem with the row–based cell methodology is that it does not easily accommodate rapidly changing technology. Design rules change very rapidly, decreasing by 15% to 20% every year. Libraries have become complex and gargantuan. A typical foundry library includes 100 to 300 functions, including SSI and MSI functions and a considerable selection of LSI functions, such as microprocessor cores and memory arrays. The trend is to include increasingly complex circuitry as cells. Maintaining these libraries now is consuming more resources and time than is practical and desirable.

New technologies are emerging that use parameterized cells to simplify library maintenance. These cells are designed with generic design–rule parameters. If the parameters are changed, the cell can be regenerated automatically. This approach greatly reduces the amount of effort required to maintain a library. The drawback to these parameterized cells is that they are offered only through certain foundries. Thus, a designer could not use a cell from one foundry, then change the parameters and use it in a design manufactured at a different foundry.

New technologies are making library–based design obsolete. Using new approaches such as layout synthesis and silicon compilation, the designer can generate each cell needed for a process, on the fly, without the need for a library. These approaches generate cells according to what is needed, in terms of both functional and electrical characteristics. The designer is not limited by the availability of functions in a library, and design rules can be incorporated quickly to regenerate cells automatically. As these tools mature, the need for library–based design will decrease dramatically.

• New Developments in Automated Layout •

The Need for Layout Synthesis

Handcrafted, whole–chip layout offers the highest performance and greatest chip density and addresses the broadest range of design problems, but lacks reusability and requires a long design cycle. The CAD/CAE industry has sought a technology that automates and accelerates the design of high–volume/high–performance ICs, while integrating handcrafting techniques.

Traditional automatic layout techniques, such as standard cells, procedural layout, and module generation, have their advantages and their disadvantages. First, the cells used by a standard–cell system and the tiles used by a module–generator program must be created. If this is to be done manually, a major effort is required. To lay out and check the 100 to 300 cells that may be needed typically would require several person–years of effort. Row–based standard cells can result in an area penalty of three to four times over handcrafting, and tiling can result in an area penalty of two times.

Standard–cell and tile libraries are not process–independent. Because a great deal of effort goes into creating libraries, those who have them try to use them for as many designs as possible. When process rules change, the library must be redone for the new process. In addition, the libraries lag behind the newest technology, because of the time required to create a new library for a new process.

Procedural layout is one method that attempts to achieve design–rule independence. However, procedural layout has proven to be impractical for generating any but very small circuits and generally is unreliable when design rules change significantly. The procedural–layout approach also replaces the problem of maintaining libraries of IC layout with the equally difficult problem of maintaining libraries of programs.

The industry seeks a layout–automation tool that shortens design time and also easily incorporates process changes to take advantage of rapid advances in fabrication technology. This means that libraries must be avoided. Custom–IC designers, in particular, want wide flexibility in automatic tools and the freedom to edit and change an automatically generated layout as desired. In addition, handcrafted–layout performance and size should not be sacrificed to gain shorter design cycles.

One solution that has been under consideration in research organizations for the past several years is an algorithmically based layout–synthesis tool that creates layout without the need for libraries. This tool has become a commercial reality only recently.

Layout Synthesis: Automatic Layout Without Libraries

Layout synthesis is the direct, automatic generation of layout from primitive devices—transistor and wires—without the use of manually predefined cells, tiles, or procedural–layout programs. Input to a layout—synthesis program is a schematic or netlist, which might consist of gates or transistors, plus a description of the IC process. The layout–synthesis program employs algorithms that emulate the techniques used in handcrafting layout. Most effort so far in layout synthesis has concentrated on MOS circuits, particularly CMOS.

In principle, layout designers have complete freedom when handcrafting layouts, as long as they obey the design rules. In practice, however, they nearly always follow certain conventions that give consistently good results. The following conventions are used almost universally for handcrafting of CMOS layouts:

   1. **Transistor grouping.** Group N transistors and P transistors together in separate common regions. The separation between N and P regions

usually is the largest spacing in the design–rule set, and there generally are more interconnections between transistors of like polarity than between those of opposite polarity. This arrangement also minimizes electrical problems that arise when opposite–polarity transistors are placed too close together.

2. **Transistor alignment.** Line up transistors vertically in rows. This allows for efficient power busing and makes it easier to keep track of design–rule relationships. Placing N and P transistors in two parallel rows helps in making N–to–P connections, which are mostly polysilicon gate connections.

3. **Transistor chaining.** Form long source–drain diffusion chains by placing together transistors having common source–drain connections. This allows the diffusion areas of adjacent transistors to be merged together, which can save significant area because diffusion extension and separation design–rule values usually are large. Minimizing diffusion area also improves circuit speed.

These rules form a transistor–level layout style that is very area–efficient for small circuits up to 20 to 30 transistors. These chains can be placed into longer rows with common power buses and well areas. Usually, well spacings are such that there are several wiring tracks at the N–to–P boundary, and these can be used for some of the connections within the row.

At the next higher level, connections between many of these smaller circuits are made in metal. The rows are stacked one above the other to form a block, possibly with routing channels between each row. The placement–and–routing algorithm that connects these rows into a block attempts to minimize the wiring required to complete the interconnections.

As an automatic–layout methodology, layout synthesis produces tighter, more efficient layouts than does the standard–cell approach. Using standard cells, the user is limited by the library selection in implementing functions. With layout synthesis, the user can create any function desired. Standard cells have boundaries between the cells, whereas layout synthesis has no boundaries to synthesized units, so these units can be merged together into chains. This saves circuit area. Layout synthesis also permits routing over synthesized units, horizontally and vertically. With standard cells, routing most often is restricted to the routing channel between cell rows.

Layout–Synthesis Applications

Layout synthesis is best used for generating random and repeated logic structures. In a repeated logic structure such as a data path, a bit slice would be synthesized, then stepped and repeated as needed. Random and repeated logic, now typically laid out by hand, could be synthesized much more quickly and with comparable area and performance.

Handcrafting is used where performance and circuit area are important factors. Peripheral logic and pad cells are a good use of handcrafting, because the pads are specialized elements. Memory and array structures are prime targets for module generators, because these structures can be constructed easily with two–dimensional arrays of abutting tiles. Standard cells can be used if there is an existing library that suits the user's needs.

Figure 8.6 shows how design–time layout synthesis can be used in conjunction with other methodologies to decrease design time. This figure shows the breakdown of circuit types by chip area and design time for a typical logic circuit such as a microprocessor. Design time for an average circuit will be reduced from 18 to 24 months to roughly 6 to 8 months if layout synthesis is used to generate random and repeated logic.

Using Layout Synthesis

Caeco Layout Synthesis is a commercial layout–synthesis product for generating random and repeated logic automatically. The cell generator normally is used to generate cells of up to 100 transistors. These cells then can be used along with handcrafted cells and other blocks, or they can be automatically placed and routed in a custom IC layout. A block generator is capable of generating multiple–row blocks of up to 5000 transistors.

The input to the layout–synthesis tool includes a logic schematic, a set of design rules, and layer assignments. The system uses basic devices, as defined in the process–definition file, which defines how each device uses each material layer and also incorporates the design rules. In addition, the user specifies a block outline in which the circuit should fit and the locations of the ports. The output is a Caeco Layout Synthesis database. The user can edit the cell after it has been generated and connect it with other elements in the design either manually, or automatically with the Caeco Blocks place–and–route package.

One main feature of this software is that it is design–rule–independent. The user has the freedom to modify the design rules and change the device definitions.

Future Directions

The flexibility of layout synthesis encourages the use of automated chip floor–planning, in which the software assists the designer in mapping the overall layout of the chip. The chip is planned by dividing the functional parts of the circuit into large blocks, then arranging those blocks efficiently on the chip.

Other automatic tools, such as module generators, do not give the designer control over the size and shape of the blocks generated. The designer must fit the blocks together after the fact, once all the blocks are generated. With layout synthesis, the user can plan block placement before generating circuitry and be sure that the generated blocks fit accordingly.

Another opportunity for automating layout is providing input at a higher level of abstraction. With a behavioral language compiler, the designer could provide a behavioral description of the desired circuit instead of a schematic. This would open up IC design to more systems–level designers, shorten the design cycle further, and allow the tool to provide full–chip synthesis if desired. Candidates for an industry–standard behavioral language for layout

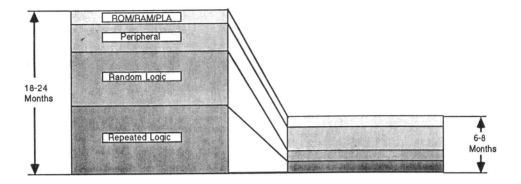

By Time

Figure 8.6: Circuit types in a typical IC layout. This figure shows how design-time layout synthesis can be used in conjunction with other methodologies to decrease design time.

synthesis include VHDL, the U.S. standard for military circuit description, and ELLA, a standard behavioral language in Europe.

Layout synthesis is used most widely in custom IC design. Synthesized cells and blocks are combined with handcrafted layout, standard cells, and layout from previous designs. Place–and–route tools are evolving into chip–composition tools that bring all these disparate elements together.

Another logical progression from layout synthesis is logic synthesis. This process automatically optimizes a logic design to reduce it to the smallest number of elements needed to produce the given function. Another form of design optimization could come from high–level techniques such as data–flow optimization, which attempts to use all processing elements as efficiently as possible in a given design.

As these advances emerge, chip size will decrease and design time will be cut considerably.

• Design Verification •

Design Verification Overview

One of the most demanding and time–consuming tasks in IC design is verification of connectivity and layout. In layout verification, all physical design data must be verified to ensure that the circuit is manufacturable, that the designer has not accidentally created shorts and open circuits, and that the circuitry in the layout directly corresponds to the network described in the engineering schematic diagrams.

The types of layout verification checks that are typically performed in this manner are:

- Design–rule checking (DRC). Spacing between two or more polygons on one or more layers; logical or Boolean operations; geometric compensation (sizing); generation of new layers; dimensional checking
- Electrical–rule checking (ERC). Area and perimeter calculations; resistance and capacitance calculations; misalignment of one shape to another; fringe characteristics between the parallel edges of two shapes
- Logic–to–layout checking. Comparison of the physical design to a logic design description (netlist); comparison of one physical design to another.

Additionally, once the physical implementation of the design is completed, the parasitic electrical properties, such as stray capacitance and interconnect resistance, must be extracted from the design and back–annotated to the original engineering schematics. This allows for simulation of the actual circuit properties, rather than the best–guess properties that were available to the engineer before the layout was completed.

Postlayout simulation typically yields a much more accurate picture of circuit performance than do simulations performed earlier in the design process. Unfortunately, the process of acquiring the data for this simulation is demanding and remains one of the most tedious and resource–intensive aspects of IC design.

Design–Rule Checking

Design–rule checks can range from simple spacing checks to complex, conjunctive checks where the result of one rule check is used as input to another. Figure 8.7 illustrates some common design–rule violations. Figure 8.8 illustrates the steps involved in performing a DRC on a typical IC–layout database.

Once the design database has been flattened and fractured (to be discussed in the fracturing section that follows), the batch design verification begins. First, a software module identifies devices in the trapezoidal database. The results of this operation are stored in temporary disk files as phantom data. Since this information is used by many of the subsequent checks, it must be able to be accessed easily and quickly.

Most batch DRCs are modular in nature. They allow the user to build complex design–rule checks by sequentially combining basic checks with connectivity and device data. This is done by describing the process design rules in the rule–description file. This can be a very tedious and error–prone phase of batch verification, because there is no automatic way to ensure that the design rules have been properly coded.

Once the DRC has finished execution, errors are annotated in a tabular fashion, and error flags are placed at the proper x,y coordinate in a GDS– II format output error cell. Typically, this cell then is placed on top of the original layout database where the errors occurred, examined, and corrected.

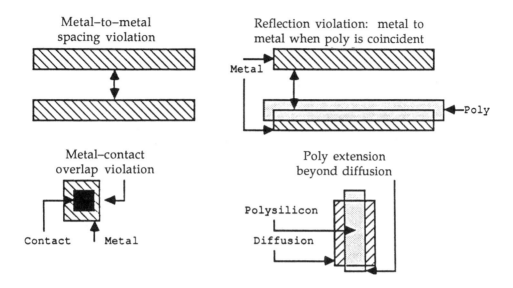

Figure 8.7: Common design–rule violations. This figure illustrates some common design–rule violations.

Fracturing

Historically, most design databases for IC layout data have been composed primarily of polygon data. The task of verifying the design–rule and electrical–rule integrity of the design has been formidable. This difficulty is due, in part, to the lack of connectivity information and to device location.

In MOS design, devices are created by the intersection of polysilicon and diffusion. When represented as polygon data, this corresponds to the polygon on the diffusion layer that is intersected by a polygon on the polysilicon layer. In the database, these two polygons have virtually no relationship, other than that they happen to intersect.

A device's actual dimensions and connectivity must be known to verify any of its properties. To determine the active gate area of the transistor, a Boolean *and* of the polygons on the diffusion and polysilicon layers must be performed. Connectivity information is determined based on where the polysilicon polygon crosses the diffusion polygon. This information then may be combined with edge–to–edge spacing checks, enclosure checks, touch–overlap checks, interference checks, and many others, to result in a complete process–design–rule verification. In view of the fact that a typical VLSI device may contain more than 500,000 transistors, and each polygon must be verified with respect to all other polygons in the design, it is no surprise that run times and disk–storage requirements for this type of verification are extremely large.

Suppliers of batch–DRC programs have taken algorithmic steps to make the task more manageable by breaking the large problems into numerous small

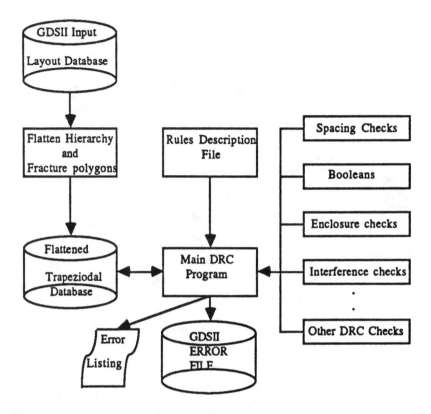

Figure 8.8: Performing a DRC on a typical IC–layout database.

problems. Most CAD systems allow the user to create polygons of up to 200 vertices. These complex polygons present a particularly difficult verification problem, since they may be part of many devices and many nodes. To deal with this circumstance efficiently, virtually all current batch–DRC programs first flatten the design hierarchy. Then, they fracture the polygon data into trapezoids (see Figure 8.9).

Reducing the complex polygons to four–sided figures allows the DRC algorithms to perform local searches of the database rather than compare each complex polygon in the design to every other complex polygon.

Batch–Mode Layout Verification

Layout verification typically is done in a batch mode, after the fact. In other words, a designer submits the chip database (either the whole chip or a section of it), after the chip is designed, to a verification program that runs in the background mode. The program is noninteractive, in that once initiated, the user cannot intervene. The program runs to completion.

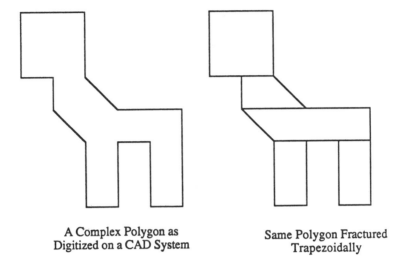

A Complex Polygon as   Same Polygon Fractured
Digitized on a CAD System   Trapezoidally

Figure 8.9: Polygon data.

Batch connectivity verification and parameter extraction use approaches similar to DRC, in that they operate on flattened trapezoidal data, generate temporary data files containing intermediate results, and produce a tabular output listing of error data. Batch design–verification programs can do a very comprehensive job of checking the integrity of layout data, but they all share some common limitations:

- Long batch execution times.
- Very large temporary disk–storage requirements.
- Loose coupling with the input data makes repair of errors difficult, requiring database translations.
- Errors found late in the design process, when they are difficult to correct.

The biggest problem with batch verification is that it is performed after the design has been at least partially completed. This means that the error may be much more difficult to correct, as it may be sandwiched into a tightly packed area. This significantly increases the difficulty, time, and expense of error correction.

An ideal solution to the design verification problem would be a CAD system that would not allow the creation of incorrect data. This concept has been called correct–by–construction in the design–automation–tools industry.

In a correct–by–construction system, the user may enter and edit data in any way, as long as no design rules or connectivity rules are violated. If a rule is violated, the system immediately stops and prompts the user with graphical feedback and a description of the error. The user then may either repair the data or force the error into the database and repair it later.

In theory, a complete correct–by–construction system would require no further design–rule or connectivity verification after the layout is complete. In practice, no one has implemented a complete correct–by–construction layout for two major reasons: First, a large amount of computational resource is required to support real–time verification on a per–user basis; second, the nature of existing CAE/CAD system architectures and databases makes implementation awkward.

Architecturally, almost all CAD systems for ICs use polygon–level databases. This comparatively unintelligent data organization is convenient for data entry and editing, but does not contain the necessary information to allow fast and accurate data verification. The only recourse available with a polygon–based system is to generate and maintain parallel data representations that do contain the necessary information for verification. This takes CPU time and disk space and causes data consistency problems as editing is performed. For these reasons, real–time verification has been impractical until recently.

On the cutting edge of database technology for IC–design systems is an approach based on parametric, device–level primitives. In this type of database, the device primitive contains two sets of information. One is a set of polygons forming a design–rule–correct transistor, and the second is a definition of the behavior of the device when it is connected to a net. With this type of information available at a high level of abstraction in the database, it is unnecessary to create or maintain any other databases in parallel with the design data to facilitate verification.

With the recent advances in the area of workstation performance, the designer now is able to perform nearly instantaneous DRC checks on localized edits. The CAD system reads a set of design–rule constraints as the designer is working and immediately flags or notifies the designer when one of the rules has been violated. At that point, the designer usually has the option of correcting the error on the spot or leaving it flagged in the database for later retrieval and correction.

This technique significantly decreases the number of times a batch DRC must be employed, by catching most basic design–rule errors as they occur. Since the quality of the data input to the batch DRC is better, the number of errors left to be found using batch–DRC tools is very small. This approach can, in many cases, improve designer productivity.

For electrical–rule checking, some CAD systems provide on–line analysis capabilities that calculate resistance and capacitance values on the fly. The system will flag the designer when the maximum allowed value has been exceeded. If the CAD system is integrated, in that it can access the logic–design database and the physical–design database at the same time, there is an added capability of connectivity checking.

From the logic database, the system reads the netlist or connectivity information, then checks that data against the designer's actions. If the designer connects a device incorrectly, the system can flag the error immediately. The error then can be corrected on the spot or left for later retrieval and correction.

A number of very significant methodological problems may hinder the further development of this technology, one of which has come to be known as the hierarchical–mismatch problem.

In the past, IC designers rarely have maintained a one–to–one mapping between the physical design hierarchy and the logic- or circuit–design hierarchy. This is because engineers typically group data with respect to functional symmetry, while layout designers group data with respect to geometric symmetry. In many cases, this leads to dramatic differences in hierarchical partitioning between layout and schematic.

Since batch design verification first flattens the entire design database, the hierarchical mapping problems do not exist. But flattening cannot be accomplished in real time. It remains to be seen whether the design automation community can fully conquer this problem.

CHAPTER 9

TESTABILITY ISSUES

• Testing as the Most Difficult Hurdle •

Before a new part type can be released to production, a test team must verify a number of things: that the manufactured part—of which the prototypes should be considered examples—will do the job it is intended to do, that it will provide the desired response under a variety of conditions, that it will not fail in the field, and that its functionality can be tested and verified before it is shipped or implemented in a board–level product. In addition to functionality, the performance level of the prototypes must be verified before the design for an ASIC part can be released to production, and a confidence level must be established. In prototype verification, this is known as the warm fuzzies.

There are two types of tests that must be completed. The first is prototype verification, in which the design team and the test engineers verify that the semiconductor designed and built actually works. The second transfers data about a part to a production tester that will sort between good and bad parts in a high–volume production environment.

Simulation patterns, or vectors, exercise a digital–logic component on a computer. However, the same digital–input words may not be usable on a multipin testing device. While VLSI testers are equipped to handle a broad range of devices, they must must be programmed to replicate the voltage, current, and digital–logic conditions the new part is likely to see in its circuit environment. The testing device may never function as fast and may never produce all the digital pulses in the same time frame as does a simulator or the actual circuit.

For example, an ASIC device may be built to play a role in a high–speed, pipelined data stream. In its operating environment, the ASIC may see a new 8-, 16-, or 32–bit data word at every clock cycle. It is possible to simulate this function on a computer and to repeat it in a real electronic system, but it is extremely difficult to test for it. Unlike the simulation program, which can offer the modeled ASIC, a new number at each clock period, effectively replicating the pipeline that the device will actually see in the system, the tester cannot easily replicate this pipeline. The tester itself is a computer machine under the control of its own software (remember: instruction–fetch/instruction–execute). It will go through several software steps of its own to present each number to the ASIC, and likely will give up at least one clock cycle for each new number. In other words, unless the tester is at least four times faster than the device it must test (an unlikely proposition), it never will replicate the pipelined speed with which new numbers are presented to the ASIC.

The entire test process, as a consequence, somehow must find a middle ground between verifying what the device is capable of doing and harnessing the capabilities and limitations of a test system. It is not simply a matter of coming up with a more powerful tester; the engineers still must write a program for this machine that adequately tests the new device. There are elements of strategy here, since knowing how a part works is different from knowing how it can be tested. In addition to knowing how a part works, the test engineers also must know how a tester works. They must figure out a way to use the tester to exercise the part so that it not only demonstrates its functions and performance capabilities, but also reveals its potential faults and weaknesses. The test engineer typically comes up with a new sequence of events for the tested part and implements them one after another on the tester.

This implementation of test strategy, in fact, is one of the most critical phases in the whole process of designing and manufacturing a new part. Silicon Compiler Systems estimates, for example, that roughly 35% of the entire design cycle is spent in creating and conducting tests. While the glamour in electrical–engineering work—the applause for devising and launching a new product—usually accrues to the design team, the test engineers have the job of certifying the product for production. They frequently are in the unglamorous position of telling marketing and design engineering—often after hundreds of thousands of dollars and dozens of person–years have been spent—that their brainchild probably will fail in the field, or, worse, that it does not work at all. It is a dirty job, say the test engineers, but somebody has to do it. With good circuit simulators, however, it is unlikely that test engineers will encounter the horror of a complete design failure. More often, testing will reveal a small design or manufacturing flaw that can be corrected iteratively.

But, too often, a test team will report—after a year of fooling around with a new design—that they do not know how to test it. Test engineers frequently are recruited from the ranks of design engineers. The designers know how the part is supposed to work, the thinking goes, so they are the best ones to figure out how to test it. Learning the capabilities of an automatic tester might come easily to a bright engineer, and devising a sequence of events for the part on the tester might take a month. Still, the part could be held out of production for an entire year while the newly recruited test engineer learns Pascal, the standard programming language of ATE. Under these circumstances, all the rapid–turnaround advantages of CAE go right out the window.

In its final phase, then, CAE depends on a growing number of programs that are designed to make it easier to harness high–speed testers. These programs do two types of jobs: First, they automatically translate simulation vectors into patterns that can be recognized and used by prototype–verification equipment or by production testers; second, they build automatic self–testing into the ASIC part, so that the part does not require a special verification program or special verification equipment. This chapter will explore each of these job types in turn.

Prototype–Verification Systems

To be useful, VLSI testers and other prototype–verification systems must be faster and smarter than the complex logic devices they are designed to test—not an easy task, when you consider that ASIC devices are built to perform a job that no other single chip can perform, or that new–generation microprocessors are built to out–run any existing processor.

Ideally, if the new processor is designed to run at 20 or 25 MHz, the tester must have a 50– or 100–MHz clock. The tester not only must be capable of putting the chip through its paces (even stressing it a bit to sense the potential for failures), it also must be able to catch every signal (even random glitches and spikes) the new device puts out. To test a 25–MHz processor, for example, it would be necessary to put a new digital word at the input of the device at the start of each clock cycle—that is, about every 80 ns. If the tester itself were running on a four–phase computer clock, it would have to be running at 100 MHz to adequately feed the input of the 25–MHz processor. To measure the parametrics generated by the device under test (DUT), the tester would have to drive all the input pins of the DUT—the clock lines, the 32 address lines, the 32 data lines, etc.—to their active state by transitioning each input pin from 0V to 5V for active high (or 5V to 0V for active low) within the appropriate clock, while simulating a load or high–impedance state (no load) on the output pins. With the exception of the Tektronix 9500–series VLSI testers, which are million–dollar machines capable of stimulating and measuring 256–pin devices at 100–MHz rates, neither prototype verification nor production testers can do this kind of job.

In practice, then, a number of special–purpose testers are employed. While their activities may call to mind the parable about a group of blind men touching different sections of an elephant, a useful picture of the performance of the new device can be assembled.

There are basically two types of testers: functional and parametric. These are analogous, in fact, to logic and circuit simulators. The functional tester verifies that the device actually performs the job it was designed to do—that it will produce the correct digital–logic words with the appropriate inputs. The parametric tester, in contrast, looks at voltages and currents and measures the frequencies with which these change. In the first case, the tester must be able to put a series of logic states on the input pins of the device and to read the logic states on the output. In the second case, the tester must apply voltages and currents and read every pin for the voltages and currents it produces.

A wafer probe extracts parametric data from a chip to verify the basic functionality of its critical transistors. The probe applies voltages to selected sections of the chip and measures the responses. The probe wires themselves are designed with microwave (very high, radio–frequency) techniques to avoid applying any kind of spurious load to the transistors being measured and to capture their subnanosecond responses.

As the switching frequency of these transistors (their ft) continues to increase with each new generation of ICs, it becomes more difficult to probe the wafers without introducing capacitive loading and other effects that are likely to distort the measurements. As a consequence, one test–equipment manufacturer, Schlumberger, has developed a noncontact method to probe a wafer using an electron beam. This method is very similar to the procedure used to generate scanning–electron–microscope photos, only in this case, the reflected electron beam is converted not into a black–and–white representation of the troughs and layers of a submicroscopic chip, but into a pattern of voltages and currents running through the probed devices. These can be plotted as on an oscilloscope screen. An interesting feature of the system built by Schlumberger is that the measured voltages and currents, the schematic representation of the IC, the polygon layout, and a scanning–electron–microscope image of the section being probed can be displayed simultaneously in the windows of a single high–resolution screen.

Whether it is a contact device or a noncontact device like Schlumberger's, however, the wafer probe verifies a certain level of electrical performance. It does not confirm the actual functionality of the part, nor does it provide a full set of parametrics. Rather, the wafer probe confirms that the semiconductor–manufacturing process was successful. The chips then can be separated from the wafer and packaged for further testing.

It is here that a prototype tester is put to use. Not only is this tester used to verify the functionality of a part, it also can be used to scale down the test vectors to shorter events that can be used on a rapid–fire production tester.

Because it must certify the functionality of the part, the prototype–verification equipment must run as fast as the parametric tester, must be readily programmable, and must couple easily with the CAE system. In many cases, it can be electrically connected with the workstation on which the ASIC circuitry was developed. But, in all cases, it must be capable of assimilating the netlists and test patterns used by a logic simulator.

Prototype verification is the specialty of Integrated Measurement Systems (IMS) of Beaverton, Oregon—now a subsidiary of Mentor. Verification is an interactive process that makes testing less of a batch–processing job by shortening the time required to put the DUT through its paces and report back to the user on the computer terminal. The faster a test can be designed, run, and analyzed; modified, rerun, and analyzed again, the faster the job of verification can be completed.

Toward this end, IMS provides a series of testers—the Logic Masters—that can be programmed and controlled from an IBM–PC. Test patterns from a CAE simulator can be uploaded and stylized for the tester. Results are displayed on the PC screen: The input stimulus, the expected response, and the actual response of the device can be seen in windows on the same screen. The computer can be used to compare the expected results with the actual results and to flag the differences as errors.

IMS software routines allow branching within the test program (that is, the program can change direction if a certain response is encountered), looping (repeat a test situation some specified number of times), and device initialization (return to beginning). Users can control patterns bit by bit and even can test the stimulus pins in three states. That is, they can send in a data high or a data low or put the pin in a high–impendance state that—though connected— does not actively affect the device under test. The test language allows the designer to incrementally vary the operating conditions (like voltages and pulses) and the margins on each pin of the tester. An internal digital–to–analog converter programs these pins to produce an output voltage in the range of –2V to +5V. Receiver threshholds are programmable from –1.85V to +5V.

Machines like the Logic Master ST provide up to 190 test pins with test–cycle rates on the order of 20 MHz. The pattern–generation channels are programmable with NRZ (non–return to zero) and DNRZ (delayed non–return to zero) data formats. Since it is important to register transitions on their leading edges (the very instant a voltage begins to rise or fall), a machine like the ST allows edges to be visualized in 1–ns increments and at a variety of voltage levels.

Hopefully, this type of interactive tool will make the process of checking out a new device easier for the test engineers. They still have the job of developing a test program for an automatic tester that will run in batch mode; that is, without operator intervention. For this purpose, the tester will need a long series of digital–test/stimulus words.

Automatic Test-Vector Generation

Frequently, thousands of digital words are generated to simulate the functions and timing sequences of a complex, digital–logic IC. While there is little correspondence between the capabilities of a simulator and the capabilities of an actual test system, a great deal of energy goes into converting the simulation patterns and vectors into a usable sequence of events for a specific tester. A number of manufacturers, consequently, are harnessing ATG software—computer programs that convert simulation vectors into test programs—to speed the design–and–test cycle. Test System Strategies (TSSI) (Beaverton, Oregon) is one of the leaders in this area, and its PC–based software develops test vectors for machines like the Fairchild Sentry and those made by IMS.

TSSI's software converts simulator inputs into a common intermediate language before generating test inputs for all the major ATE systems. On one side, TSSI connects with logic simulators including Calma's TEGAS, Daisy's DLS, Gateway's Verilog, GenRad's HILO, Mentor's Quicksim, Silvar–Lisco's Helix, Simucad's Silos, and Teradyne's LASER (though not Cadat's simulator). On the other side, it generates vectors for a large number of production testers.

Automatic test generation may be one of the value–added features that converts silicon compilation from an experimental tool into a widely used commercial program. This is the thinking behind Silicon Compiler Systems' ATG option. This addition to its Genesil design tool kit is designed to trace all circuit paths in a new design and come up with set of test vectors needed to achieve user–specified levels of test coverage.

In Silicon Compiler Systems' conception, the modules constructed by the silicon compiler are effectively black boxes, and designers spend little time learning how to develop test vectors for them. The ATG option can be used to generate test vectors at any stage of the design and can be run either interactively or in batch mode. Useful in pinpointing trouble spots, ATG can be run interactively during the layout phase to quickly highlight the architectural features that are the easiest and the hardest to test.

The program works with Silicon Compiler Systems' proprietary logic simulator, Lsim. It uses a 16–value algebraic notation for various logic and fault conditions to model indeterminate states and uses a proprietary extension to the popular D algorithm for path tracing. The ATG application extends Genesil's functional simulator beyond normal operations into the time domain, by examining the events surrounding each storage element, a technique called *time unrolling*, which makes all events—even sequential logic—appear to be a combinational sequence. The program remembers the states that all storage elements exhibit at their nodes as a function of time. Test sequences are generated by analyzing the combinational circuits and finding paths that get at all possible fault areas of the device.

In most cases, the designer can simply run the ATG program and obtain good fault coverage. The program performs static fault analysis by examining the logically distinct groups in a circuit and locating any portions that are isolated and, thus, difficult to test. ATG uses algorithms in the functional simulator to justify or trace back optimal paths. From any point from within an object, the simulator's algorithms trace backward to find observable inputs. Likewise, the program can ripple data from that point to any of the observable outputs. For a gate buried deep inside a circuit, there are many paths from the output all the way back to the primary inputs. The program picks the test vectors required to exercise that part of the circuit and also finds the vectors that analyze several potential faults simultaneously. One vector, for example, may be able to fully cover stuck–at–1 and stuck–at–0 faults at many different nodes. By choosing vectors that can detect multiple faults, ATG helps to minimize test time.

The concept of unrolling time—of storing remembered states—is memory–intensive, and typically has been implemented in mainframe environments. Because the sequential circuit is expanded into a combinational one, a complete copy of the circuit is required for every event in the time window for all states to be recorded. In other words, a linear increase in circuit complexity increases memory requirements exponentially. Since each copy of the circuit represents one time frame (vector), limiting the complexity restricts the length of the test sequence. As a result, most test generators using this principle perform reasonably well on only circuits no larger than 1000 gates.

Still, there is a trade–off among the execution time for the ATG program, the sequential depth, and the degree of test coverage. If, for example, the chip has a large sequential depth—a long series of sequential logic—and the ATG program is invoked using a small depth, the program will run quickly on an Apollo or Sun workstation, but will result in poor test coverage; that is, large areas of the chip will be left untested.

During analysis, designers can vary the sequential depth—the number of discrete time windows used for such analysis. The value of sequential depth corresponds to how deeply the hardware and bus structures are nested; that is, how many clocks it will take to move a digital test pattern from the inputs to the outputs. For example, for a single chip that has three stages of pipelining between the input and output pins, three clock cycles are required to propagate input values through to the outputs. The user must specify a sequential depth of three to generate a test sequence for this pipeline.

In operation, the test designer may wish to run the ATG program longer (commit more CPU time) or assign a greater sequential depth. Seed vectors culled from the Lsim program can be inserted manually to accelerate the ATG program. For example, by setting the inputs of certain structures (like counters) with a seed vector, the designer can reduce the number of cycles required to propagate all signals through the circuit. If (say) a 4–bit counter that contains all zeros (0000) is subsequently loaded with a seed vector containing all ones (1111), the next clock cycle would clear the circuit back to all zeros automatically, thus skipping an entire 16–stage increment loop from 0000 to 1111.

The advantage of ATG programs like Silicon Compiler Systems' is that they develop test vectors for both sequential and combinational circuits without the addition of bulky test structures to the chip layout. More typically, the inner nodes of a complex logic circuit will be inaccessible to the stimulus applied by a test system. In these cases, it makes sense to build test–pattern generators right into the ASIC device, as a way to guarantee the testability of the final product.

Built–in Test Capability

Built–in self–test capability (called BIST) accomplishes two tasks. First, it can minimize the job that external testing must accomplish. Second, self–testing can check the inaccessible regions of complex VLSI designs, where a great deal of logic often is buried inside the chip that cannot be accessed through the pins of the packaged device.

For ASIC and other IC designs, self–test logic can impose some difficult trade–offs on design teams. On the one hand, the self–test should detect as many areas of a chip as possible to minimize external testing. On the other hand, the number of self–test circuits must be limited to avoid a significant increase in die size and also to prevent any impact on clock speed. Since even external tests cannot find all the possible faults in a microprocessor, a reasonable self–test goal might be to find, say, at least half of all faults.

One of the difficulties in designing a self–test mechanism is predicting its effectiveness. Evaluating self–test circuitry for its fault–finding capability could be done by comparing the self–test results obtained with a variety of good and bad dies. However, that would hold up production until some sort of confidence level were established on the self–test capability. Consequently, self–test circuitry—like any other device function—should be simulated and the simulation fault–graded before the chip is produced.

The grandfather of the self–test techniques used in production of semicustom ICs is level–sensitive–scan design (LSSD), developed by IBM. Practically all BIST these days uses some form of scan design. It is a technique that, in principle, guarantees that all the nodes of a complex logic array will be accessible to an IC tester. LSSD exposes the inner logic of a complex design through built–in logic blocks that can be pulsed one after another to reveal their responses to a digital test pattern.

With scan testing, shift–register latches are designed into all address and I/O pins. The inner sections of a device then are tested by serially shifting in a test vector through a scan–input pin and shifting the output to a scan–output pin. The required logic blocks include scanning registers and serial rings that, under test, will record the status of gates within combinational logic circuits that cannot be accessed by any other means.

While much of the simple combinational logic used in a circuit—*and, or* and *nand* gates—may be completely accessible through a carefully thought–out stimulus pattern, more complex logic will need other ways to reveal its functionality. A D flip–flop, for example, is the basic element of a memory cell and, like any storage cell, may not give a readable output until many clocks have passed. Some other mechanism is required to read the cell on one clock (that is, before a valid output appears). In these cases, another clock line may be added to the flip–flop that is at a frequency different from the system clock's. The additional clock line will force the flip–flop to reveal something of its state to the shift registers around it.

Because this method relies on a serial scan chain, it can reduce the number of additional signal pins required for testing. However, it significantly lengthens the time it takes to perform the test, since extra cycles are required to shift in the address and data inputs and shift out the memory output. This method also does not readily allow memory blocks to be tested at normal cycle times, and ATE still is required for pattern generation.

Instead of applying digital test patterns from a tester through a long serial scan chain, it is possible for self–test logic on the chip to generate its own signature; that is, a long digital word peculiar to that chip. While there are a variety of peripheral components on the chip used to generate signature words, the LFSR (linear–feedback shift register) typically is the key mechanism. The LFSR operates in successive stages, feeding output patterns from sections of the

DUT back to the input or intermediate stages of LFSR through exclusive–*or* (*xor*) gates. These registers either can generate pseudorandom test vectors for test–input stimuli or (as in memory testing) can compress a series of output–response vectors into a single parallel vector. The final signature of the register— the one that appears after all test results have been cycled through—is compared to an expected value in a comparator in the output scan–chain circuits.

The LFSR generates a signature by dividing the digital input to the register by a seemingly arbitrary polynomial. In this technique, the output data of a test is fed into the parallel inputs of the LFSR and shifted through the register in successive stages. After the first digital word is shifted through the register, for example, a quotient appears at the output, while the remainder of the shifting process still is stored in the internal stages of the register. It is in the feedback process that the shift register will execute its characteristic polynomial; that is, a polynomial can be effected by feeding the quotient back to the LFSR while a remainder still is being shifted through. The feedback points are selected with the primitive polynomial corresponding to the shift–register size.

The polynomial, however, is selected in such a way that numbers generated by the shift register will appear to be statistically random. Assume, for example, that a three–stage LFSR has a polynomial of $x^3 + x + 1$. This register will sequence through $(2^3 - 1) = 7$ unique vectors before repeating. Suppose that the input is held at zero and the register is initialized to 100; in this case, the register will generate seven unique vectors starting from 100 and ending with 011: 100 (1), 101 (2), 110 (3), 111 (4), 001 (5), 010 (6), 011 (7). The register cannot be initialized to 000 (since the input is held at 0). If this occurred, the vectors generated always would be zero.

When the LFSR is used to compress a series of test responses into one vector, the parallel mode will require extra *xor* gates to combine the data outputs of the logic under test and the output of the previous shift–register element. After shifting the entire sequence, the final vector stored in the shift register is the summation of the remainders of the polynomial divisions. This final vector then can be compared with the signature of an expected value.

The signature–analysis method minimizes the amount of chip real estate devoted to testing. If you try to compare the serially output test data with its correct value for each clock cycle, you would need a large on–chip ROM to store the right answers. This might be easier to implement on a board–level tester, but there would be no space for such a ROM on a chip. In addition, taking something like a check sum (a number generated from the data patterns themselves) of all outputs over all clock cycles easily could give an answer that is useless for self–test purposes, since check sums can just as easily be generated by faults as by correct data patterns. Instead, signature analysis is used to accumulate only one possible answer.

This method is especially useful for testing large internal structures of a chip (which often are not accessible through I/O tester pins), such as RAM and ROM spaces or user–programmable logic areas. On microprocessor parts, instruction decoders frequently are exercised with LFSRs, since the activity of these blocks is difficult to either control or monitor with external tests.

This type of test scheme, in fact, is capable of exercising memory blocks in a variety of ways that would tax external testers. Memory test patterns range from minimal functional tests such as March and checkerboard patterns—which test each cell location for a 0 and a 1 and also check for any cell–to–cell shorts or interactions—to complex tests such as the Galpat and sliding–diagonal patterns. The minimal patterns verify functionality, while the more complex patterns detect disturbance–type phenomena. Frequently, it does not pay for an ASIC designer to run these complex patterns with production or in–circuit testers. On–chip testing, however, ensures functionality by using more complex patterns during device characterization in the product–development phase.

In a typical scan–test implementation of an embedded memory block, for example, the shift–register scan chain shifts in the test vectors serially from a single input during the scan mode. These test vectors are loaded into the address buffer and data–input latches and registers, so that they will be written to the memory as a parallel data byte. After writing the memory array with latched address and data inputs, memory–read cycles transfer the memory contents to data–output scan latches. The latched data then is shifted serially to a scan–out for verification.

A self–test structure was used on Intel's 80386 processor, as a specific example, to exercise 52.5% of the chip's 285,000 transistors. The circuits needed for signature analysis included a parity tree with two levels of exclusive–*or* gates, the LFSR required to generate a signature, and a comparator that stores two correct signatures. One signature was used by the comparator to check the ROM and instruction–decoder signature; the other signature was for the remaining tests. Actually, three LFSRs were used to generate a 32–bit signature.

One advantage of this self–diagnostic method is a reduction in the number of additional pads and pins required for testing. Since the LFSR generates its own test pattern, and an on–chip comparator verifies the results of a test, the only external signals required are the ones that say, "Start the test, time it this way, and let me know when you are finished": an auto–test mode pin (AT), an auto–test clock pin (ATC), and a pass/fail signal line. The auto–test clock can be run at normal memory–cycle time, allowing the memory to be tested at the rated operating speed.

Unlike scan testing, which uses an external test–pattern generator, practically all the input patterns needed for self–diagnostics are implemented directly on the chip. However, the more extensive the test patterns—the bits used in the LSFR—the more chip real estate is required for test and the greater the delays through the LFSR. Here, too, some kind of test algorithm is needed to optimize the test procedure, optimize the pattern–generation logic design, and reduce testing time. Otherwise, the testing logic begins to consume more silicon space and design time than the original circuit did.

Test–Synthesis Programs

As the design process becomes more automated, the manual insertion of BIST logic can undermine the quick turnaround gained by automating other parts of the product–development phase. There is a growing interest, consequently, in programs that automatically insert scanning logic and other self–test capabilities into a digital–logic device.

One of the first commercial programs to accomplish this is Aida's synthesis program, part of its ATPG (automatic test–pattern generation) package. This program adds in the scanning circuits required to implement LSSD on a completed gate–array design. Aida's synthesis program and library examine each logic cell (D flip–flops, for example) and determine what logic should be added to convert it into a scannable logic cell. In many cases, the synthesis program adds scanning registers, serial rings, and additional clock lines that provide the scannable inputs and outputs for a logic cell. While little can be done about the 10% or 15% extra chip space required, this automatic synthesis program ensures the testability of gate arrays—in some cases, to 100%.

The synthesis package currently works, for instance, with Fujitsu Microelectronics' 20K gate arrays, mapping out additional logic blocks and providing additional pin–outs required for the chips to implement a level–sensitive scan. The output of the synthesis program is a netlist that is compatible with Fujitsu's gate–array simulation and layout programs. While the package must run with Aida software on an Apollo workstation or IBM mainframe host, translators are available for converting Daisy and Mentor files into Aida–compatible schematics.

Since LSSD provides a way to test a finished IC, test–vector generation is completely automatic, provided by the synthesis program. However, the vectors can be executed only on those IC testers equipped for level–sensitive scanning. The Fairchild Sentry 20 is the primary such tester, and test vectors are provided in this format.

A very similar program, geared toward standard–cell designs, was developed by Tangent Systems (Santa Clara, California). This synthesis program provides IC testability circuits, but minimizes the die size required to accommodate them. While logic–synthesis programs (especially those using LSSD) ensure testability by adding scanning logic to an IC, the penalty can be a larger die size—and, consequently, a more expensive chip. Tangent's solution to this problem is a synthesis program that uses a much simplified version of LSSD. Called TanTest, the program is used in conjunction with Tangent's standard–cell layout program, which runs on VAX hosts.

First, the TanTest software performs a design audit to verify that there are no feedback loops or previously scannable cells within the circuit logic. A report of the design audit is generated for the user. In the next stage, TanTest performs a testability synthesis in which the D flip–flops in a circuit are converted to scannable cells.

The synthesis program is modeled after an AT&T program called Titus, which adds only secondary inputs and test–output points to the flip–flops, but not additional clock frequencies. This program is intended to eliminate some of the cumbersome counting circuitry required to accommodate the multiphased clocking of LSSD. The elimination of the additional logic helps to create a smaller chip and, in principle, makes it easier to test.

The original Tangent placement–and–routing package ensures a small die size by integrating timing analysis (identifying and upholding critical timing paths) with the layout process in successive iterations on the computer. The TanTest synthesis program, similarly, minimizes the penalty on scanning chains by running in iterative steps along with the placement–and–routing package.

In the next step of the TanTest program, test vectors are generated that provide tester access to the scan chains. The program includes built–in fault simulation, since the test vectors generated also will reveal the proportion of inner nodes covered by the test scan. In the final step of the TanTest program, a test file is generated in a HILO–compatible format. This test file is usable with GenRad testers, as well as with other machines.

Other noncommercial efforts are under way to develop software that will automatically inject scanning logic into a design without extracting a penalty in chip real estate. One scan–test scheme, developed at the AT&T Bell Laboratories, provides a partial scan capability with no extra logic overhead. This approach is part of a program that synthesizes chip layouts from behavioral models and automatically implements BIST logic in VLSI devices, as well as in PLD–based circuit packs. The major advantage of this scheme is that it eliminates the multiple clocks ordinarily required for LSSD.

The basic idea behind the program is to selectively replace memory elements (for example, flip–flops) in the device with a specialized flip–flop cell. These flip–flops, which replace D flip–flops in a circuit, use an exclusive–*or* gate, with each input driven by a *nand* gate. This combination yields four modes of operation: initialization (B0=0, B1=0), shift (B0=0, B1=1), system (B0=1, B1=0), and self–test (B0=1, B1=1). These cells are interconnected to form a circular chain of self–test flip–flops. Any sequence, from initialization, to pattern generation, to scanning (the shift mode), to neutral (equivalent to system mode) can be propagated through the scan chain just by toggling lines B0 and B1. The shift mode configures the self–test logic into a partial scan chain. In system mode, the flip–flops behave as normal D–type units, performing the intended system function. The self–test mode performs an exclusive–*or* operation on the system data input and the output data from the previous flip–flop in the scan chain.

When configured for self–test operation, the basic system architecture also includes an SAR (signature–analysis register) in the scan chain. This register is needed to effectively dissect the output of the scan chain during system diagnostics. Additional control circuitry manages the movement of data through the chain and holds the resultant signature on the SAR until it can be read by the test machine.

When applied to experimental VLSI devices, this BIST approach costs an additional 19% in chip real estate, while providing better than 90% fault coverage. However, this level of fault coverage can be extended by applying an external series of functional tests in conjunction with the partial–scan design mode.

Another BIST program, developed at the Virginia Polytechnic Institute and State University (Blacksburg, Virginia), automatically inserts on–chip self–testing hardware in a circuit described in VHDL. Based on what Virginia Polytechnic calls BILBO (built–in logic block observation), the technique combines scan–path testing methodology with on–chip, pseudorandom–pattern–generation and signature–analysis techniques.

In operation of the program, the design structure is extracted from a VHDL circuit description. Where it finds strictly combinational logic blocks in the design, the program automatically allocates testing resources, such as pseudorandom–pattern generators and multiple–input signature registers. This resource allocation is followed by the organization of scan paths, which are used to locate test registers and collect signatures from the other blocks in the design.

Depending on the resource allocation, a test session is scheduled for each combinational logic block. As a final step, control signals for distinguishing between several functional modes are distributed to the multifunctional register design. A key to this assignment is the recognition of an I–path through the circuit. An I–path is a route through which data can be transmitted without undergoing any change. These paths are used by the program to place registers and transmit test patterns and responses.

While there is no information available concerning the run time for a program like this, the analysis of the circuit blocks and paths, the test scheduling and control–signal distribution, and the insertion of required registers also are performed by the software algorithms. Those self–test resources that cannot be allocated automatically are assigned using placement rules entered by the user. Both the software algorithms and the rule–based systems are implemented with an artificial–intelligence language called Prolog.

Most of the efforts at BIST of VLSI devices focus on scan–path and signature analysis. While these programs are geared toward combinational logic and can be used to test large block structures like memories and PLAs, they may have difficulty in testing other structures. The largest number of these synthesis programs, however, still are regarded as experimental efforts, with few commercial implementations. In addition, the expense of implementing a BIST usually is not justified unless it is used to exercise a very large, complex device. This type of self–test logic rarely is implemented on small, special–function ASIC devices.

CAE–to–Board Test Links

Rather than implementing self–test on large semiconductor devices, there probably is a larger commercial potential in self–testing—even test–vector generation—for PCBs. Self–test could be used for board–level testing in two phases: First, the board tester would ask each VLSI component, "Does your self–test say you are OK?" Then, the tester would check the remaining board circuits and connections. Standards for a test technique like this, called *boundary scan*, are being evaluated by IBM, AT&T, Plessey, Philips, and others.

For one thing, the increased use of SMDs and custom ICs—ASICs or PLDs—makes board testing more difficult. Most automatic board testers are bed–of–

nails devices, which inject a test stimulus in one section of the board and measure the responses of the circuitry from probes at another section of the board. With their closely spaced and inaccessible leads, SMDs often prove impossible to test using in–circuit testing techniques. Typically, the test engineer then must adopt a cluster technique to test the block of ICs containing the ASICs and/or SMDs as a single functional unit. But if the board tester's library of elements does not contain the appropriate vectors to stimulate and measure responses for custom devices, the engineer must create them.

Board–test engineers struggle with the same difficulties as do the test engineers within semiconductor houses. Typically, they have only limited knowledge of the detailed operation of the device or IC cluster. And although design engineers may thoroughly understand the board tester's detailed operation, they may not totally understand the physical constraints under which it operates and the often subtle effects these constraints impose on the testing of the ASIC, PLD, or cluster.

Consequently, a communication path is needed between CAE and board–test activities. Ideally, the CAE system must be able to pass netlists, functional models, stimulus waveforms, and simulation results to the test environment. Tester–specific test descriptions and test–set evaluation capabilities also must exist in the design environment. CAE–to–ATE software links that incorporate knowledge of the timing and physical constraints of the board tester simplify test creation by generating the required functional tests from simulation results. Such a package should be equally useful to design engineers and test engineers.

About the only example of a CAE–to–board–est link is HP's EDS/3065 test–program generator (TPG). This package links the HP EDS (electronic design system) with the HP–3065 family of combinational PCB testers—a family that includes both in–circuit and full functional testing capabilities. The HP EDS/3065 TPG runs on the 68020–based HP–9000 series–300 workstation, along with design–capture and design–verification tools.

The test–program generator effectively converts the database from a HILO–3 logic simulator to a PCF (pattern–capture format), the general–purpose test–vector format used by the HP–3065 family of board testers. As with many other conversion programs, a great deal of hand–tweaking may be required. The netlist may need to be revised to ensure that all the connectivity patterns and directions are specified. The user may have to come up with names for devices that are not in the test–generation library. However, this type of ATG does provide the user with a sensible starting point.

The test–vector files produced by the test–program generator are transferred to the HP–3065 board tester, where they are compiled into executable functional tests for the custom devices and/or IC clusters. An error file may be produced to highlight the inevitable errors and incompatibilities between the simulation results and the HP–3065 board tester. The test designer then can correct the errors and recompile the stimulus files while still in the CAE environment. In principle, the HP EDS/3065 TPG is capable of generating up to 100,000 PCF test vectors in a single execution.

Although the HP EDS/3065 TPG may be used by both design engineers and test engineers, there are trade–offs in making it accessible to both. A test–

environment tool, running on the board–test system and generating test programs from simulation results, automates a time–consuming and error–prone process. Its disadvantage is that it does not contribute to solving the test engineer's major problem: understanding the detailed function of a custom device or cluster of ICs. It does not increase communication between design and test departments, nor does it bring the design engineer's expertise into the test process. Since there is no guarantee that the simulation results provided by the design engineer are compatible with the board–test system, there is no assurance that test programs can be generated from them or that the tests are comprehensive or complete. Additionally, if simulation results are modified to make them compatible with the board tester, there is no guarantee that the tests generated from them represent the actual function of the design, nor that they represent full fault coverage.

However, there is no way to bypass the test process. Maintaining a link between CAE and test, then, is critical to ensuring the rapid turnaround that is the direct result of automating the design process.

The Movement to Zero Defects

The effort to build in testability for a VLSI part during its design phases is a clear recognition throughout the electronics industry that quality control is not something that manufacturers can test and screen as an afterthought. The notion of quality (obtaining zero defects), as it is now being preached and implemented in a majority of U.S. semiconductor companies, is something that must be designed into a product and maintained throughout its life–cycle. Whether this guarantees working silicon on the first pass through a foundry, allows fewer defects in the prototype–evaluation stage, or lowers the chance of a failure in the field is a debatable issue. The fact is that the American semiconductor industry is shipping with much lower defect rates than at any time in its history.

This lower defect rate, frankly, is more a response to Japanese competition than a consequence of design automation. Whether this effort will save the U.S. electronics industry and whether the industry will revive itself well enough to finally benefit from the faster turnaround with lower defect rates made possible by design automation are issues that will be touched upon in Chapter 10.

• Creating Effective Links Between CAE and ATE •

There is little need to argue the merits of linking CAE to ATE. The sheer volume and complexity of today's device designs and simulation and test–vector files demand some form of automated CAE/ATE translation or conversion. Manually converting 50,000 or more simulation vectors to a test program simply is not practical, not from the standpoint of human endurance, nor from the economics of product time to market. Thus, automating CAE/ATE file conversions is a foregone conclusion. Now it is a question of "What is the best conversion approach?"

Unfortunately, most of today's answers focus on the problem end points, the CAE simulation waveforms, and the available ATE resources. This can lead to oversimplifications and assumptions that ultimately must be paid for in test–program debugging time. By recognizing some key simulation–to–test conversion considerations, many of the potential pitfalls and weak links in translation processes can be avoided. The payoff is that test–program generation and debugging time often can be reduced from weeks to days.

The Waveform Test Plan

Often, CAE–to–ATE translation facilities are created on the spur of the moment to solve an immediate problem. The result is an ad–hoc link between a specific CAE simulator and a specific ATE system or tester. While the link may be well executed and quite serviceable, its survival is questionable. What happens when the design facility adds different simulators? What happens when the test facility modifies existing testers or adds different tester models?

Things rarely stay the same for long. What may have started as a fairly clean link from a specific simulator to a specific tester evolves into a hodgepodge of links and link modifications that tries to accommodate equipment upgrades and expansions. Much of it may have been created on the fly to serve immediate needs and often is poorly documented. The result is a set of translation code that grows more cumbersome with each addition and eventually collapses under the burden of its own confusion.

To avoid such entanglements, it is best to begin any translation process with a clear and unambiguous waveform test plan. The relationship of this plan to the translation process is shown in Figure 9.1. The key attributes of a waveform test plan are:
1. A tester–independent description of the design behavior to be verified during the functional testing process
2. Accurately timed stimulus waveforms reflecting the input–timing specifications of the DUT
3. Accurately timed response waveforms reflecting DUT output–timing specifications.

The main virtue of a waveform test plan is that it can be implemented in a standard waveform format. As indicated in Figure 9.1, an input converter changes the raw simulation output to the standard waveform format. These standardized waveforms then can be operated on by generic tools to condition the waveform files to meet specific tester requirements. The conditioned waveforms then can be translated to a tester–specific program with a pattern–bridge program.

By using a standard waveform format, various translation links can be created by adding simulator–specific input converters and tester–specific rules checkers and pattern bridges. The core tools never change. The CAE/ATE links are implemented as needed with different input and output modules. Thus, a

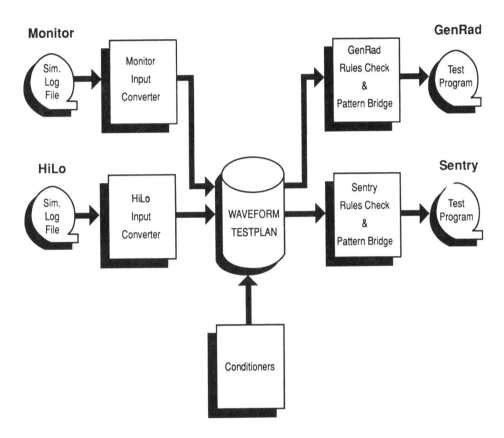

Figure 9.1: Relationship of a waveform test plan to the translation process.

simulation log file from any CAE workstation can be converted to the standard waveform format. The resulting waveform test plan then can be rules–checked against any number of available testers to find the best resource match for test–program generation. Moreover, the entire process can be implemented on a minicomputer or supermini. Expensive tester resources do not have to be tied up in program development.

Simulation–Vector Capture

The first stage of any CAE/ATE link is simulation–vector capture. There are two basic approaches that can be taken: The vector states can be sampled, or the vectors can be captured as raw events. The latter, raw–events capture, is more complex, but it provides a complete description of the waveforms by capturing all state transitions (events) and their locations. This high–fidelity approach is virtually a necessity for efficient translation of simulation vectors from asynchronous–device designs.

Synchronous devices, on the other hand, do not always require high–fidelity vector capture. In fact, raw–events translation can become unnecessarily complicated for simpler devices. For this reason, the greater simplicity of sampling methods may be preferable.

The Pitfalls of Sampling

Unfortunately, sampling often is chosen as the vector–capture method regardless of device type or complexity. Sampling is attractive because of its initial simplicity and low technology requirements. It can be done with a sampling program or even with a simulator's existing sampling facility. The result is a series of equally spaced samples of waveform states, as indicated in Figure 9.2.

This method may be adequate for simple synchronous devices employing uniform clocks and data formats, but there is a loss of timing information. The sample strobes fall on the waveform states, but miss the edge locations.

A simulation waveform can be represented on a tester as return–to–one and has two cycles with different pulse widths. This width change represents the designer's intent to check a change in clock duty cycle. To sample this waveform, or any other, for a translator, tester cycle boundaries need to be assigned to the waveforms. Then, sampling is set for some location within each cycle.

For example, mid–cycle sampling can be selected. The resulting translator waveform recreates the clock states, but misses the state changes. The result is uniform clock pulse width, which misses the designer's original intent to check the effect of a change in clock duty cycle. Changing sample location produces even more dismal results—no clock translation at all.

The point is that sample placement within a cycle has to be done carefully, to make sure that states are sampled. But even when that is done, state changes still are missed.

For example, a pulse format may be DNRZ in the first two cycles and change to R1 (return to one) in the third cycle. The pulse may have its trailing edge changed to a different time value to simulate a worst–case test. In this case, a translated waveform from mid–cycle sampling will pass the device, but will not include the simulation's intended worst–case test condition. The sampling translator's waveform will fail the device, and the test engineer will have to debug the vector set on an ATE system. In either case, the designer's original intent is lost.

Avoiding Sampling Pitfalls

A tempting solution for these problems is to increase the sampling density. If one sample per cycle is not covering all cases, then three, four, or more per cycle might be adequate. Indeed, sample density can be increased to the full resolution of the simulator if need be.

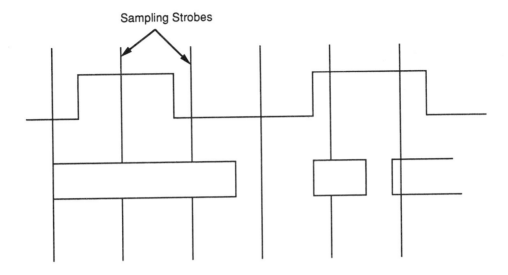

Figure 9.2: Sampling. A series of equally spaced samples of waveform states.

Increased sample density most certainly will affect sample file size. Increased sample density also can create other problems. For example, the sample rate can mix with related waveform rates, such as a uniform clock. This can create beat frequencies that inject unexpected cycle variations into the sample train. The result can be anomalies in the translated waveforms that are artifacts of the sampling process, rather than representations of the true waveform.

Also, uniform high–resolution sampling makes no distinction between artifacts and actual waveform anomalies. It captures unstable states or setup activity indiscriminately. For example, an output cycle might change states several times over a "don't–care" interval before reaching its valid state. With dense sampling, all these states—the valid and the invalid—are captured. At some point before testing, a decision will need to be made, based on device specifications, about which states to keep as valid data and which to discard.

A more appropriate approach is to use fewer samples and place them more judiciously. For example, shapes can be preserved by running through the simulation file and placing samples just before and after event transitions. Another approach is to create a histogram of the simulation data, as shown in Figure 9.3. An intelligent sampling routine then can detect the stable regions within a cycle and make some automatic decisions about optimum sample placement.

Either approach, shape capture or histogram placement, can be used to avoid a wide range of pitfalls normally associated with simulation–vector sampling. There still are some key assumptions, though. One is that the simulation waveforms are not overly complex. Another is that the waveforms

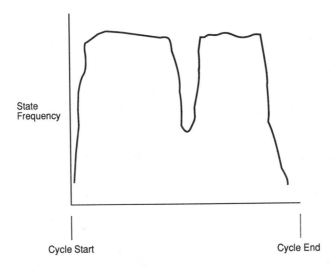

State
Frequency

Cycle Start   Cycle End

Figure 9.3: A histogram of the simulation data. From this, an intelligent sampling routine can detect the stable regions within a cycle and make some decisions about optimum sample placement.

are synchronous enough to provide readily identifiable regions of stability in any given cycle.

When these assumptions begin to break down, adequate sampling becomes more difficult, and the resulting waveform data complexities result in more translation problems. The cure in this case is to move to the high–fidelity approach embodied by event capture.

The Effects of Device Specifications

In any CAE/ATE translation or conversion process, device specifications must be taken into account sooner or later. Simulations embody what a device is capable of. They do not, however, represent the intent or specification of the device. But the device's actual operation is the ultimate goal. For example, if an output becomes valid 73 ns after a rising clock edge, the actual device must change some time before that. It has to reach the new state and settle out by the clock time. In doing that, it may experience numerous settling transitions. Ironically, the more accurate the simulator, the better the settling transitions are modeled. Excluding those simulation transitions from waveforms imported to a tester requires impressing the device specifications onto the simulation waveforms.

One way to do this is to consider the target tester resources and manually assign cycle times, timing sets, strobes, and so forth. For simpler devices, this is not particularly difficult. In fact, assignment of tester cycle times is a prerequisite for vector capture by sampling methods.

Another approach is to create a waveform test plan, where the waveforms themselves represent the device specifications. This also can be done with sampled vectors. However, this approach is most amenable to event data.

For the most part, the two approaches are inverses of each other. With sampling methods, the data is captured and then modified to fit the tester. As a result, tester strobe placement must be used to impress device specifications. With event capture, device specifications are impressed on the waveforms. Then, the waveforms are matched to the available tester resources.

The differences in approach necessitate differences in tools for creating the CAE/ATE link. This is illustrated in Figure 9.4, which shows both the sampling and high–fidelity translation approaches. In the sampling case, edges are not preserved and vectors are created directly from the standard waveform format by applying device specifications and tester resources. In the high–fidelity case, which applies to more complex or asynchronous devices, device specifications are impressed on the standard waveform format selectively, using generic conditioning tools. Then, conditioned waveforms are converted to tester–specific code.

Dealing with Simulator Artifacts and Tester Realities

The necessity for waveform conditioning arises from some basic differences between simulators and testers. These differences dominate more and more as device and simulation complexity increases. As a result, high–fidelity waveform capture and conditioning become imperative, especially for asynchronous devices.

The basic difference between simulators and testers is that simulators operate in a logic domain and testers operate in a physical domain. Compounding this difference is the fact that simulators can be operated under assumptions or conditions that simply cannot be matched in reality. Logic simulators make simplifying assumptions from circuit simulators so that they can run orders of magnitudes faster. The result, more often than not, is a gaping disparity between simulation results and tester realities.

For example, how does the simulator model device rise time? The simulator uses a single model for the device, but not all testers provide corresponding application environments for the device. Real–life device rise time is always a function of the environment that the device pin is looking into. This includes skew–rate reductions due to the loading effects of device fixturing. This and other simulation–artifact problems must be dealt with by various forms of data flagging or conditioning. The more common problems and solutions are discussed next.

Apply Valid Data Specifications. When simulating synchronous logic, meaningless information often is generated for output signals before or during circuit–settling intervals. This is encountered most often with simulators that ignore device rise and fall times or tester skew. To keep these simulator artifacts from complicating test programs or causing unnecessary test failures,

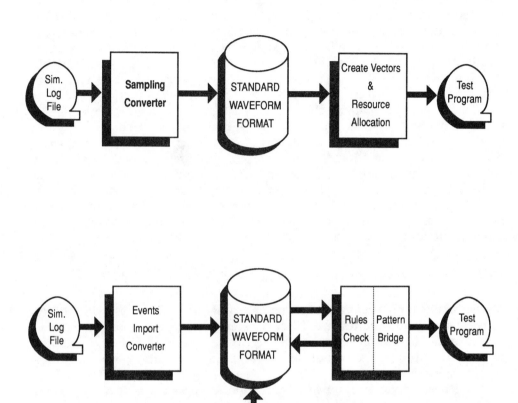

Figure 9.4: Different tools for creating the CAE/ATE link. This shows both the sampling and high–fidelity translation approaches.

regions of invalid data should be masked out of the conversion process. Guardbands also should be set up to mask out ambiguity in transition thresholds or to deal with devices whose rise times differ from their fall times.

Remove Small Pulses. Since circuit behavior is modeled with nominal timing delays, simulator output may include small pulses. These artifacts can be caused by reconvergent fan–out or race conditions that are not present in the actual device. Such extraneous pulses add difficulty to test–program generation and, if included in the test, can cause otherwise good devices to fail testing. Therefore, it is wise to identify and remove such artifacts before test–program generation.

Move Timing Edges or Align I/O Boundaries. The nominal timing delays of simulators can lead to misalignment of edges that actually should be simultaneous. This is particularly troublesome for bi–directional signals and the signals that control them, since edge misalignment can cause unwarranted test failures. Dealing with edge alignment is best done with a *move* tool or a tool that snaps I/O transitions to nearby state changes on other signals.

Synthesize New Signals. It may be necessary to create a signal not included in the simulation output file. For example, a high–frequency clock signal might be omitted from the simulation file to keep file size down. This clock signal must be rederived for the test program.

Synchronize Signal Edges. Derived I/O control signals, or signals that have been conditioned by moving edges around, may have to have their edges resynchronized. This is particularly important for I/O state changes and the signals being controlled.

Debugging Economics

In considering all the various issues involved in converting simulation files to ATE programs, a general test philosophy should begin to emerge. This philosophy impresses device specifications and test realities onto the simulation waveforms. Unfortunately, an opposing philosophy often evolves from typical ad–hoc approaches to CAE/ATE translation. This ad–hoc philosophy imposes arbitrarily derived waveform cycles onto tester realities, which invariably turns out to be an open invitation to numerous obscure bugs in the initial test program.

The price, of course, is extensive debugging time. Worse yet, the debugging is done on the target tester. The vectors are run and looped on errors, printouts are studied, etc. Then the process is repeated for the next bug. A million–dollar (or more) test system gets tied up as a development–and–debugging tool. In some cases, the debug tie–up can last for several weeks.

A more economical approach is to capture the simulation vectors and express them in a normalized standard–events format on a workstation or superminicomputer. With the appropriate software tools, device specifications can be impressed on the standard–events file, simulator artifacts can be removed, and tester–compatibility issues can be resolved with resource-allocation software or emulators. This structured development environment avoids the weak links in other approaches by dealing with key issues in a structured atmosphere. This eliminates overall debugging time. It also saves money, because the bulk of the work is done on a separate system that is less expensive than the target tester, and final verification and debugging on the actual tester take a few hours instead of the usual weeks.

• The Role of Prototype Verification in ASIC Development •

The need for ASIC prototype–verification tools has been driven by a basic change in the technology available to electronic design engineers for designing systems. The ability to implement system architectures with custom ICs lands the designer in the middle of a new realm of measurement needs. Rather than relying on well–characterized components that are connected at the circuit–board level, the designer is forced to understand and debug system–integration problems that occur inside components. This problem makes it necessary to reexamine the verification process during the design cycle. This section will examine the struggle of ASIC users and instrumentation suppliers to establish a prototype–verification process in the design cycle that allows confidence in committing a design to volume manufacturing.

Changes in Electronic Systems Technology

As the technology available for the development of electronic systems has changed, the tools required to successfully develop these new systems have been forced to change as well. In the early 1960s, most designs were done with discrete devices, using analog–design techniques. Inputs and outputs were few in number and were very well isolated according to the function they performed. An oscilloscope could deliver the information needed to verify that a function was performing within its expected range of operation. Engineers could easily maintain expected performance in their heads at this level of complexity.

By the mid–1960s, digital design was becoming the leading–edge technology. Designers soon discovered that the standard oscilloscope could not deliver the signals required to analyze the complex interactions between multiple digital inputs and outputs. The first response of the instrumentation suppliers was to multiplex oscilloscope channels, but this approach soon was replaced by a tool specifically created for the job—the logic analyzer. Thus, a new verification tool grew out of the change in design technology from analog to digital.

Similarly, the microprocessor–development system grew from the use of microprocessors in systems design. This change had an even broader effect on the design process than did the change from analog to digital. With the microprocessor came custom software and the software engineer. And once software was embedded within the system, software integration and verification emerged as critical tasks in the system–development process. These debugging tasks lengthened and complicated the design process, especially since designers now could change functions that were implemented in software with relative ease and cost efficiency. Thus, the microprocessor–development system

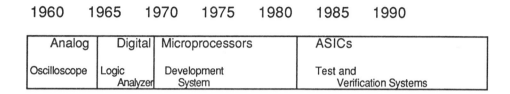

| 1960 | 1965 | 1970 | 1975 | 1980 | 1985 | 1990 |

Analog	Digital	Microprocessors	ASICs
Oscilloscope	Logic Analyzer	Development System	Test and Verification Systems

Figure 9.5: Changes in leading–edge technology.

met the need to analyze the system function changes introduced during the debugging process (see Figure 9.5).

The ASIC Edge

The advent of custom ICs as a technology for systems development has the potential for an even greater impact on the design cycle. There already are ASIC design specialists in most major companies who have taken on the responsibility of ASIC development for the system team. The integration task has been complicated by another custom element (the ASIC), but in this case one that may be changed only with a large cost and time penalty. For this reason, the tool that is required for ASIC verification must provide complete analysis of performance in a fixed environment and be targeted toward preventing change. The ASIC–verification system should help the engineer determine ways to force change in other areas of the system to obtain the desired performance, as well as indicate how the ASIC could be changed.

The impact of the ASIC on the design process puts new pressures on prototype verification, not because the ASIC is easy to change, like software, but because it costs a great deal to modify it. This greater emphasis on the part being correct has led to the ASIC verification system. This is the first time in the history of systems development that the systems engineer has been faced with this type of problem. PCBs could be changed easily with a wire or a cut run to keep manufacturing going if a small problem were found after production release. Software continues to change in complex systems long after release to production. ASICs force systems engineers to commit their systems to manufacturing with major functions hidden inside components that are expensive to alter and difficult to verify.

ASIC–verification tools must be capable of inferring the behavior of the device from its external pins—another problem not faced by designers in the past. It always has been possible to partition circuits to look inside a function and understand its operation. For analog design, this was accomplished by tracing a signal path with a scope; for digital design, by capturing various logic outputs inside a function on the PCB with a logic analyzer; and for software, by analyzing the microcode as the program executed. ASICs present designers with a complex function that must be measured as a single entity. They can make only inferential measurements to determine the operation of functions hidden between the input and output pins.

Evolving the Design Cycle of ASIC Verification

The design cycle itself has not changed over time in its major parts or objectives. It is a process in which an engineer transmits an idea into volume production. The engineer's job, simplified to the lowest level, is to ask three questions: Can I design one? Did I design one? Can I commit to manufacturing thousands? This is really the design cycle, though it is customarily expressed in functional terms such as concept definition, design, debugging, and release to manufacturing.

Can I Design One? This question currently is being answered with the aid of the CAE tools that help to put an idea in a form that allows analysis by computer. Software models and functional simulation make it possible for the designer to break the problem into manageable blocks for analysis. Functions that have a complexity exceeding the human's ability to track interactions can be simulated to provide some assurance that the implementation is possible.

Did I Design One? This is the first question answered by the verification system in the ASIC design cycle. Before ASICs, the question was answered by verifying system functional performance when all of the components were integrated together. When the system ran for the first time, the designer had an answer. Getting to that answer often involved several days or weeks of debugging, during which the designer partitioned the functional blocks and brought separate functions to life individually. In contrast, an ASIC typically forms a major portion of the circuit. System debugging is complicated by the fact that several major functions often are contained in one block, and the designer has limited ability to isolate them.

The verification system allows designers to partition a circuit in a different manner. First, they can verify the ASIC itself by matching its functionality to that predicted by the simulation; then, they can integrate the system with confidence that the ASIC is completely functional. This allows them to focus on other functions in the system during the debugging process. Thus, the question is broken down into two parts: "Did I design a functional ASIC?" and "Did I design a functional system?" This is the same functional partitioning exercise that designers are used to, but without the verification system's ability to provide a known environment for the ASIC, the task cannot be partitioned to provide an answer.

Can I Commit to Manufacturing Thousands? Commitment to manufacturing is the final objective of the designer. ASICs have made this aspect of the engineer's job much more risky, because functions implemented in silicon cannot be altered easily on the manufacturing floor or in the field, as could previous technologies. As a result, there is a need for more complete characterization and rigid checks for compliance with the expected behavior of the circuit functions implemented in the ASIC.

It may be possible to verify that a system performs the intended task without separately verifying the ASIC, but with what certainty can the commitment to production be made? The functional performance of the system depends on ASIC performance, and once a commitment to manufacturing has been made, the ASIC design cannot be altered without shutting down the production line. Yet, how many PCB designs are released to production that have no runs cut, wire or components added, or software modified after a few systems are in the field?

This aspect of the design cycle—commitment to manufacturing—is where the verification system proves most valuable to the design engineer. It provides the power necessary to analyze an ASIC to the point where a change will not be required after the system is released to production.

The Search for Tools

The value offered by ASICs in optimizing system performance forces designers to use the technology even though its use complicates the design cycle. Thus, as ASICs gained popularity in the 1980s, both designers and test engineers experienced in IC development and engineers new to ASIC design recognized that they needed appropriate tools to help them make the decisions necessary to complete the transfer of new products into production.

They first looked to familiar instruments and systems to get the answers needed. Manufacturing ATE was an alternative that had the power to give a confident answer, but ATE systems were costly, difficult to use, and not readily accessible to design groups. Many ASIC designers can talk about the midnight shifts on a Sentry IC tester, trying to write test programs to verify a device.

Logic analyzers and pattern generators were much more familiar tools to the design engineer and seemed to provide a better alternative for analyzing ASIC performance. However, while the functional capability is contained within the instruments, it is difficult to cluster them together as a system for ASIC verification. Also, even if the investment is made to write the control software and the link to the simulation pattern, an instrument cluster does not provide the known environment required for verification. In addition, there is too little control over timing conditions and too much timing uncertainty to allow critical measurements with instrument clusters. Engineers who have completed the process of assembling an instrument–cluster solution often have found that, even if they could prove functionality, there was no way to make the additional measurements necessary to commit to manufacturing with confidence.

Early Attempts at Functional Verification Systems. The first verification systems were targeted primarily at the debugging portion of the ASIC design process. These tools provided links to simulators and the input/output performance to determine that the ASIC was functional and that it matched the expected results provided by simulation. The focus was on the question, "Did I design one?" Typically, these instruments either provided the functionality of an instrument cluster in a prepackaged product with a simulator link, such as the Mentor Hardware Verification System, or were very slow functional testers that operated at microprocessor speeds, sending device inputs and comparing results in software, like the Cadic STM4000.

These first tools did fill a need in the verification process, but were not directed at the major question: "Can I commit to manufacturing thousands?" To be confident that the ASIC would not require change in the future, full characterization was needed in a known environment. Early tools did not provide that capability and were not readily accepted in the design process.

The First Verification System. The first true ASIC verification system emerged when the capability was available in a dedicated system to answer the question "Can I commit to manufacturing thousands?" The introduction of the Logic Master by IMS in 1984 provided a baseline for the functional requirements of an ASIC verification system. It not only focused on the need to debug an IC functionally, but also provided the controlled environment necessary for analysis and the system–measurement capability needed for IC verification.

The Changing Focus of Verification

Originally, vendors and design engineers focused on the functional aspects of ASIC verification. This approach to the market met with resistance from several fronts. Designers expected their devices to work, CAE companies told the designers their tools would make them work, and ASIC vendors told the designers that they would test the ASICs to ensure that they would work. The experience of the first sales attempts soon illustrated that functional verification was not simply a question of "Does the device pass the test vectors that were run on the simulator?"—but instead was a process of gaining additional information about the device through its performance in a controlled environment over a range of conditions. The interactive ease of vector change allowed users to try different functions and conditions that may not have been looked at in simulation to ensure proper performance.

Simulation and vendor testing are not perfect answers. In fact, the success rate for ASIC designers who rely on these methods rather than performing verification is much less than 100%. This is why functional–verification tools have become essential. These tools find problems in prototype devices and errors in simulator models, saving companies thousands of dollars in future design iterations.

Speed–and–Timing Analysis. Another problem faced by ASIC designers is running functional vectors at speed. Most vendors will not test at speed, even with extra NRE costs, because their ATE systems simply do not have the speed necessary for ASIC processes. Engineers have found that, using a verification system, they can run their devices at higher speeds to verify performance or isolate problems. Since many devices (ECL devices, for example) have clock rates that exceed the capability of even the most advanced test instrumentation, the ability of the device to run at speed may not always be verified by running functional vectors at full clock rates. This problem is addressed very well in verification systems that have timing resolution capable of measuring critical–delay paths and the setup and hold characteristics of the IC. The results of these measurements can be used to predict the maximum speed performance of the device under various conditions.

Verification systems have significantly easier access to timing control for edges and sampling than do ATE systems. Therefore, the designer can analyze device performance to a much greater depth than can the ASIC vendor. Such analysis has, in many cases, shown either timing problems in the initial prototypes or margins that could not be expected to be maintained in manufacturing. The ability to isolate these problems does not necessarily mean that a design change must be made on the array. Many times, the designer will be able to compensate for the problems in the PCB and thus prevent costly redesign and future production–line shutdowns. This is a case where the prototype system functions because of a statistically favorable matching of delay components, but duplicating this performance in volume is not ensured. Here, verification tools begin to seriously address the question of commitment to volume production, but they do not truly provide the necessary level of confidence.

Measuring DC Parametrics. The verification–system tool necessary to answer the question "Can I commit to manufacturing thousands?" is the DC–parametrics measurement unit. DC parametrics measurement is most important in the verification of devices that have some process uncertainty or where new I/O cells are involved. Parametric measurement ensures that the IC will meet the interface requirements of the target system properly and will continue to operate over the expected ranges of temperature and loading conditions.

Characterization Tools. New tools offered by verification system vendors are software programs targeted at making the characterization of devices easier. Waveform displays, Schmoo plots, automated timing analysis, data logging, and links to databases and data–management tools such as Lotus are being offered to ease the tasks of data collection and analysis. These new tools, again, are aimed at building confidence in the designer's decision to commit to production.

Impact of User Demands on Verification–System Performance

Specification Lockouts and FWD. The basic tool set of the verification system now is in place, and several vendors are offering various combinations of these tools to designers and test engineers. The market has matured to the point where the basics are defined, and vendors are rattling their sabers over the

FWD (faster–wider–deeper) aspects of system architecture, looking for the ultimate lockout specification. This has fostered various user concerns and questions about specifications that become much more significant in the purchase process.

Confidence in Decisions. If we review the development history of the verification system and how it has helped designers, it was not a question of specifications that drove the market. The basic goal of verification systems is confidence: confidence in the answers to the questions "Did I design one?" and "Can I commit to manufacturing thousands?" Certainly, the specifications of the system are important in meeting basic performance criteria, but, more importantly, what are the conditions under which the specifications are valid? How do timing accuracy and skew affect the measurements being made?

What is most important to the designer committing a product to manufacturing is confidence that the decision is correct. The aspects of the verification system that breed confidence go beyond FWD. They include well–defined specifications or visible indications of current system performance, such as diagnostics and automatic calibration; the accessibility and experience of applications personnel; and the vendor's commitment to providing support and helping to ensure that measurements are a true indication of device performance.

The role of prototype verification in ASIC development is to provide answers to the questions a designer must ask to complete a design cycle. Verification–tool vendors must focus features, performance, applications support, and education toward providing the user with confidence that each phase of the design process has been completed successfully. The success of the design engineer, test engineer, product, and company depend on a correct decision that commits the product to manufacturing. Successful verification tools are those that provide the most confidence in answering the questions "Did I design one?" and "Can I commit to manufacturing thousands?"

CHAPTER 10

THE FUTURE OF COMPUTER-AIDED ENGINEERING

• Introduction •

This chapter makes some pointed remarks about the future of computer–aided engineering. Throughout this text, we have described the kinds of manipulations that a computer must go through to aid engineers in their design activities. We have been rather insistent that this process makes no sense unless the computer can do things—simulation, routing, layout—faster and better than the human operators can. CAE, in fact, is a response to the need to bring increasingly complex electronic products to market quicker. We also have indicated some of the bottlenecks: the places where data–file conversion slows this process down, where vital steps are lost in the race against the clock. Understanding how the various CAE programs work by themselves on a computer and how they work (or fail to work) with each other is key to understanding CAE as a business for hardware and software companies.

In this chapter, we look at the future of the CAE industry and examine its implications for the entire American electronics industry. Several trends will impact the future: Some are technological; others are business and market trends. The technology trends—the movement toward color graphics and increased 3–D rendering capability—are difficult to describe, but fairly easy to deal with. They point to the merging of 2–D CAE and 3–D mechanical–CAD applications. The business trend—the competition in the electronics industry from foreign industrial conglomerates—is fairly easy to describe, but tremendously difficult to deal with. This points to a new level of integration, not just of engineering databases, but of entire companies and industries.

• Computational Requirements of 3–D Graphics •

There is an obvious future in integrating mechanical CAD with electrical engineering. This remains a challenging area, since the computational requirements of mechanical CAD, in many cases, will be more difficult to meet than those of electrical engineering. This can be seen most clearly with computer graphics–display requirements.

The majority of electrical–engineering work, for example, is performed on 2–D flat screens. While a very–high–resolution display (1280 x 1024 pixels) is required to comfortably visualize a complex circuit (or to divide the screen into multiple viewing windows), the flat 2–D display requirement means that each pixel need not be very deep. That is, the scanning mechanism on the CRT needs only to turn each pixel on or off as it scans across the screen. A black–and–white image, in fact, will display almost everything an engineer needs to see with electrical CAE.

The integration of mechanical–engineering programs into CAE establishes a requirement for color and, inevitably, for a 3–D modeling capability. For example, the thermal analysis of PCBs or semiconductor surface areas requires color to portray hot and cold areas. The mechanical modeling of PBCs and their enclosures requires at least a 3–D wire–frame capability. This elevates the cost of a graphics workstation and the run time on its mainframe computer host.

Where color is used to make the screen easier to read (as, for example, in displaying multiple waveforms for analysis on a single x–y axis), the color pixels merely need to be turned on or off by the display's scanning mechanism. Usually, three circuit boards, representing RGB, are all that is required to produce any color combination. Most electrical–CAE work, even thermal modeling, requires that each pixel—whether it is red, green, or blue—merely be turned on or off. But the color requirement is easily three times more difficult to meet than a monochrome requirement since, at any instant, three pixel generators must be activated instead of one. This means that three times more memory and three times more scanning speed will be required.

In addition, by simply turning on or off red, green, and blue pixel generators, there is a choice of only eight displayable colors. This is 2^3, or 2^n, where n is the number of color planes (3—red, green, blue). A multilayer circuit board or a complex IC layout may need more than need eight colors to visualize its complexity on a computer graphics screen. One way to accomplish this is, instead of merely turning each pixel on or off, to increase the number of color-pixel generators. Another way is to vary the light–intensity level of each pixel.

The depiction of 3–D images requires an even higher level of computer-graphics sophistication. To portray a sense of depth, each pixel must reflect a different level of light intensity. The brighter pixels will portray sections of an object in the foreground; the darker pixels will portray sections of an object receding from the viewer into the background. The computer–graphic machinery must not just turn each pixel on or off, but must calculate the level of light intensity for each pixel and activate a mechanism capable of scaling the light intensity at that point. For color displays, the computer calculates the light intensity for each of the RGB color planes.

To understand the complexity of this computational work, it is necessary to recognize the number of pixel points with which the computer must deal. For a 1280– x 1024–pixel screen, the computer must deal with almost 2 million pixels. To prevent a fatiguing screen flicker, these pixels much be refreshed (totally redrawn) 60 times per second. Even for a 2–D black–and–white drawing, the computer must refresh 120 million pixels each second. For a color screen, merely turning each RGB pixel on or off would force the computer to choose among eight possible colors (2^3) at each pixel location. The average viewer can distinguish eight bits of light intensity at each pixel point; that is, the viewer usually can distinguish among 256 (2^8) distinct intensity levels. If an 8–bit light–intensity level is added to each color board, the computer is forced to choose among approximately 16 million color/light–intensity combinations (2^{24} or 2^3 x 2^8) at each pixel location. This means that the computer controlling the graphics screen must make about (120 million x 16 million) pixel display choices each second.

A mainframe computer typically is required to crank for many hours in the background just to transform a 3–D scene into an image that can be painted pixel by pixel, scan–line by scan–line onto a 2–D computer screen. For example, the computations frequently involve perspective projection, hidden–line and surface removal, depth cuing, and illumination modeling. Illumination modeling, for instance, requires the computer to figure out where the light comes from in any particular picture, both as an original source and as it may bounce from a reflective surface, and then to calculate pixel by pixel the areas of the screen that require light and shading.

Manipulating 3–D Images

In executing a 3–D rendering program, a mainframe CPU first generates a data flow for models, called a display list. Within an application program, this is a sequence of displayed objects, expressed as primitives such as line, polyline, and polygon. (The interrelationships between these can be arranged hierarchically.) Traversing the display list produces a sequence of data in world coordinates. Often, this data represents polygon vertices and also can represent control points and other data for parametric surfaces; as a result, the data must be *tessellated*; that is, converted to a polygonal approximation of the surface.

Polygons expressed in 3–D world coordinates then must be transformed geometrically into a form suitable for display on a CRT or 2–D raster device. Transformations include not just 3–D–to–2–D translation, but also scaling, rotation, perspective projection, and clipping. The result is a series of polygon vertices supplied in coordinates for a specific CRT. In addition, the 2–D coordinates must have RGB color values that can be modified according to the degree of illumination.

The next operation is a scan–conversion, or rasterization, process, which interpolates between the vertices of the polygon and the associated color data to determine which pixels should be illuminated and by which color. After this operation, visibility detection (that is, hidden–surface removal) interpolates depth (sometimes called z–axis) information to determine which polygons are obscured from the observer's view. Color values are written to the frame buffer, and depth values are written to the Z–buffer, which, with its associated hardware, supplies hidden–surface removal.

Finally, the display–generation operation takes each pixel's color data from the frame buffer, sequences it in the line–by–line order needed by the CRT, and converts it to an analog signal. This block also produces the required timing and control signals.

Not surprisingly, it can take hours for a mainframe or small supercomputer to calculate the pixel–display coordinates of a single elaborately colored, textured, and shaded object. The degree of complication increases as the user attempts to rotate the object to see a different view or to visualize the relationships among objects as they move in concert or randomly on the computer screen. Calculating all the coordinates can tie up a Cray–type supercomputer for hours at a time. Since a Cray–2 sells for approximately $15 million, and time–sharing can cost more than $7000 per hour, the depiction of motion on finely shaded and textured objects is required only for the most well–funded projects.

As with other kinds of computer simulations, there are two ways to speed up the computation of complex, 3–D images. One method is to build dedicated hardware for graphics rendering and computations. This is the goal of 3–D workstation vendors such as Silicon Graphics, Evans and Sutherland, Megatek, Ramtek, and even HP with its SRX (solids–rendering accelerator). There even is an emerging generation of superworkstations or graphics supercomputers, led by manufacturers such as Ardent Computer Corporation and Stellar Computer, which combine powerful graphics–rendering capability (for example, 600,000 10–pixel vectors per second) with the vector–processing capability of supercomputers (for example, 40 to 60 MFLOPS). These machines are targeted specifically at mainframe computer applications, such as molecular modeling, mechanical stress analysis, and wind–tunnel simulations, which would benefit from graphical depiction.

The other method of speeding the computations is through algorithm development. The computational task can be made practical, for example, by simplifying the image, reducing the number of textures and light sources, settling for a crude surface depiction rather than the smooth surface, or letting a skeletal structure or framework serve as a representation of the entire object. By reducing the 3–D image down to a wire frame, the number of computations is reduced to something that can be handled by a PC.

However, to integrate a 3–D model into the electrical CAE environment, the wire frame still must share the computer screen and computational resources with the circuit, the netlist compiler, the logic simulator, the waveform display, and the documentation package. Consequently, the integration of 3–D images with 2–D electrical CAD will require some concerted software efforts.

• Integrating Mechanical CAD •

Not only is there a need for development in machinery that can render 3–D images, there also is a need to integrate mechanical CAD with electrical CAE. Some of the specialized electrical–CAE vendors are attempting to develop mechanical–CAD software packages that will expand their utility to their customers. Noteworthy manufacturers making strides in this direction include Mentor, Valid, and Calma. Since Calma's strength has been in systems that depict physical layout, especially IC layout, movement to mechanical modeling systems is a natural evolution. Because of its strong engineering customer base and a line of powerful workstations capable of depicting finely shaded 3–D objects, HP is another company to watch in the thrust to integrate electrical with mechanical CAD.

Another strong contender in this area is Integraph, which offers a line of both stand–alone workstations (based on the Fairchild Clipper RISC processor chips) and graphics terminals using DEC's VAX computers as their hosts. Because its strength typically has been the mechanical–drafting area, Integraph's efforts to integrate a broad selection of electrical–CAE software tools may give this company an interesting possibility of success in the movement to integrate divergent software packages into one system.

However, Mentor deserves a leadership position with the introduction of a CAE system designed specifically for electronic–system package design. The system Mentor calls the Package Station harnesses drafting and geometric–modeling databases and thermal–modeling tools for PCBs to a 3–D graphics–display capability. The system provides a clear view of how a PCB will fit into its enclosure, as well as a thermal map of the PCBs. It can be used to determine not only physical clearances within an enclosure, but also places where fans and heat sinks may be required for cooling.

• Thermal–Analysis Packages •

Typically, thermal analysis has the required mainframe resources to run finite–element–analysis programs using finite–difference techniques. The surface of a PCB or an IC can be modeled as a mesh of connected thermal nodes. To calculate the thermal characteristics of PCBs and components, the program determines steady–state temperatures over a regularly spaced grid of nodes. Like a PCB autorouter, the computation time depends primarily on the number of components and the number of nodes for which temperatures are calculated. A good compromise between computation time and resolution results from using the default number of nodes provided by the program for each board topology.

This calculation is as difficult as setting up and interpreting a SPICE run on a mainframe. In addition to run–time considerations, thermal analysis requires development time for thermal models and setup time for data.

One of the first CAE manufacturers to offer a complete thermal–analysis package is Valid. The company's Thermo–STAT program provides an integrated suite of tools for thermal, reliability, and noise–margin analysis within the PCB design environment.

Like a simulator, Thermo–STAT uses three types of information: the placement of components on a board (a netlist), descriptions of the components' thermal characteristics (thermal models), and a description of the board's operating environment. Component–placement data can be taken directly from Valid's Allegro PCB–layout database, from Scientific Calculation's SCICARDS PCB–layout system, or from a Computervision system using file–conversion facilities for Thermo–STAT.

Each component's thermal characteristics are called from a library of models that includes about 2000 devices. The thermal characteristics of the component are made up of several factors, including the junction–to–case conductance, the thermal case–to–board conductance, and the presence or absence of a heat sink. For devices that are not covered by the library, Thermo–STAT includes intelligent default values based on certain IC technologies: An ECL semiconductor device, for example, will tend to run much hotter than a CMOS VLSI part; a power transistor will run hotter than a small–signal device, etc. To obtain greater accuracy than the default values are likely to give, users can enter their own thermal information from data sheets.

The third type of information Thermo–STAT needs is a parametric description of the board's operating environment. These parameters include the adjacent PCB temperature, board–to–board spacing, altitude (to account for the effects of atmospheric density), gravitational orientation (to determine the effects of natural convection), forced–air–flow velocity, and inlet–air temperature. Both natural and forced–convection heat–transfer mechanisms are modeled, allowing the engineer to simulate the natural rising of the dissipated heat, as well as the additional cooling factors provided by fans. (Radiation mechanisms also are considered in the analysis; the designer can input values for adjacent board temperatures that may contribute an additional heat load or, possibly, even help to remove heat.)

The program analyzes the input information to calculate temperature values for individual components and the entire PCB surface and then displays the results graphically. On a PCB, heat generally flows from the center of the board to the edges. If all four edges are conducting heat from the board, the isothermal contours probably will appear as a set of concentric rings. All the points on a specific isotherm have the same temperature. As a consequence, heat flow from hot areas to cold areas will be across the isothermal contours, rather than along them. In addition to the isotherms, the operating temperatures of the board's components will be displayed graphically as hotspots—blocks whose color indicates a component's temperature range.

As well as displaying results in graphic form, the Thermo–STAT generates a text report that includes all the environmental conditions that governed the analysis: each component's location, size, thermal characteristics, and case and junction temperatures; the temperatures on the PCB's surface; and the temperature of the air that drifts off the board.

A unique application of the Thermo–STAT data is to use it for a noise-budget analysis, which reveals any components that are especially susceptible to noise. Heat increases a semiconductor's susceptibility to noise, because temperature affects the device's junction–voltage threshold. If heat causes enough of a shift in the voltages at which two connected devices operate, an additional shift due to electrical noise is more likely to cause logic errors. This approach is especially valuable for predicting the performance of ECL devices, which depend for their speed on short interconnection distances and small voltage shifts to register high–low states.

Despite the progress of manufacturers like Mentor and Valid toward bringing mechanical–CAD programs into an electrical–engineering environment (as with vanilla CAE), a great deal of integration work still needs to be done. Many of the large mainframe–computer vendors such as IBM, DEC, and HP have a variety of electrical–engineering and mechanical–engineering software packages that run on their machines, but the job of integrating these packages is an ongoing effort.

• CAE as a Big–Company Business •

As demonstrated throughout this text, CAE is not one job or one computer program: It is a patchwork of many different programs designed to run on many different computers. Schematic entry is designed to run interactively on PCs and workstations; logic simulation is a totally different program that runs as a batch–processing job on a mainframe or minicomputer; SPICE simulation is an even more complex job, requiring more computational muscle and long run times. Autoplacement–and–routing is a long batch–processing job that, nonetheless, attempts to leave a window open for human intervention and interaction. Even in this case, the autoplacement–and–routing programs for ICs are different from those for PCBs. There are, in fact, a half dozen different placement–and–routing programs for ICs and many more proprietary programs developed by semiconductor manufacturers for their own use. On top of that, test programs and test–generation routines proliferate.

In the short term, CAE has been an interesting business opportunity for Silicon Valley start–up companies and venture–funding organizations. CAE companies, in fact, have been built by some of the same forces as have other Silicon Valley start–ups. Here is a hypothetical example: Two engineers at a major semiconductor manufacturing plant come up with a new way of automating gate–array placement and routing, one that does not require mainframe comput-ational resources, but could be run on a 32–bit workstation with results almost as good as on the mainframe. Instead of selling the idea back to their company (they tried, but "management wouldn't listen"), they start their own firm to develop, manufacture, and market this new software. In a positive scenario, they work 16–hour days for two or three years and build the organization up to 300 employees with $15 million in revenues. Though profit margins are slim, they continue to grow at a rate of 150% per year. A venture–capital company takes the little CAE company public—offers its stock for sale on the NASDAQ over–the–counter exchange. The two engineers who founded the company now are millionaires and are free to try out some new ideas with a new company.

This scenario depends on a certain vision of the electronics market: Traditionally, American electronics companies are too small to produce all elements of a product in–house. Rather, the responsibility for designing, prototyping, evaluating, and eventually producing a new system is parceled out among sometimes dozens of separate companies.

As long as the American electronics industry remains fragmented in this way, partitioned into niches, the issue of design compatibility need not be taken seriously. That is, as long as the circuit is designed and simulated by one company, the PCB laid out and manufactured by a second company, the board purchased and integrated by still another company, the issue of design compatibility does not become serious. Each software and hardware supplier—the gate–array router, in our example—brings something valuable and unique to the CAE process. Each company can buy, invent, and use its own specialized hardware and software, and the interfaces among them need not be very elaborate.

Where the systems manufacturer is vertically integrated, however—where the board user and the circuit designer are in the same organization, working on different aspects of the same product—file compatibility between one department's program and another's is absolutely critical. Designing a front–to–back CAE system requires tight software integration among the various packages in the system. This question, too, is one of resources: in this case, the personpower required to do the software porting–and–patching job.

Even if we assume a positive market environment, there still are problems and difficulties. Even with 300 employees, the new CAE company does not have enough software engineers to bring about the tight integration required to make the gate–array package run on all or most of the available workstations, nor will the company be able handle the design rules and feature sets of all gate–array manufacturers. It is a point solution, rather than a generalized one. It represents an improvement of only one point in the CAE process, rather than of the entire cycle. In addition, this point solution frequently leaves users in the position of porting the software from one UNIX workstation to another or making patches between the software and items (like gate–array design rules) already existing in their databases.

The proliferation of different workstation hardwares and software programs can appear bright and positive: The CAE business, at times, has resembled a supermarket, in which many dozens of computers and software packages can be pulled off–the–shelf and put into use. In this supermarket, there are dozens of high–performance graphics workstations and PCs, as well as specialized software for schematic entry, logic simulation, and layout—though few easy ways to get from one function to another. While some companies—EDA Systems, for example—may make software conversions part of their businesses, the engineering firm that attempts to construct a front–to–back design capability frequently finds that it is constructing a patchwork of barely related and barely compatible programs, whose run–time efficiency is severely impaired because of the software patches and overlays that must be stuck into the program just to get everything to work together.

Because of these problems, users of these electronic products no longer may want to visit a CAE supermarket; they are not interested in a variety of packages that must be glued together. The biggest purchasers of CAE technology, so far, are those with the resources and personpower to integrate the diverse software and hardware elements into one coherent system for their own use. Primarily, these purchasers include the larger American semiconductor manufacturers (National, Intel, Texas Instruments), the vertically integrated computer and instrument manufacturers (IBM, DEC, HP, Tektronix), the vertically integrated aerospace companies (Boeing, Hughes, McDonnell–Douglas), and, because of their increasing use of electronics, the automobile manufacturers (Ford, GM, Chrysler). But even these users of CAE software and hardware, with their insistence on standards and open systems, in fact may be willing to live with a slower logic simulator and a slower router, as long as the two packages mesh together well.

Not surprisingly, the electronics industry has had frequent recessions and shakeouts. It is a dynamic industry with many challenges and changes, but also is riddled with fatalities. The most innovative companies of one period can be minor players in the next. Some may be acquired by larger companies; some may vanish; others may persist in a barely conscious, barely profitable state— sometimes called "the undead"—for years. With such short product life cycles, there is little loyalty in the electronics industry, and those companies that survive have some thick–skinned managers, technologists, and financial people. "Look around you," I was bid at freshman orientation in engineering school, "look at the person on your right; look at the person on your left. Four years from now one of these people won't be here." The same can be said of participants in the CAE industry.

For these reasons, CAE should not be regarded as a playground for a Silicon Valley start–up. It is a serious business, requiring big–company resources to make it work. Only the larger systems vendors are capable of building and marketing front–to–back solutions. The most successful players in the CAE market will not be those with an ideal point solution—a package that does one or more CAE jobs well—but those who can support the entire design cycle. This market increasingly will belong to large systems vendors like DEC and HP. This suggests that the electronics industry no longer will be dominated by a large number of small aggressive companies (cowboys) that seem to get so much of the glamour of the electronics companies (if not the revenues), but by a small number of large, vertically integrated electronics–manufacturing firms—those with the ability to manufacture all parts of a system under one roof, or, more realistically, within the same organization.

• The Trend Toward Vertical Integration •

The trend in the world electronics market points to vertical integration. That is, instead of parceling the design of an electronic system among many suppliers, vendors, and engineering groups, the vertically integrated manufacturer uses the economy of scale that comes from keeping many aspects of the design and manufacturing process in–house. With the electronics marketplace becoming a worldwide global market, the major competitors are not the small, technologically innovative companies, but large manufacturing conglomerates. American dominance in this area is being superseded by vertically integrated Japanese companies and, in some cases, European industrial giants. The only way American firms can compete with these conglomerates is with the same economy of scale. They must, through intelligent merger and acquisition activity, embrace the same level of vertical integration as do their foreign business competitors.

One alternative is a strategic partnership, in which separate companies form alliances to work together toward the same business goals. In this way, two or more companies can work together as if they were part of the same horizontally or vertically integrated conglomerate and still retain part of their independence. This is a keynote among American semiconductor manufacturers, whose market and technology dominance (especially in semiconductor memory parts like dynamic RAMs) has been conceded to the Japanese. Research consortiums like the Semiconductor Research Corporation (Research Triangle Park, North Carolina) and Sematech (Austin, Texas) are designed to pool efforts and avoid redundancy of device and manufacturing technology. Sematech, for example, was formed not just with contributions from commercial semiconductor makers like National Semiconductor, but also with the support of semiconductor users like IBM and AT&T. Over a five–year period extending to 1992, as one goal, the members of the Sematech consortium hope to derive a high–volume, low–cost method of X–ray lithography for manufacturing ICs with 0.35–μm feature sizes. It is through these strategic alliances that the American semiconductor industry hopes to recapture world dominance from the Japanese.

These efforts at cooperation run counter to the American laws and prejudices against monopoly conglomerates. The Japanese and other Asian competitors, however, have no such prejudice against monopolies. In addition, they do not need to show quarter–by–quarter earnings to shareholder groups and can put long–term investments in place more readily than can most American firms. While the devaluation of the American dollar against the Japanese yen makes foreign goods—even semiconductors—more expensive inside the U.S. and gives American manufacturers a small window of opportunity, many economic strategists see mergers, acquisitions, and alliances—a massive pooling of resources—as the only way to come from behind in a difficult worldwide market.

The tendency of small American manufacturers go their own way—the American cultural trend of independence and rugged individualism, usually expressed in the Silicon Valley start–up company—is beginning to be seen as a strategic disaster for the American electronics industry, whose best results appear to be hit and run for enterpreneurs and capitalists in certain markets. Unfortunately, the electronics industry (especially in semiconductors) requires too much capital investment in manufacturing technology for little companies to succeed. It is just not that easy these days to grow a garage shop into a $100–million electronics firm, the pattern followed by Silicon Valley start–ups of the 1960s and 1970s. There are not enough niche markets to support that kind of growth, and it takes big–company muscle to compete in worldwide commodity markets, such as consumer electronics, business computers, telecommunications, or even the newer markets like home energy management, which represents a hybrid of consumer (low–cost) and industrial (rugged and functional) electronics. The small start–up company no longer may be the ideal model for competitiveness in the electronics industry.

As a consequence, American manufacturers are slowly revising their CAE strategy (and its relation to CAD and CAM) along lines resembling those of the European manufacturing giants. The European model calls for large mainframe capabilities and the integration of all types of electronic–circuit and manufacturing data on one large database. The American model parcels the CAE, CAD, and CAM functions among different machines and databases, develops specialized software and computational machinery to serve the needs of these specialized areas, and then attempts to forge artificial links between design and engineering, engineering and manufacturing, engineering and test, and test and manufacturing.

Among the European manufacturers and the largest American manufacturers such as IBM, DEC, and HP, there traditionally is a concern for mainframe computational resources, large databases, and improved techniques for organizing, querying, and manipulating these databases. But this need for ultrasophisticated database management—as a way to integrate CAD and CAM—is being seen by other organizations as well.

• Increased Database Requirements •

As more and more American electronics firms become vertically integrated, the manufacturing database will swell and the need for mainframe computer resources will be obvious. Within the semiconductor houses, we already have seen mainframe resources applied to the problems of design rule checking. Every new IC design, if it is to be fabricated with a company's manufacturing processes, must have the dimensions of its transistors and switches checked against the manufacturing design rules. These rules reside on a mainframe database, and the process of checking the dimensions of new designs against the manufacturing design rules is a batch–processing job that runs on a mainframe computer in the middle of the night.

But as American semiconductor manufacturers become increasingly integrated with larger systems and equipment manufacturers, the size of the database and the constraints it may impose increase exponentially. What we foresee is an integration, not only of CAE databases, but of CAD and manufacturing databases as well. While still new among American manufacturers, CIM is part of the computer–usage strategies of European conglomerates like N.V. Philips and Siemens AG.

At N.V. Philips, for example, there is an insistence on continuity from design inputs to manufacturing outputs. The same CAE system that is used to describe a circuit schematic not only must be able to place parts on a PCB, but also must deliver the solder masks and drilling tapes for manufacturing that PCB. Within COMPASS (Computer–Aided Systems and Services), an internal support group at Philips, the CAE system used by many of the company's divisions represents an attempt to vertically integrate an entire consumer product line (like the CD—compact disc player), from its initial conceptual stages to its final production runs, onto one system.

Here, the manufacturing database must contain not just electronic–circuit information, such as schematics and printed–circuit layouts, but also mechanical–assembly drawings and sketches depicting the final appearance of the assembled consumer product. In many Philips products, for example, PCBs assume odd sizes to ensure a compact fit with rotating parts (like motors and front–panel displays) without creating problems of RFI and other signal cross talk. In other words, since the design of a PCB depends on the mechanical constraints imposed by the enclosure in which it sits, both the PCB and the enclosure should be visible on the same computer–graphics screen.

In this environment, it is essential that schematic drawings, product specifications, simulation data, and physical–layout and manufacturing–process constraints reside in the same database and be accessible at once to the same project team. It is, first and foremost, a database requirement. To integrate all the database information, Philips, like other European manufacturers, is harnessing much of its effort to large mainframes and minicomputer systems. The need to integrate all aspects of the design and manufacturing processes on the same system creates a choice of flexibility over performance. While many of the existing CAE systems guarantee high performance in selected areas such as schematic entry, simulation, and layout—for example, Philips' Research Labs chose Mentor as the supplier of the layout system for its 4–Mbit DRAMs—there often is no way to mix mechanical– and electrical engineering tasks, along with mainframe–database–management and project–tracking (largely operating–system) functions.

Philips' COMPASS group built its PCB design system around the Computervision CGP 200X hardware and CADDS 4X software. Philips believes this choice reflects a compromise (leaving aside the financial stability of Computervision, now owned by Prime Computer): It is willing to accept a lower level of performance if it can gain database flexibility.

While a mainframe–based system like Computervision's provides flexibility, it was not a turnkey system. Philips' use of the CADDS software was tailored to include both analog PCB design (with its special requirements for straight–through signal paths and large metal areas for shielding and ground planes) and Philips' own manufacturing design rules. These rules include circuit–board trace widths and solder–mask restraints—ground planes, shields, and high–frequency transmission lines for the analog boards—which are entered manually by users. Since Philips also manufactures its boards in–house, the CAE system user must constantly check the manuals and guidebooks to be sure that the ground planes and other metallization areas input to the system are consistent with Philips' board–manufacturing processes. Circuit boards for the CD–ROM device, for example, include SMDs with 0.15–mm pin centers. There are few commercial CAE systems that can handle this type of fine line spacing.

The careful reference to design rules provides no savings in time over hand–drawn PCB layout systems, but does make it easier to track design changes. Ideally, the layout system should put the board rules on–line with the layout editor.

Though Philips is one of Europe's most influential manufacturers, the company does not assume it has the power to drive CAE standards. While the ESPRIT research projects are cited as one way of overcoming European manufacturers' resistance to standardization efforts, Philips' own goals are closer to what COMPASS managers call a limitation of variety within the company (according to its own manufacturing contingencies), rather than an industry–wide standard.

Any CAE/CAD/CAM system, viewed in this light, may tend to stifle a designer's creativity in the movement toward rapid product turnaround. Ideally, the system should provide a workable balance between a designer's personal innovation and the automation of the design and manufacturing processes.

Many industry leaders are coming to believe that the proliferation of PCs and indvidual workstations, though they are inexpensive, has created an uncontrollable situation in the corporate environment. Not only is it difficult to integrate these very specialized products into the design and manufacturing processes, it also is difficult to supervise the labor of individual workstation users. In many corporations, there is a thinking process that insists on tying CAE and other workstation activities to the corporate mainframe, regardless of how inefficient this may seem. By tying all individual computers to a central host computer, marketing, engineering, and manufacturing groups all can work from the same database. Accessing this database may be slow for individuals, but the corporation has some assurance that the computerized efforts of different groups will be somewhat compatible and that these groups will function with at least some concern for overall corporate goals.

This is the viewpoint of Philips, one of the giants in European electronics manufacturing, and can be considered typical of European sentiment toward computational resources for CAE applications. European electronics manufacturers, it turns out, have become very sophisticated CAE users. Their wish lists will be extremely influential in defining the requirements for the next generation of CAE systems.

• Integrating CAE, CAD/CAM, and CIM •

In recent years, there has been a confusing proliferation of engineering aids— software tools—designed to promote workstation productivity. The proliferation of general–purpose graphics workstations and PCs that can be equipped with software for engineering drawings also has made it difficult to distinguish electrical engineering from CAD, CAM, electronic publishing, or other disciplines that appear to make good use of workstation technology. In the early stages of workstation automation, corporations referred to CAD and CAM in the same breath. Throughout this book, we have used the term CAE for electrical–engineering work. However, we should not forget that the term CAE makes no clear distinction between computer–aided mechanical engineering and computer–aided electrical engineering. Consequently, some manufacturers use CAE to refer to mechanical–engineering activities, the calculation of stresses (forces and heat) on mechanical parts, and EDA to refer to electrical engineering. For consistency, we will use CAE to refer to electrical–engineering work and MCAD (mechanical CAD) to refer to mechanical–engineering work.

With the movement toward vertical integration and mainframe databases, most of these programs and disciplines now can be grouped together under an umbrella called CIM. A NASA/NRC (National Aeronautics and Space Administration/Nuclear Regulatory Commission) study conducted in 1984 predicted that CIM—the linking of all corporate activities to one database— could result in the following:

- A 15% to 20% reduction in personnel costs
- A 15% to 30% reduction in engineering design costs
- A 30% to 60% reduction in overall lead time (that is, time to market)
- A 30% to 60% reduction of work in process
- A 40% to 70% gain in overall production
- A 200% to 300% gain in capital–equipment operating time
- A 200% to 500% gain in product quality
- A 300% to 3500% gain in engineering productivity.

Referring to this study in a 1987 Dataquest presentation, IBM saw the essential requirements of CIM as follows: first, building a database; second, establishing a data–communications network to disseminate this data; third, using the database for administrative decision–making; and, finally, putting engineering and manufacturing under computer control. The progress of automation, suggested the IBM presenter, typically has been in the reverse order: A Booz, Allen & Hamilton study conducted in 1986 suggested that of all the American investments in factory automation, 95% were in equipment. Only 4% of the total investment was in linking cells, and only 1% reflected anything like CIM–database construction.

Putting all these tools to work on the same computer—a mainframe—and building a database that can be used by many different kinds of programs within an organization is a mammoth undertaking. Not only is there the problem of integrating electrical–engineering CAE tools into one coherent system, there is the additional problem of integrating the tools for MCAD and those for CAM and CIM. Just as engineers can appear to be working at cross–purposes with marketers, the software tools developed for manufacturing layout can be totally incompatible with those used by engineering. All the productivity gains implied in the use of workstations by engineers can go out the window as manufacturing and test experts struggle to decipher the electronic files that engineers provide.

The terms CAD/CAM and CIM are coming to refer not just to specific disciplines, but also to a corporate strategy for building, using, and integrating these tools. The future of an entire industry, in fact, will rest on how well these strategies are formulated and implemented.

• Improving the Effectiveness of the Engineering Process •

While dealing with the work of engineers and the overall process of engineering, this book does not focus on the traditional automation of engineering design and analysis tasks. Rather, its focus is on the greater engineering environment: the support of the design processes and the many other functions that are necessary for the engineering process. Often, these still are viewed as a great gray area. Yet, unless all parts of the engineering process benefit from advances in technology, major gains in overall engineering effectiveness will be difficult to achieve.

While they may seem mundane in comparison to the mainstream design functions, tasks such as document control, revision control, project management, engineering–information distribution, and engineering communications are critical to the overall process of product design and support. Corporations now speak of their libraries of hundreds of thousands of drawings, of the millions of pages of technical information they must publish, of the thousands of design changes that must be approved and implemented, and of how these functions can become major bottlenecks in the engineering process. Engineering, charged with developing new products and continually enhancing existing products, is being buffeted by technological change and by new competitive and economic pressures. Whereas a five–year design–through–manufacturing cycle once was considered adequate for a new aircraft engine or automobile transmission, increased competition now requires that these lengthy cycles be radically shortened.

The old ways of designing and bringing new products to market and supporting them through their life cycles are no longer adequate. Technology is moving too rapidly to preserve old and manual processes: Information must be accessed, managed, and updated faster; more must be accomplished in less time; quality must be improved; resources must be managed better.

Although technology has provided better tools to help engineers in their design work, the manual portions of the engineering process are becoming increasingly harmful obstacles to the overall process. We can produce better designs, faster, with CAD workstations, but we have increasing difficulty in managing the growing libraries of engineering drawings and data that are produced by the CAD systems. While we are increasing the productivity of the information creators, we are not necessarily improving the processes of information distribution to the users.

For those companies that have invested heavily in automation, the investmentsfrequently have been oriented to automating tasks. Yet, the tasks that make up a process frequently have been automated with different technologies. For instance, different design departments use different types of CAD workstations, an electronic–mail system may be dictated by the corporation, office–automation committees select different solutions from different vendors, and individual professionals select their favorite PCs or workstations.

When you have to request, implement, approve, and distribute a critically important engineering change—and you cannot use an integrated CAD, project management, office automation, electronic mail, and documentation system— you lose time trying to patch together this engineering change out of differing automation technologies. While there may be pockets of productivity gains, the overall process suffers, and productivity may be lost because the various computer solutions cannot be integrated easily and information does not flow smoothly throughout the process.

As we automate, we are confronted with two alternatives: to automate jobs that previously were performed manually or to use automation to streamline a process. When the first approach is taken, we might be able to introduce some productivity gains within the task itself, but we may have created yet another island of automation. What appeared to be the solution may have introduced a new set of problems. With the latter approach, we may have to rethink the tasks and the process entirely and then apply automation tools more creatively.

The Engineering Process

Engineering is a process that starts with the conception of a product and includes product definition, design, prototyping and testing. The process extends into manufacturing, particularly the delivery of buildable designs to the manufacturing department. It also includes the ongoing support of the product during its life cycle. This includes the production of user documents (such as installation and service information) and the support and enhancement of products after their delivery.

While we can outline and take complex processes from inception through design and manufacturing to deliverable products, the actual engineering processes are fragmented by division into projects, tasks, and subprocesses. Organizational boundaries—such as development engineering, manufacturing engineering, and service engineering—can create further divisions. Yet, if major gains in engineering effectiveness are to be achieved, we must address the whole process, rather than automating the pieces and then depending on the telephone, committee meeting, and paper to join the tasks into a process.

Engineering Effectiveness

Engineering effectiveness can be defined as delivering better designs to manufacturing faster and at less cost. For some organizations, this is expressed as reducing the time to market. It also means developing products that are more reliable and easier to build, service, and use—at less cost.

The Players

We traditionally think of engineering as being staffed by personnel busily occupied in design (which is correct), but it is much more. It also includes creators of information (plans, specifications, designs); implementers, supervisors, and managers (of projects, departments, work groups); and supporters (drafters, technicians, administrators, writers). Very few corporate strategies today have addressed the issue of providing all these participants with a compatible set of work tools, so that their work and the information that they use and produce can be fully shared or integrated.

But the mission of engineering is not solely to benefit engineering. The design, information, and documentation that emanate from engineering have a destination: manufacturing, service, customers, etc. Few corporations have addressed the integration of the tools used by the engineering creators of information and those used by the users of such information. For example, can the design created on the CAD engineer's workstation be transmitted and displayed on the service engineer's terminal? The answer is, probably not—instead, the design must be printed on paper, stored in a master library, copied onto microfiche, and mailed to the field–service sites. Assuming that the drawing is accessible electronically at the service engineer's terminal or workstation, we should ask if there is a method whereby the service engineer not only can ask for the right drawing, but also can be assured that the latest released version, with the most up–to–date changes, is being displayed. In most cases, the answer again is probably not. When a change to an original drawing must be distributed, it usually must be slowly propagated through the paper, people, and microfiche processes, rather than being disseminated by taking advantage of rapid electronic communications.

Information Distribution: A Paper Problem

Engineering documentation often is treated as an afterthought. Yet, it is part of the process, it has to occur, and there are support groups to handle it. Life is not simple: The problem and its implications are immense. Given the serial and task–oriented nature of the engineering process, almost every step or work group involved generates its own documentation, from the original project and design proposals through the plans, specifications, schedules, designs, test data, etc.

To proceed from one step to the next usually requires approvals and signed documentation—not to mention the final and frequently voluminous documentation required to support the product in the field: service, user, and installation documentation. Even small changes must be rippled back through the documentation, and the change process itself generates more documentation: change requests, change orders, and change notifications. Hence, the engineering process, even with CAD and CAE technology, reverts to a manual paper morass at each step. While computer programs can compute the most complex analyses in seconds, it may take months to get the results described, documented, printed, and distributed.

For example, the service and user documentation of many high–tech products—computers, aircraft, missiles—takes up more space than does the product itself; the paperwork in a recent proposal from a defense contractor for a new missile weighed several tons; and documentation for a new missile consisted of 80,000 pages.

To the high costs of producing documentation must be added the complexities of storage and distribution of paper–based information and the penalties of distributing information that is not up to date. It has been estimated, for example, that of the 125,000 different manuals in use by the U.S. Navy, 25% are out of date at any given time.

Properly used, electronic technology will help relieve many of the delays, costs, and other penalties associated with paper–based information delivery.

Search For a Name

While engineering processes usually are well defined and the various engineering disciplines are well organized, there still is no nomenclature or accepted discipline for addressing the problems just described. We are faced with the challenge of applying technology across the entire engineering process to gain efficiency.

There is, indeed, project management that can be systematized and applied to ensure the completion of projects on time and within budget. But project management does not cover the entire process or organization of engineering. There are references to engineering management, to computer–aided engineering, and to computer–integrated engineering. At DEC, there is a marketing group called the Engineering Systems Group, with three focused discipline units: two to address design and analysis (electronic, mechanical, and software) requirements, and one to focus on the overall process of engineering. The latter is called the Engineering Support Systems (ESS) Group.

What Is Needed

To address the problems just described, engineering management needs a vision of the ideal environment. It needs to define engineering effectiveness and develop a plan to achieve it. This will require a view of the whole process, an understanding of how the various tasks can be better integrated and how technology can be used to streamline the entire process. Electronic technology certainly can be used to automate many tasks that now are accomplished manually and to reduce the heavy dependence on paper–based information distribution.

Technology and its proper application and integration will help streamline the engineering process. But technology will be only part of the success equation; management, organization, and planning will complete the equation.

Acronyms and Abbreviations

2–D	two–dimensional
3–D	three–dimensional
AC	alternating current
ALU	arithmetic logic unit
AMD	advanced micro devices
AMI	American Microcircuits, Inc.
ANSI	American National Standards Institute
ARPA	Advanced Research Projects Agency
ASCII	American Standard Code for Information Interchange
ASD	analog system design
ASIC	applications–specific integrated circuit
ASP	average selling price
AT	auto–test mode pin
ATC	auto–test clock pin
ATE	automatic test equipment
ATG	automatic test generation
ATPG	automatic test–pattern generation
AV	circuit gain
BiCMOS	bipolar CMOS
BILBO	built–in logic–block observation
BiMOS	bipolar MOS
BIOS	basic I/O system
BIST	built–in self–test
BJT	bipolar junction transistor
BORIS	block–oriented interactive system
BSD	Berkeley Software Distribution
C	capacitance
CAD	computer–aided engineering
CADAT	computer–aided design and text
CAE	computer–aided engineering
CAM	computer–aided manufacturing
CD	compact disc
CDC	Control Data Corporation
CIF	Calpoly's intermediate file
CIM	computer–integrated manufacturing
CISC	complex–instruction set computing
CLK	clock

CMOS	complementary metal oxide silicon
CNC	computer numeric control
COMPASS	Computer–Aided Systems and Service
CoSim	cosimulator processor
CPU	central processing unit
CRT	cathode–ray tube
CSMA/CD	carrier sense multi–access with collision detection
DAC	Design Automation Conference
Db	decibel
DC	direct current
DEC	Data Equipment Corporation
Deg	degree of arc
DFT	discrete Fourier transform
DIP	dual in–line package
DLS	Daisy Logic Simulator
DNRZ	delayed non-return to zero
DoD	Department of Defense
DOS	disk operating system
DRAM	dynamic random–access memory
DRC	design–rule checking
DUT	device under test
ECAD	electronic computer–aided design
ECL	emitter–coupled logic
EDA	electronic design automation
EDIF	electronic design interchange format
EES	Electrical Engineering Software
EGA	enhanced graphics adapter
EIA	Electronic Industry Association
ERC	electrical–rule checking
ESS	Engineering Support Systems
FA	full adder
fC	corner frequency
FDDI	fiber–distributed data interface
FET	field–effect transistor
FM	frequency modulation
ft	switching frequency
FTP	file transfer protocol
FWD	faster–wider–deeper
GaAs	gallium arsenide
GB	gigabyte; one billion bytes
GDT	generator development tool
GHz	gigahertz; one billion hertz
GKS	graphic kernel system

HCMOS	high–speed CMOS
HDL	hardware description language
HP	Hewlett–Packard
IC	integrated circuit
IEEE	Institute of Electrical and Electronic Engineers
IGES	initial graphics exchange specification
IIL	integrated injection logic
IMP	International Microelectronic Products
IMS	Integrated Measurement Systems
INRIA	National Institute for Research in Computer Science and Automation
IPC	interprocess communication
ISO	International Standards Organization
I/O	input/output
JFET	junction field–effect transistor
k	Kiloohm; one thousand ohms
KB	kilobyte; one thousand bytes
kbit	kilobit; one thousand bits
KFLOPS	thousand floating–point operations per second
kHz	kilohertz; one thousand hertz
LAN	local–area network
LCC	leadless chip carrier
LE	logic evaluator
LED	light–emitting diode
LFSR	linear–feedback shift register
LSI	large–scale integrated
LSS	logic–synthesis system
LSSD	level–sensitive–scan design
LVS	layout versus schematic
mA	milliamp; one thousandth of an amp
MB	megabyte; one million bytes
Mbit	megabit; one million bits
MCAD	mechancial computer–aided design
MCC	Microelectronics and Computer Technology Corporation
MFLOPS	million floating–point operations per second
MHz	megahertz; one million hertz
mil	0.001 inch; one thousandth of an inch
min–max	minimum–maximum
MIPS	million instructions per second
MIS	management information systems
MIT	Massachusetts Institute of Technology

mm	millimeter; one thousandth of a meter
MMU	memory–management unit
MOS	metal oxide on silicon
MOSEC	metal–oxide seminconductor emitter–coupler
MOSFET	metal–oxide field–effect transistor
ms	millisecond; one thousandth of a second
MSI	medium–scale integrated
MS–DOS	Microsoft disk operating system
MTBF	mean time between failures
mV	millivolt; one thousandth of a volt
NAS	National Advanced Sytems
NASA	National Aeronautics and Space Administration
NC	numerically controlled
NCR	National Cash Register
NFS	network file system
NMSO	negative–well MOS
NRE	non–recurring engineering
NRZ	non–return to zero
ns	nanosecond; one billionth of a second
NV	node voltage
OE	output enable
OEM	original equipment manufacturer
op amp	operational amplifier
OSI	open systems interconnect
PAL	programmable array logic
PARC	Palo Alto Research Center
PC	personal computer
PCAD	Personal CAD Systems
PCB	printed circuit board
PCF	pattern–capture format
PC–DOS	personal computer disk operating system
PerSim	personal simulator processor
pf	picofarad; one trillionth of a farad
PFG	probabilistic fault grading
PGA	pin–grid array
PHIGS	Programmer's Hierarchical Graphics System
PLA	programmable logic array
PLD	programmable logic device
PMOS	positive–well MOS
PMX	physical modeling extension
PROM	programmable read–only memory

R	resistance
RAM	random–access memory
RC	resistance–capacitance
RF	radio frequency
RFI	radio–frequency interference
RFS	remote file system
RGB	red; green; blue
RISC	reduced–instruction set computing
RMS	root mean square
ROI	return on investment
ROM	read–only memory
rsh	remote shell
SAR	signature–analysis register
SCALD	structured computer–aided logic design
SDE	system development engine
SMD	surface–mounted device
SMT	surface–mount technology
SNA	system network architecture
SOA	safe operating area
SOS	silicon on sapphire
SPARC	scalable processor architecture
SPICE	simulation program with integrated circuit emphasis
SQL	Structured Query Language
SRAM	static random–access memory
SRX	solids–rendering accelerator
SSI	small–scale integrated
TPG	test–program generator
TSSI	Test System Strategies, Inc.
TTL	transistor–to–transistor logic
V	volt
VDI	virtual device interface
VHSIC	very–high–speed integrated circuit
VLSI	very–large–scale integrated
WAN	wide–area network
XL	accelerated
μA	microamp; one millionth of an amp
μf	microfarad; one millionth of a farad
μm	micron; one millionth of a meter
μs	microsecond; one millionth of a second

Index